Il Trittico, Turandot,
and Puccini's Late Style

MUSICAL MEANING AND INTERPRETATION

Robert S. Hatten, editor

Il Trittico, Turandot,
and Puccini's Late Style

ANDREW DAVIS

Indiana University Press

Bloomington & Indianapolis

This book is a publication of

Indiana University Press
601 North Morton Street
Bloomington, Indiana 47404-3797 USA

www.iupress.indiana.edu

Telephone orders   800-842-6796
Fax orders   812-855-7931
Orders by e-mail   iuporder@indiana.edu

♾ The paper used in this publication
meets the minimum requirements of
the American National Standard for
Information Sciences—Permanence
of Paper for Printed Library
Materials, ANSI Z39.48-1992.

Manufactured in the United
States of America

Library of Congress Cataloging-
in-Publication Data

Davis, Andrew C., [date–]
   Il trittico, Turandot, and Puccini's
late style / Andrew Davis.
       p. cm. — (Musical meaning
and interpretation)
   Includes bibliographical
references and index.
   ISBN 978-0-253-35514-0 (cloth : alk. paper)
1. Puccini, Giacomo, 1858–1924. Trittico.
2. Puccini, Giacomo, 1858–1924. Turandot.
3. Opera—20th century. I. Title.
   ML410.P89D33 2010
   782.1092—dc22

                                      2010003084

1   2   3   4   5   15   14   13   12   11   10

For my family, without whom none of this would be possible

CONTENTS

ACKNOWLEDGMENTS

Sometimes it seems the people who contribute to a project like this are too numerous to thank. Any omissions here are unintentional, and I regret them; any errors or shortcomings that remain in the book are my own.

I am grateful to the University of Houston for a New Faculty Research Program grant that allowed me to write a substantial portion of the manuscript in the summer of 2005, and to the Moores School of Music for course releases and for generous funding that supported travel to domestic and international conferences at which I met valuable colleagues and presented some of these ideas.

Many individuals have contributed to my work. David Ashley White has provided immense personal and professional support, and Robert Hatten has been unwavering in supporting all aspects of my career for years now; I will always be grateful to both of them. Jürgen Maehder has been extraordinarily generous with his support, time, and expertise on a wide range of topics in Puccini studies. Peter Ross has likewise been gracious in sharing his expertise on Italian verse and librettos. Helen Greenwald helped me obtain the Ricordi first-edition librettos for Puccini's last four operas. Nicholas Baragwanath, Deborah Burton, Michele Girardi, Howard Pollack, Gabriela Biagi Ravenni, David Rosen, Matteo Sansone, and Alexandra Wilson all supported my work, constructively critiqued my ideas and analyses, or read portions of my manuscript. Sandra Celli-Harris was generous with her time in helping me with the Italian translations, which are better as a result of her expertise; Buck

Ross also provided valuable translation advice. Gregory Malone helped me interpret the actuarial tables, which would have been impenetrable without his assistance. Johanne Cassar provided me a copy of her unpublished dissertation. John Grimmett was my research assistant in the semester in which I finished the manuscript; his efforts saved me hours of work, and I am grateful to him and to the University of Houston for providing him a Provost's Undergraduate Research Scholarship. Under my supervision, Adam Hudlow was writing his master's thesis on the vocal music of Richard Strauss—whose strategies are similar to Puccini's in so many respects—while I was finishing this manuscript, and his work informed some of my ideas. Numerous other graduate students, many of them trained opera singers, in my opera history and analysis seminars at the University of Houston have helped me form ideas on this material. Jane Behnken of Indiana University Press provided valuable editorial advice, and both she and Katherine Baber have been generous with their time in handling my manuscript. And the anonymous reviewers for Indiana University Press provided penetrating critiques that only made the book better.

I must thank my family, with whom I know this project caused countless hours of lost time. In fact, I wrote this book during a time of significant personal challenges, during which I was constantly reminded of Dante's immortal opening: "Nel mezzo del cammin di nostra vita / mi ritrovai per una selva oscura, / ché la diritta via era smarrita."

Finally, I am grateful to Puccini for all the enjoyment his music has brought me.

NOTE ON SCORES, LIBRETTOS,
AND TRANSLATIONS

Published editions for each of Puccini's last four operas are widely available; as such I have assumed throughout the book that readers have access to the scores, and I have not provided musical examples for all passages discussed in the text. For *Il trittico*, all score references, including references to rehearsal numbers, are to *Il trittico in Full Score: Il tabarro, Suor Angelica, Gianni Schicchi* (Mineola, New York: Dover, 1996).

This publication contains reprints of the following full orchestral scores:

Il tabarro: opera in un atto. Partitura: nuova edizione riveduta e corretta. Milan: Ricordi, 1956 (© 1918, 1917; plate no. P.R. 118; Schickling 85.E.3C). This is itself a reprint of the second edition of the full score: Milan: Ricordi, 1927; © 1927; plate no. 120480; Schickling 85.E.3B. The second edition is a reprint, with Michele's new monologue ("Nulla! . . . Silenzio! . . ." replaces "Scorri, fiume eterno!"), of the first: Milan: Ricordi, 1919; © 1918; plate no. 117710; Schickling 85.E.2A.

Suor Angelica: opera in un atto. Partitura: nuova edizione riveduta e corretta. Milan: Ricordi, 1958 (© 1918; plate no. P.R. 115; Schickling 87.E.3C). Reprint of the second edition of the full score: Milan: Ricordi, 1927; © 1927; plate no. 120481; Schickling 87.E.3A. The second edition is the first full score printed without Angelica's "Amici fiori."

Gianni Schicchi: opera in un atto. Partitura: nuova edizione riveduta e corretta. Milan: Ricordi, 1957 (© 1918; plate no. P.R. 114; Schickling 88.E.2G). Reprint of the second edition of the full score: Milan: Ricordi,

1927; © 1927; plate no. 120482; Schickling 88.E.2D. The second edition is a reprint of the first: Milan: Ricordi, 1918; © 1918; plate no. 117712; Schickling 88.E.2A.

For *Turandot*, all score references are to *Turandot: Dramma lirico in tre atti e cinque quadri*. Partitura: nuova edizione riveduta e corretta. Milan, Ricordi, 1958; reprint Milan: Ricordi, 2000 (© 1926; plate no. P.R. 117; Schickling 91.E.2H). This is the fourth edition of the full score and essentially a reprint of the first: Milan: Ricordi, 1926; ©1926; plate no. 119761; Schickling 91.E.2A. All the full scores have the Alfano II (revised) ending. The first piano-vocal edition has Alfano I (Milan: Ricordi, 1926; ©1926; plate no. 119772; Schickling 91.E.1), as does the first German piano-vocal edition (Milan: Ricordi, 1926; ©1924, 1925, and 1926; plate no. 120150; Schickling 91.E.1A); all other piano-vocal scores were printed with Alfano II.

Unless otherwise indicated, all libretto citations are to the Ricordi first editions: *Il tabarro, Suor Angelica, Gianni Schicchi* (Milan: Ricordi, 1918; Ricordi plate no. 116999); and *Turandot: Dramma lirico in tre atti e cinque quadri* (Milan: Ricordi, 1926; Ricordi plate no. 119773). I have used these as my source material because they are the closest approximations we have to the librettos for the first performances, even though in reality this is somewhat of an oversimplification: various librettos were often published specifically for particular performances, to satisfy requirements of copyright law, or for other reasons; they exist in numerous forms, published and unpublished, and almost none of these correspond exactly to the texts in the scores. As such, it remains nearly impossible to identify a libretto's definitive version, or even the version that Puccini set to music.[1]

Note also that the only way of ascertaining the first-edition texts is to view a copy of the first edition itself: numerous publications claim to reproduce the first editions, but so far I have found none that do so reliably, especially with regard to textual-formal issues such as line length and stanzaic structure. A good example is Ricordi's own *Puccini: Le Prime*, in the series *Le Prime: Libretti della prima rappresentazione*, which claims to reproduce "the original versions of the librettos" Puccini set to music (Milan: Ricordi, 2002: 5), but the text in this publication does not agree completely with that of the first edition (plate no. 116999), even though nowhere is there citation of another source for the text. The Garzanti edition edited by Enrico Maria Ferrando (*Tutti i libretti di Puccini,* Milan: Garzanti, 1984) also contains problematic discrepancies, despite citing as its source the final versions of the librettos handed to Puccini by his librettists. Again, more than indicating any shortcomings in these various editions, the inconsistencies underscore the difficulty of identifying the definitive source for any libretto.

Unless otherwise indicated, all Italian translations are my own. Libretto translations are mine also, although I relied to some extent on published English translations, as noted in the text.

Il Trittico, Turandot,
and Puccini's Late Style

Hearing Puccini

This book has grown out of a deep fascination with the experience of Puccini's operas: the ways the music on the stage moves the listeners in the theater. Like many commentators on Puccini from his own lifetime and more recently, I have always found in his music a contrast between the new, or unfamiliar, and the traditional (in the sense of stylistically Romantic), or familiar. This feature of Puccini was clear to me from my earliest experiences with this music—the times when I first discovered opera, attended Puccini productions, or listened to recordings—what I anticipated and what I heard were often two very different things. As a scholar, I found this frustrating; it was a feature of Puccini's work that was easy to hear but not at all easy to explain, and much of my work in opera analysis since has been devoted to trying to account for this discrepancy. My thinking on the subject has been heavily influenced by the work of Carolyn Abbate, Gary Tomlinson, Lawrence Kramer, and the captivating work of French psychoanalyst Michel Poizat, each of whom has addressed, in different theoretical contexts, the kinds of experiences I had while listening to Puccini.[1] One of the most useful ideas in this literature for describing analytically what I heard, and thus one that underlies a considerable portion of this book, is that of opera as *uncanny*. This is the idea that part of opera's fascination lies in its capacity to produce an objectified singing voice—a voice heard not simply as sound, but also as a tangible object of fascination—and, moreover, in how the art form exploits this capacity by overtly inviting listeners to aurally revel in the singers on the stage. And while this book is not overtly semiotic,

I have been heavily influenced by the musical semiotics of Robert Hatten, in which marked oppositions of style types, genres, and topics—as well as expressive manipulations of conventional, background formal schemata—are the tools with which composers create meaning in music.

Puccini seemed to me a master of the musical phenomena these writers were describing. As a listener, my attention gravitated naturally toward moments when I could hear, as a result of striking contrasts in the musical language, the composer turning attention in the music toward the singing voice. The voice became objectified in these moments, precisely the moments in which I also found the music to be the most traditional and the most familiar—in the sense that this was the music I expected when I came to the opera house or put on the recording. This was no coincidence, of course, and indeed all these impressions of Puccini—his music as a mix of new and old, as familiar and unfamiliar, and as music that shifts the focus of attention—are related. All stem from Puccini's strategically mixing a traditionally Italian operatic language with a compositional approach that borrows from contemporary European musical trends. The method is *strategic* because Puccini does more than simply mix the two styles: he systematically withholds until pivotal dramatic junctures the most traditional of his musical tokens in order to heighten their effect on his listening audience. As a result, the most traditionally Italian lyric music in these works becomes rhetorically charged, or *marked,* so that its appearance forces a shift of listeners' attention away from the music as music per se and onto the performer's presence on the stage, and, more specifically, the performer's *voice.* Anyone who loves this music is likely familiar with this remarkable effect. As Poizat has suggested, it can trigger irrational, somewhat hyperbolic emotional responses—often physically manifested in tears; it also accounts in part for Puccini's reputation as a sentimentalist—a tugger of heart strings. This effect shapes much of what I have to say here.

This book offers analyses of Puccini's last four operas as a lens through which to view what I consider his *late style:* the works that most clearly exhibit this strategic approach to incorporating contrasting musical styles. This approach is evident throughout Puccini's oeuvre, but, as the result of an evolution I will discuss more thoroughly in the epilogue, it becomes the governing aesthetic in the three one-acts of *Il trittico—Il tabarro, Suor Angelica,* and *Gianni Schicchi*—that premiered in New York in December 1918, and in the final, unfinished *Turandot,* premiered posthumously in Milan in April 1926. These four works come at the end of what is generally regarded as a three-phase career that produced a dozen operas. Puccini's two early works, *Le villi* and *Edgar,* never entered the standard repertory but have enjoyed a resurgence in popular and critical appreciation.[2] His four mature works—*Manon Lescaut, La bohème, Tosca,* and *Madama Butterfly*—remain among the most often-produced operas in theaters worldwide. And his late works—*La fanciulla del West, La rondine, Il trittico,* and *Turandot*—together comprise a gradual move toward a newer, less conventional, and in some ways more experimental compositional approach that found its ultimate manifestation in *Il trittico* and *Turandot.* The tortured genesis of the latter dates to the three and a half years preceding his untimely death in November 1924 from complications related to throat cancer.

All six late works, moreover, followed a long personal and professional crisis for Puccini that ensued between *Butterfly* and *La fanciulla.* Puccini had a debilitating automobile accident in February 1903 that necessitated a long and frustrating convalescence. *Butterfly* premiered unsuccessfully one year later at La Scala in Milan, sending Puccini into what has been described as "suicidal despair."[3] Critics and others, including his publisher and longtime confidant, Giulio Ricordi, called for Puccini to undertake a more novel, ambitious work—further complicating his search for a new libretto after *Butterfly.* His marriage to Elvira Bonturi Gemignani—with whom he had been living since 1885 but whose husband had died only the day after Puccini's car accident in February 1903, and thus whom he had been able to formally marry only in January 1904—became increasingly troubled, not least because of Puccini's own series of affairs with other women. Finally, in these years he wrestled with an interest in, but continuing ambivalence toward, contemporary literary trends, with influences that included the work of Gabriele D'Annunzio (with whom he considered a collaboration that was never brought to fruition), Oscar Wilde, and, later, avant-gardists Luigi Pirandello and Pier Maria Rosso di San Secondo.[4]

This understanding of Puccini's late style as having crystallized most clearly in *Il trittico* and *Turandot* excludes from the book consideration of the other two operas normally understood as emerging from his late period, *La fanciulla del West* and *La rondine*. *Fanciulla* has long been considered a transitional experiment for Puccini, and any detailed exploration of Puccini's move in it away from the mature, lyric style he cultivated in *Manon Lescaut, La bohème, Tosca,* and *Butterfly* and toward a more continuous, recitative style that suppresses conventional lyricism could easily be the subject of another book-length study. *Rondine* has likewise long been considered something of an anomaly in Puccini's career—Puccini's own conception of an operetta, written on a commission from the impresarios of Vienna's Carltheater, premiered (because of the ongoing world war) in Monte Carlo, and published not by Casa Ricordi but by Ricordi's rival in Milan, Lorenzo Sonzogno. Stylistically, the piece lies somewhat closer to the music of Puccini's middle period than to the other late works.

The analytical point of departure for this book is Puccini's strategic use of *stylistic plurality*. This term describes heterogeneous music in which diverse styles are exploited to such a degree that the contrasts among them—rather than the styles themselves—become the focal point for the listening audience. This is music that can be said to be written *with styles* rather than *in a style*. In much of Puccini's music under consideration here, the interpretative value of this hermeneutic approach is obvious and unproblematic. *Turandot* in particular is characterized by the use of at least three separate, discrete stylistic categories, some of which involve traditional, Romantic music and others of which consciously undercut it. Ashbrook and Powers were two of the first to discuss this aspect of the work in their 1991 book on *Turandot*, and Jürgen Maehder has for years now described the piece as a "sophisticated game" of generic-stylistic interactions.[5] But in other of Puccini's works, including the three operas of the *Trittico*, the stylistic plurality is less apparent: here it takes the form not of several discrete stylistic categories, but rather of a binary opposition between music that suppresses the conventional lyric style on the one hand and music that exploits it on the other. The contrasts and tension between the two approaches become the central aesthetic concern in these three works—just as in *Turandot* the main point of interest is not the styles themselves but rather how Puccini handles them structurally and exploits their dissimilarities. In the end, this hermeneutic approach yields a common understanding of all four of Puccini's last operas: each systematically suppresses the most conventional, familiar musical idioms in the service of heightening the already potent affective power of Puccini's most traditional, lyric writing.

This book comprises seven chapters: an opening theoretical chapter, another on Puccini's idiosyncratic brand of the Italian lyric style, a chapter on each of his last four works, and an epilogue. Chapter 1 constructs the theoretical apparatus, with special attention to stylistic plurality as a theoretical notion and its role in this music's capacity for emotional, expressive impact on its theater audiences. Regarding the latter, two overlapping constructs from recent music analysis, one from musical semiotics and another from narrative theory, prove particularly useful. One is Robert Hatten's *levels of discourse,* a paradigm borrowed from literary criticism but which is also, as Hatten has shown, applicable to music;[6] the other is Carolyn Abbate's notion of musical *voices,* an idea that in a musical performance sound is perceived as originating not from a single source but rather from multiple sources—multiple voices—where some of these engage in the act of narration and others do not.

Chapter 2 is a detailed exploration of Puccini's conventional lyric style. Using as a framework recent analyses from the secondary Puccini literature, the chapter explains, in examples from the last four works, aspects of Puccini's lyric strategies in his melody, orchestration, harmony, voice leading, and local and large-scale metric structures. These analyses—unlike much of the published work on Puccini, which is more musicological and less overtly theoretical—also seek to situate Puccini's music in a broader analytical context and thus draw on approaches that have proven important for understanding tonal (often instrumental) music but that have never before been applied systematically in an attempt to understand Puccini. Especially important in this regard are the Schenkerian theories of rhythm and meter from the work of Carl Schachter and William Rothstein.[7] These approaches are valuable because so much of Puccini's expressive power can be said to lie in his ability to manipulate the listener's sense of time, which he accomplishes in part by employing a metric structure highly regular at its underlying background levels but highly irregular and elastic at its surface levels.

Chapters 3–6 comprise, respectively, detailed investigations of structure and design in *Tabarro, Angelica, Gianni Schicchi,* and *Turandot.* These analyses all involve in-depth consideration of Puccini's engagement with nineteenth-century Italian operatic conventions of form and design known collectively in recent literature as *la solita forma.* This is a complex subject in Puccini studies: the *solita forma* is a rubric generally regarded as applicable to Italian opera through mid-Verdi, though Harold Powers and Philip Gossett have compellingly shown that even Verdi's late works (especially *Aïda*) conform to—or, better, are rooted in but *expressively deform*—such formal conventions much more than would appear to be the case on the surface. This runs contrary to the notion, widespread in the Verdi literature, that Verdi did his best to *shed* or *avoid* the constraints of the old formal structures, an idea that should be understood as grossly oversimplified at best or simply incorrect at worst.[8] The relevance of the *solita forma* for Puccini and his late nineteenth- and early twentieth-century contemporaries is less clear: a 2001 Lucca conference devoted to this subject produced, among other important work, a seminal article by Verdi scholar David Rosen that explores the potential of the *solita forma* as a framework for understanding Puccini's formal designs. Michele Girardi had, before this, raised the question in his award-winning 1995 life-and-works study, and the issue is traceable in Puccini studies to William Ashbrook and Harold Powers' study of *Turandot.*[9] I view the discussion as ongoing and the issue as far from settled: clearly the *solita forma* conventions remain distantly removed from Puccini's formal strategies in large portions of his works, but just as clearly, it seems, Puccini's scores and librettos—especially those of the last four works, more so than the eight preceding operas—provide compelling evidence that on some occasions the conventions are not entirely irrelevant. More to the point, *hearing* Puccini's music *with this question in mind*—with the conventions in the cognitive background, as a framework within which the music moves and against which we measure its temporal unfolding—provides fascinating opportunities to interpret its theatrical effect and expressive meaning.

A speculative epilogue explores in more detail the notion of Puccini's late style as it relates to certain aspects of his biography—especially a depression that apparently afflicted him early but that seems to have grown more severe over the last twenty or so years of his life. This, combined with other disabilities and illnesses (either temporary, such as the physical debilitation following his car accident; chronic, such as the diabetes he first mentions in his correspondence around 1903; or terminal—the sore throat first reported toward the end of 1923, which, unbeknownst to Puccini, was the result of a malignant tumor under his epiglottis) that appear to have had a significant impact on both his frame of mind and his creative output, may account for the move in his music toward what we can view retrospectively as a late style.

The best musical analyses bring to light ways of hearing the music one may never have stumbled upon intuitively but that, once studied and fully considered, have the potential to inform one's listening experience and thus—especially in opera—enhance one's understanding of the music's expressive, theatrical power. I hope to have contributed to the Puccini conversation a historically informed examination of his late music that complements the best recent work on the subject and that does some justice to—in meaningful and audible ways—Puccini's considerable theatrical achievements.

ONE

Stylistic Plurality, Narrative, Levels of Discourse, and Voice

Il trittico and *Turandot* provide good laboratories for exploring the technical means behind the theatrical efficacy of Puccini's late operas. One feature emerges above all others as key to these works' identities: each is distinguished by a musical-stylistic plurality in which multiple, distinct musical styles or compositional approaches are juxtaposed in time and space in the service of formal organization and expressive effect. The trend toward mixing apparently incompatible styles in a single musical work has become an important topic for discussion in recent musicology. A wide body of literature has recognized its importance in modern music, both operatic and symphonic;[1] and much of the recent Puccini literature, especially that which leans toward a view of him as a modern composer seeking to assimilate contemporary trends in European music and theater, has explored the pluralistic character of his late music.[2]

Defining stylistically heterogeneous music as such is not as straightforward as it may seem. It could be said, for example, that a composer's *style* is to employ a variety of stylistic references, or that the style of a particular work is one that mixes various compositional approaches. Perhaps, in other words, *Puccini's style* is simply to *mix styles,* and maybe in reality—in the broadest possible view—the late works are not as variegated as they seem. The point seems to hinge on the level at which we locate *style:* it can reside at the level of a single work (e.g., "the style of *Turandot*"), a group of works (perhaps works that employ similar compositional strategies and which were composed around the same time—"Puccini's mature style," for example, in reference to his work of the 1890s and early 1900s), a single composer ("Puccini's style"), a group of composers ("the style of the *giovane scuola italiana*"), a genre ("the style of nineteenth-century Italian opera"), or a historical era ("the late-Romantic style"); many other levels may be possible.[3] In asserting here that Puccini's late operas exhibit stylistic plurality, I posit style as located *below* the level of the whole work—below, certainly, the level of "Puccini's style" or "the style of the *giovane scuola italiana*." Doing so allows for attention to two important components in the style construct and its analysis: *compositional choice* and *symbolic competency*. First, modern composers have numerous styles at their disposal, and music composition entails, among other decisions, choices of which style to use at various moments in the work. Second, from an analyst's point of view, interpreting a composer's strategic deployment of the available options presupposes a competency—that is, an understanding, shared by the composer and listener alike—in the symbolic, expressive potential of the styles and their interactions.[4]

Consider in this context some of the definitions of style employed by recent authors. Larry Starr calls it "a mutually understood [between listener and composer] context within which communication may take place with some ease and fluency"; Leonard Meyer calls it "a replication of patterning, either in human behavior or in the artifacts produced by human behavior, that results from a series of choices made within some set of constraints."[5] Puccini's late music is stylistically heterogeneous in both of these views, and recent writers on Puccini have expanded on this point. Ivanka Stoïanova has described *Turandot* as a "patchwork quilt" of disparate musical fragments, each linked as a temporal chain of "boxes" or "sonorous panels" in which each panel has its own uniform character; Carner has described *Turandot* as a "remarkable fusion" of separate stylistic elements, all of which appear, independently, in Puccini's earlier work; and Girardi has described Puccini's late operas as moving toward "multistylistic experimentation."[6]

But consider also that to claim stylistic pluralism as the single most important feature of Puccini's late operas may be doing nothing more than pointing out the obvious, that his operas follow in a long line of works employing a wide variety of styles in the service of the broadest possible range of musical-dramatic expression. Indeed, as numerous writers have noted, the technique is fundamental to the genre itself and overt in the music of Monteverdi, Handel, Mozart, Wagner, Mahler, Strauss, Verdi (especially late Verdi), and Berg, among many other composers of dramatic and symphonic (especially programmatic) music. Carl Dahlhaus, for example, aptly observed that "the musical-dramatic means available to composers of opera, and the principles from which they can proceed, are uncommonly heterogeneous by comparison with those in other musical or theatrical genres. This has less to do with differences in the stylistic traditions converging in one work than with the divergences between the forms in which music fulfills dramaturgical functions," and, similarly, "The musical means at an opera composer's command are so heterogeneous that we can scarcely speak of 'operatic' style as we speak of 'symphonic' or 'chamber-music' style."[7] In Puccini's case, the important question becomes not whether stylistic pluralism is *present* (it is, by my definition), but rather *how* and *for what expressive purpose* the various styles are used and, moreover, whether the pluralistic elements are compatible and integrated or whether they pose a threat to the musical-dramatic integrity and coherence of the work.[8] In Puccini's late music, the styles are expressive and they rise to the level of the *raison d'être* of the works themselves: indeed, invoking Starr's definition and understanding *style* as a *frame* confining a composer's musical language to a certain mutually recognized conceptual space, we may say that Puccini's late operas break this frame so often that they may best be regarded not as composed *in a style* but as composed *with styles*.[9] Contrasting styles are elemental to every aspect of this music, especially its formal organization, its narrative expression, and its theatrical efficacy; more than abstract compositional tools, these are very real, essential components of the means by which these works move their theater audiences.

It seems natural that Puccini would have made a move at some point in his career toward stylistic plurality, given his desire both to respond to his critics' and publisher's demands for more novelty in his operas, and to maintain a high level of interest among members of the opera-going public—with whose approval Puccini was obsessed throughout his career. This latter concern especially was an important motivating force: Puccini knew that most members of his audience (at least as he and many other Italian opera composers of his generation understood them) came to the opera house with some awareness of the traditional, nineteenth-century, Italian repertoire, and that they would recognize references to, and departures from, the language of that repertoire in Puccini's own music. Thus it also follows that stylistic plurality should have entailed for Puccini not simply a mixture of styles broadly defined, but more specifically a juxtaposition of compositional procedures recognized as conventional with others recognized as unconventional—or, more specifically still, those of a traditional, Italian, Romantic stylistic language with those of a newer, less conventional, more international approach.

Loyalty toward nineteenth-century Italian-opera traditions and, more generally, toward the musical language of his Tuscan heritage is one of the clearest features of Puccini's music. Alexandra Wilson has recently established that Puccini's reputation in the popular Italian media of his time was built precisely on this feature of his work,[10] and even today his reputation for many rests on the notion that his operas represent the Italian tradition at its zenith. He consistently exhibited concern for the most fundamental qualities of traditional Italian opera, including, among others, direct appeals to his audience's emotions, incorporation of uniquely Italian cultural elements, and a concern for the procedures of musical-dramatic form and design developed over the course of several preceding generations. Such concerns surface often in his correspondence throughout his career: he wrote, for example, to Gabriele D'Annunzio, while discussing a possible collaboration, "But give me a great love scene. Will it be possible? On this subject? And above all each act would have its own great emotion to fling at the audience"; to Giuseppe Adami, in reference to Adami's *Turandot* libretto, "It could also be that in conserving the masks *with discretion,* one would have a regional element that, in the middle of so much Chinese mannerism (such as it is), would bring a local touch, and above all a sincere one" (emphasis in original); and to friend and confidant Riccardo Schnabl Rossi, "*Turandot* is sleeping: it wants a big aria in the second [act]; I need to insert it, and I need . . . to find it."[11]

But whether explicitly expressed or not, Puccini's concern for traditional facets of Italian opera is always evident in his music—in, among other parameters, his melodies, harmonic procedures, and dramaturgical aesthetics. Some are obvious: the long, fluid melodies, for example, or the lyric vocal-orchestral climaxes, or the relative simplicity of the melodic and harmonic language (especially at the most expressive moments in the scores). Others are more subtle: a psychological realism and directness of affect—both of which contribute to his reputation for being able to establish a bond between composer and spectator, and, as a result, move the spectator emotionally—and a certain (perceived, if not real) sincerity, humanity, and immediacy of sentiment, all of which are characteristic in traditional Italian opera and which remained important in Puccini's work throughout his career. All of his works—even the late operas—exhibit these features to some extent; all have a large role in explaining how he managed to ensure his operas remained comprehensible to the widest possible listening audience.

Among all these aspects of his compositional approach, one in particular has garnered extensive musicological attention in recent years: his attitude toward existing notions of how a piece of Italian musical theater should be formally constructed. These notions can be understood collectively within the rubric of the *solita forma* (literally "the usual form"): the loosely codified yet highly formalized, complex network of Italian musical-dramatic formal conventions that began to take their definitive nineteenth-century shapes around the time of Rossini. These conventions were well established in Italy by the mid-nineteenth century. They informed the views of Italian composers, librettists, and critics alike, and they governed the way most of the content—plot, text, and music—was to be organized and delivered in an *ottocento* opera, shaping as such nearly every facet of the operatic complex, from dramatic action to verbal structure to musical setting.

The term *solita forma* originates in a single, now-famous line from the work of the nineteenth-century Florentine scientist, doctor, philosopher, music critic, and composer Abramo Basevi—specifically, from his *Studio sulle opere di Giuseppe Verdi*. In this work, in passing and in the middle of a discussion of Verdi's Rigoletto-Sparafucile duet, Basevi makes note of "la solita forma dei duetti, cioè . . . quella che vuole un *tempo d'attacco*, l'*adagio*, il *tempo di mezzo*, e la *Cabaletta*" ("the usual form of duets, that is . . . with a *tempo d'attacco, adagio, tempo di mezzo,* and *Cabaletta*")—his point being that the Rigoletto-Sparafucile duet does not fit the mold.[12] The simplicity and dispassion of Basevi's statement belies its (often controversial) status as the source of most recent

Italian-opera analysis that takes as its focus—whether in operas of Rossini, Bellini, Donizetti, Verdi, Puccini, or others—underlying "melodramatic structures": "the conventional presumptions about how a particular kind of piece is supposed to work that lie behind any specific piece of that kind."[13] Such analysis rests on the historically informed presumption that the dominant organizing force in this repertoire—nineteenth-century Italian melodrama[14]—is a particular patterning in the sequence of musical genres or textures, all supported with coincident articulations in the organization of the poetic verse. Genres may include the *rondò, cabaletta, stretta, ritornello, pezzo concertato,* and others, while textures may include, for example, the *recitative, parlante armonico, parlante melodico,* and aria.

The words *texture* and *genre* in Italian opera can be problematic. The standard terminology for defining textures comes from Basevi, who identifies a continuous hierarchy of textures that describes the most typical relationships between voice and orchestra found in nineteenth-century Italian opera and that progresses from least to most melodic: "a sort of chain may be constructed between the various categories of vocal music, placing in succession simple recitative, obbligato recitative, harmonic parlante, melodic parlante, and finally aria."[15] Practically speaking, Puccini and his late nineteenth- and early twentieth-century Italian contemporaries continued to use these same textures, even though theirs sometimes differed from Verdi's and they tended to employ the *parlante* textures far more extensively than Verdi ever did. *Genre* is also difficult in that it may refer, for example, to "comic opera," "serious opera," or "opera semiseria," but I prefer to allow for a wider definition that includes a more complex generic hierarchy and thus generic categories such as "overtures," "arias," "duets," "ensembles," "finales," and even "*tempi d'attacco*" or "*cabalette*"—or indeed any other category encompassing structures or groups of structures with normative patterns in their music and text against which we may measure a composer's choices in order to expressively interpret the music.[16] Note also that much confusion is avoided if one distinguishes between the *textural* meaning of the common terms "aria" and "recitative" and the *structural* meanings of the same terms; "aria," for example, refers to a texture in which the voice carries all the melodic material while the orchestra has a purely accompanimental role, whereas the same word refers in a structural sense to a closed lyric set piece for a single character, perhaps in multiple movements exhibiting a variety of textures.[17]

At the largest level the *solita forma* is a schema comprising a series of four movements (or five: a *scena*—the *recitative*[18]—may precede the four core movements, even though Basevi himself never mentions this), all with typical, identifiable characteristics in their music and text. Following recent work in cognitive theory, by *schema* (pl. *schemata*) I mean a normative model—a "packet of knowledge"—we can use to interpret and compare any number of immediate, real-world experiences.[19] Schemata can take the form of a *prototype,* or an ideal type, which usually exists only in the abstract and the constituent features of which are intuited by an observer from features common in a variety of similar experiences in comparable contexts. It can be an *exemplar,* a model example of something (a style or genre, for instance) but not necessarily a prototype, with which one is intimately familiar and which thus may serve as a yardstick against which one can measure other similar constructs (e.g., the Parthenon is, for many, an exemplar of Classical Greek architecture). Or it can be a *hypothesis,* derived from experience and intended to explain, as Robert Gjerdingen has phrased it, "the nature of things and their meaning."[20] In most recent studies of musical form and design and especially in this book, a schema is best understood as a prototype: an ideal shape or organizational pattern abstracted from the common formal features in comparable musical genres. The formal prototype for almost all Classical and Romantic orchestral music and much chamber music, for example, is the sonata; likewise, the formal prototype for almost all Italian arias written in the first half of the eighteenth century is the da capo.

Understanding exemplars, prototypes, and their relationship to schemata is important because it will help dispel the rather traditional, oversimplified notion that an exemplar of something (a form, style, or genre, among others) necessarily contains all the constituent features of its underlying schema.[21] This is simply not true, and as cognitive beings we construct exemplars, prototypes, and schemata very differently, in much more complex ways. Exemplars need not exhibit all the features of a schema—or, more generally, a *category*—in order to be understood as a member of a category or as representative of a prototype; some exemplars will necessarily be better examples of their categories than others.

Conversely, an exemplar need not exhibit all a category's distinguishing characteristics in order to be understood as belonging in that category; in fact, no member of any category—no exemplar of any schema—will ever constitute a perfect example. Contrast this with the more traditional view of categorization, in which a category is defined only by features shared among all its members; this means no member of a category could be a better example of that category than any other.[22] But, practically speaking, this cannot be true: we know from basic intuition that some sonata-form movements, for example, comprise better examples of the sonata form than others. In some sense, then, an unqualified judgment on whether an exemplar is or is not a member of a category, or based on an underlying schema, is impossible. Rather, membership in categories is graded: some exemplars necessarily will have more or less membership than others. The *most* representative examples approach the status of *prototypes*.

Using schemata to interpret musical form and design is a dialectictal process: musical features function as cues for a schema, and, conversely, a schema's presence guides the search for and detection of features in the music. A modulation from tonic to dominant in a Classical orchestral movement may signal an emerging sonata form; in an *ottocento* opera, a shift from a *parlante melodico* texture in a relatively fast tempo to an aria texture in a slower tempo may signal a shift from the first movement (the *tempo d'attacco*) to the second (the *adagio*) of a multi-movement *solita forma*. On the other hand, the generic title "overture" for a Classical orchestral piece implies that the sonata form is the governing schema; thus, no matter how unusual the ensuing form may appear to be (the first modulation we hear is from tonic to subdominant instead of dominant, for example), we should interpret it as a deformed sonata.[23] Likewise, two characters on stage in an *ottocento* opera signal that the *solita forma* of a duet is the governing schema, and thus not only does it imply the necessity of the tempo change described earlier (and many other such events) even before it happens, but it also implies that we should interpret the scene as a deformed duet no matter how unusual the ensuing form may be. In each scenario, departures from the schematic norms beg the questions "why?" and "what does it mean?"—*not* the questions, "is this a sonata?" or "is this a duet?" The deformations present opportunities for meaningful, expressive interpretation.

Consider also that the tendency to oversimplify the relationship between a schema and its features surfaces often in basic music theory pedagogy, especially in the pedagogy of musical forms (but also in, for example, voice-leading pedagogy), and most readers who have experience teaching such topics will find it familiar. Instructors often (and, presumably, inadvertently) present the sonata form, for example, in ways that encourage students to seek out the "perfect" model sonata—one that adheres exactly to the sonata schema—in, perhaps, music of the Classic period; when students fail to find it, they become frustrated and question the utility of such oversimplified notions (or—worse—arrive at the naïve conclusion that "rules exist in order to be broken"). But, of course, no perfect sonata form exists in the real, living musical tradition, just as, in Italian opera, there is no perfect multi-movement set piece—no prototypical exemplar of Basevi's *solita forma;* both exist only in the abstract, and to even seek out such a thing is to completely miss the point of why we identify such schemata to begin with. For analysts, schemata allow us to make predictions and form expectations about what we hear; they provide an interpretive context, or interpretive frame, for various events or features we experience in the music. Without the schemata, everything we hear becomes simply an ad hoc series of events with no meaning, because we have no context in which to interpret them and no model against which to make meaningful comparisons. For example, a theme in a non-tonic key in a Beethoven recapitulation has significance, and thus meaning, precisely because the relevant schema—the sonata— implies that it must be (and thus we expect it to be) in the tonic; the lack of a concluding *cabaletta* in a Verdi duet is likewise meaningful because the schema demands its presence. Without a schema in the cognitive background, there is nothing at all unusual—and thus nothing at all meaningful—about either event.

These principles occupy central positions in recent work on formal design in music, wherein *form* is understood not as an inherent property of the music itself but rather as something a listener *constructs* by measuring what is heard against established schemata. When what is heard departs from what a schema implies should occur, the music is understood as being *in dialogue* with the schema; thus all form in music is in some sense *dialogic.* In James Hepokoski's formulation, "The concept of 'form' is not primarily a property of the printed page or sounding surface. Instead, 'form' resides more properly in the composer- and listener-activated process of measuring what one hears against what one is invited to expect. . . . Form exists in that conceptual dialogue with implicit generic norms, which exist outside of the material surface of the printed page and its acoustic realization." Constructs such as *sonata form* in Classical instrumental music and *la solita forma* in *ottocento* opera are thus "sets of tools for understanding" (read: sets of tools for interpreting) a piece of music more so than they are criteria that must be satisfied before we allow a piece a label such as "sonata" or "duet."[24] Ultimately, understanding music according to such formal schemata requires invoking a complex network of generic expectations; meaning and expression in musical form and structure therefore reside ultimately in the dialogue between our immediate musical experience and the relevant underlying schemata and all its implications.

These kinds of musical expectations, and thus ultimately these kinds of interpretations, are possible in *ottocento* opera in part because the individual components of the formal schema—in this case understood as movements, as in movements of a symphony or a quartet—have their own distinguishing, prototypical musical-dramatic characteristics.[25] The schema for multi-movement set pieces—duets, arias, central finales—is the pattern of textures and genres Basevi referred to as the *solita forma*, and, as Basevi's remark indicates, the formal prototype is that of the *grand duet* as it appears in Verdi's music through the 1871 *Aïda*.[26] Dramatically, each of the schema's four movements is either *kinetic* (that is, *active,* in the sense that the plot moves) or *static* (that is, more *reflective* and without plot development):[27] the *tempo d'attacco* and *tempo di mezzo* are kinetic, while the *adagio* and *cabaletta* are static. This forms a double cycle of action-reaction, action-reaction that is key to understanding large-scale Italian operatic form. Textually, the *tempo d'attacco* is typically marked in the verse by a shift from the *versi sciolti* (literally "loose verse," comprising in Verdi unrhymed, ungrouped lines seven or eleven syllables in length—*settenari* and *endecasillabi,* respectively)[28] of the *recitative* to the *versi lirici* ("lyric verse": rhymed lines grouped into stanzas usually comprising four, six, or eight lines, all in the same meter). Musically, many *tempi d'attacco* are complex and multisectional, where some of the internal sections may be rather lyric and thus easily mistaken for a separate *adagio* movement. The actual *adagio* (some call it, more generically, the "cantabile" or "slow movement," or simply refer to it with its actual tempo designation, which may or may not be ada-gio),[29] the first of the two lyric movements, typically comprises parallel statements (*proposta* and *risposta*) for each singer on the same or similar music, followed by an interlude (perhaps more dialogue) and often *a due* (i.e., simultaneous) singing in a coda. The *tempo di mezzo* follows and normally introduces a new character or some kind of major, irreversible change in the dramatic situation; this in turn justifies the lyric release characteristic of the *cabaletta,* which is always faster in tempo than the *adagio* and comprises parallel thematic statements for each character (similar to the *adagio*), a transition, and a complete repetition of the main thematic material *a due* (the latter is perhaps the most distinguish-ing feature of *cabalette*).

One of the most crucial aspects of organization in nineteenth-cen-tury Italian opera is that the musical and textual schema are intertwined: expectations for the *musical* form—the succession of genres, textures, and tempos—govern the *textual* form.[30] That is to say, the librettist plans the libretto with the musical schema—the *solita forma*—in mind, so that when the composer goes to set text to music, the musical form is already articulated in the libretto. This may seem troubling for those who would seek to find dramatic veracity, or indeed dramatic viability, in *ottocento* librettos: their internal structure and indeed their shapes at the largest levels derive from situations for which specific compositional procedures and formal patterns are already predetermined. Broadly speaking, dra-matic action is shaped not only by conventional notions of character, plot, and situation but also by prescriptions for generic-formal articu-lations in both music and libretto. Moreover, an understanding of the *solita forma* as a schema means that, in practice, this was not a rigid mold into which a scenario was poured and from which a set piece emerged; rather, this was a flexible formal-organizational pattern, the effectiveness of which resided in its ability to accommodate expansions, contractions, and other deformations in the hands of composers or librettists seeking novel ways of managing dramatic situations—similar to, as mentioned, how the expressive power of a sonata form lies in large part in its capacity to accommodate deformations of formal norms anticipated by the lis-tener. Indeed, in *ottocento* operas and classical sonata forms alike, defor-mations of the schema were the *norm,* not the *exception,* and in almost all cases it can be established that the deformations were *intentional* (even if not *conscious*) on the part of the composer and thus imbued with dramatic meaning. For such strategies to be effective, of course, listeners had to have understood the underlying schemata and internalized them to an extent that allowed them to recognize and interpret deformations of the normative schemes as they happened, in real time, in the theater (just as, again, a sonata form's capacity for communicating meaning depends on a listener's *a priori* fluency with normal sonata prototypes).[31]

Puccini's relationship to the *solita forma* schema is complex, and our understanding of it continues to evolve. While, as mentioned, authors have for decades recognized the presence of stylistic plurality in Puccini (Carner's biography was first published in 1958), recognition of the *solita forma* in this music is much more recent and can be traced to the 1991 publication of William Ashbrook and Harold Powers' *Puccini's "Turandot": The End of the Great Tradition*. The issue remained important in Michele Girardi's *Giacomo Puccini: L'arte internazionale di un musicista italiano,* published shortly thereafter, in 1995. Ashbrook and Powers see the conventional schemata as the main governing force behind *Turandot*'s formal organization, while in Girardi's view they interact with numerous other simultaneously unfolding formal processes. More recent writers have followed Girardi's lead and adopted more caution: most take the view that the sweeping spirit of social and political upheaval characteristic of the *Italia umbertina* period spilled over into opera,[32] such that Italian opera of the era exhibits a gradual move away from the more conventional, nineteenth-century formal strategies and toward newer forms much more freely tailored to the drama—forms that allowed for a greater sense of dramatic realism. Thus by the time of Puccini's maturity the *solita forma,* practically speaking, may no longer have existed as a formula to which Puccini adhered (in the sense that Verdi used it overtly, explicitly, as a model on which his scenes were constructed), but nevertheless may have continued to exist as a schema that could be integrated with other organizational approaches and invoked for expressive effect. That is, even if each opera became more of an ad hoc construction in which the dramatic action had more control over the musical design—and in which conventional elements (genres, textures, verse forms and meters, etc.) remained present but also became divorced from their normal formal functions, to be used only in accordance with dramatic logic—the conventional formal schemata continued to be relevant as prototypes on which a composer could draw to communicate meaning and against which the music and its organization can be measured and interpreted. My sense here is that Puccini's organizational strategy in the late works is one in which he achieves the "best of two worlds," so to speak:[33] he retained—or, better, *used strategically*—the traditional, high *ottocento* style and its related formal schemata, integrated within a well-developed language in which he also assimilated contemporary, *episodic* approaches to form and design. This position on Puccini's relationship more generally with *ottocento* conventions resonates with parallel, ongoing research in Puccini studies that suggests Puccini may have been predisposed toward engaging with other *ottocento* schemata in other areas of his compositional technique.[34]

At the same time, that the other side of Puccini's stylistic pluralism should involve newer, less conventional, and more internationally informed strategies should also come as no surprise, given his well-documented, lifelong interest in introducing unconventional features into his work. Most recent Puccini research addresses this point in some detail. Commentators have pointed out that international influences, many at odds with Italian conventions and aesthetics—including the German symphonic tradition, French harmonic and orchestrational traditions, and, to a lesser extent, aspects of Wagnerian chromaticism, among others—are clear even in Puccini's earliest compositions, including the Mass (1880) and the *Preludio sinfonico* in A (1882); that while his first opera, *Le villi,* is designated generically as an *opera-ballo,* the ballet is actually a more integral part of this work than in other contemporary Italian works of the same genre, a feature that places it—like so much of what Puccini wrote throughout his career—closer to the French tradition; that his tendency to rely less on the traditional Italian formal schemes and more on ad-hoc, through-composed, or even symphonic forms as large-scale frameworks for his operas clearly dates from the time of *Manon Lescaut, La bohème,* and even the earliest works, *Le villi* and *Edgar;* that *Tosca* is more indebted to French realism than to the so-called Italian *verismo* (for more on which, see chapter 3); and that *La fanciulla del West* borrows heavily from early expressionism and other trends in the fin-de-siècle European theater—as is clear in the interiority of its text, its realistic characters, and those characters' expressions of an unusually wide spectrum of human passions and obsessions.[35] Indeed, his unconventionality was an important topic in contemporary Puccini criticism; Fausto Torrefranca himself, infamous for lambasting Puccini's lack of creativity, among other perceived sins, also criticized him, somewhat ironically for modern readers, for abandoning his national heritage in favor of an unconventional, "international" style.

These conventional and unconventional strategies work together to expand the richness of Puccini's late work, not only in the sense that they introduce to the music an expanded expressive palette, but also because they expand the range of experiential levels on which listeners may engage with each piece. That is to say, in Puccini's late operas, stylistic plurality has the effect of revealing openly the mechanical means with which the works are constructed—means which, in more conventional works, would have been more carefully concealed—and thus also has the secondary effect of diverting spectators' attention away from purely musical or dramatic matters and onto more structural-technical concerns. This is not a flaw, certainly, but rather an aesthetic effect known in the theater as *distancing*. It was first introduced in the Italian theater by Pirandello and is similar to what Bertolt Brecht famously called *alienation* (Gr. *Verfremdung*): the act of suppressing viewers' empathetic responses in the interest of forcing them to consider a work of art in a more objective, detached manner, as an intellectual exercise or an artistic statement, rather than as pure entertainment.[36] In Puccini, the force of these effects stems mainly from his innovative approach to formal design, which, again, was an approach rooted in the music of the *giovane scuola italiana*—the group of Italian composers, including Puccini, who matured in the 1880s. All four operas under consideration here are more accurately described with respect to their formal organization not as fully organic or conventional, but rather as episodic. Much of Puccini's late music—especially *Turandot*, but also all three panels of the *Trittico*—proceeds according to a series of discrete episodes, each articulated with a discrete style and each contrasting with neighboring episodes in such a way as to produce obvious musical seams. The seams capture attention, even if only momentarily, and thus function aesthetically as distancing devices that draw attention away from the drama and toward the piece's underlying structural mechanics.[37]

The pluralism also has another important effect: that of making explicit the nature of these works as performances. An important aspect of Puccini's strategy involves not only his juxtaposing conventional and unconventional styles, but also his reserving, or strategically withholding, the conventional, Italian Romantic or lyric style so as to heighten its expressive impact. The strategy exploits the capacity of opera as an art form for foregrounding the physical presence on stage of the opera singer and the sound of that singer's voice. Some of the theoretical apparatus developed by Carolyn Abbate and Robert Hatten will make this clearer.[38]

Abbate's work is in narrative theory, specifically *narrative pragmatics,* which accounts for how, when, and why music (or anything, or anyone, else) narrates. This is work oriented more generally toward *musical phenomenology,* with its primary concerns not structuralist notions of the music per se—how it is constructed, how it coheres, what it means, etc.—but rather the *experience* of music and its effects on its listening audience. Narrative pragmatics holds that "we do well to examine narrative activities rather than the events that they describe, to examine forms of enunciation rather than forms taken by utterance."[39] Central for Abbate is the rather unusual idea that music does not narrate by tracing dramatic events in sound, and that, as a result, music is not (indeed, cannot be) narrating all the time. This is different from traditional narrative analyses of music, including most opera analyses, almost all of which attempt to explain *what* music narrates—its narrated content—by invoking what Abbate calls a "miming model": "the composer invents a musical work that acts out or expresses psychological or physical events in a noisy and yet incorporeal sonic miming."[40] But because systematically explaining *what* music narrates can be difficult, if not impossible, refocusing attention on *how* music narrates makes it possible to account for narrativity without recourse to descriptions of what the music might be saying. Narrativity thus becomes something we can understand as a *state of being,* so to speak, a state that a piece of music can acquire, lose, and acquire again in the course of its evolution—rather than a persistent, ever-present quality inherent in the music itself. More often than not, in fact, music *lacks* narrative qualities: musical narration is *expressive* precisely because it is an occasional, striking, "rare and peculiar act."[41]

Abbate's notion of narrativity in music is related to Robert Hatten's notion of shifting levels of musical discourse. These are rhetorical changes defined as musical analogues to literary shifts from direct discourse to indirect discourse or narration.[42] Music, like literature, has the capacity to project multiple discursive levels (for Abbate, to "speak in multiple voices"), levels delineated in literature with, for example, distinctions among tenses or points of view: a shift to the past tense can indicate a shift to another level, as can a shift from the first to the third person.[43] Many such shifts produce discursive distance or detachment between a voice and its content; in these cases the voice can be described as *diegetic* (i.e., *distanced* or *distance-inducing*),[44] and, because diegesis is a quality inherent in all narrations (because narrating a tale requires detachment between speaker and content), when a musical voice is diegetic we can think of that voice as *narrative*. But how does this happen in music? Music has no past tense, no apparent distinction between points of view, and no obvious means of acquiring diegesis (especially in absolute music; an obvious example of diegetic music in opera is the music traditionally known as *musica in scena:* music originating from a sound source other than the pit orchestra, such as an on-stage ensemble, or *banda*).[45] Nevertheless, it can invoke different "ways of speaking" that effect the same kinds of discursive shifts. These may involve rhetorically charged or emphasized (often coded) harmonic progressions; sudden or unusual (again, coded) tonal shifts; orchestrational changes; disruptions in the flow of musical time with fermatas, cadenzas, or other metric manipulations; quotations of or modified references to another work (intertextuality); and shifts of style or topical register.

The last of these is key for Puccini: because narrativity in music is a rare and unusual state—a "zone of non-congruence"[46]—we might say that the late operas shift their level of discourse and enter the non-congruent zone (adopt the narrating voice) by invoking—rarely—the conventional, Italian Romantic style. This may seem counterintuitive: is the Romantic style "rare and peculiar" and thus non-congruent, while all other styles are, by default, normative? Or is it the other way around: is the Romantic style Puccini's *normal* mode of speaking while all other modes are peculiar? It *should* be the latter, of course—in Puccini, the expectation is often for stylistic conventionality—but the former is more accurate: in strategically withholding the familiar Romantic music until key dramatic moments, Puccini *makes* that language sound non-normative. The new styles are left to become the norm, while the old style becomes novel; the prevailing musical continuum is overtly non-Romantic, while the Romantic music intrudes, occasionally, for expressive and theatrical effect. The Romantic style even has the sense of a past tense: it recalls the past, literally, by invoking the *ottocento* tradition, in sharp contrast with the newer—present tense—styles borrowed from contemporary European repertoires.

Certain features of the Romantic style make it amenable to diegesis as I have described it here. The first is its familiarity: the more familiar the style, the more it stands out, especially if everything around it is less familiar. This is a complex issue, especially as it regards understanding Puccini in a contemporary context, because it is hard to assert with any specificity exactly what music Puccini's audiences were familiar with when they entered the opera house. But Wilson has recently established that Puccini's listeners received his music according to an essentially binary, familiar-versus-unfamiliar opposition. Contemporary reviews of *Turandot,* for example, consistently indicate that critics heard two kinds of music in the opera: the Romantic music, heard as sincere, authentic, and familiar—because it recalled all the (idealized) qualities Italian audiences were seeking in Puccini's music—and the non-Romantic or modern music, which was insincere, inauthentic, and unfamiliar (read: un-Italian). The latter seems to have prevented these critics from engaging with the work in any meaningful way; it made the piece's characters rigid, cold, mechanistic, and artificial (especially Turandot, Calaf, and the three masks), and it made the piece as a whole baffling and impenetrable. In the end, they found it impossible to discern the authentic Puccini: was he a traditional Italian composer, or not?[47]

The second is the centrality of the voice. Italian opera had long been melody- and voice-driven; think no further than Verdi and his subjugating the orchestra, harmony, and counterpoint in favor of unencumbered lyric singing (such favorites as "Sempre libera," "Questa o quella," or even, later, "O terra addio" are all exemplary). Puccini follows suit in his late works, adopting in his Romantic style a melody- and voice-centered quality that remains conspicuously absent from his non-Romantic music. Every time he shifts to the Romantic mode, the singing voice emerges from the texture with striking clarity; when the shift goes the other direction, the voice retreats into the background—or at the very least assumes less prominence, yielding to other, now more equal elements in the texture. This is key to the diegesis: the style change itself diverts listeners' attention onto the musical seam thus created; when that change involves a shift toward the familiar, Romantic style, the emergent centrality of the singing voice directs that attention not only onto the style change per se but specifically onto the sound of the voice itself, in the sense that the voice becomes a pure sonic *object*—a *voice-object,* as it were. Abbate is relevant here: what occurs is a "radical autonomization of the human voice" in which "the sound of the singing voice becomes, as it were, a 'voice-object' and the sole center for the listener's attention. That attention is drawn away from words, plot, character, and even music as it resides in the orchestra, or music as formal gestures, or as abstract shape. . . . [At these moments] the 'presence of the performer' may well suddenly emerge to impede the listener's contemplation."[48] The presence of the singer is suddenly more apparent than ever; the nature of the work as a physical act of performance—sometimes an obviously difficult one, when the singing is virtuosic—is explicit.

The presence of sonic voice-objects speaks in a very meaningful way to how powerful this music is for theater audiences (finding listeners who describe the experience of being "riveted," "on the edge of their seats," during a Puccini aria, for example, is easy), to how deftly Puccini manipulated music and musical language in the service of theatrical effect, and to how remarkable was his musical achievement, in that he found a way to incorporate the newest compositional strategies and, at the same time, maintain a wide audience not simply by including in his work gratuitous lyric sentimentality—moments that "tug at the heart strings," as one often hears this notion rather oversimplistically rendered—but by adroitly *using*—indeed, *exploiting*—Italian stylistic conventions in the service of extraordinary theatrical effects. And note the important point that these effects are inherent in the music: they depend neither on the identity of the performer nor on the quality of the performance (poor singers, or poor performances, can also break the theatrical illusion, but it may be painful rather than pleasurable; Abbate notes, "we are aware at these junctures [the discursive shifts]—painfully, if the high C is missed—that we witness a performance").[49]

It would nevertheless be an oversimplification to say that in late Puccini the discursive level shifts and the voice-object emerges in exactly the same way, with exactly the same force, every time the music shifts to the Romantic style; clearly, some passages emphasize the voice more strongly than others and thus make the voice-object more apparent. Equally oversimplified would be an assertion that all the non-Romantic music in these works deemphasizes the sound of the singing voice just as strongly as the Romantic music emphasizes it; indeed, some of the non-Romantic styles—certain varieties of exoticism in *Turandot* among them—foreground the voice rather strongly. But not all discursive shifts are equal, nor need they be. Recall that the level of discourse shifts not because of any specific feature of the music per se, but rather because some music stands out as different, or novel, relative to other music in the same work; the expressive significance lies in the *opposition* of one musical style against another. This is a key principle in *markedness theory*, which holds not only that *meaning* (i.e., what is *signified*) stems from the *difference* in a binary opposition of terms (i.e., *signs*), but also that such oppositions tend to be asymmetrical, or weighted.[50] Until recently, the "man/woman" opposition was a good example: "man" referred either to the human race without regard to gender or, more specifically, only to the male members of that group, whereas "woman" referred only to females; "woman" was the marked term, "man" unmarked. In late Puccini, the opposed styles are not equal. Rather, one—the Romantic—is *marked:* it invokes, very specifically, the nineteenth-century Italian operatic tradition. The "unmarked," non-Romantic styles draw on a wide range of modern, avant-garde, international compositional strategies—some of which, indeed, may be Italian or Italian-influenced and may strongly emphasize the presence of the singing voice in the texture.

None of this, incidentally, should be considered a commentary on the experiential effects or aesthetics of post-Romantic, early twentieth-century modern music, and none of the theatrical effects described here are necessarily more acute for listeners for whom modern music is unfamiliar, uncomfortable, or unpleasant. Nor do listeners have to *enjoy* the Romantic music in Puccini to experience discursive shifts, objectified voices, and broken theatrical illusions. That modern music may be just as pleasing for some—or, indeed, more pleasing (certainly more pleasing for many listeners than Romantic Italian opera)—is not entirely relevant; the fact, moreover, that we can no longer encounter Puccini's late operas with an early twentieth-century Italian ear—one for which the Romantic Italian idioms were still understood as musical norms, no matter how rarely composers were employing them in the contemporary repertoire—does not change the effects of the stylistic contrasts. The key, again, is in the opposition of the Romantic versus non-Romantic styles: even though Puccini's non-Romantic styles no longer sound challenging, or even dissonant, to our modern ears, they still sound *different* from the traditional Italian idioms, and Puccini still marks the traditional idioms as rare and special relative to the other idioms he employs. Certainly the effects may be stronger for listeners who enter the opera house in a conscious search for the lyrical, Puccinian language they love—they find it only rarely in the late works; when they do, they receive it with enormous satisfaction—but the same effects are available even for those who do not, or for those who have no prior knowledge of what is or is not commonly regarded as Puccinian. The universality of Puccini's effects, in large part, explains what makes this music so powerful, effective, and timeless.

TWO

The Romantic Style in Late Puccini

Hearing Puccini's Romantic style as the marked, non-congruent music in the late works requires a more detailed understanding of some of its most salient features and their expressive functions. All of these are seemingly deployed with one goal in mind: the foregrounding of the singing voice above all other textural components. The style is characterized most boldly in the melodic dimension and by its adoption therein of an expansive, lyrical manner solidly in the Italian operatic tradition. Other features are also important; some are more subtle and less immediately apparent. Many, especially in the harmonic and voice-leading dimensions, are designed to negate or undermine, in some way, the traditional sense of musical motion through time; achieving such an effect may be as simple as deploying an ostinato or another form of repetition in a way that purges the music of its harmonic variety, or it may be more complex—and may involve, for example, a reversion toward non-functional voice leading, a systematic undercutting of the normative dominant function so essential in all tonal music, or a use of musical meter in an elastic fashion that alternately suspends, then accelerates, the progress of musical time.

MELODY AND ORCHESTRATION IN THE STYLE

Puccini's lyric melodic style derives directly from *ottocento* Italian opera,[1] specifically from the *primo ottocento* of *bel canto* opera—Rossini, Bellini, and Donizetti—as well as from the mature style of Verdi and, perhaps even more important for Puccini, from both the French style of Massenet and the Italian style (melodically somewhat less measured and less formulaic than Verdi's) of late nineteenth-century Italian masters Leoncavallo, Mascagni, Giordano, and Catalani—composers of the *giovane scuola italiana*.[2] Puccini's idiom is characterized by an essentially diatonic style and by what seems to be a rather tight control of leaps. His melodic writing in the late works can by no means be characterized as predominantly conjunct, but the leaps he does employ seem to be restricted vis-à-vis (1) their position—the largest of them tend to occur at melodic climaxes; (2) their harmonic context—they often arpeggiate diatonic triads, often the tonic triad; and (3) their immediate intervallic neighborhood: like most great melodists, Puccini appears to have adhered, consciously or not, to the traditional contrapuntal principle that a large leap should be followed by motion (often stepwise) in the opposite direction.

Calaf's "Non piangere, Liù," from *Turandot* Act I (R43),[3] provides a good example of this style. The melody moves stepwise until the poignant "per quel sorriso" (R43.7–8; "for that smile"—i.e., the smile that Calaf apparently, one day long ago, offered Liù), at which time the line leaps from B♭ to E♭. Shortly thereafter ("Il tuo signore"), the line leaps from B♭ to G♭, which, as with the previous leap, also arpeggiates safely within the supporting harmony (G♭ major here, E♭ minor before). The final lyric section of Turandot's "In questa Reggia" (Act II; the whole aria begins at R43) behaves similarly but is somewhat more expansive: this theme ("Mai nessun m'avrà," at R47 in strings and high winds and in the voice in the measures immediately following) leaps much more frequently, almost always within the G♭-major tonic triad or, interestingly, from E♭ to a member of the tonic triad, where E♭ is an upper neighbor to the fifth scale-degree D♭, and an important motivic pitch in the theme. The motion from E♭ creates some occasional leaps through dissonant intervals, as in the major ninth in R47.4. And one of the most well-known melodies in all of Puccini's late output is the theme from Lauretta's "O mio babbino caro," from *Gianni Schicchi* (R40). This tune is somewhat more overtly metered than the most prototypically Puccinian melodies because of the folk-like simplicity of the pastorale topic—a topic cued with, among other signifiers, the $\frac{6}{8}$ meter, the moderately slow tempo (andantino), the "ingenuo" marking (for the naïve Lauretta), and the complete absence of dotted rhythms.[4] But it also exhibits features common in most of Puccini's Romantic-style themes: many of the leaps arpeggiate the tonic triad (see R40.3–4; see also R40.1–2, where the arpeggiation is filled in stepwise with the G and F on their way to E♭); many, such as most of those in R40.17–20, are followed by motion in the opposite direction (which, especially with the characteristic pastorale rhythms, contributes to a certain rocking quality that makes this aria among Puccini's more distinctive).

Puccini's lyric style is also marked by a distinctive orchestrational approach, the most notable characteristic of which is the tendency to double the vocal melody in the strings (or even winds) at the unison or—more often—at the octave or multiple octaves. This technique, known as the *violinata* or *sviolinata,* is employed throughout Italian opera, though Puccini almost certainly was directly influenced in this regard by the late nineteenth-century *giovane scuola italiana.* Puccini used it, as did others at the time, as a device that *lowers* the music stylistically and moves the stylistic level closer to the linguistic level, giving both music and text a very strong sense of affective immediacy.[5] Moreover, it at once simplifies the musical texture and heightens the emotional register—and thus the discursive level—of the vocal melody; it emphasizes and underlines the melodic line itself, such that the melody has more directness and more prominence—more energy, and indeed more brute force—than it would otherwise have had in a standard homophonic, melody-and-accompaniment-type texture; and it lends an exceptionally rich, expansive quality to the overall sound characteristic of much of Puccini's music. In this regard, he seems to have used the *violinata* to manipulate the music's affective intensity by strategically expanding or contracting the orchestral doubling. Among many others, "Non piangere, Liù" is a good example (see example 2.1): the first doubling of the voice occurs at "Il tuo signore" (emphasized anyway, as previously noted, by the melodic leap to the high G♭), where the viola doubles the tenor at the unison before being quickly joined by the flute, doubling at the octave; by the time the first part of the piece concludes (R44), the doubling has expanded to include cellos, both violins, and some of the winds, all doubling at the unison or the octave. Puccini makes a momentary retreat (doubling the voice with violins and cellos only, at, for example, R45.3) before unleashing the full textural force of the *violinata,* duplicating the vocal melody at the

EXAMPLE 2.1. *Turandot* I, "Non piangere, Liù."

122

P.R. 117

EXAMPLE 2.1. *continued*

EXAMPLE 2.1. *continued*

P. R. 117

EXAMPLE 2.1. *continued*

EXAMPLE 2.1. *continued*

EXAMPLE 2.1. *continued*

EXAMPLE 2.1. *continued*

unison, octave, and double octave, at "che non cade" (R45.4) and again at the climactic "che non sorride più" (R45.10).

HARMONY AND VOICE LEADING IN THE STYLE

As noted, many of the strategies Puccini employs in his Romantic style, especially those in the harmonic and voice-leading dimensions, are designed to undermine musical motion. The affective result is that the music often seems to slip into what sounds like a suspended state of zero-gravity in which the melody hangs, freely, unbound to conventions of harmony, tonality, or voice leading; the melody seems to float, unencumbered, on top of a pool of musical background—a pool that exists, as does any pool, in a confined area in which it cannot flow or otherwise move coherently in any single, perceivable direction. The result, as with most of Puccini's Romantic-style strategies, is that the melody is foregrounded above all other textural elements.

The effect can be achieved with almost any kind of musical repetition—or, indeed, anything that suppresses change in any musical dimension. Sometimes the suppression results from something as simple as an ostinato or oscillation that robs the music of its potential for motion. The second part of "Non piangere, Liù" (starting at R45.3), for example, comprises a progression oscillating between tonic and subdominant in E♭ minor, with an attendant bass ostinato alternating among two pitches, E♭ and A♭. The opening of both Calaf's "Nessun dorma," from *Turandot* Act III (R4), and Rinuccio's "Firenze è come un albero fiorito," from *Gianni Schicchi* (R30), behave similarly: in "Nessun dorma" a bass ostinato between G and E♭ supports motion from tonic harmony to a nonfunctional chromatic chord, while in "Firenze" an ostinato in the strings and winds (one subjected to some melodic but not rhythmic variation) sustains tonic harmony over a pedal B♭ and emphasizes—in that its melodic contour is similar—Rinuccio's potent, rising diatonic melody.

More subtle means of achieving the effect include turns toward nonfunctional voice leading, including the systematic undercutting of the dominant function through the use of modal dominants (i.e., dominants with lowered leading tones), dominants that resolve non-functionally, or simply no dominant at all. Often these strategies occur in conjunction with one another: an unresolved dominant leads, for example, to an extended passage of non-functional voice leading, or non-functional voice leading persists through a cadence in such a way that it seems to *prevent* the appearance of the normal, functional dominant. Regarding non-functional voice leading, in Puccini this often takes the form of the same kind of harmonic parallelism known in the early-twentieth-century impressionistic music of Debussy and others as *planing*—usually parallel fifths and octaves, though also parallel dissonant intervals such as sevenths, ninths, or tritones. A straightforward example is in the middle section (at R31.5) of the three-part "Firenze" in *Gianni Schicchi*: this is Rinuccio's ode to the river Arno, and as such the parallel motion clearly invokes the river—obvious text-painting of a kind Puccini seemed particularly fond of, as he invoked similar parallel motion to represent the river Seine at the opening of *Il tabarro*. The planing in "Firenze" is both consonant and dissonant: parallel triads at "L'Arno prima di correre alla foce" (R31.5) become parallel seventh chords at "canta, baciando piazza Santa Croce" (R31.9). The opening of Turandot's "In questa Reggia" (R44) exhibits similar dissonant planing: the string ostinato (beginning at R44.3) includes the typical parallel fifths but also, again, dissonant parallel sevenths. Unlike in "Firenze," however, the sevenths here seem to result from a misalignment of members of the $F\sharp$-minor tonic triad: that is, this is a deformation of a simpler ostinato with alternating tonic and dominant triads, the root motion of which is still audible in the bass (example 2.2 compares what Puccini wrote with a hypothetical, normative version of the same ostinato—one that preserves the characteristic parallelism but also the underlying tonic-dominant harmonic motion). This is a very clear example of what I call *stylistic integration,* a phenomenon in Puccini's language to be discussed in more detail in chapter 6, in which tokens from various style types *trope* to produce a new expressive meaning.[6] Here, the troping adds a dissonant, dark, urgent color to the sound that seems entirely suitable for Turandot's Princess Lo-u-Ling narrative—in which, in her first extended monologue in the opera, she recounts a tormented past that explains her aversion to men and marriage.

Non-functional dominants are ubiquitous in Puccini's Romantic style. Often they take the form of modal dominants lacking functional leading tones (that is, minor dominant triads), as in the case of the $C\sharp$-minor triads in the oscillating "In questa Reggia" progression (R44.3ff;

a) written:

b) normalized:

EXAMPLE 2.2. Ostinato in *Turandot* II, "In questa Reggia":
(a) written and (b) normalized versions.

see example 2.2). There, however, the dominants are essentially surface decorations and do not articulate the piece's harmonic design in any kind of structural sense; other of Puccini's modal dominants occur in some very prominent structural positions. A good example is at the final cadence in Luigi's "Hai ben ragione" from *Il tabarro* (example 2.3), where a modal dominant (a G-minor triad in the key of C minor) appears in one of the most structural of all harmonic locations: the final structural cadence in the tonic key (two bars before R46).

Perhaps the most common of all Puccini's strategies for undercutting the dominant function is the use of no dominant at all—which is to say, the use of harmonies that substitute for real, functional dominant chords. Like the modal dominants, some of these are obvious; others are buried deep in the harmonic structure of their respective pieces. Good examples of the former occur in *Gianni Schicchi*, in "Firenze è come un albero fiorito" and "O mio babbino caro," both of which employ prominent, substitute dominants in almost exactly the same way: they substitute a supertonic in place of the normative dominant at a final cadence.

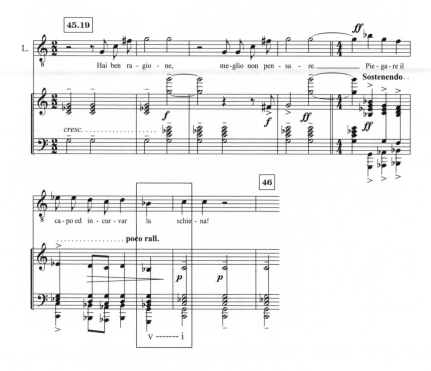

EXAMPLE 2.3. *Il tabarro*, "Hai ben ragione."

At the end of the first part of "Firenze" (a measure before R31), tonic B♭ is approached not with dominant F but with supertonic C minor;[7] likewise, at Lauretta's final cadence the final tonic A♭ (last syllable of "pieta," two before R41) is approached through the supertonic, B♭ minor. In both instances the progression could easily be rewritten to include a dominant between the penultimate ii and the final I, and thus each sounds like it skips the dominant, moving directly from a predominant-functioning ii chord to the tonic. A striking example of the latter occurs in the opening lyric movement of Angelica's "Senza mamma" (example 2.4): the fifths sequence beginning at "ed aleggiare intorno a mei" (ii-V-iii-vi-IV in F major) prolongs predominant function and strongly implies that a dominant should follow; the following ii chord (at "sei qui") breaks the fifths sequence but remains functionally predominant. But the normative dominant is denied by a return to the IV (at "baci"); another ii chord and a completely non-functional iii intervene before tonic F

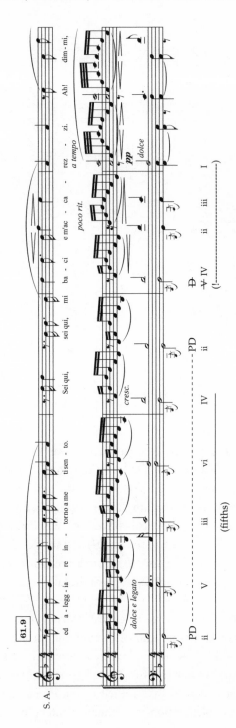

EXAMPLE 2.4. *Suor Angelica*, "Senza mamma."

major returns—with no dominant preparation—and the theme begins anew.

"Non piangere, Liù" (*Turandot* I, R43) is a somewhat more involved example of the same strategy. The aria is in two large parts: part 1 contains two smaller subsections (at R43.1 and R43.12); part 2 (R45.3) is essentially an abbreviated, varied reprise of part 1. Part 1 ends on a dominant harmony (but a weak dominant in the second—$\frac{4}{3}$—inversion; see R44.9); part 2 ends on a strong cadence in the tonic E♭ minor. This final cadence involves a straightforward substitute dominant, not the supertonic this time but the subdominant, which supports Calaf's climactic high B♭ (at R45.10) and the presence of which derives from the tonic-subdominant-tonic oscillation that supports the entire second part of the aria. The oscillation has, in essence, continued right through an obvious cadential moment, having gathered, it seems, unstoppable momentum in the previous seven measures and overridden the normative harmonic progression—which should have included a dominant supporting the high B♭ (indeed, the progression could easily be rewritten to include this chord). The gesture is especially meaningful: the aria is the start of a relentless pursuit by Calaf of the Princess Turandot—a pursuit he proves unwilling to abandon, even at the threat of death.

Part 1 of the piece is considerably more complex. As mentioned, it concludes (at "strade," R44.9) on a weak—second inversion—dominant seventh chord in place of what we might have expected, given tonal and stylistic norms, to be a strong, root-position dominant dividing the piece in half and setting up the return of the tonic and the main theme in part 2. This much is simple; the origins of the V_3^4 are less obvious. It seems at first that Puccini simply substituted the second scale degree (F) in the bass in place of an implied scale-degree five (B♭), but this explanation is not entirely satisfying: in a rather uncanny way, it is not the bass F that sounds unusual but rather the upper voices (the other members of the dominant seventh: B♭, D, and A♭) that seem much more out of place. Closer inspection reveals that other normative pitches, and harmonies, have been *deleted* from the progression, in much the same way as the dominant was deleted from the final cadences in "O mio babbino" and "Firenze."

This harmonic and metric structure is shown in example 2.5, which suggests that the first part of "Non piangere, Liù" is a badly deformed version—deformed metrically and harmonically—of a rather idiomatic musical structure. A hypothetical normative version is given in example 2.5a: the structure is an 8-bar classical period with an antecedent arriving on dominant (a minor, modal dominant—but this could easily be a major, functional dominant) in the fourth bar and a consequent proceeding through a descending fifths cycle (in which the first chord in every two-chord pair is metrically weak and sounds like a pickup to the following chord) to an authentic cadence in the eighth bar. What Puccini wrote—the deformed version of the structure—is shown in example 2.5b, in the form of a *durational reduction* in which every notated measure in the score (one whole-note value) becomes a quarter note in the reduction; thus one measure in the reduction (a *hypermeasure*) represents one four-bar phrase in the score.[8] Because Puccini's meter is elastic and his music often expands and contracts at the largest metric levels, some hypermeasures in any durational reduction may look unusual: m. 1, for example, is contracted (it lacks the last eighth note of its fourth beat) because this measure in the score has been cut in half (and has, in fact, simply been appended to the end of R43.5, which contains three half notes instead of two). Deformations here include the extension of the antecedent's concluding dominant into hypermeasure 5, which delays the onset of the fifths sequence; the omission of the vi chord (originally in m. 6) from the progression so that the bass proceeds directly from G♭ to F rather than passing first through C; and an elliptical condensation of harmony and voice leading such that when the bass proceeds to the second scale degree F, the upper voices move not to members of the expected ii but immediately to members of the dominant seventh—which produces a weak dominant and a linear, modal bass at the cadence. Note more specifically the expressive role of the metric elasticity, a hallmark of Puccini's Romantic style and important in heightening the affective intensity of the structural deformations: the lengthening of the minor dominant in the middle of the progression sounds like a relaxation, in which the music seems to *wait* for Calaf to finish repeating a melodic motive; but the deletion of the vi and ensuing harmonic condensation make the structure sound impatient, or hurried. The acceleration this produces seems especially effective, given the inexorable tonic-subdominant oscillation that ensues beginning at hypermeasure 9 and continues, as discussed previously, through the aria's final cadence. The structure

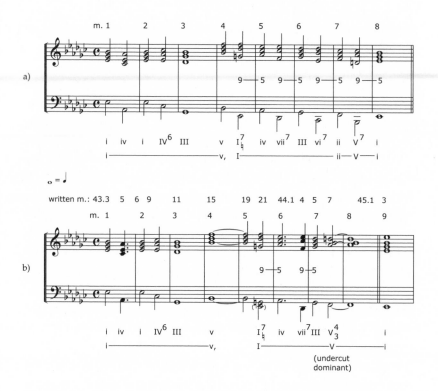

EXAMPLE 2.5. Harmonic and metric structure in *Turandot* I, "Non piangere, Liù": (a) hypothetical normative structure; (b) deformed (written) structure.

first *weakens* the dominant, then *overwhelms* it, a small-scale reflection of Calaf's weakening Liù ("If one distant day I smiled at you, then for that smile, my sweet girl, [I ask you to] make gentle for him [Timur, Calaf's father and Liù's master] the road into exile") before the force of events completely overwhelms her (so much so that she takes her own life in the third act).[9]

Finally, perhaps the most well-known example of undercut dominant function in all of Puccini may be the final cadence in "Nessun dorma" (*Turandot* III, R4), a good example of Puccini's using a real dominant but resolving it nonfunctionally. Here, the dominant itself receives heavy emphasis—as if Puccini wanted to highlight its rarity in the style—in the form of an upward leap in the voice to the second scale degree E and a fermata on the same pitch (first syllable of "vincerò," three bars before R6). But, although the vocal line resolves as the supporting harmony implies it should, from E to tonic D (last syllable of "vincerò"), the harmony fails to cooperate and shifts instead to a subdominant G-major triad—which itself is sustained for two bars before yielding to the by-then desperately needed tonic. Here, the choice of subdominant to undercut dominant function is a local-level realization of a large-scale problem in the piece's tonality. The aria is a binary design in which part 2 is a varied repetition of part 1; each large part subdivides into two smaller parts (thus 1_{A-B}, 2_{A-B}). Both A sections are in G, but both B sections—in which Calaf sings the main lyric theme—are in D. This means the D-major triad at the start of the first B (R4.10, at "Ma il mistero") sounds initially like dominant harmony, and its role as the real tonic is not clarified until the end of the entire aria, in the move from the G-major to the D-major triad (now understood as subdominant moving to tonic) at the final cadence. Even the cadence at the end of part 1 is no help: here dominant (A major) moves to subdominant (G major), but the progression does not continue; G major becomes tonic, and the A section repeats. And, interestingly, while D sounds like dominant at its initial appearance (R4.10), when section A repeats, G—the original tonic—now sounds like *subdominant* because of the strongly articulated D major in section B. The whole aria, in fact, is a good example of Puccini's general fascination with subdominant harmony, even at levels deep within the opera's harmonic structure.

After all this tonal ambiguity, the final tonic D major at the aria's end seems especially meaningful. While the most important event here structurally is the thematized denial of the normative, functional resolution of dominant to tonic and the momentary tonal vertigo it creates,[10] at the same time the final tonic has an enormously effective dramatic impact, in large part because of its very direct, immediate meaning: it signals Calaf's affirmation of final victory ("vincerò"—"I will be victorious"), while the clearly coded, highly suggestive subdominant is the plagal "amen"—here in the sense of a "so be it."

One of the best examples of Puccini's synthesizing these procedures is in the first Giorgetta-Luigi duet in *Il tabarro*, in the movement beginning "È ben altro il mio sogno" (R48).[11] This exhibits an expanded form of a traditional schema known in the secondary literature as the *lyric form* or *lyric prototype,* in which a 16-bar theme groups in four, four-bar phrases with the thematic profile A A' B A". The initial A sections remain in the tonic key, the B section departs from it, and the final A returns to it.[12] In "È ben altro il mio sogno" the A sections each comprise a two-phrase period, with a weak cadence at the end of an antecedent (R48.9) and a strong cadence at the end of a consequent (R49.13). Each arrives half way through its consequent on a dominant harmony (R49.4–5), the strength and structural prominence of which strongly suggests that the tonic should immediately follow. But each time, the harmony makes an abrupt, surprising shift directly to the subdominant (R49.6). This entails juxtaposing two root-position triads a step apart and thus also motion in parallel fifths and octaves; as such, Puccini uses the event to initiate a descent through a series of parallel root-position harmonies, V-IV-iii-ii7, that occupies nearly the entire second half of the consequent phrase. A quick, punctuating functional dominant follows at R49.12—complete with a rapid, condensed summary in the voices and orchestra of the final harmonic descent (see the descending sixteenths)—to achieve the final tonic B♭.

The shift from dominant to subdominant is, again, heavily marked. Heard against the background of the normative tonal-harmonic schemata (resolution of dominants to tonics, for example) against which it seems we must measure Puccini's music, the move never ceases to surprise, despite its becoming a stock harmonic device in the style; that it is followed here with an extended passage of decidedly non-functional harmonic parallelism underscores the effect all the more. Time, tonality, and all sense of forward musical motion seem suspended; the melody floats, unfettered, above the harmonic surface. In each instance the V–IV move supports a crucial line in the text, the large theme of which is Giorgetta and Luigi's longing to escape their weary, nomadic bargeworker's life on the Seine and return to the idyllic surroundings of their native Belleville—to this day one of the more storied Paris suburbs. Emphasized in the first A section is Giorgetta's "questa logora vita vagabonda" ("this weary nomadic life," R49.4–6), where the harmony itself—which literally wanders off course—actually *becomes* the figurative vagabond, or wanderer, with which Giorgetta and Luigi no longer wish to be identified;[13] in the second A section the text is Giorgetta's "Noi non possiamo vivere sull'acqua" ("We can't live on the water," R50.9–10), which explicitly invokes the imagery to which I referred earlier, that of a harmonic pool of water on which the melody floats.

In the last A section, the same harmonic shift and non-functional voice leading again support a critical line in the text. But full appreciation of this moment requires a short survey of another of Puccini's core Romantic-style strategies: that of undercutting a deep structural, rising melodic arpeggiation through the tonic triad.[14] These arpeggiations are common in Puccini, probably because they effectively increase forward momentum in the music toward a melodic climax—itself usually the completion of the prolonged, sometimes diverted arpeggiation. "Non piangere, Liù" (*Turandot* I, R43) for example, occupies itself entirely with this kind of event: the aria's melody achieves a rising arpeggiation through the tonic triad, from B♭ through E♭ to G♭—the latter of which is heard as the goal for which the aria strives. This melodic structure reaches completion (that is, returns, through a linear, stepwise descent, to the tonic scale degree) only in the concertato movement that concludes the act, where the melody repeatedly, and resolutely, descends stepwise from G♭ to E♭. This produces an enormous amount of unresolved tension in the aria itself, even though the piece does conclude with a cadence in the tonic E♭ minor.

The "È ben altro il mio sogno" melody behaves very similarly, except that this time the full arpeggiation is completed and resolved, in a magnificent gesture of theatricality, within the boundaries of the movement itself. This melody is built on a rising theme that partially fills in stepwise an arpeggiation through the B♭-major tonic triad: D-F-B♭-D-F. The momentum of this rising arpeggiation implies that it may want to continue all the way to the high tonic B♭. But in sections A and A', the line rises from the high F only stepwise to a rather unsatisfying G (R48.6). The G is unsatisfying in that the note denies the anticipated high B♭; G is, notably, emphasized by one of Puccini's characteristic melodic gestures in the voice, the upward leap of an octave and a step from F to G—exactly the same gesture I noted earlier in "In questa Reggia," namely, a wide leap from a member of the tonic triad to the sixth scale degree, the latter functioning motivically as an upper-neighbor to scale-degree five. But in the concluding and climactic A" section (beginning at R53.1), Giorgetta and Luigi, now finally singing *a due,* reach the pinnacle of their longing for a permanent home in the Paris suburbs and proclaim, in an ecstatic delirium, to hear Paris—the city they can see from the river but the "fascino immortal" ("eternal charm") of which remains for them permanently out of reach—"ci grida con mille voci liete," "crying out to us with a thousand happy voices" (see R53.12–17). This vocal climax has been *saved*, as is typical in the style, for the non-functional harmonic space: at exactly the moment the melody finally completes its upward arpeggiation and achieves high B♭, the harmony makes the dominant-to-subdominant shift, and the non-functional parallel voice leading ensues. Paris cries out, but the possibility for infinite happiness it holds is at once grasped—fleetingly, at the high B♭ over the subdominant—and denied, by the emphatic undercutting of functionality in the descending parallel motion. The parallelism carries the music toward a final cadence that embodies the momentary satisfaction (however elusive it may be in the long term) for Giorgetta and Luigi, whose fantasy is now complete—if only in their own minds.

METRIC QUALITIES OF THE STYLE

A metric hallmark of Puccini's Romantic style is its elasticity: the flow of musical time is constantly ebbing and flowing, accelerating and decelerating, stretching and contracting in ways that lend the music a kind of free, improvised quality that, to the ear alone, may sound more closely related to performance practice than to any specific compositional procedures on Puccini's part.[15] That is, the listener easily gains the impression that the singers (or perhaps the conductor) are manipulating the flow of musical time in order to provide maximum opportunity for showcasing their vocal prowess. And, indeed, some of this is performance-related: rubato is an important aspect of performance practice in this music, and there is no evidence Puccini ever wished it to be otherwise—even though he was unspecific about the amount and precise location of the rubato.[16] But, interestingly, closer observation reveals that most of what one hears in this regard is controlled by—has been *predetermined* by—the *composer*, not the performers. Much of what in Puccini sounds like rubato—acceleration and deceleration of the tempo relative to a stable, consistent background pulse—is actually *not* directly a result of rubato or, indeed, of any conscious choice at all on the part of the performers, but rather is tightly controlled in the score by Puccini himself.

The simplest, most obvious examples of this are the fermatas Puccini tends to add at vocal climaxes, of which we have already seen several examples: Lauretta's E♭ just before the final cadence in "O mio babbino caro" (*Schicchi,* four bars before R41), Turandot's high B setting up the final lyric section of "In questa Reggia" (one before R47 in Act II), Calaf's high B♭ at the end of "Non piangere, Liù" (*Turandot* I, four before R46), and Calaf's cadential E in "Nessun dorma" (Act III, three before R6)—which, strangely enough, is not the vocal climax. Calaf proceeds after the cadence to arpeggiate the subdominant G-major triad and quickly reach a climactic high B, on which (again, strangely) Puccini writes no fermata but on which a fermata is always added by the singer.[17] Similar examples include, among many others, Angelica's A in the coda of the first lyric section of "Senza mamma" (three before R63), where the fermata serves to delay the orchestra's supporting chord so that, for just a brief but sumptuous moment, we can luxuriate in the sound of the pure, unaccompanied voice-object; the end of Rinunccio's "Firenze è come un albero fiorito" (*Schicchi,* two before R33), which actually has no fermata (it would run counter to the persistent rhythmic character of the Tuscan *stornello*),[18] but rather the marking *poco rit.,* which has the same effect—that of stretching time to allow the voice sufficient opportunity to wallow in the musical climax; and, in "È ben altro il mio sogno" from *Tabarro,* the orchestral fermata on the *fortissimo (fortississimo* in the trumpets) tonic triad just before the onset of the final section (R53)—a fermata which, even though not in the voice part, just as effectively expands musical time at a climax and delays, ever so slightly, the anxiously anticipated *a due* singing for Giorgetta and Luigi.

But there are far more subtle aspects of Puccini's metric elasticity, some of which appeared in Calaf's "Non piangere, Liù" (see example 2.5). There, he achieved a deformation in both metric and harmonic structures by lengthening a modal dominant chord in the fourth hypermeasure, by subsequently resuming a normal harmonic rhythm (about two chords per hypermeasure, or one every two notated bars), and by creating a harmonic condensation in hypermeasures 7 and 8 (which produces what sounds like a weak and abnormally long dominant). Both lengthened dominants create a metric expansion, common in the style, that produces a sense of swelling or waiting—waiting, perhaps, for the next important event or, as is often the case in Puccini, the next vocal climax. The metric structure in "Non piangere" is even rather elastic in the more normative antecedent phrase, in which Puccini truncates the fourth notated measure by half (and, as mentioned, actually appends this shortened measure—one half note—onto the end of the third notated measure). This is a metric compression, also common in the style, that produces a sense of impatience—a sense that the music has somehow skipped forward in time.

Angelica's "Senza mamma" behaves similarly. The first lyric movement ("Ora che sei un angelo del cielo," example 2.6) opens in a quadruple hypermeter (i.e., one produced by recurring groupings of four notated measures of $\frac{4}{4}$ time), but this large-level meter is not completely regular: the numbers beneath the staves in example 2.6 indicate that the first hypermeasure is expanded by two notated beats (last two beats in R61.5) and the second is contracted by one complete notated measure. The latter of these deformations creates the rather strange sensation—strange even while common in this music and essential to the experience of it—that the vocal phrase beginning at "ed aleggiare," heard as the *beginning* of a metric unit (i.e., a hypermetric downbeat) because of the change in orchestration and the entrance of the voice, is a large-scale downbeat that arrives too early.

Later, the final lyric section of the same aria ("La grazia è discesa, dal cielo," example 2.7) opens, as Hepokoski has observed,[19] with a threefold repetition of an eight-bar, sequential theme. This music also has a distinctly anapestic rhythm that comes from the highly unusual *novenario* verse (i.e., verse with nine syllables per line; a typical line of *novenario* sounds like an abbreviated line of *decasillabo*—ten syllables—without the initial syllable but with the same anapestic rhythm. The *novenario* is unusual because it appears nowhere in the operas of Verdi, and in fact nowhere in Italian opera before Boito's *Mefistofele* of 1868).[20] The last measure of every eight-bar unit is elided with the first measure of the next, and the last unit is expanded once in the middle and again at the end. The effects are the same each time. The elisions at the end of every phrase (see R64.8 and R64.15 in example 2.7) are impatient metric contractions, in that in each case what should have been a regular hypermetric unit of four notated measures instead becomes a truncated unit of only three (the fourth is reinterpreted as the downbeat of the next). In the third cycle, beat two in the first hypermeasure expands by four full

EXAMPLE 2.6. Hypermeter in *Suor Angelica*, "Senza mamma."

notated measures;[21] the theme resumes afterward exactly as in the first two cycles, as if the metric disturbance never happened. And at the end, Puccini lengthens the final beat of the penultimate hypermeasure by a full notated bar, so that the music *waits* for the dominant resolution and tonic closure. This last expansion, incidentally, is the most common in the late style: one located at the *end* of a hypermetric unit that suspends musical motion, or stalls time, in order to make the music—and thus the listener—wait for the next large-scale downbeat and a resumption of the regular temporal flow. Similar examples occur in, among many other places, "È ben altro il mio sogno," "Hai ben ragione," "Firenze è come un albero fiorito," and "O mio babbino caro."[22]

These expansions and contractions often result from what appears, on the surface, to be rather metrically complex music. Such complexity is not as obvious in "Senza mamma," where the elasticity stems predominantly from additions or subtractions of either complete measures or their regular subdivisions (that is, full measures or half measures), but it does become evident in a piece like "È ben altro il mio sogno," in which we can hear a fundamentally regular—albeit elastic—large-scale metric structure that belies the complexity of the notated score. The score exhibits mixed (changing) meters—see R48–49—in which the meter sign continually changes to reflect whole or partial beat units added to or subtracted from each measure. The first three measures of the opening pair of phrases, for example, are in the normative $\frac{2}{4}$ (the phrase begins at R48.2, on "sogno"); the fourth and fifth measures each have an extra beat (both are in $\frac{3}{4}$); the sixth subtracts the added beat and returns to $\frac{2}{4}$; the seventh subtracts an eighth note (and has three eighths instead of four, and a meter sign of $\frac{3}{8}$) before the eighth and final measure adds back not only the lost eighth but an extra quarter as well (thus the $\frac{3}{4}$).

The aural experience of the piece, however, is quite different: the effect is not one of continually changing meters and thus metric irregularity, but rather an essentially regular temporal flow that ever so slightly accelerates and decelerates as the phrase unfolds—again, an effect of controlled, written rubato. This aural experience is graphically depicted in example 2.8, a durational reduction of the piece's first eight phrases (R48–49.13 and R49.15–R51). As in the durational reduction seen earlier, of "Non piangere, Liù" (example 2.5), every measure in the score becomes one beat (one quarter note) in the reduction, so that one measure in the

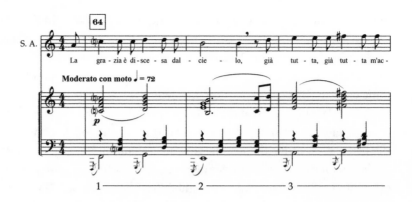

EXAMPLE 2.7. *Suor Angelica*, "Senza mamma."

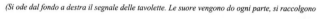

(Si ode dal fondo a destra il segnale delle tavolette. Le suore vengono do ogni parte, si raccolgono

e tutte in fila si avviano verso le celle; le teoria bianca entra

EXAMPLE 2.7. *continued*

EXAMPLE 2.7. *continued*

reduction (one hypermeasure) is equivalent to one four-bar phrase in the score. The regular but elastic nature of the meter produces hypermeasures with sometimes more or sometimes less than four quarter notes. A hypermeasure with too many beats will sound like a metric expansion (temporal deceleration); a truncated hypermeasure will sound like a metric contraction (temporal acceleration).[23] The first and third hypermeasures are good examples of the common procedure mentioned earlier, that of expanding the ends of hypermetric units: each is expanded, the first by half a hyperbeat and the third by a full hyperbeat, so that each immediately subsequent measure (mm. 2 and 4) in effect must wait on the first and third to finish. Exactly the opposite procedure occurs in m. 2, which now sounds hurried because the third beat is truncated (this is the notated measure of $\frac{3}{8}$). Perhaps the most interesting music of all is in hypermeasure 4, where the meter expands significantly—so much so that the temporal flow seems to almost come to a complete stop. Every beat in the reduction is expanded by one quarter note; the first beat even has two extra quarters. This expansion coincides exactly—certainly not coincidentally—with the move in the harmony from dominant to subdominant (at the downbeat of hypermeasure 4) and the shift to nonfunctional harmonic space, such that the tonal vertigo produced in the harmonic motion is reinforced by a similarly vertiginous quality in the meter. Such shifts effect complete and total focus on the singing voice-object, especially at the very end (at "Parigi ci grida con mille voci liete"), when Giorgetta and Luigi reach (at "con"), *a due*, their climactic high B♭.

Much of Puccini's metric elasticity stems directly from his texts. Most employ a freely recitative verse, either pure *endecasillabo sciolto*—ungrouped, unrhymed lines of eleven syllables each—or a freer, but heightened, occasionally rhyming mix of *endecasillabo, settenario* (seven syllables), and *quinario* (five syllables) that originates in librettos of Boito and that James Hepokoski has called rhymed *scena* verse.[24] Both examples discussed here—"Ora che sei un angelo del cielo" and "È ben altro il mio sogno"—use mostly *endecasillabo*, the freest of all the Italian verse meters with respect to its internal accent structure and the meter poets use to achieve a more natural, recitative, conversational quality in the text that lies closer to spoken prose. This kind of text was quite common around the time of late Puccini—this is the period, after all, that saw the advent of Italian *Literaturoper* and a gradual severing of

EXAMPLE 2.8. Metric structure in *Il tabarro*, "È ben altro il mio sogno," first eight phrases. Phrases 5–8 comprise a nearly identical, reorchestrated, repeat of phrases 1–4. Hypermeasure 1 beat 4: ♩. first time only; ♩ second time.

conventional relationships between musical rhythm and Italian poetic meters—but the problem of how to deal with it musically remained a difficult one.[25] Various composers tried various solutions. Some imposed strict musical regularity on a highly metrically irregular text, a rather procrustean solution in which the verse sounds forced into a regular metric framework and retains neither its natural rhythm nor its speech-like quality. Others tried to make the music strictly adhere to the irregular declamation patterns in the text by frequently changing meters, changing tempos, and all but abandoning any coherent motivic or thematic framework. Others—mainly Ildebrando Pizzetti—employed a monotone declamation with complete rhythmic flexibility, such that one hears in the vocal rhythms almost no recognizable metric patterns, and indeed almost no meter, whatsoever. Still others tried to compromise by writing a regular metric structure in the music, fixing with respect to the musical meter both the rate of declamation and the position of each line's beginning and end, thus treating the internal accents in each line with a flexibility that maintained some of the speech-like quality of the original text. None of these solutions to the problem proved very effective, which probably accounts at least in part for the theatrical failure of works like Franchetti's *La figlia di Iorio*, Mascagni's *Parisina*, and Pizzetti's *Fedra,* among others. Frustration with the issue among these *generazione dell'ottanta* composers—a group of composers from the generation following Puccini's, born in the 1880s—led to the rise of Italian neoclassicism following the first World War.[26]

But Puccini found an effective solution, one similar to but not exactly the same as—and ultimately more flexible and much more theatrically effective than—the last of the four approaches described earlier. He managed to gracefully accommodate both the meter of the text and the metric regularity essential in the lyric, Romantic style without forcing his texts into a rigid musical frame or forcing the music to blindly adhere to the text's flexible internal rhythms. Indeed, this is one of Puccini's great insights: that the freely declamatory text common in modern Italian librettos required neither an abandonment of the declamatory rhythmic patterns in the text itself nor of the conventional, regular metric prototypes in the music. As such, the latter observation especially is yet more evidence of Puccini's allegiance to various conventional musical (here metric, as opposed to formal or harmonic) schemata. The result—which helped make him more theatrically successful than any of his contemporaries—is an ingenious, effortless give and take: the declamation accelerates and decelerates to keep pace with the musical meter, while the musical meter allows for slight expansions and contractions so that the text can be declaimed as naturally as possible. Imagine trying to lower an irregularly shaped house onto a regularly shaped foundation, the dimensions of which do not match those of the house. Either could be altered to accommodate the other, but a more effective solution aesthetically might be to compromise. Both foundation and house can be slightly altered—some angles adjusted, some corners cut, some dimensions stretched, others contracted; eventually they can be made to align, even if the dimensions of neither are exactly what they would have been if house and foundation remained separate. This describes Puccini's music: think of the music as the (inherently regular) foundation onto which the (inherently irregular) text is placed. Each can be subtly adjusted in order to achieve a harmonic symbiosis between the two.

A preponderance of *triple* hypermeter—that is, a use of rather unusual groupings of *three* (rather than the more normal two or four) measures at the level of either the phrase or phrase groups—is one more idiosyncratic metric feature of Puccini's Romantic style. It warrants attention here as related, indirectly, to issues of metric elasticity. This feature is not prototypical of the style, but rather acts in dialogue with its metric norms. Often, in Puccini, triple hypermeter arises from a regrouping of a prototypical number of measures that could have (or should have) been grouped in pairs or fours (2+2+2+2 or 4+4)—8-bar units, in other words, grouped irregularly to produce imbalance and instability at the larger metric levels of the music. Most of the time, in Puccini, isolated instances of the procedure yield the same sense of surprise described earlier (a triple hypermetric unit sounds like an abruptly truncated quadruple unit, and the music sounds impatient or hurried), but in Turandot's "In questa Reggia," for example, Puccini applied the procedure systematically to yield a thoroughly irregular structure at the highest levels of the hypermeter.[27]

Example 2.9 is a durational reduction and bass-line sketch of the entire lyric section of the aria, from R44.3 through R50 (the aria proper begins with the *recitative* at R43). As before, one beat in the reduction (one hyperbeat) represents one measure in the score. At the phrase level, the music is almost completely normal: most phrases are two or four bars long. Some are expanded at their ends to create the typically Puccinian temporal elongation, as in the sixth, eighth, and last hypermeasures; one is contracted (the twelfth). But triple groupings persist at the larger metric levels. Part A comprises eight hypermeasures of music but, as shown with brackets in the example (top line), they group irregularly as 3+3+2, where the end of each large group is articulated by a pause in the soprano solo, a statement by the chorus (R44.13–14 and R46.1–2 in the score), and a subsequent change of tonic (from F♯ to D back to F♯). Part B consists almost entirely of a rising bass line—first by step through a whole-tone cycle from G♭ to F♯, then from E♭ to F♯ and on to A♭ and B♭—where each step in the bass lasts two notated measures (two quarter notes in the reduction). The "Mai nessun m'avrà" theme (in D at R47.9) articulates a large-scale downbeat at the change to the two-sharp key signature; three bass steps (thus one triple hypermeasure) later, the tonal deflection to E♭ and Calaf's entrance articulate another; and, again three bass steps (and another triple hypermeasure) later, the return of the "Mai nessun m'avrà" theme, now in A♭ with different text, marks another. The last begins with an elision—the last beat of the twelfth hypermeasure is the first beat of the thirteenth—that cuts short the climactic *a due* for

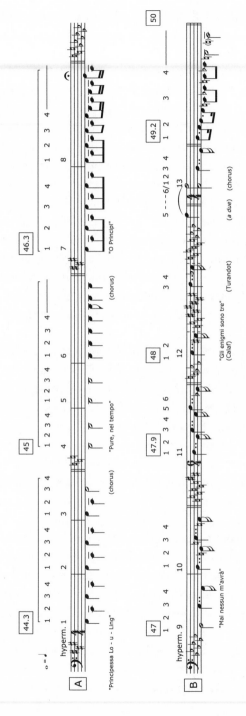

EXAMPLE 2.9. Bass and metric structure in *Turandot* II, "In questa Reggia."

Turandot and Calaf. Finally, parts A and B are each triple at the largest metric level, in that each comprises three large parts (3+3+2 hypermeasures in part A; 2+2+2 in part B).

Other examples of triple hypermeter in Puccini can be traced directly to the use of an unusual form in the text, which in turn demands an unusual musical form. The first and third parts of Rinuccio's "Firenze è come un albero fiorito" (Table 2.1a shows the text from the first) each comprise, for example, one *sestina* (i.e., six lines) of lyric *endecasillabo* verse. This is interesting, and unusual, if we put it in a larger stylistic and generic context: again, the procedure is not prototypical but rather in a dialogue with *ottocento* norms. The movement directly follows Rinuccio's own *recitative* ("Avete torto," R28), which itself emerges out of a large choral movement ("Dunque era vero," R16), and thus all indications are that we should expect in "Firenze" a solo lyric aria (an *aria di sortita,* or entrance aria) for the leading tenor that engages with one of two conventional genres: either the *romanza* or the *cavatina. Romanze* are one-movement arias in *versi lirici* almost always preceded by *recitative* in *versi sciolti,* while *cavatine* are full, four-movement arias in the conventional *solita forma* mold (with a *scena, adagio, tempo di mezzo,* and *cabaletta*) sung at a major character's first entrance on stage (as an *aria di sortita*); the lack of another lyric movement, or indeed any further solo singing for Rinuccio at all, after "Firenze" makes this a *romanza* (see chapter 5 for a full discussion of formal organization in *Gianni Schicchi*).[28] Moreover, as early as the 1830s and 1840s, the normative text form for lyric movements in Italian opera had become the *ottava:* an eight-line stanza. Normative texts for such movements exhibit a property Verdi referred to as *cadenza regolare,* in which grammatical syntax consistently aligns with the poetry. Enjambment—running a sentence over from one couplet or stanza into another—would generally be avoided, and each line would comprise an independent clause in the grammar. The normative musical setting of such text is at a rate of one line for every two measures of music, such that *accenti comuni* almost always fall on downbeats of every other measure, and in order to ensure that the poetry and musical settings are compatible (specifically, that the poetry allows for music that adheres to the norm of duple groupings at all levels of the hypermetric structure), the verse normally includes lines grouped in pairs (distiches), pairs of distiches grouped in quatrains

TABLE 2.1. *Gianni Schicchi,* "Firenze è come un albero fiorito," part 1

a. Text form

			mm.
Rinuccio	11	Firenze è come un albero fiorito,	
	11	che in piazza dei Signori ha tronco e fronde,	1–4
	11	ma le radici forze nuove apportano	
	11	dalle convalli limpide e feconde;	5–8
	11	E Firenze germoglia ed alle stelle	
	11	salgon palagi saldi e torri snelle!	9–12

b. Musical form

1	2	3	4	5	6	7	8^1	9	10	11	12
bi^2				ci				bi		ci	
I ———————————————————————— V								I ———————— I (!)			
lines 1–2				lines 3–4				lines 5–6			

Notes

1. Measure 8 is expanded by two beats (by the added $\frac{2}{4}$ measure at R30.10).
2. "Bi" and "ci" are the now-standard abbreviations referring to the "basic idea" and "contrasting idea" components of any conventional antecedent or consequent phrase. See William E. Caplin, *Classical Form: A Theory of Formal Functions for the Instrumental Music of Haydn, Mozart, and Beethoven* (New York: Oxford University Press, 1998), esp. 49–58.

(four-line stanzas), and a pair of quatrains grouped as an *ottava.* The resulting 2+2+2+2 scheme in the poetry yields in music the ubiquitous 16-bar lyric prototype, the A A B A form discussed earlier.

Clear right from the opening of "Firenze" is that in most respects, the text and Puccini's setting of it are completely conventional: the declamation pattern is absolutely regular, at a rate of one text line (and thus one *accento comune*) for every two bars of music (the shift later in part 2—at R31.5—to a line of text for every four measures of music is aurally imperceptible). This suggests in turn that the large musical form might also proceed according to a conventional design—perhaps the lyric prototype. But the lyric prototype requires that m. 5 (music for text line 3) repeat motivic material from m. 1 (music for text line 1). That this does not happen here rules out the lyric form, but at the same time introduces another highly conventional prototype with which the piece may be in dialogue, the possibility of which is strengthened by the arrival in m. 8 of a cadence in the dominant F (i.e., a half cadence with respect to the piece's home tonic of B♭): the classical period, here with antecedent and consequent phrases of eight bars each. In conventional (parallel) periods, the beginning of the consequent recalls the beginning of the antecedent, as happens here, with Rinuccio's rising scalar figure at m. 9 recalling a similar gesture from m. 1. But instead of completing its consequent in a conventional fashion, the period quickly dissolves and arrives at full cadential closure surprisingly early, at the end of its twelfth measure (see Table 2.1b). The consequent sounds truncated, and the form severely unbalanced. Indeed, this is such an abrupt ending that it sounds as if Puccini ran out of material and had to find a way to quickly close the music—which, in a way, is what happened: the *sestina* lacks two lines that would have (in a normal *ottava*) provided for four more bars of music. Thus the text provides opportunity for a striking musical gesture: as soon as the musical form begins to crystallize into a classic prototype, Puccini swiftly amputates it, as if to make a decisive rejection of convention in a way that echoes in music the central point in Rinuccio's text—and, indeed, one of the central points in the opera as a whole: "Viva la gente nuova e Gianni Schicchi!" ("Long live the newcomers and Gianni Schicchi").

As in these two examples, Puccini's triple hypermeters create in the music a distinctly audible sense of irregularity or, better, *flexibility*—and, as such, his tendency toward triple hypermeter is another manifestation of the metric elasticity characteristic in his Romantic style. Moreover, as most of Puccini's triple groupings occur at the larger (and thus not as immediately audible) levels of the hypermeter, their effect can be a rather uncanny one of occasionally not knowing exactly *why* the music sounds so unbalanced. That is: informed listeners expect, almost subconsciously, hypermetric regularity in the form of duple and quadruple groupings at the largest levels of metric organization; when a musical unit (on almost any level) closes before allowing a normal grouping to be completed—as in "Firenze" or any of the large groupings in "In questa Reggia," especially the first two (first six hypermeasures)—the effect is one of that unit having been truncated, and the closure can sound abrupt. But when that closure is so strong and so stylistically marked in other musical dimensions, as in the cadences at the ends of parts 1 and 3 of "Firenze" or the end of the brief A♭-major *a due* section of "In questa Reggia" (where, in both instances, harmony, melody, and voice become the focal points), this can overcome the sense that the music has somehow been destabilized formally and metrically. The result, then, is a sense, often fleeting, that something in the music is not quite right, but that the music is so satisfying that whatever is wrong must not be important. As such, this is a near-perfect example of what makes Puccini's late style so innovative: he found a way to not only *preserve* but also *strategically deploy* the traditional, high *ottocento* style, along with the lyric singing so elemental to it, while at the same time assimilating more contemporary compositional approaches, especially in the area of form and design.

THREE

Expressive Uses of Convention in *Il tabarro*

An examination of formal and expressive strategies in Puccini's late operas naturally begins with *Il tabarro*, not only because this is the opening, anchoring work for the *Trittico* but also because the piece is a definitive example of Puccini's strategies in the late works—especially the systematic withholding of the lyric, Romantic style so as to make its presence rare, peculiar, and striking. In *Tabarro* as in both *Angelica* and *Schicchi*, the effect is achieved through Puccini's use of two contrasting musical languages, one overtly Romantic and the other equally overtly non-Romantic, in an expressive opposition: the Romantic language becomes fully manifest, and thus the work's level of discourse shifts, once in the piece. In *Tabarro* this occurs in the first duet for Giorgetta and Luigi, just before the work's halfway mark, where the shift is cued by the emergence of stylistic traits explored in chapter 2—lyric singing, textural isolation of the melody, harmonic non-functionality, systematic undercutting of dominant function, metric elasticity, suspension of musical time, and others—and, in a far less obvious but equally important strategic maneuver, by Puccini's invoking the organizational schemata of the nineteenth-century melodrama: the conventions of *la solita forma*.

PUCCINI'S TRIPTYCH

Mosco Carner has observed the parallel in Puccini's *Trittico* with the three volumes of Dante's *Divine Comedy: Inferno, Purgatorio,* and *Paradiso*.[1] Even if *Gianni Schicchi* is the only one of Puccini's three panels derived directly from Dante, the parallel is apt in that, at least in one reading of the work's meaning, Puccini's three move in a generally negative to positive direction, from darkness to light, despair to bliss, hopelessness and total despondency to the optimism of a brighter future.[2] Dante may have been one source of Puccini's inspiration for the idea (he even apparently considered a three-part work based entirely on Dante after reading the *Divine Comedy*); another may have been his interest—widespread in contemporary Italy—in French literature and theater, in particular the Grand Guignol, in which short plays in contrasting styles and genres were commonly joined to make a single evening of theater. Grand Guignol often included a violent horror piece, something sentimental, and a comedy, exactly the grouping in Puccini's triptych and a generic scheme that integrates a principle from ancient Greek theater, in which a satyr play—a Greek comic form similar to a modern burlesque, with themes of sexuality, drinking, and other forms of raucous entertainment, so named because it includes a chorus of satyrs—served to lighten the atmosphere following a series of tragedies.[3] In any case, it is well known that by the time of his starting work on *Il tabarro* he had been considering the idea of joining together three works of varying *tinte* for quite some time[4]—at least since September 1904, in the period of crisis following the disastrous Milan premiere of *Madama Butterfly*, at which time he apparently considered setting three stories by Maxim Gorky and told Illica "I insist on three colors";[5] he wrote to future Casa Ricordi director Carlo Clausetti some years later, on March 19, 1907, during his agonizing search for a new subject: "I am constantly depressed about the [next] libretto. I will no longer do *The Woman and the Puppet*. Another kind of idea has come to me: a while ago I had considered doing three different sketches (3 acts) by Gorky, taken from *The Vagabonds* and *In the Steppes;* I had chosen [in September 1904] *The Raft* and the *26 and One:* but I was missing a strong and dramatic third for the evening's finale, and I couldn't manage to find it in anything else by Gorky."[6] And evidence of a tendency on Puccini's part toward somewhat unconventional, experimental dramaturgy had surfaced at least as early as *La bohème* (in which, in Act II, Puccini's highlighting each character in a series of rapid shifts of focus resembles procedures later adopted in film) and *Madama Butterfly* (in which the original second act was abnormally long relative to contemporary theatrical norms).[7]

The three one-acts, furthermore, hold a unique position in the context of Puccini's career and, indeed, in the context of Italian opera and even Western European opera more generally.[8] One-act operas were far less common, and far less successful, in the Italian tradition than in the German: by the time of *Trittico*, German opera had Strauss's *Salome* and *Elektra*, Schoenberg's *Erwartung* (more properly a *monodrama*) and *Die Glückliche Hand* (a *Drama mit Musik*), and Zemlinsky's *Eine Florentinische Tragödie*. More would follow, including Hindemith's *Mörder, Hoffnung der Frauen; Das Nusch-Nuschi;* and *Sancta Susanna;* Strauss's *Daphne* and *Capriccio;* and Schoenberg's *Von Heute auf Morgen,* among others. But many Italian one-acts were failures (among them Mascagni's *Zanetto* and Mancinelli's *25 Paolo e Francesca*), even though the Sonzogno competition in the 1880s and 90s was important in encouraging their composition and production. Besides the three in Puccini's *Trittico,* the most successful example is *Cavalleria rusticana,* although even *Pagliacci* was also originally in one act (before Leoncavallo decided he needed a curtain before beginning the play-within-the-play). Moreover, as Girardi has pointed out, there were no precedents in Europe at the time for three works of varying *tinte* and genres having been conceived as a single, organic whole, even though there were examples of two or even three one-acts performed in succession in a single night in the theater (including *Cavalleria rusticana* and *Pagliacci,* Busoni's *Arlecchino* and *Turandot,* Bartók's *Bluebeard's Castle* and *The Wooden Prince,* and Hindemith's *Mörder, Hoffnung der Frauen* and *Das Nusch-Nuschi*).

And, though clearly the main dramaturgic premise behind Puccini's *Trittico* is the stylistic-generic contrast among the three individual works, the trilogy was, again, conceived as a whole and given a collective title, and there is ample evidence for unity among the three pieces.[9] Each compresses its events into one act, with no scene change (and as such culminates a long-developing tendency in Puccini's works toward tighter concentration of dramatic action); each has in it a death (or at least evidence that one has recently occurred); and each has as an underlying theme an escape from present circumstances in search of a new and better life. In *Tabarro* escape is close—Paris looms in the background—but unattainable; in *Angelica* escape is possible only in death (suicide, followed by divine intervention and pardon); in *Schicchi,* finally, escape (from the stuffy life of the old aristocracy) not only looms, as in *Tabarro,* in the background (now in the form not of Paris but of the Florence cityscape) but is ultimately attained, so that the whole triptych closes with a vision of the present transformed into the future. Many have also noted the three settings' backward progression through time, from the 1890s Paris of *Il tabarro,* to *Suor Angelica* at the end of the seventeenth century (in, notably, an unspecified place), to *Gianni Schicchi* in 1299 Florence. And Girardi has observed the central role in each piece of both *time—Tabarro's* focus on the past, the unrelenting passage of time in *Angelica,* and *Schicchi's* concentration on the present and future, in its strong rejection of the past—and *place,* Puccini's musical setting of which serves in all three works a dual, structural-descriptive function, establishing an atmosphere but also providing an orchestral, narrative continuity.[10]

Beyond all these are more abstract commonalities binding the three panels into a unified whole. The most important of these, almost paradoxically, is the contrast among the three *tinte*—that is, the *disunity* of the three panels. This disunity was initially a point of concern for Puccini. He apparently first considered, between March and May 1900, the idea of an opera that would draw together various episodes of a single dramatic work—at the time, it was the three *Tartarin* episodes by Alphonse Daudet—and, as mentioned, he had returned to a similar, now more developed idea by September 1904, when he considered a trilogy on stories of Gorky. But at that time he was troubled with the challenges to dramatic realism such an endeavor might present; the problem of a single singer performing multiple roles in the same evening seems to have been especially troublesome to him. In the March 19, 1907, letter to Clausetti mentioned earlier, he also wrote, "Then [in 1904] I thought about the idea [the trilogy] again and didn't find it practical: three different things that would then be performed by the same singers would break the illusion and damage the representative truth. And so I abandoned the idea."[11] Ricordi had eventually vetoed the idea anyway in light of financial concerns.

But by 1918, when he was actively engaged in the composition of *Trittico,* this no longer posed a problem for him, as is apparent in an April letter to Clausetti in which he agreed to allow the same singer to perform Giorgetta and Lauretta, or Lauretta and Angelica, and also agreed that the first and last works could use the same tenor and baritone: "For *Tabarro*, other than Galeffi we need someone else, a woman who could also do *Schicchi*; but *Schicchi* needs a petite ingénue with a fresh sounding voice, lacking dramatic weight, etc. Dalla Rizza, who wouldn't be ideal for S. A. [*Suor Angelica*], could easily do Lauretta in G. S. [*Gianni Schicchi*]."[12] Indeed, even as early as 1907 this issue apparently had ceased to trouble him, so far had his aesthetic evolved and so committed had he become to the idea of juxtaposing contrasting genres. The letter to Clausetti of March 19 ends, "Now I'm thinking about it [the trilogy] again, not about the sketches but about Gorky, who I believe is still working at Capri."[13] And though the more general notion of contrasting stylistic and expressive registers was an important part of a larger aesthetic movement dating in literature from the 1870s and in opera from the 1890s, and as such had long been essential in Puccini's own musical language, *Il trittico* is the developmental zenith of this trend in Puccini's output.[14] It represents his near-complete renunciation of traditional Italian operatic dramaturgy—in which the norm is an organic, unilinear narrative structure with the natural flow of real time mirrored in the music—in favor of a more multiform, variegated dramaturgic structure that juxtaposes traditionally distinct theatrical genres and their musical-stylistic corollaries.[15]

In *Il trittico*, furthermore, is a unity residing not only in the disjunctions among the three panels, but also in the way those disunities are deployed musically and structurally on more a local level, within each work. That is, while the entire triptych is based on juxtaposing contrasting genres and styles on the largest possible level—among complete operas—each piece of the whole individually exhibits stylistic contrast within itself, deployed with an almost identical strategy in each work. Specifically, each establishes at its opening one style, or one *tinta* that encapsulates its atmosphere and that persists throughout almost the entire work; each decisively shifts, once, to a contrasting style. In terms of Hatten and Abbate, each work establishes one prevailing (lower) level of discourse and then shifts—in a gesture at once musical, dramatic, and theatrical—only once, to a higher level. In every case the lower level is marked by a non-Romantic musical language, while the higher is marked by a clear shift to the more traditionally Italian, Romantic style; as mentioned, the shift occurs both in the musical style itself *and* in the work's formal design, in that the clearest stylistic shifts are supported with attendant references to the formal conventions of nineteenth-century Italian melodrama.

PUCCINI'S CLOAK

Il tabarro is, as noted, the first of Puccini's panels but chronologically the last in terms of its setting. Puccini and librettist Adami retained many elements from French playwright Didier Gold's *pièce noire, La Houppelande*[16]—"The Cloak"—all of which have been ably summarized by Carner and, more recently, Girardi.[17] Present are most of Gold's characters and their ages:

- Georgette (Puccini's Giorgetta), 25
- Georgette's husband Michel (Michele), 50
- Louis (Luigi), 20
- The aptly nicknamed Goujon ("Il Tinca," or "tench," where a tench is a fish—incidentally, as Carner has noted, not exactly the same species as a goujon—known for its capacity to survive in less than ideal conditions), 35
- La Taupe ("Il Talpa," or the "mole"), 55
- La Taupe's wife La Furette ("La Frugola": literally "one who rummages," but also the stock, *Lumpenproletariat* character of the "rag-picker" common in veristic dramas), 50

In Gold, as in Puccini, Georgette and Louis share a birthplace in the Paris suburbs, a fascination with the city of Paris, and a frustration at the nomadic life in which they both find themselves entangled. Gone are some of Gold's details (in the play, Georgette is the seductress who lures the younger stevedore Louis; both Georgette and Louis have moral compasses mostly suppressed in Puccini and Adami's more basely erotic version of the tale), one of his characters (Goujon's wife), and an extra murder (Goujon murders his wife in a quayside tavern after discovering her with two other men; her promiscuity is the motivation for his fondness for drink, the latter an aspect of his character Puccini and Adami retained). Its repugnant violence and its focus on urban, working-class characters make *Il tabarro* perhaps the best example in all of Puccini's output of the movement often known as Italian *verismo*, even if a broader definition of this genre—one that accounts for the narrative, stylistic, and expressive qualities present in most operatic and literary *verismo*—suggests that all of Puccini's work, and his stylistic orientation in general, comes out of this aesthetic.[18]

One aspect of Puccini's style for which such an understanding is relevant is his distinctive musical characterization of place—his constant obsession with finding just the right way to capture in music the *atmosphere,* or local color, unique to each of his settings. Again, this quality of his work betrays his assimilation of strategies derived from the *giovane scuola italiana* in the late nineteenth century, whose operas are marked by, among many other features, a strong musical orientation toward the work's geographic or social milieu. The sense of locale is critical to all three of the *Trittico* panels: in each, the non-Romantic music that characterizes the place is likewise the music that provides for the prevailing stylistic homogeneity; the music marked as more conventionally Romantic is almost always less place-specific (Rinuccio's Tuscan *stornello* in *Gianni Schicchi,* "Firenze è come un albero fiorito," is an exception). In *Il tabarro* specifically, the homogeneity results from Puccini's use of musical material based almost exclusively on ostinatos and other forms of incessantly repeated pitch and rhythmic motives, so that the music exhibits almost throughout a static quality that denies or undercuts any traditional sense of motion through time (thus in some ways these themes reflect one of Puccini's more general stylistic traits, that of a tendency to suppress musical motion—as discussed in more detail in chapter 2).

Most writers have identified three main themes in *Tabarro:* one linked with the Seine river, one linked with Giorgetta and Luigi's clandestine love affair, and another linked with Michele and his cloak (in which he hides Luigi's dead body after murdering him at the end, having caught him on his way to Giorgetta's barge cabin for another rendezvous).[19] The river theme opens the work (as has often been noted, Puccini's instructions in the score are for the curtain to be opened *before* the music begins) and sets the tone for the whole opera, in that the theme establishes unrelenting repetition and monotony as the distinguishing musical characteristics of both local and large-scale levels of the structure. On the local level (R0.1–5), the theme is clearly constructed to mimic the qualities of the Seine as it meanders through Paris: the unceasing presence, usually in the bass voice, of a rhythmic ostinato (constant eighths—and even these lack definition because of the muffled pizzicato) evokes the perpetual, unstoppable flow of the river, a metaphor for the slow, tedious passage of time for the stevedores mired in a bleak, transient life of hard physical labor. The ostinato supports a modal, wandering melody (like the wandering river) with a series of parallel open fifths (these lend the music an ancient sound perhaps appropriate for the cathedral of Notre Dame, which, according to Puccini's instructions, should be visible in the set's background)[20] exhibiting tonal ambiguity (the opening bass note, G, seems best understood as the fourth scale degree and not the tonic, which is D); to this texture is added (at R1.7) a more active, rising motive and its variation (at R2), both of which suggest a surge in the river's motion but both of which ultimately fail to break free from the relentless, directionless flow of the river music. On a larger level, the music exhibits the same repetitive qualities: the opening two and a half minutes of the opera comprise three repetitions of a musical block lasting, respectively, 27, 38, and 38 beats in the compound meter (see example 3.1). The key shifts up a half step to E♭ minor as more stevedores enter from the hold at R2.7; the hemiola at R2.9 provides a momentary break from the rhythmic monotony and suggests more variation in the river's flow. This entire section exhibits stasis in every dimension: melodic, rhythmic, metric (here, unlike in "È ben altro il mio sogno," the changing meters ensure that the music is essentially ametric, with nothing more than a constantly articulated pulse), harmonic (all the sonorities are variants of the initial open fifths), and tonal (both locally—the bass line seems to have trouble moving away from D, for example—and globally—the tonic changes only once, at the shift to E♭).[21]

The adultery theme exhibits the same properties. It first appears at R12, when Luigi summons a passing organ grinder (vivid Parisian local color), Giorgetta invites Luigi to dance, and the eroticism is overt ("Io capisco una musica sola: quella che fa ballare"—"I only understand one kind of music: dance music"); it reappears (at R57) in the second duet for Giorgetta and Luigi (I will return presently to the issue of the work's formal design), then again in the finale (at R87 and R97). It comprises a short, cadential figure in the minor mode (in C at R12, C♯ at R57, G at R87, and C again at R97), only four beats long and incessantly repeated every time it appears. The definitive statement is in the duet at R57, when

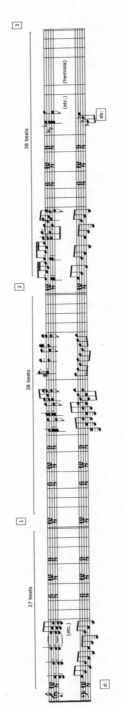

EXAMPLE 3.1. Sketch of *Il tabarro*, Ro–R3. Three-fold repetition of the river music.

Giorgetta and Luigi passionately reminisce on the pleasures of their relationship—the existence of which Michele remains unaware—and mull their fears (of being discovered), frustrations (from always having to hide), and hopes (of escape). Here the theme repeats no fewer than fourteen and a half times before the music finally moves on to something new at R59.6, at Giorgetta's "Ah, se fossimo soli, lontani" ("Ah, if only we were alone, far away"). The repetition seems never-ending: the constant return to the C♯ in the bass alone would have been enough to produce a rather frustrating tonal stasis, but Puccini goes further in also pairing this with the same kind of stasis in the voice, in which the lines for both Giorgetta and Luigi struggle to break away from the fifth scale degree, G♯, used here almost as a reciting tone. The stasis persists even when the ostinato breaks off at R59.6: the tonic remains on C♯, and the voices remain stalled on G♯.

The cloak theme is withheld until late in the work, in the last duet, that of Giorgetta and Michele. This is one of the most painful sections of the whole opera—far more so than the base, gruesome murder and hiding of the corpse at the end. The hopelessness is palpable: Giorgetta makes it explicit at the duet's opening (two bars before R72), in her "Come è difficile esser felice" ("How hard it is to be happy") and poignant shift up a half step from C♯ to D.[22] There follows a lyrical theme (sketched in the top system of example 3.2), which Carner has associated with Michele's despair over his broken relationship with Giorgetta,[23] that may seem at first stylistically Romantic—or at least may seem to have Romantic potential. But this music never fully develops any of the hallmark characteristics of Puccini's Romantic style, and the style itself remains nothing more than a distant hope—an unrealized potential, and as such a metaphor, perhaps, for both the Giorgetta-Michele relationship and the lives of the story's characters more generally, the future of both of which remain only distant potentials, never to be realized. The theme, in fact, only goes as far as suggesting traditional Romanticism for four measures (R72.1–4), after which its potential to expand into a fully conventional, lyric theme is denied—or, better, forcibly suppressed: the melody not only fails to break away from a static oscillation around A, B, and C (see the cellos at R72) but, in an even clearer non-Romantic gesture, veers off to the chromatic, functionally ambiguous B♭ (A♯?) at R72.5, never to return to the lyricism of its opening until the whole process repeats itself again at 72.13 (indeed, before that time the music dissolves into an even more static, more chromatic state—see the aimlessly oscillating material at R72.7 and 10). Furthermore, as if to encapsulate even more clearly the characters' frustrations, this cycle of stylistic Romanticism followed by dissolution repeats (as shown in example 3.2) not once but five times, with only minor variations in each repetition.

Here we have for the only time in the opera a more nuanced glimpse into the causes of the relationship's demise, which go well beyond the far more obvious fact that Giorgetta is half Michele's age: there apparently was a son who died as an infant, and the ensuing strain on the relationship was too much for either of them to handle. Michele insists on bringing up this painful episode, which occurred only a year before, much to Giorgetta's dismay (and here we also glimpse very clearly some of her moral misgivings about her adulterous affair, an aspect of her character that Puccini and Adami, as noted, drew from Gold's play). When he arrives, at the end of the fifth cycle, at "vi raccoglievo insieme nel tabarro" ("I used to gather [all three of] us together in [my] cloak"), the cloak theme appears so as to coincide with the word *tabarro*, and more repetition ensues. We hear the theme three times in succession (bottom line in example 3.2), first on G, then down a step (to F and E♭) in each of the next two statements, as if the music descends, with Michele, deeper into despair.

The stasis and homogeneity are deployed in other more subtle ways as well, forming an important part of the music for *Il tabarro* even when, on the surface, Puccini avoids obvious, incessant thematic repetition. Michele's monologue—where *monologues* are "tightly organized pieces that cannot properly be called arias [because they lack the characteristic formal, textural, and thematic expansiveness]"[24]—at the end of the work ("Nulla! . . . Silenzio! . . . ," R86) is a good example.[25] The piece is in C minor, a choice of tonality that proves difficult to explain in the traditional language of opera analysis. If traditional associations between characters and keys exist at all in Puccini's music—and in fact evidence for their presence is not strong—C minor seems to be associated with Giorgetta and Luigi, not Michele. C minor is the key in which the adultery theme first appears (R12); the key of Luigi's "Hai ben ragione" (R44); and the original key of the second duet for Giorgetta and Luigi (R57), before Puccini transposed it up a half step to C♯. Thus it seems surprising that

EXAMPLE 3.2. Sketch of *Il tabarro*, R72. Thematic organization in the Giorgetta-Michele duet.

Michele's monologue should be in the same key—never before in the opera has he been linked with it—even though interpretations, however improbable, are always possible: perhaps, for example, C minor indicates that the illicit Giorgetta-Luigi affair is the motivating force behind his monologue. Much more plausible, though, is an explanation that relates directly to the role of stasis as the governing aesthetic in most of this opera's music: Puccini returns to C throughout the work in an effort to maintain tonal stasis; the key is unmarked, and thus not always linked directly to specific characters or plot elements.[26]

The monologue is a single, continuous, closed lyric movement for Michele in three short parts, each delineated texturally and thematically. The first (R86.2) and last (R88) exhibit a texture closer to a true aria but one probably more properly designated either *arioso* or, in the standard nineteenth-century terminology, *parlante armonico*, mainly because of the way—very typical of Puccini's style, even in his lyric movements— the orchestra carries the thematic content and the voice enters and exits freely in a manner known as *musica di conversazione*. This latter term refers to a procedure from the late nineteenth-century music of the *giovane scuola italiana* and the move therein toward a more equal balance between voice and orchestra; the orchestra takes over some of the thematic functions formerly reserved exclusively for the voice, and the voice engages in a freer dialogue with the thematic material in the orchestra.[27] The monologue's middle part (R86.12) shifts between this and another texture better thought of either as a true *parlante armonico* (in which the voice carries little actual thematic material) or even a more traditional *recitative* (especially at R87). The framing sections are in C minor and use the full cloak theme, now expanded into a full, 8-bar theme in a modified lyric form (A A B A; example 3.3 shows part 1), complete with internal tonal motion that had earlier been denied: the theme now tonicizes the relative major E♭ in bars 5–6 before returning to its C-minor home. The middle section is in the very distantly related E minor and revolves around neighbor motion in the voice from B to A and a new, rather agitated ostinato in the bass.

This music may also seem stylistically Romantic, especially with the expansion of the cloak motive into a full lyric theme and more lyric expansion in Michele's part, but in fact the Romanticism is again forcibly suppressed: the music never manages to break away from the repetition

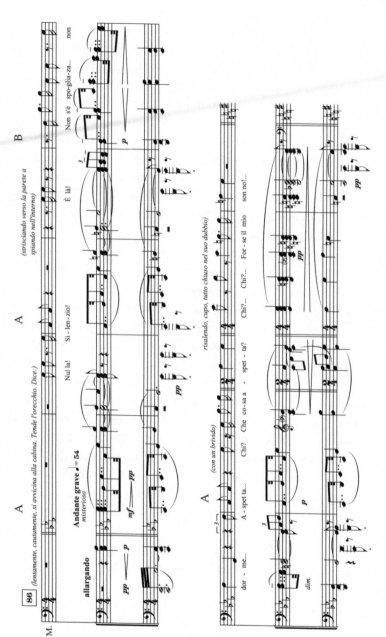

EXAMPLE 3.3. *Il tabarro*, Michele's monologue, first part.

of a very limited number of motivic ideas, and it never achieves true lyric expansion of the kind discussed in chapter 2. The expansion is so short-lived that it really introduces no significant departure from the prevailing homogeneity; the welcome motivic contrast in bars 5–6 (B in the lyric design) only becomes a source of frustration when the music returns almost immediately to the main cloak motive and then dissolves into two concluding measures (R86.10–11) that wander somewhat aimlessly both tonally and melodically (it seems aimless, at least, until the final tonic C minor crystallizes on the second beat of R86.11). If this music truly exhibited the Romantic style, we likely would have heard some kind of Puccinian cadence here, probably in the tonic or another, closely related key, probably with an attendant vocal climax for the singer. Even the form's middle section seems at first to be another area of contrast and thus a refreshing departure from the obsessive uniformity, but, as mentioned, first another ostinato appears in the bass and suppresses any potential for real tonal or melodic motion. Even the neighboring B-A motive in the voice comprises a variation on the appoggiatura figure (A♭-G) that concludes the cloak theme itself (see the brackets in examples 3.4a and b) and thus represents no real departure from, or even true expansion of, the cloak theme. The adultery theme and its incessant ostinato reappears (R87), briefly, as Michele turns his attention to Luigi as possibly the stevedore with whom Giorgetta has been unfaithful, and this theme then dissolves (R87.5) into more unremitting repetition, now of the last three beats of the cloak motive, over a long dominant (G) pedal that sets up the return of the concluding A section. Thus there is no lyric expansion, no stylistic Romanticism—and indeed no escape, either for the music, mired in stasis, or for Luigi, mired in a lonely, hopeless life dissolving before his eyes.

Again, Puccini deploys stylistic contrast in *Il tabarro* in a way that shifts the music's discursive level once in the opera. This occurs in the section of the work that includes Luigi's "Hai ben ragione," Giorgetta's "È ben altro il mio sogno," and the *a due* "Ma chi lascia il sobborgo" for Giorgetta and Luigi. This entire unit of the work is best conceived as a large, multi-movement, Giorgetta-Luigi duet, the first of two duets for the pair of lovers and one consistent with Puccini's late-style strategies described earlier. This duet, central to the opera in every sense—musical

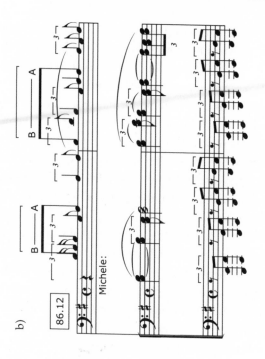

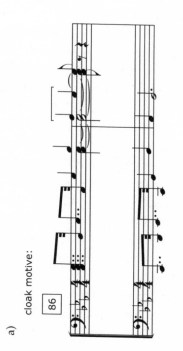

EXAMPLE 3-4. Motivic stasis in *Il tabarro*, Michele's monologue.

structure, dramatic organization, plot, and characterization—exhibits stylistic Romanticism not only in its vocal and orchestral writing but also in its formal design, in which it invokes the nineteenth-century melodramatic conventions of *la solita forma*.

A dialogue with conventional formal procedures begins to emerge at "Hai ben ragione" (R44).[28] This is a closed, lyric movement for Luigi that is much more overtly Romantic than any of the music that precedes it, most of which has the static, homogeneous, and emphatically non-Romantic qualities discussed previously. Even so, the simple presence of a single closed lyric movement for the tenor, whether in a conventional style or not, does not yet suggest anything out of the ordinary in an organizational sense. Puccini's large-scale formal strategies almost always involve some kind of episodically organized music in a continuous *parlante* texture in which characters enter and exit freely. Occasionally one finds closed lyric movements such as this one or even Michele's monologue, but one of these movements alone does not necessarily invoke a conventional nineteenth-century formal design. "Hai ben ragione," however, is followed closely with another lyric movement, "È ben altro il mio sogno," also unequivocally in the Romantic style and now for the *prima donna* Giorgetta, and which, furthermore, culminates with traditional *a due* singing for both the tenor and soprano. This particular *succession* of movements strongly suggests that Puccini may have entered here into dialogue with the *solita forma* of the *ottocento* grand duet, in four main sections (ostensibly *tempo d'attacco, adagio, tempo di mezzo*, and *cabaletta*) often preceded by a fifth (the *scena*, or *recitative*; see chapter 1 for more details). The reference emerges here in *Tabarro* if an informed listener bears in mind that the full, four-movement form of a duet grows out of a very simple underlying formal-dramatic principle—two progressions through a cycle of, first, active (kinetic) confrontation between two characters and, second, inactive (static) parallel, then *a due*, lyric singing—and then realizes that this principle aptly accommodates the sequence of events in this part of *Tabarro*. Starting at R41, the music proceeds through four discrete sections that comprise, in turn, kinetic confrontation (the conversation between Talpa, Tinca, Frugola, Luigi, and Michele beginning with "To'! Guarda la mia vecchia! ... Che narravi?"); static, lyric singing (Luigi's "Hai ben ragione"); and—repeating the cycle—more kinetic confrontation (more dialogue, now among Talpa, Tinca, Frugola, and Giorgetta); and more static, lyric singing (Giorgetta's "È ben altro il mio sogno" and the *a due* "Ma chi lascia il sobborgo"). The music thus implies that we can hear the entire block of the opera from R41 through R57 as a single set piece—structurally a *duet,* and again, the first of two for Giorgetta and Luigi in the opera—the parts of which fulfill the formal functions of, even if not all the precise musical, textual, and dramaturgical characteristics of, *tempo d'attacco, adagio, tempo di mezzo,* and *cabaletta.* (Note again here the *structural,* not *textural,* meaning of another common operatic term, in this case *duet.* Structurally, a *duet* is a confrontation between two characters played out over the four movements of the *solita forma;* texturally, it refers to two characters singing together. The structural sense of the word implies the textural sense, but does not require it; that is, most duets include simultaneous—*a due*—singing, but this kind of texture comprises only a small part of even the most conventional duet structures, and some duets avoid it altogether.)[29]

Table 3.1 gives the full text for the duet (minus a short dialogue at the end—the coda) and the four-movement division delineated in Puccini's musical setting—an organizational scheme, as suggested in the figure, that approximates the conventional formal functions of the nineteenth-century melodrama. Table 3.2 summarizes the duet's musical, dramatic, and textual organization. I will comment on the text first, since in some respects this is the most problematic aspect of the duet: the text does not clearly articulate the four-part formal prototype. This is not a total surprise, of course, given that the librettist was Adami, who tended, at least in his other librettos for Puccini (*La rondine* and *Turandot*—the latter a collaboration with Renato Simoni), toward an extremely loose versification of his texts, and given that conventional text forms were all but obsolete at the time anyway.[30] Indeed, the most likely explanation for the underlying formal strategy here is that Adami probably never intended to invoke the *solita forma* at all, but rather Puccini imposed on Adami's verse his own (musical) reference to the conventional formal model in order to reinforce the discursive shift in the music toward the conventional, Romantic Italian vocal style.

The verse in every section but two exhibits exactly the same property: loosely organized lines of *endecasillabo* and *settenario* verse not clearly grouped into stanzas but occasionally rhymed. This is the kind of

TABLE 3.1. Text in Il tabarro, first Giorgetta-Luigi duet

Part 1 (≈*tempo d'attacco*)

1	Il Talpa	11	To'! guarda la mia vecchia!... Che narravi?	
2	La Frugola	11	Parlavo con Giorgetta del soriano.	
3	Michele	7	O Luigi, domani	
4		7	si carica del ferro.	
5		7	Vieni a darci una mano?	
6	Luigi	11	Verrò, padrone.	
	Il Tinca		Buona notte a tutti.	
7	Il Talpa	11	Hai tanta fretta?	
	La Frugola		Corri già a ubbriacarti?	
8		11	Ah! se fossi tua moglie!	
	Il Tinca		Che fareste?	
9	La Frugola	11	Ti pesterei finché non la smettessi	
10		11	di passare le notti all'osteria.	
11		11	Non ti vergogni?	
	Il Tinca		No. Fa bene il vino!	b
12		11	S'affogano i pensieri di rivolta:	d
13		7	ché se bevo non penso,	b
14		7	e se penso non rido!	b

Part 2 (≈*adagio*)

15	Luigi	11	Hai ben ragione; meglio non pensare,	a
16		11	piegare il capo ed incurvar la schiena.	b
17		11	Per noi la vita non ha più valore	a
18		11	ed ogni gioia si converte in pena.	b
19		11	I sacchi in groppa e giù la testa a terra.	b
20		11	Se guardi in alto, bada alla frustata.	b
21		11	Il pane lo guadagni col sudore,	a
22		11	e l'ora dell'amore va rubata ...	b
23		11	Va rubata fra spasimi e paure	a
24		11	che offuscano l'ebbrezza più divina.	b
25		11	Tutto è conteso, tutto ci è rapito ...	c
26		11	la giornata è già buia alla mattina.	b
27		11	Hai ben ragione: meglio non pensare.	a

Part 3 (≈*tempo di mezzo*)

28	Il Tinca	7	Segui il mio esempio: bevi.	
29	Giorgetta	7	Basta!	
	Il Tinca		Non parlo più!	
30		11	A domani, ragazzi, e state bene!	
31	Il Talpa	11	Ce ne andiamo anche noi? Son stanco morto.	
32	La Frugola	7	Ah! quando mai potremo	
33		7	comprarci una bicocca?	
34		7	Là ci riposeremo.	
35	Giorgetta	11	È la tua fissazione la campagna!	
36	La Frugola	8	Ho sognato una casetta	a
37		8	con un piccolo orticello.	b
38		8	Quattro muri, stretta stretta,	a
39		8	e due pini per ombrello.	b
40		8	Il mio vecchio steso al sole,	c
41		8	ai miei piedi *Caporale,*	c
42		8	e aspettar così la morte	c
43		8	ch'è il rimedio d'ogni male!	c

Part 4 (≈*cabaletta*)

44	Giorgetta	7	È ben altro il mio sogno!	a
45		11	Son nata nel sobborgo e solo l'aria	b
46		11	di Parigi m'esalta e mi nutrisce!	c
47		11	Oh! se Michele, un giorno, abbandonasse	c
48		11	questa logora vita vagabonda!	b
49		7×2	Non si vive là dentro, fra il letto ed il fornello!	a
50		11	Tu avessi visto la mia stanza, un tempo!	a
51	La Frugola	11	Dove abitavi?	
	Giorgetta		Non lo sai?	
	Luigi		Belleville!	c (b)
52	Giorgetta	7	Luigi lo conosce!	c
53	Luigi	7	Anch'io ci sono nato!	a
54	Giorgetta	7	Come me, l'ha nel sangue!	c
55	Luigi	7	Non ci si può staccare!	c

TABLE 3.1. *continued*

56	Giorgetta	7	Bisogna aver provato!	a
57		11	Belleville è il nostro suolo e il nostro mondo!	a
58		11	Noi non possiamo vivere sull'acqua!	b
59		11	Bisogna calpestare il marciapiede!...	c
60		11	Là c'è una casa, là ci sono amici,	[d]
61		11	festosi incontri, piene confidenze...	c
62	Luigi	7×2	Ci si conosce tutti! S'è tutti una famiglia!	b
63	Giorgetta	11	Al mattino, il lavoro che ci aspetta.	b
64		11	Alla sera i ritorni in comitiva...	a
65		7	Botteghe che s'accendono	c
66		7	di luci e di lusinghe...	a
67		7	vetture che s'incrociano,	a
68		7	domeniche chiassose,	c
69		7	piccole gite in due	c
70		7	al Bosco di Boulogne!	c
71		5	Balli all'aperto	c
72		7	e intimità amorose!?...	b
73		11	È difficile dire cosa sia	b
74		11	quest'ansia, questa strana nostalgia...	c
75	a2	11	Ma chi lascia il sobborgo vuol tornare,	c
76		11	e chi ritorna non si può staccare.	b
77		11	C'è là in fondo Parigi che ci grida	c
78		11	con mille voci il fascino immortale!...	[e]

TABLE 3.2. Summary of musical, dramatic, and textual organization in *Il tabarro*, first Giorgetta-Luigi duet

Section:	1 (≈*tempo d'attacco*)	2 (≈*adagio*)	3 (≈*tempo di mezzo*)	4 (≈*cabaletta*)	*coda*
Location:	R41	R44	R46.2	R48 (*a2* at R53.1)	R54
Text:	Talpa: "Tò'! Guarda la mia vecchia! . . . Che narravi?"	"Hai ben ragione"	Tinca: "Segui il mio esempio: bevi."	"È ben altro il mio sogno" (R48); "Ma chi lascia il sobborgo" *a2*	Frugola: "Adesso ti capisco"
Tempo:	Andante moderato come il I.º tempo	Allegro moderato con moto (R43.1); Appena meno (R44.8); Andante moderato (R45)	Andante mosso (R46.6); Allegretto mosso (R47)	Andante mosso (R48); Andante con moto (R53.1)	Sostenendo molto (R54); Andante moderato (R56)
Personnel:	enter Talpa, Luigi, and Michele; enter stevedores; all characters now on stage; dialogue: all except Giorgetta; exit Michele	Luigi	Tinca, Talpa, Giorgetta, Frugola ("Ho sognato una casetta," R47); exit Tinca	Giorgetta (R48); Giorgetta and Luigi (R53.1)	Talpa and Frugola (reprise "Ho sognato una casetta"); exit Frugola and Talpa; Giorgetta and Luigi remain
Key:	d (R41); C (*brindisi* reprise, R43.1)	c	a (R46.6), d (R47)	B♭	B♭; ends on enharmonic V of C♯
Verse (see figure 3.1):	rhymed *scena* verse	libretto: three quatrains plus one line (4+4+4+1) *endecasillabo lirici*; score: three quatrains plus one distich (4+4+4+2) *endecasillabo lirici*	rhymed *scena* verse; Frugola: two quatrains (4+4) *ottonario lirici*	rhymed *scena* verse, 4+4+2 / 4+4+2 / 4+4+3 / 4	*versi sciolti* (except "Ho sognato" reprise)

verse common in recitative sections of almost any late-nineteenth century Italian opera, a heightened form of traditional recitative *scena* verse (i.e., *versi sciolti*) that James Hepokoski has called "rhymed *scena*."[31] Sometimes this will include *quinari* mixed among the *settenari* and *endecasillabi* (Boito's *Otello* and *Falstaff* librettos are good examples), and while this appears to occur once in this example, at line 71, this is probably a misprint in the published libretto (see n. 44). Only twice do we find traditional *versi lirici*: once at Luigi's "Hai ben ragione," where Adami writes three quatrains plus a distich of lyric *endecasillabi*, and again at the interlude for Frugola—"Ho sognato una casetta," for which Adami used two quatrains of lyric *ottonario*—in the middle of the putative *tempo di mezzo*.

But strictly speaking, in the most normative formal prototypes, *versi sciolti* appear only in the introductory *scena;* the text shifts to *versi lirici* at the *tempo d'attacco* and the *versi sciolti* normally do not return. (The change to *versi lirici* is, in fact, one of the features that helps mark the boundary between the *scena* and the *tempo d'attacco,* a boundary that otherwise may be hard to locate.)[32] Here in *Tabarro,* even if we accept that the *tempo d'attacco* and *tempo di mezzo* might reasonably employ rhymed *scena* verse in place of *versi lirici* in order to produce the kind of naturalistic, speech-like dialogue Puccini clearly sought in these kinetic movements, the problem remains that even the putative *cabaletta*—the second of the two static, lyric movements—employs this same kind of verse. And, because of the two stanzas of lyric *ottonario* for Frugola ("Ho sognato") in the *tempo di mezzo,* the *cabaletta's* opening is articulated, oddly, not by a shift from rhymed *scena* verse to *versi lirici,* but rather by precisely the opposite move, from *versi lirici* backward to rhymed *scena* verse. Even Luigi's ("Hai ben ragione") fourteen lines of lyric *endecasillabo*—the most conventional text in the duet, in that this is lyric verse for a lyric movement—can be regarded as a reference to a nonstandard procedure. *Endecasillabo* is a less common choice for a lyric meter, though it is by no means uncommon, and there are examples even in late Verdi and early Puccini. But, in almost all cases, the choice of *endecasillabo* for a lyric meter should be interpreted as expressively marked, as generally this is a meter reserved for *versi sciolti* because of its highly flexible internal accent pattern. Moreover, in the strictest formal sense, the use of three quatrains here instead of two is also atypical (and it produces a continuous, through-composed musical structure—shown in example

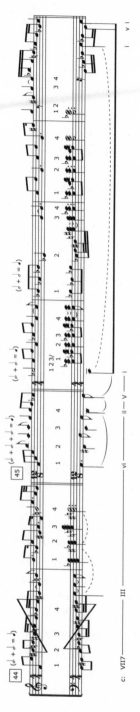

EXAMPLE 3.5. Harmonic and metric structure in *Il tabarro*, "Hai ben ragione."

3.5, to which we will return presently—that makes no apparent reference to any standard, two- or three-part formal model).[33]

Incidentally, understanding the entire block of the opera from "To'! Guarda la mia vecchia!" to "Ma chi lascia il sobborgo" as a Giorgetta-Luigi duet necessitates understanding Frugola's two quatrains of *ottonario* as belonging to a multisectional *tempo di mezzo*—for which there are plenty of formal precedents, even in the most conventional duets.[34] Such an interpretation also reinforces Frugola's role *outside* the traditional dramatic space. Her text effects a detour that breaks the work's narrative continuity; in this sense, her character is a tool, a distancing device through which the discourse shifts inward, to a state of interiority and anti-subjectivity that is similar in some respects to that which emerges in the stylistically Romantic passages.[35] This shift can be understood as analogous to the dramatic shift expected in the most normative *tempi di mezzo*, which often include the introduction on stage of a new character who introduces some kind of irreversible change—a detour—in the dramatic situation.

Furthermore, Frugola's highly regular, rhythmic *ottonario* verse contrasts markedly with the rest of Adami's loosely organized, more conversational rhymed *scena* verse (and even with Luigi's *endecasillabo*, lyric though it is); and her music, just as in her earlier "Se tu sapessi" (R32.3), is extremely repetitive (see her repeated D at the opening), with a constantly articulated pulse point and a highly regular meter (in sharp contrast to Puccini's typically elastic meters). The music, like the verse, sounds *mechanistic* in relation to everything around it—as if it were mechanically produced (on a music box, perhaps)—and conveys a *puppet* quality that depersonalizes the character and prevents the audience from empathetically identifying with her. That she has no name (only a generic nickname) reinforces this effect, as does her representation, as noted, of a stock character: the rag picker, or Marx's *Lumpenproletariat*. The mechanical quality of her music and text is a stock characteristic Puccini may have borrowed from the aesthetics of contemporary straight theater, some of which dictated that actors be masked or, in more radical formulations, replaced completely with puppets or synthesized (metaphorically) with machines, all in the interest of dehumanizing them and undermining any possibility of reproducing reality on the stage—any attempt at which was viewed as dishonest or misleading.

These same kinds of mechanical characters appear elsewhere in Puccini's work, including, most notably, as the three masks in *Turandot*—the best examples besides Frugola herself.[36]

Musically, the duet exhibits many features of the *solita forma* schema but introduces interesting, expressive departures from others. The opening section (R41) is typical of a *tempo d'attacco*. The return of the river music (which already has an initiatory quality because it opened the opera) strongly articulates the beginning of a new formal-dramatic section, a restart of the relentlessly repetitive musical cycling characteristic of the piece more broadly.[37] The entrance on stage of all the characters (including Michele and all the stevedores) reinforces the sense of a musical-dramatic attack;[38] the music moves freely in and out of various textures, anywhere from *parlante armonico* (the opening dialogue over the river music) to *recitative* (Frugola's "Ti pesterei finché non la smettessi"). Sometimes the kinetic dialogue, in which all but Giorgetta participate, is rapid-fire (in, for example, the exchange between Frugola, Tinca, and Talpa), and the music exhibits the multiple sections typical of many conventional *tempi d'attacco*: here the *brindisi* (reprised from R7) is, like Frugola's "Ho sognato" in the *tempo di mezzo*, a lower-level unit within the larger movement.[39]

Dramatic action stagnates for the first time at Luigi's "Hai ben ragione" (example 3.5 shows the large-scale harmonic and metric structure—the latter in the manner of the durational reductions in chapter 2), his lament on the miserable state of his life (or, better, his Marxist tirade against the oppression of the working class).[40] This music may initially sound as if it belongs to either the *romanza* or *cavatina* genres, where, again, a *romanza* is a one-movement aria in *versi lirici* (preceded by *recitative*), while a *cavatina* is a full, four-movement *aria di sortita* following the conventional *solita forma* schema. "Hai ben ragione" may be considered Luigi's entrance aria, although even this is not clear, as Luigi has been on stage for some time prior to his singing this piece and any sense of *entrance* has surely been lost. In his late works, however, Puccini withholds entrance arias for major characters until deeper and deeper into the operas.[41] "Hai ben ragione" also sets *versi lirici* in one movement and has no leading recitative; as such, it matches neither the traditional *romanza* nor *cavatina* definitions. Only a retrospective hearing clarifies the matter, and renders moot the *romanza* versus *cavatina* question. The piece functions as the *adagio* movement in a four-movement duet, and thus implies no need for a *recitative* (in a duet, the *adagio* would only have leading *recitative* if it were preceded directly by the *scena*—that is, if the piece skipped the *tempo d'attacco;* precedent for this certainly exists, even as early as Donizetti and Verdi, though it is not the norm).[42] But the genre issue is still not completely clear. This is a typical *adagio* movement only insofar as it sets lyric verse in a relatively slow tempo; otherwise there is nothing about it that suggests it should be part of a duet. It lacks the conventional setting of parallel stanzas for the two main characters followed by a coda with *a due* singing in unison, parallel thirds, or parallel sixths, and in fact it includes no participation of any kind from Giorgetta.

The action-reaction cycle resumes again at the *tempo di mezzo* (at Tinca's "Segui il mio esempio," his direct response to Luigi), which comprises a return to dialogue in a *parlante* texture (here more *parlante melodico* than before), characters either exiting the stage (Tinca) or preparing to do so (Frugola and Talpa), and Frugola interrupting the scene with her "Ho sognato," about her dreams of a cottage in the country with her cat. Action then stagnates for the second and final time at "È ben altro il mio sogno," the homage to Paris and Belleville and the first opportunity for significant participation in the piece by Giorgetta. The movement fills the formal function of the *cabaletta* in the most general sense, in its status as a lyric, static, dramatically conclusive movement in a new meter and a tempo noticeably faster than that of the *adagio.* But the formal particulars are more complex:[43] here Adami's libretto (see table 3.1) has ten lines (two quatrains and a distich) basically for Giorgetta alone (lines 45–54; Frugola and Luigi interject at the end); ten more lines (lines 55–64; again, two quatrains and a distich) for Giorgetta and Luigi, with no *a due;* eleven lines again for Giorgetta alone (lines 65–75);[44] and a concluding quatrain sung *a due* (lines 76–79). Musically, this produces an A (the first 10 lines)–A (next 10)–B (next 11)–A (last 4) form in which the A sections are closed periods in the tonic B♭, B is a transition that prolongs the dominant (a dominant pedal begins at R52), and the last A repeats the original period, now sung *a due.* This is essentially the lyric prototype, now expanded to include both characters and finish with *a due* singing.

More importantly for our dialogue with the *solita forma,* it also mirrors the form of a conventional *cabaletta.* These normally comprise a thematic statement by the first character (often a 16- or 32-bar period), a restatement of the same (sometimes contrasting) material by the second character, a transitional ritornello, and a repetition of the original material by both characters *a due*—almost exactly the form of "È ben altro il mio sogno." In fact, the movement's organization is so similar to that of the traditional *cabaletta* that the reference is nearly impossible to miss. Furthermore, even were it not as similar—and we have no reason to think it should be, as *cabalette* were largely out of fashion even as early as the late 1860s as a result of a general trend toward an acceleration of musical pacing and a concomitant tendency for composers to avoid the time-consuming, full *cabaletta* form—we might still invoke William Ashbrook's notion of the "*cabaletta*-function," defined as a "short appendix" at the end of a truncated version of the standard *solita forma* in an aria or duet, normally differentiated in tonality and tempo, involving musical repetition, and heightening the emotional intensity to produce a dramatic climax. All of these characteristics describe with precision "È ben altro il mio sogno."[45]

There remain, then, only two potential interpretive problems with invoking the duet form as an underlying schema. The first is simpler, and involves the relationship between the two participating characters and their music. As noted, there is nothing in the *adagio* that structurally suggests that the underlying formal prototype should be that of the duet. Likewise, in the *cabaletta,* Giorgetta and Luigi have unequal roles, with Giorgetta carrying the bulk of the thematic material and Luigi participating only in the second and last A sections (he never sings an independent thematic statement of his own, as he should in a *cabaletta,* and he remains subsidiary to Giorgetta for the entire movement). Indeed, the close proximity of these lyric statements for Luigi ("Hai ben ragione") and Giorgetta ("È ben altro") also suggests, however weakly, that these may comprise not separate, large-scale movements but rather the normative parallel statements (*proposta* and *risposta*) of *a single slow movement.*[46] But the differences in tempo ("Hai ben ragione" is clearly slower), tonality (Luigi sings in C, Giorgetta in B♭), meter (duple for Luigi versus triple for Giorgetta), and thematic content (the two have nothing in common) all mitigate against such a reading and support hearing "Hai ben ragione" and "È ben altro" as separate movements.

Such deformations of the normal formal prototypes are expressive in the context of the opera as a whole. Giorgetta's lack of ability to participate in the duet's slow movement (and, indeed, her near-complete lack of participation in any of the music before the *cabaletta*: she has only two lines before "È ben altro," both in the *tempo di mezzo*) reflects her general lack of ability to take control of her life's circumstances. The unusual, through-composed form of "Hai ben ragione" (see example 3.5) squelches—overwhelms, really—Luigi's latent Marxist inclinations and his valiant attempt to refuse to accept his situation in life.[47] The descending fifths cycle (VII–III–vi–ii–V–i in C minor) leading to a structural downbeat (R45.5) and a longer section in the tonic represents in music a gradually accelerating, downward spiral that traps Luigi in his own misery, at once ruling out any possibility of escape—his life will never change, his situation is hopeless—and foreshadowing the doom that awaits him. And Giorgetta's dominance in the *cabaletta*, in which she finally emerges in the texture with some force—force of personality, perhaps—and leads (drags) Luigi into the *a due*, is almost a holdover from Gold, in which Giorgetta (not Luigi) initiates and prolongs the adulterous affair.

The second problem is more complex. Recent secondary literature on Puccini seems to have arrived at the (very reasonable) position—not a *conclusion*, really, as the issue remains open for debate—that conventional *ottocento* forms play little role in Puccini's organizational strategies,[48] and that in Puccini's music these forms exist not in whole but only in part, in "free-floating remnants" that vaguely recall the conventional forms, genres, and textures but that have been stripped of their traditional formal functions in an otherwise ad hoc, episodically organized musical language.[49] Furthermore, to assert that Puccini *used* or *made reference to* formal conventions as part of a larger expressive strategy concomitantly implies that his audience may have known—and even that he may have expected them to know—the conventions, and that this audience may even have *expected him* to *use* those conventions. But certainly not all this can be true. Perhaps at the very least it would be reasonable to think Puccini may have expected some of his audience—the connoisseurs—to have some familiarity with the conventional *ottocento* style, and that these same listeners may have been able to recognize a reference to older organizational strategies, however deformed, that recalled those in, say, Verdi's music. On the other hand, it seems much less reasonable to assume that Puccini's listeners—even the most educated among them—would have been *expecting* Puccini to invoke conventional formal models, again however skillfully disguised.

Note the contrast here with Verdi's audience, at least a portion of which, if some contemporary writings—Basevi's critical study of early Verdi and the correspondence of Verdi's student Emanuele Muzio—are any indication, was aware of both the organizational conventions and Verdi's strategic, expressive uses of them.[50] But even this point is not as self-evident as it seems, and it may well be difficult, if not impossible, to ascertain what Verdi's audience was expecting upon entering the opera house. To project the assumptions and expectations of a contemporary critic or composer, much less someone like Basevi, onto even a small portion of Verdi's listening audience may indeed be untenable, as Roger Parker has so eloquently argued.[51] Basevi, in particular, was a composer well out of the mainstream (this rendered him rather unsuccessful as a composer and author, which, in turn, according to Parker, may have given him reason to be envious and hypercritical of Verdi). His famous *Studio sulle opere di Giuseppe Verdi* was a technical treatise for other composers, not for the general public, and thus not a good example of the most typical nineteenth-century approach to music criticism. And in fact he is not as concerned as some modern writers make him seem with large-scale form and design, preferring the vast majority of the time a consideration of *form* on a much more local level—that is, the form of the internal movements of what we now think of as a larger, coherent four-part scheme.

My own view is that while Parker is convincing when he asserts that Basevi alone cannot possibly represent a nineteenth-century critical understanding of Verdi, let alone a general public's understanding, and that while modern analysts may rely unduly on the argument that *solita forma* analyses are *authentic* (and thus, by implication, somehow *privileged*) because they use contemporary criticism as their point of departure, none of this makes the analyses of Powers, Moreen, Gossett, and others any less convincing. Parker, in fact, never takes issue with the point that Verdi's music relies (as does music of, say, Mozart and

Beethoven) on normative, formal-generic schemata for its expressive effect, and in fact Parker seems to have no trouble with these analyses *per se*. He challenges only these analysts' tendency to invoke Verdi's *intentions* and the *expectations of Verdi's audience* as a point of departure—both of which may be interesting speculative arguments, but neither of which are necessary for the analyses to suggest viable, persuasive, compelling ways of hearing this music.

Puccini's audience, on the other hand, would have been at once more diverse and, at least in some segments, less educated than Verdi's—and thus ascertaining its expectations is even more difficult. Puccini—beyond being able to assume some familiarity with *ottocento* style—may also have been able to assume that many would be familiar with not only contemporary Italian opera, but also contemporary French and German opera. But he probably never would have assumed that anyone *expected* the use of the old formal prototypes, as these had been in a process of dissolution that began around the 1880s or, by some accounts, even earlier.[52] None of this, however, renders untenable my assertion that Puccini's late music relies in large part on a move toward a pluralistic musical style, and that such a move entailed, among many other facets, his occasionally invoking older, conventional nineteenth-century schemata as part of a strategic effort to sound more stylistically Romantic. Neither an audience's familiarity with conventional forms nor an expectation that Puccini may use them are prerequisites for Puccini's being able to use such a strategy expressively. We can assume that audiences noticed the reversions to Romanticism in other aspects of the musical language— Wilson, as mentioned, has established very convincingly that contemporary audiences heard *two* Puccinis in the late operas: one honest, sincere, sentimental, and conservative (read: Romantic and Italian), the other superficial, insincere, emotionally detached, and progressive (read: new and international)[53]—but whether they noticed the conventional formal designs he employed to support such reversions ultimately does not matter. The desired effects—marked rhetorical shifts in the level of discourse and an attendant shift of attention to the voice-object—may be stronger for those who did notice these references, but the effects were, and still are, present, even for those who did not.

This in turn suggests a crucial point: how *Puccini's* audience heard this music is completely separate from how a *modern* audience hears it.

Modern audiences bring much more to the listening experience, including, of course, knowledge of recent, modern music, but also a different level of familiarity with conventional music that predates Puccini. Modern listeners may be (probably are, in fact) even more familiar with, for example, Rossini and early Verdi than Puccini's own audiences were, and this familiarity has an enormous impact on how one hears and interprets the music. A listener who knows Rossini and Verdi well will hear Puccini completely differently from one who knows only, say, Berg and Strauss. For this reason, invoking conventional formal prototypes as a framework within which to hear this music is not only reasonable but eminently appropriate, in that it provides fascinating opportunities for expressive interpretation and new ways of hearing rich layers of musical meaning in this repertoire.

Even the issue of Puccini's *intentions*—was he intentionally invoking the *solita forma* or not?—is not entirely clear, nor ultimately does it need to be. We can produce meaningful interpretations of this music that account for the myriad ways listeners may experience it—interpretations that bring about new ways of hearing it, ways that may never have arisen intuitively but that, once available, may strongly color one's experience of the music and change the way one understands its theatrical effects—without being bound by what Puccini may or may not have *intended*. There need be no intention at all on Puccini's part in order for us to hear the music as I am suggesting. But this is not to say that there is no evidence for intentionality on Puccini's part: we have seen that in at least one instance in *Il tabarro*, for example, he seems to have imposed on Adami's verse structure a musical form—one that hews closely to conventional models—that was not readily apparent in the verse alone. This means, in turn, that in some sense not only did Puccini himself enter abstractly into a dialogue with conventional formal models, but he also *invited his listeners into the dialogue.* Here we should be cognizant of David Rosen's point that to assert that Puccini may have employed such a strategy *intentionally* is not the same thing as asserting that he did it *consciously.*[54]

What, then, *is* needed in order to hear in Puccini a dialogue with conventional forms, especially if we do not necessarily approach these operas—if we do not necessarily enter into the listening experience—with *a priori* expectations of hearing conventional formal prototypes?

Something *in the music itself* must initiate the expressive dialogue. If some event or series of events in the piece (a succession of genres or textures, for example, such as *Il tabarro*'s two lyric movements in close proximity) makes a clear enough reference to one or more facets of a conventional model, it may be that other references will follow from this, or even that we as listeners will *seek them out*. Again, in any well-formed cognitive schema, the presence of an underlying prototype will guide detection of that prototype's features, just as, conversely, the appearance of individual features themselves will help point to the relevance of some particular prototype. To be completely realistic, moreover, such references really need to come as *series* of events, not as *single* events; an interpretive strategy relying on the latter can easily get out of hand and may lead, for example, to any slow lyric movement being designated a potential *adagio*—and clearly, this could quickly become meaningless. In any case, it does seem reasonable that Puccini should have made such occasional references a part of his work more generally; it goes hand in hand with the larger strategy of a stylistically heterogeneous language. But *occasional* is the key word here: the most meaningful reading of Puccini seems to be one that strikes a compromise between finding *solite forme* everywhere—subsuming nearly every part of an opera into one of the four standard movements—and finding them nowhere—viewing an opera as organized in an entirely new and ad hoc fashion. Each point of view seems equally unlikely and equally unproductive analytically.[55]

In that spirit, I will survey here, in less detail, the organization of the rest of *Il tabarro*. The essential point is that nowhere in the work is there another reference to conventional formal models as clear as the one in the first duet for Giorgetta and Luigi—just as nowhere else in the work does the music clearly make a discursive shift to the marked, Romantic mode. Thus, the piece is a good example of Puccini's organizational strategies in his late works: most of them are best described as *episodic*, wherein a series of discrete musical-dramatic episodes governed mainly by an interest in moving the dramatic narrative as realistically and efficiently as possible integrate, occasionally and for expressive effect, with fundamentally conventional formal schemata.

Table 3.3 summarizes these points: the opera comprises two large parts (typical of Puccini's first acts and one-acts, all of which are bipartite, with one kinetic half devoted to *ambience* and another static half devoted to *characters*);[56] within these is a series of three set pieces, all duets, framed by an introduction that establishes the predominant *tinta* and a finale in which the dénouement unfolds. Evidence for a certain underlying conventionality in Puccini's formal thinking, at least at the largest structural levels, lies in the series of three duets (and note that here again *duet* has a *structural*, not a *textural* meaning—these are *duets* in the sense that each sets a two-character confrontation across multiple movements or episodes). That all of *Il tabarro*, except the introduction and finale, is subsumed into duets places the piece firmly in the nineteenth-century tradition of the "opera of duets"; this is Paolo Fabbri's coinage that contrasts, very broadly, nineteenth-century operas with those of the eighteenth century, most of which are best understood as "operas of arias."[57] In this regard *Il tabarro*—again, on the largest formal level—is even somewhat *more* conventional than one might expect, in that the importance of the duet as the driving organizational force in Italian opera had diminished by about 1890. As Jay Nicolaisen has explained, by that time a freer, episodic organization governed more by dramatic concerns than by conventional formal models (similar to that of *Il tabarro*'s introduction and finale) had become widespread.[58] This observation is consistent with Puccini's general tendency, already noted, toward a stylistic reversion—a move *backward*, closer to *ottocento* norms—late in his career, at least with regard to his use of formal conventions, all of which together function in this music as neoclassicizing devices—as they do in, for example, Richard Strauss's *Ariadne auf Naxos* and *Capriccio*.

At more local levels, *Tabarro* exhibits a less conventional formal organization everywhere but, as discussed, in the first duet for Giorgetta and Luigi. The piece's local-level unconventionality is consistent with its decidedly non-Romantic style, employed everywhere but in the lyric movements of that first duet. That is, while Puccini's Romantic style entails a concomitant reference to conventional formal prototypes, his stylistically non-Romantic music scrupulously avoids such references. The second Giorgetta-Luigi duet (duet 2), in which the two first passionately express frustration at maintaining their secret affair (Luigi wants unfettered access to Giorgetta but cannot obtain it as long as he works for Michele) and then arrange another rendezvous for later that night,

TABLE 3.3. Formal organization in *Il tabarro*

	Large formal function	Small formal function or movement	Personnel	Keys	Elapsed time[1]
R0 PART 1	INTRODUCTION		orchestra (river theme)	d	
3		episode 1	Giorgetta + Michele	a	
6		episode 2	+ stevedores		
7		*brindisi*	(Luigi/Talpa/Tinca)	C	
12		adultery theme		c	
13.5		waltz	(+ organ grinder)	E♭	
17.7		episode 3	+ Michele		
24			+ song vendor	G	
30		episode 4	+ Frugola	a	
32.3		"Se tu sapessi"		d	
41	DUET 1 (Giorgetta/Luigi)	part 1 (≈*tempo d'attacco*)	all except Giorgetta	d	
44		part 2 (≈*adagio*)	Luigi	c	16' 39" (62% of part 1)
46		part 3 (≈*tempo di mezzo*)	Tinca, Giorgetta, Talpa, Frugola	a, d	
48		part 4 (≈*cabaletta*)	Giorgetta, Giorgetta/Luigi *a2*	B♭	
54		coda	Frugola, Talpa		

	Label	Section	Characters	Key	Duration
57	PART 2 — DUET 2 (Giorgetta/Luigi)	A	Giorgetta/Luigi	c♯	26′ 43″ (50% of total)
60		(*recitative*)	Michele/Luigi		
62		B	Giorgetta/Luigi		
64.5				A	
66		A		c♯	
67		(*recitative*)	Giorgetta		
69.4		B	Luigi	A	
70		A		c♯	
72	DUET 3 (Giorgetta/Michele)	part 1	Giorgetta/Michele	d	35′ 00″ (66% of total)
77.5			Michele		
78		part 2	Giorgetta/Michele (brief *a2*)	D♭, E♭	
79		part 3	Giorgetta/Michele	E♭	
80			Michele		
84	FINALE		2 lovers offstage	a	43′ 01″ (62.5% of part 2)
86		monologue	Michele	c	

TABLE 3.3. *continued*

Large formal function	Small formal function or movement	Personnel	Keys	Elapsed time[1]
90	pantomime (murder)	Michele/Luigi		
96	conclusion	Michele/Giorgetta		
				total 52' 48"

Note

1. Shows the total elapsed real time (not elapsed measures) at the designated location. Timings are from the 1999 Antonio Pappano recording on EMI Classics (7243 5 56587 2 2).

provides a good example. This is a rondo in five parts (a form Puccini was apparently fond of in this period: he used it again in *Turandot* Act I, in the trio for the ministers), A B A B A, modified (from the traditional A B A C A) so as to maintain the high degree of formal-thematic stasis that governs almost all of *Tabarro*. All three A sections (R57, 66, and 70; the first was discussed earlier) revolve around incessant repetition of the adultery theme in C$\sharp$ minor; the first two dissolve into *recitatives* (just before R60 and just after R67, respectively) that function as transitions to the B sections (R64.5 and 69.4). The first *recitative* is longer and in two parts, one for Luigi and Michele (Luigi asks to disembark at Rouen) and another (R62), much more agitated, for Luigi and Giorgetta (the latter challenges the former's faithfulness; Luigi responds that he wants to disembark because he can no longer share Giorgetta with Michele). The second is shorter and mainly for Giorgetta (she will signal Luigi later with a lighted match). Both B sections are more lyrical, in the third-related A major (and thus also brighter), and more passionate and overtly erotic: the first is for both, while the second (like the last) is for Luigi alone (on the "Folle di gelosia"—"the madness of jealousy"). The final A comprises only Luigi's climactic emotional release on the high G$\sharp$, a "sharpened" reiteration, as Helen Greenwald has noted, of his earlier release—in the first duet—on the high G at the end of "Hai ben ragione."[59]

The static rondo design overpowers any possible reference to the *solita forma*. Certainly there may be ways of hearing in this duet a four-movement, double cycle of kinesis-stasis (the most obvious is to hear the A and B sections as the kinetic-static pairs and the last A as a coda), but any of these seem to run roughshod over the more important formal principle at work here, that of a circling, repetitive thematic-tonal design that traps the characters into a world from which there is no escape (not to mention that the *adagio* and *cabaletta* in such a scheme would have absolutely none of the musical characteristics of their traditional counterparts). This should not be completely unexpected, in that generically this duet (along with the next one, for Giorgetta and Michele) is in the tradition of the *dialogue duet* or, better, the *duologue,* both of which entail an illicit, secret, or otherwise problematized exchange between characters, usually set in a continuous *parlante* texture and not adhering closely to normative formal prototypes. The illicit nature of their content thus places them *outside* the realms of both normal dramatic activity and normal musical forms.[60]

In this regard one of the most notable features of the second Giorgetta-Luigi duet in *Tabarro* is its careful suppression of *a due* singing, which makes the entire piece extraordinarily tense. As listeners, we badly want—need—an *a due* as a way of releasing some of the pent-up energy between the characters; the best opportunity here would have been in either of the lyrical B sections, but the second of these contains not even a single line for Giorgetta, while the first seems to squelch the chance for simultaneous singing at every turn (note especially the rapid exchange of thematic material around R65 that denies both singers several opportunities to join their voices). The strategy is expressive: there can be no *a due* for Giorgetta and Luigi here because it has already occurred in the *cabaletta* of the first (far more conventional and far more optimistic) duet. Indeed, the end of that earlier *cabaletta* and the *a due* release were only the beginning of a course on which Giorgetta and Luigi move further and further apart, a course that ends tragically and violently with Luigi's murder.

Duet 2 ends with a coda and a very strong cadence in C♯ minor (71.7), from which the piece moves directly—with no intervening transitional material—into duet 3, now for Giorgetta and Michele. This duet provides one final glimpse into what might have been for husband and wife and unfolds in a three-part structure now considerably more episodic. Earlier I discussed the first part (R72), a conversational episode for both characters in a *parlante armonico* texture and comprising a churning, quintuple cycle of a theme known as "Michele's despair," followed directly (R77.5) by three descending iterations of the cloak theme. The second part (R78) is a lyrical episode in D♭, initiated by Michele and complete with an *a due* (R78.5). Finally, the third—which begins (R79) with both characters in dialogue but moves into what is essentially a long monologue in E♭ for Michele (beginning and ending with "Resta vicino a me," at R80 and R82.5, respectively)—returns to the *parlante* texture of the opening but also freely incorporates textures closer to both recitative and aria (or, more properly, *arioso*—there is none of the metric regularity here associated with a true aria). The piece completely rejects any possible reference to conventionality (there simply is no way to hear a double kinetic-static cycle), and indeed at the largest level the piece seems all about denying even the simplest of conventional gestures, including, again, *a due* singing. The thematic cycling at the opening lends an impression of repeated stopping and restarting, in which the music tries to expand into a full lyric theme but is denied each time, only to have to return to where it began and try again. When an *a due* texture does appear (R78.5), it dissolves almost as soon as it begins (it lasts but four bars). Finally, the climax of the third section ("Resta vicino a me," R82.4) sounds in some sense like an attempt to initiate a fourth—perhaps another lyric episode with another opportunity for an *a due* (Giorgetta does actually re-enter, at R83.2)—but the orchestra continues to churn endlessly (the material is a variation on the river theme), stifling any lyric expansion that may have been possible. The music thus confirms what the audience knows already: the relationship is over; time will continue to relentlessly churn away, and the future is hopeless. Giorgetta's "Buona notte, Michele . . . casco dal sonno" ("Good night, Michele . . . I'm falling asleep"; the libretto has "Buona notte, Michele . . . Ho tanto sonno") is at once disingenuous—her aim is to be available to meet Luigi—and final, as if to cut off the conversation, once and for all. Michele likewise gives up, wrenching the tonality a tritone away, to A, at his vulgar "Sgualdrina!" ("Whore!").

Only the introduction and finale remain. The introduction comprises an orchestral opening followed by a long, episodically organized section in a *parlante* texture (the orchestra carries the thematic content almost exclusively) with occasional interludes that move (as is typical for Puccini) toward more expansive, lyric singing—although never does the music develop into a full aria texture. Entering and exiting characters delineate the episodic segments: Giorgetta remains on stage all the time (the action revolves around her); successive episodes add Michele (R3), the stevedores (at R6, in an episode that comprises, in order: a traditional *brindisi* in C at R7, in three verses for, respectively, Luigi, Talpa, and Tinca; the adultery theme at R12 in C minor; and the organ grinder's waltz in E♭ at 13.5, in a classic A B A C A rondo design), Michele again followed by the song vendor (R17.7 and 24, respectively), and finally Frugola (R30, in an episode that includes her "Se tu sapessi" in D at R32.3). The finale opens (R84) with two lovers singing offstage (showing us what might have been in this dismal tale, in which any hope for a happy ending has long since been lost—if indeed it was ever present at all) followed by Michele's monologue ("Nulla! . . . Silenzio! . . .," R86—discussed previously), the pantomime (R90, in which Michele ambushes and murders Luigi), and a very short, final, morbid conclusion (R96) for Giorgetta and Michele.

The form as a whole exhibits masterful proportioning. Girardi has observed this as well—"The drama is organized according to golden section proportions"[61]—without providing, oddly enough, a specific explanation of what he means. He apparently has in mind numbers of measures, as nowhere does his analysis refer to clock timings: his part 2 ("Peripeteia") begins at m. 870, just over 60 percent of the way through the total of 1439; his part 3 ("Catastrophe") begins at m. 1220, which (somewhat less obviously now) is just over 61 percent of the way through the 570 measures that comprise parts 2 and 3 together. Even more interesting is that Puccini's proportioning measured in terms of clock time confirms Girardi's intuition on the role of the golden section—but only if we take the form given in table 3.3 as a point of departure. That is, the opera lasts just under fifty-three minutes,[62] parts 1 and 2 divide the piece almost exactly in half; the first lyric movement in the most conventional duet (Luigi's *adagio*, "Hai ben ragione," in duet 1)—by any account one of the more salient formal articulations in the score—begins roughly at the golden section of the large part 1 (about 62 percent of the way through); duet 3 (at Giorgetta's "Come è difficile esser felice"—which opens the only duet for her and Michele and likewise provides a salient formal articulation) starts at the golden section for the whole opera (again, about 62 percent of the way through); and the finale (at Michele's "Sgualdrina") begins roughly at the golden section (62.5 percent) of part 2.[63]

This proportional scheme very effectively controls the theatrical experience of *Tabarro* by imparting a sensation that the opera *accelerates* toward its conclusion. The structural articulations occur more frequently as the piece progresses. The first major articulation in part 1 (the first duet) occurs roughly two-thirds of the way through, but then another (the second duet) occurs at the halfway point of the whole opera, and two more (the third duet and the finale) follow in relatively quick succession, at about one-third and just under two-thirds of the way through part 2. The murder, of course, occurs very close to the end (with about two and a half minutes left), and from the moment Luigi dies until

Giorgetta's discovery of the body (right at the end) the tension is thick enough to be almost unbearable.[64]

Thus ends the first, darkest, and most violent panel in Puccini's triptych. Not only does *Tabarro* provide a gripping, tremendously effective piece of theater to open the set of three one-acts, but the work also functions as a structural, strategic prototype for all the operas that follow—including *Angelica* and *Schicchi*, which follow in the same evening, and *Turandot*, which premiered more than seven years later. In *Tabarro*, Puccini established a method of integrating a more contemporary, episodic, formal approach—one consistent with most contemporary European opera and one which, for Puccini, originates in the Italian-opera aesthetics of the 1880s and 90s—with strategies that rely on older, conventional, nineteenth-century formal-dramatic schemata. And, more than being integration for integration's sake, and even more than being the backward, retrogressive stylistic turn that often typifies many composers' late styles, Puccini's is an integration of organizational strategies for expressive effect. The interpretive key to this music therefore lies in the interaction, or the dialogue, between the two approaches. *Il tabarro* suppresses the most traditional Italianate style and its supporting formal schemata in all instances save for one: the central, pivotal duet for the two leading characters, in which the lyric style flourishes within a formal design in dialogue with the most conventional nineteenth-century models. In that single juncture, the work reaches an expressive, emotional height striking in and of itself but even more powerful when heard within the interpretive framework provided by the dialogic design. The work is thus a classic example of Puccini's expressive uses of convention and, even more importantly, the expressive power of form in music.

FOUR

Formal Multivalence in *Suor Angelica*

Even with the intervening intermission, the monophonic, ancient chant-like opening of *Suor Angelica* could not be more striking in its divergence from the intensely violent ending just witnessed in *Il tabarro*. But the contrast masks the fact that *Angelica*'s opening exhibits nearly the same organizational procedures as the opening of *Il tabarro,* and that this foreshadows striking similarities between these works at the broadest, most generic levels of their forms. Both works, indeed, exhibit nearly precisely the same strategies in their formal designs: both comprise a series of set pieces framed by an introduction establishing the *tinta* and a conclusion containing the dénouement; both expressively integrate a contemporary, episodic organizational approach with a more traditional approach based on conventional formal schemata; and each fully shifts its level of discourse only once, when a reference to the conventional formal schema of the *ottocento* melodrama underscores a clear, complete shift to the lyric, Romantic style. But *Angelica* also exhibits distinctly more *formal multivalence* than *Tabarro,* in that here Puccini employed what Hepokoski has called "multiple strategies of structure-building"— not all of which support one another at all times—in the service of expressing in the opera's structure the deep psychological tension that torments its main character to the point of her taking her own life.[1]

Both of the *Trittico*'s last two panels, *Angelica* and *Gianni Schicchi,* stand as mostly original creations of Puccini's new librettist Giovacchino Forzano. *Schicchi* was spun out from a passage in Dante, while *Angelica* was apparently completely original—though not without precedent and possible models.[2] The most likely of these, as many have noted, seems to be Massenet's *Le jongleur de Notre Dame* of 1902, on a libretto by Maurice Léna borrowed from a medieval legend: the work is in the medieval tradition of the miracle play, as is Forzano's *Angelica*, and takes for its setting a historic (fourteenth century for Massenet, end of the seventeenth century for Puccini) cloister (Massenet, unlike Puccini, names the place specifically: the Abbey of Cluny). Both end with divine intervention of the Virgin, bathed in light, and the death of the protagonist to the sound of a heavenly choir (in Massenet a statue of the Virgin extends a final blessing to the minstrel juggler, while in Puccini an apparition of the Virgin offers absolution to a dying Angelica); each employs singers of a single gender—all males in Massenet's monastery, all females in Puccini's convent—and thus each has a similarly persistent uniformity of sound and timbre; and both (as Girardi has observed) reflect a contemporary vogue for medieval subjects also evident in, among others, Debussy's incidental music for D'Annunzio's *Le martyre de Saint Sébastian* (1911) and Bartók's *Bluebeard's Castle* (1918, on Maurice Maeterlinck's play *Arianne et Barbe-Bleue*—set "in legendary times" with a medieval flavor).[3] Other of Puccini's and Forzano's models may have included Belgian symbolist Georges Rodenbach's 1892 novella, *Bruges-la-mort* (which has a similarly persistent religious *tinta*); Manzoni's classic Italian Romantic novel of 1828, *I promessi sposi;* and (especially for Puccini) the vocal works "La Sulamite" by Chabrier and "La damoiselle élue" by Debussy (both for all female voices, Chabrier's including a mezzo soloist).[4]

Girardi's observation on the special significance of Puccini's collaboration with the young Forzano (1884–1970) also seems relevant here,[5] especially in light of Puccini's concern for visual effects in *Il trittico* and for the near-complete uniformity of musical color within each of the three operas—color used, as seen in *Tabarro,* as a foil to the infrequent turns toward musical Romanticism. Forzano, a native of Borgo San Lorenzo near Florence, was at one time an operatic baritone, a journalist, and an attorney (serving occasionally as a legal advisor for Puccini) before becoming a playwright and author of over thirty librettos for Puccini, Franchetti, Mascagni, Leoncavallo, and Wolf-Ferrari. But perhaps the most important among all his professional interests and activities was stage directing, in which he was involved for most of his career. He produced all of his more than twenty plays himself; was resident stage director at *La Scala* in the early 1920s (he revived Puccini's *Trittico* there in 1922 and staged the *Turandot* premiere in 1926) and, at various other times, was engaged as guest director in Rome and at Covent Garden; and in the early 1930s took his interest in directing into the burgeoning world of film, directing and filming some of his plays under the auspices of his own production company. He was one of the early directors (others include German Max Reinhardt, Swiss Adolphe Appia, and Briton Edward Gordon Craig) responsible for making stage direction into an art form of its own, in which the director exercises a certain amount of creativity independent of the author of the work in production. As such, he seems the ideal directorial choice for Puccini, who we know was eminently concerned with visual and stage effects, and experimentations with both, in all three *Trittico* panels; for evidence one need look only as far as his very lengthy description of the Princess's entrance in *Angelica* and the long descriptions of the *mise-en-scène* at the openings of *Tabarro* and *Schicchi*.[6]

As mentioned, numerous parallels connect *Il tabarro* with *Suor Angelica*, even if some of these are masked by the obvious differences in the two operas' surface *tinte*. Like *Tabarro*, *Angelica* takes place in the space of a few hours at most, beginning at sunset (specified in the opening stage directions: "Tramonto di primavera. Un raggio di sole batte al disopra del getto della fonte"—"Sunset in Spring. A ray of sunlight hits the spray from the fountain") and ending later the same night. Forzano organized the libretto into seven tableaux (divisions Puccini sometimes respected in the music but sometimes did not—an issue to which we will return shortly), marked *La preghiera* (prayer), *Le punizioni* (penance), *La ricreazione* (recreation), *Il ritorno dalla cerca* (return from the quest—i.e., from soliciting offerings), *La Zia Principessa* (the Princess Aunt), *La grazia* (grace), and *Il miracolo* (the miracle). Puccini called for a total of fifteen female voices (adding boys' and men's voices in the miracle scene, at the ancient Marian hymn "O gloriosa virginum," R81): eight nuns, including sopranos Angelica, Genovieffa, Osmina, and Dulcina as well as the higher-ranking (and, notably, unnamed) mezzos *La Badessa* (Abbess), *La Maestra della Novizie* (mistress of the novices), *La Suora Zelatrice* (literally "the zealous sister"—the one responsible for discipline), and *La Suora Infermiera* ("infirmary sister"); two *novizie* ("novices"); two *cercatrice* (literally "searchers"—those who seek offerings or donations); two lay sisters (*converse*); and Angelica's aristocratic aunt, the *Zia Principessa* (which, as many have observed, is Puccini's only significant contralto role).

As in *Tabarro*, musically *Angelica* comprises a relentlessly homogeneous, static language in which Puccini systematically suppresses the Romantic, lyric style almost throughout, reverting to it (and thus shifting the discursive level) only once, in a similarly dramatic, theatrical gesture. The prevailing language in *Angelica* is, again as in *Tabarro*, a metaphor for the monotony and hopelessness that plagues its characters' lives, especially Angelica's. The convent for her is nothing short of a prison, one offering no hope of escape and no hope of return to the normal, maternal life for which she longs; just as the music suppresses progression, change, and, it seems, the flow of time itself, so too does Angelica perceive time as slow and oppressive—as psychologically stifling for her as the convent's physical walls. The uniformity of the female voices, of course—even with the natural contrast among sopranos and mezzos—lends an unrelenting uniformity to the timbre. Other of Puccini's strategies include a brightly colored ("pastel-tinted," as Hepokoski calls it)[7] orchestration emphasizing the timbral transparency of the harp, winds, and muted or pizzicato strings; a sacred *colore locale* that entails musical reference to a learned or ancient contrapuntal style and that produces a sense of time suspended (in that the music is stylistically backward-looking);[8] a pervasive use of modality and dissonance, the latter often involving the same kinds of impressionistic parallelism or planing seen in *Tabarro* and again in *Turandot;* cyclic repetition of blocks of material (similar to the repetitive sections of *Tabarro*) that create an impression of the music progressing nowhere; and a strategic suppression of extended singing in the lyric, Romantic style. All capture well the monotony of monastic life as well as the pseudo-religious *tinta* and the pure (Hepokoski: "faux-pure"),[9] almost surreal world of the convent.

Typical of the orchestrational color in the piece is the episode (R13), near the beginning and just after the *Zelatrice* has given permission for recreation, in which Genovieffa excitedly announces that she has seen sunlight hitting the courtyard fountain (an event that, insofar as it happens only three times a year, provides reason for celebration but also marks the unceasing passage of time): short fragments in flutes, oboes, and clarinets accompany the sisters' "Un altr'anno è passato" ("Another year has passed"). Muted strings follow (R14) with a *moderato e soste-nuto* expansion of the same motive, and the passage concludes with five lines of highly regular *ottonario* for Genovieffa (R15.3; "O sorella in pio lavoro"—"O sisters in pious works"), with orchestral support now from the winds only (pizzicato strings return to the texture, with the chorus of sisters, at R16). The "sunlight" music—the orchestral interlude (R8) in which the sisters scatter throughout the cloister grounds—earlier in the same episode exhibits similar strategies, now with a luminous combination of winds, harp, triangle, and pizzicato violins colorfully juxtaposed against a richer blend of violas, cellos, and basses.

Typical of the sacred *colore locale* is the motive known as the "litany refrain" (example 4.1), a recurring fragment (always with Latin text, if text is present) comprising a composed-out double-neighbor motive over a plagal progression, sometimes accompanied by harp to provide an ancient, lute-like effect (see the statement at R46.5, for example); the *converse*'s penitential "Cristo Signore, / Sposo d'Amore" (R5), which—though not quite Fuxian two-voice counterpoint—recalls the strict counterpoint of an earlier era; and Angelica's own cadence (R26.6) in the episode in which wasps have stung one of the sisters and Angelica is compelled to assist—apparently because she has expertise with remedies made from herbs and flowers. The latter (a deformed Phrygian cadence, with the lowest voice descending a half step) is rather unusual and contrasts markedly with the immediately preceding, rather frenetic music for the infirmary sister. Indeed, time seems to pause momentarily, not because of a shift to the Romantic style but because of the harmonically non-functional, religious punctuation. It clearly underlines in music Angelica's "Aspettate, ho un'erba e un fiori" ("Wait, I have an herb and a flower"), making us wait for the infirmary sister's "Suor Angelica ha sempre una ricetta" ("Sister Angelica always has a [good] recipe")—a critical sequence in the plot, as we discover later, when (after quoting the infirmary sister's line, at R69.3) Angelica poisons herself with a solution she makes from herbs and flowers.[10]

Typical of the work's dissonance is the music (R34) in which attention first turns toward the arrival of a grand coach and a visitor in the *parlatorio*: this tonally ambiguous, extremely static passage emphasizes the whole-tone collection, both in the supporting chord (a French aug-

EXAMPLE 4.1. *Suor Angelica,* "litany refrain" (sacred *colore locale*).

mented sixth—a whole-tone subset) in clarinets, bass clarinets, bassoons, and horns, and in the ornamented flute line, which is modal (mixolydian on E♭) but emphasizes D♭, E♭, F, and G—all pitches from the same whole-tone collection as the supporting chord. Shortly afterward (beginning just before R35), a pedal F supports upper voices first centering on dissonant Gs and Ds (see R35) and then moving quickly to a frenzied, highly chromatic passage in which the stasis finally abates; the diatonic music for "Da gran signori" ("A noble family's [coach]"; R36) emerges from the latter.

Cyclic repetition is important in *Suor Angelica* right from the start—again, just as in *Il tabarro:* the two works' openings closely resemble one another with regard to their expressive and organizational strategies. In *Angelica* as in *Tabarro,* the initial music sets the *tinta* for work: the key of C major, a corollary for purity; a monophonic, 4-bar melody that invokes ancient chant, orchestrated in distant, off-stage chimes (the distance is reinforced by the closed curtain—a marked contrast with *Tabarro,* in which, again, the curtain is open before the music begins); parallel triads (R0.5–8) in the ethereal muted strings and celeste, each with an extra note for impressionistic dissonance; a chorus of nuns chanting an overtly religious "Ave Maria"; and an ornamental, obbligato piccolo that adds an additional touch of (faux) purity to the already other-worldly sound. And, still as in *Tabarro,* globally the music establishes stasis and homogeneity as central themes: the entire opening *preghiera* tableau comprises about four minutes of music, organized as four nearly identical, slowly-unfolding repetitions of an 8-bar unit, itself comprising two almost identical four-bar phrases (*a* and *b* in example 4.2). The first 8-bar unit is entirely instrumental; the second, third, and fourth include the chorus of sisters (mm. 5–8 of the third is for Angelica alone); and a varied, expanded ten-bar coda complete with the obligatory 4–3 suspension at the contrapuntal cadence closes the tableau. Incidentally, Puccini was fond of this cadence in this piece, returning to it often as a device

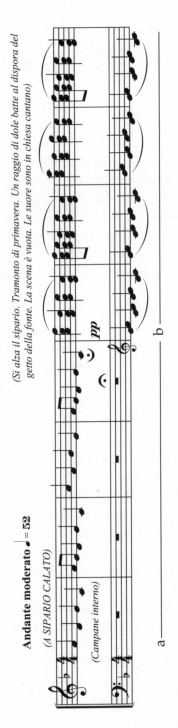

EXAMPLE 4.2. *Suor Angelica*, opening theme.

to evoke the sacred *colore locale*. Another example appears at the end of Genovieffa's "Soave Signor mio" monologue (two bars before R20), where it emerges idiomatically out of a modal texture in E♭, in support of Genovieffa's "Perdonami, Signore, / Tu che sei l'Agnus Dei" ("Forgive me, Lord, you who are the Lamb of God").[11]

Numerous other examples of cyclic repetition pervade the score. The best of these is perhaps what I am calling the "Abbess" episode, which begins (R40) when the Abbess enters and summons Angelica into the *parlatorio* to meet the Princess and ends at the Princess's "Il Principe Gualtiero vostro padre" (R44.2)—and, as such, runs over Forzano's own *La Zia Principessa* designation, itself placed just before the lengthy, well-known description of the Princess's entrance. This begins Angelica's anxious waiting, and the slow, relentless monotony of the music mirrors the crushing tension of not knowing what news the Princess can possibly have brought. The episode (example 4.3) comprises three parts, each involving its own cyclic repetition: the first (A), in which a composed-out double-neighbor motive (i.e., E-F-D-E) related to the litany refrain degenerates into seemingly interminable stasis (R40.5–10), then repeats (R40.11) in a kind of breathless *canto spezzato* for Angelica and in a non-normative, inverted form (i.e., E-D-F-E) that literally turns Angelica's world upside down; the second (B), in which every measure is a varied repetition of the previous and which includes the sisters' "Requiem æternam" for Bianca Rosa, overheard from the cemetery; and the last (C), involving a seemingly never-ending cycle of seven repetitions of a single, basic three-bar unit (itself comprising a one-bar arpeggiated motive in C♯ minor and a two-bar chromatically-related chord. The arpeggiated motive changes at R43.4, at the Princess's entrance. Its opening intervals invert—yet another turning upside down of Angelica's world—and it begins to move rhythmically at half the speed and in a more broken fashion, both gestures effecting a palpable increase in tension.[12]

Regarding Puccini's strategic avoidance of extended lyric singing, Angelica's short monologue, "I desideri sono i fior dei vivi" ("Desires are the flowers of the living") deserves comment.[13] Here idiosyncrasies in music, text, and formal organization produce a forcible suppressionvof the Romantic style similar to that observed in *Il tabarro*, in the Giorgetta-Michele duet and in Michele's monologue. "I desideri" is the musical centerpiece of *Angelica*'s long, introductory episode that begins with

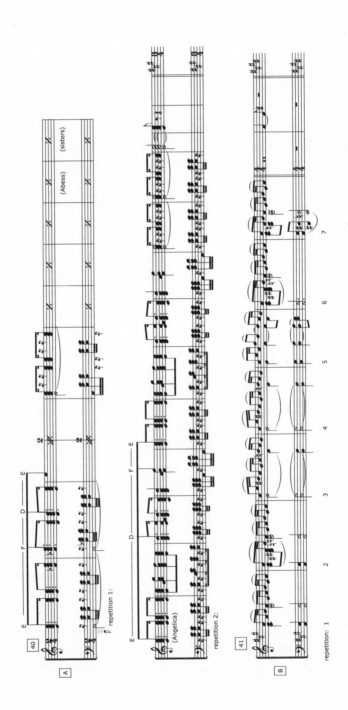

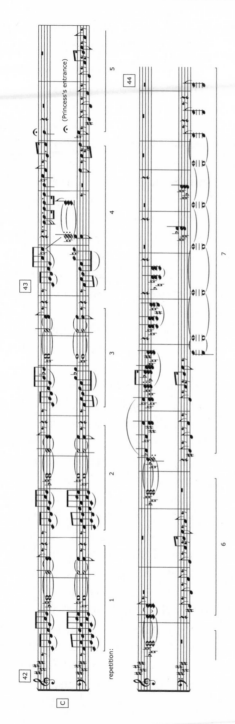

EXAMPLE 4.3. Sketch of *Suor Angelica*, R40. Thematic organization and cyclic repetition in *Suor Angelica*, "Abbess" episode.

sunlight hitting the fountain, continues with Genovieffa suggesting that the sisters take some golden water to the deceased Bianca Rosa's grave, and finally turns toward a discussion among Angelica, Genovieffa, the *Zelatrice,* and others on the place of worldly desires in the monastic life (they have no place, according to the *Zelatrice*). As such, in the largest possible sense the monologue and what follows it underscores the prevailing religious *tinta,* the establishment of which is the focus of this entire introductory episode; but it also marks the beginning of a stylistic shift toward the contrasting Romantic style and away from the homogeneous color characteristic of the rest of the piece. "I desideri" is, indeed, musically Romantic, in stark contrast with (and emerging abruptly and unexpectedly from) the preceding, persistently monorhythmic music for Genovieffa and the chorus of sisters. It exhibits several of the important stylistic traits explored in chapter 2, including triple metric groupings at the phrase level and a suppression of the dominant function at a significant structural juncture (approaching R17, where the bass descends through G and F on its way to the tonic E♭ instead of first moving through the dominant B♭—a linear, modal cadence that recalls Calaf's in "Non piangere, Liù").

The triple metric groupings lend the monologue a rather unbalanced and unsettled quality that renders the experience of the piece as frustrating for the listener as the suppressed desires are for Angelica. The idiosyncratic metric structure grows out of an unusual feature of Angelica's text: a single line of *settenario* at line 4, in the middle of two quatrains of otherwise strict, lyric *endecasillabo* verse (see table 4.1a). The declamation begins regularly, if slowly, with one text line per four measures of music (compare table 4.1b); but, apparently because of the shortened line 4, Puccini compresses both lines 3 and 4 into one four-bar phrase, producing a grouping of three (rather than a more normative four) phrases for the first quatrain. The second quatrain, furthermore, even with no variation in its verse meter (it comprises four lines of strict *endecasillabo*), maintains the large-scale irregularity: line 5 occupies four measures and seems to resume the regular text and metric flow, but Puccini compresses lines 6 and 7 into four bars before finishing with line 8 and a return to the normal four-bar declamatory rhythm—all resulting in another triple grouping at the phrase level. Globally, the setting produces a disconcerting, agitated effect: Angelica begins slowly

TABLE 4.1. Text and musical organization in *Suor Angelica*, "I desideri sono i fior dei vivi"

a. Text form

			mm.
Angelica	11	I desideri sono i fior dei vivi,	1–4
	11	non fioriscon nel regno delle morte,	5–8
	11	perché la Madre Vergine soccorre,	9–12
	7	e in Sua benignità	
	11	liberamente al desiar precorre;	13–16
	11	prima che un desiderio sia fiorito	17–20
	11	la Madre delle Madri l'ha esaudito.	
	11	O sorella, la morte è vita bella!	21–24

b. Musical form

1	2	3	4	5	6	7	8	9	10	11	12	13	14	15	16	17	18	19	20	21	22	23	24
bi^1				ci				(ci?)				bi				ci				(ci?)			
I ——————										— V —		I ——											I
line 1				line 2				lines 3–4				line 5				lines 6–7				line 8			

TABLE 4.1. *continued*

c. Hypothetical normal-period form setting two quatrains of text

1	2	3	4	5	6	7	8	9	10	11	12	13	14	15	16
bi				ci				bi				ci			
I———————————V								I———————————I							
lines 1–2				lines 3–4				lines 5–6				lines 7–8			

Note

1. For the abbreviations "bi" and "ci," see table 2.1, n. 2.

and regularly (lines 1–2), accelerates (lines 3–4), catches her breath and resumes a regular pace (line 5), then accelerates again even more markedly than before (lines 6–7, the metric compression of which necessitates a very rapid declamation because both are *endecasillabi*—see especially the setting of line 7), before slowing somewhat for the final cadence.

Musically, the piece engages with the classic period design (similar to Rinuccio's "Firenze è come un albero fiorito" from *Gianni Schicchi*; see example 2.10): a four-bar basic idea and a four-bar contrasting idea imply (even with no dominant in the eighth measure) that the basic idea should return in m. 9 (compare the prototypical period shown in table 4.1c), but this is thwarted by the appearance of more new material and a noticeably more recitative text setting in mm. 9–12. Arrival on the dominant (m. 11), completion of the first quatrain, and resumption of the basic idea in m. 13 all clarify that the first twelve measures function as a three-part antecedent, and the period concludes with an equally irregular three-part consequent. The monologue ends climactically with the "la morte è vita bella" ("death is life more beautiful") motive in the tonic E♭. Named as such by Hepokoski,[14] this motive comprises a texted head ("O sorella, la morte è vita bella") and an untexted tail; the untexted tail returns later in the opera, a half step higher, just before Angelica drinks the suicidal poison (five bars before R77). The texted head portion is also remarkably similar to (and even in the same key as the initial statement of) the "Gli enigma sono tre, una è la vita" motive at the end of Turandot's aria, "In questa Reggia" (see *Turandot*, Act II, a bar before R48).

Just as important for creating the perceived suppression of a full engagement with the Romantic style here is the monologue's brevity—or, more specifically, the fact that it ends just as soon as we start to hear some sense of large-scale regularity in the succession of two, three-phrase groups. It sounds like it ends as soon as it begins, in other words, and it leaves the listener wanting more—some kind of repetition, perhaps, or some kind of fuller engagement with a multi-movement form. The ending, indeed, is as abrupt as the beginning: the *Zelatrice*'s "Noi non possiamo / nemmen da vive avere desiderî" cuts short Angelica's lyric excursion with the heavy hand of discipline. And the effect is highly expressive: "I desideri" is unsatisfying not only because of its unsettling irregularity but also because it suppresses its Romantic potential—just as the convent (here personified in the *Zelatrice*) suppresses Angelica's desires. There will be no expression of worldly needs; no further lyric singing; no expansion into a fully developed, Romantic theme (we have only the frustratingly short, despondent "la morte è vita bella"); and, as a consequence, no full-scale engagement with conventional formal schemata.

At the largest formal level, as mentioned, Puccini's strategies in *Angelica* are the same as in *Tabarro* (see table 4.2 for the organization in *Angelica*): an introduction and a finale frame a series of set pieces—in this case two: a duet, and a scene and aria—such that the overall design is episodic but in which the episodes occasionally make strategic, expressive references to *ottocento* formal schemata. At the same time, *Angelica*'s distinctly more multivalent quality adds a layer of formal complexity not present in the previous work. *Multivalence* refers here to what several other authors have described as a situation in which multiple musical components work simultaneously, but often independently, toward building form and structure, such that the structure embeds multiple forms rather than a single form; some of these may not coincide with or otherwise support one another and thus may yield a work that is, while perhaps *coherent,* not necessarily *unified.*[15] As such, *Angelica* is a perfect example, in that it comprises no fewer than three structure-building strategies. The first is Forzano's seven libretto tableaux, already mentioned (see table 4.2, column 2). The second is Puccini's own series of musically delineated episodes, some of which coincide with Forzano's tableaux but some of which do not (table 4.2, column 4).

The third is a *rotational form* (table 4.2, column 6): this is a term coined by Hepokoski to describe a structural process involving cyclical restatements of thematic materials (marked A, B, C, and D in table 4.2) in which each cycle preserves the order of themes: "an ordered arrangement of diverse thematic modules that is subjected to a (usually varied or altered) recycling, or several recyclings, later on in the work."[16] Many rotational forms, including this one, also involve a goal-directed process known as *teleological genesis:* this describes a strategy in which a composer withholds one of the thematic modules—usually the last one in a multi-part cycle—from earlier rotations in favor of releasing it later as a climactic, culminating gesture in the form. In *Angelica* this is module D, which is withheld from the first rotation (beginning at R36.2) only to

TABLE 4.2. Formal organization in *Suor Angelica*

Libretto tableau	Large formal function	Small formal function or movement	Personnel	Rotational formal function	Keys
R0 La preghiera	INTRODUCTION		orchestra, chorus (Angelica solo)		F
3.5 Le punizioni		episode: discipline	Zelatrice, converse, Maestra delle Novizie, Osmina, chorus		
7 La ricreazione		episode: light	Zelatrice		A
8		orchestral interlude			
9.2		"O sorelle! Sorelle!"	Genovieffa		E♭
15.3		"O sorella in pio lavoro"	Genovieffa		
16.5		"I desideri"	Angelica		e♭
19		"Soave Signor mio"	Genovieffa		
24		episode: wasps	Suora Infermiera, Angelica, chorus		
29 Il ritorno dalla cerca		episode: *cercatrice*	cercatrice, Dolcina, Zelatrice, chorus, Angelica		

TABLE 4.2. *continued*

Libretto tableau	Large formal function	Small formal function or movement	Personnel	Rotational formal function	Keys
36.2		"Da gran signori"	*cercatrice*, Angelica, chorus	ROTATION 1 A	F
39		"O Madre eletta"	Angelica, Genovieffa	B	a
40		episode: Abbess	Abbess, Angelica	C	a
41		"Requiem aeternam"	chorus offstage	(digression)	A
42		"È venuta a trovarvi"	Abbess, Angelica		C#
43.4 *La Zia Principessa*					
44.2	DUET	part 1 (≈*tempo d'attacco*)	Princess, Angelica		C#
		part 2 (≈*adagio*)			
50.4		"Nel silenzio"	Princess		C#
52		"Tutto ho offerto"	Angelica		a
56.6		pantomime			a
60 *La grazia*	SCENE AND ARIA	part 1 (≈*scena*)	Angelica		a

Measures		Performer	ROTATION 2		
	part 2 (≈*adagio*)				
61	"Ora che sei"		A		F
61.17	"Oh! dolce fine"		B		a
62	"Dillo alla mamma"		C		
63	part 3 (≈*tempo di mezzo*)	Genovieffa, chorus		(pause)	A
64	part 4 (≈*cabaletta*)	Angelica		D (*telos*)	C

Measures		Performer	ROTATION 3		
	FINALE				
66.3	pantomime	Angelica	A		F
67.6			B		a
69	episode: self-poisoning	Angelica, offstage chorus	C		
	"Suor Angelica ha sempre una ricetta"[1]				
75	"Addio, buone sorelle"			(pause)	D, E
81	episode: hallucination	Angelica, offstage chorus		D (*telos*)	C
81	*Il miracolo*				

Note

1. Not present until the third (1922) edition of the piano-vocal score (this is the location of the "aria dei fiori": "Amici fiori, voi mi compensate," originally R70 to R74). See chap. 4 note 10. For a revised libretto see, for example, Ferrando, ed., *Tutti i libretti di Puccini*, 469.

appear in the second (at R64) and again in the third (R82)—the latter functioning as the concluding gesture for the entire opera.[17]

All three organizational strategies interact expressively throughout the piece. Most notable, perhaps, is the way in which the piece becomes gradually less multivalent: that is, more and more of the structure-building strategies tend to support one another as the piece moves toward its close. This creates an audible sense that the piece is directed very strongly, both musically and dramatically, toward its ending, which helps make the ending just as powerful theatrically as—even though it could hardly be more different dramatically from—the violent ending of *Il tabarro.*

The introduction provides a good example of the multivalence. This initial, expository section lasts about half the opera; contained in it are the beginnings of five of Forzano's tableaux (*La preghiera, Le punizioni, La ricreazione, Il ritorno dalla cerca,* and *La Zia Principessa;* most of the latter overlaps with the first set piece) but also six complete, discrete musical-dramatic episodes. The first two—a choral-orchestral introduction (in which, as mentioned, Angelica sings alone briefly) and a "discipline" episode (in which the *Zelatrice* reprimands two novices)—coincide exactly with Forzano's *preghiera* and *punizioni* tableaux. Puccini divided Forzano's *ricreazione* into two episodes, one dealing with "light" (which hits the courtyard fountain and turns its water gold) and the other with "wasps" (which have stung one of the sisters). The former begins with the *Zelatrice*'s order for recreation and ends with "I desideri"; the latter, as mentioned, is dramatically essential (because we learn of Angelica's expertise with flowers and herbs) and a section we know even Puccini himself conceived of as an independent formal unit.[18]

Puccini likewise divided Forzano's *ritorno dalla cerca* in two, the first part comprising the return of the *cercatrice* with offerings (and, importantly, the first notice of a grand coach having arrived at the convent) and the second an episode for the Abbess and Angelica (beginning when the Abbess enters and dismisses the other nuns, who finally have water for Bianca Rosa's grave). This part of the piece in particular is especially multivalent: as we have seen, in terms of style and approach to structure, all the music from the Abbess's entrance (R40) to the start of the Princess's "Il Principe Gualtiero" (R44.2) is one coherent formal unit based entirely on monotonous, cyclic repetition—a metaphor, again, for the oppressive tension in Angelica's desperate, anxious waiting for news from her family. Tonally and motivically, however, a new section seems to begin when the Abbess identifies the visitor in the *parlatorio* (R42, just before "È venuta a trovarvi / vostra Zia Principessa"—"Your aunt, the Princess, has come to find you"), a result of two coincident, strongly initiatory musical gestures: the key shifts to the Princess's C♯ minor, and a motive that will later accompany the opening movement in her duet with Angelica appears for the first time.[19] Puccini perhaps had in mind Forzano's own formal demarcation here, as this is roughly where the *La Zia Principessa* tableau begins in the libretto. To add to the complexity, this is also where the rotational form begins to churn below the structural surface, adding a deep-level reinforcement of the inexorable cyclic repetition. The initial rotational cycle coincides neither with Puccini's episodes nor with Forzano's tableaux: its first two modules are the music for the coach ("Da gran signori," R36.2) and Angelica's prayer to the Virgin ("O Madre eletta, leggimi nel cuore," R39)—both from the *cercatrice* episode—while the last block is the opening music in the Abbess episode (R40.1–10).

The multivalence abates in the finale, especially toward the end. This begins at "La grazia è discesa, dal cielo" (R66.3), about halfway through Forzano's *La grazia* tableau and immediately after Angelica's scene and aria. It coincides exactly with the full, final rotational cycle, in which modules A and B are treated dramatically as a bipartite pantomime (in which Angelica gathers flowers for her suicidal poison) and module C (along with some subsequent non-rotational material) as the self-poisoning episode for Angelica. The final, teleological D module coincides both with the last of Forzano's tableau (*Il miracolo*) and the last of Puccini's episodes, in which the now fully hallucinatory Angelica has a dying vision of the Virgin and a child (Angelica's dead son, apparently, although nothing discounts the possibility that this may be the Virgin's *own* son—that is, Christ)[20] to the rather mysterious, distant sounds of an offstage orchestra and chorus—the latter, again, the only part of the work with music for male voices. The coincidence of structural strategies, especially at "O gloriosa virginum" (R81), clearly makes the moment a kind of fulfillment—a *telos*—a final, magnificent release of energy for Angelica at the moment of her death. That Puccini uses for the finale the rotational *telos* music (module D) emphasizes the effect; even more striking, as we will see presently, is the fact that this music is exactly the fully Romantic-style music used for the end of Angelica's scene and aria (see R66), and that this allows the work's level of discourse to shift one last time here at the end, a marvelously effective expressive device that suggests in music the now-total detachment from reality of the dying, hallucinating Angelica.

The formal design is at its most expressive, and occasionally its most multivalent, in the two set pieces that comprise about the middle twenty minutes of the opera: a duet for Angelica and the Princess and a scene and aria for Angelica. The scene and aria for Angelica is especially important: except for the final tableau, this is the only time the opera fully shifts its level of discourse, wherein a reference to *ottocento* formal prototypes underscores a clear, complete shift to the lyric, Romantic style.

Angelica's scene immediately suggests a four-part design with an embedded double musical-dramatic cycle—not necessarily the conventional kinetic-static cycle, but a modified double cycle nevertheless. The first two parts are child-centered (one at R60, "Senza mamma," focusing on the dead child; another at R61 now focusing on the living child— i.e., the child as a reincarnated angel in heaven: "Ora che sei un angelo del cielo" ["Now that you are an angel in heaven"]); the next two are grace-centered (one at R63, a return of the sisters from the cemetery and an acknowledgement of grace delivered: "Sorella, o buona sorella, / la Vergine ha accolto la prece" ["Sister, good sister, the Virgin has answered your prayer"]; another at R64, "La grazia è discesa, dal cielo" ["Grace has descended from heaven"]: Angelica's acceptance of grace).

Verse meter, text distribution, tonality, and texture in the scene work to articulate the same double cycle (see table 4.3). The first part (at "Senza mamma") comprises four quatrains in a curious mix of short meters—*quaternario, quinario,* and *senario*—probably written so as to facilitate the nervous, labored musical setting in a freer, *parlante* texture, in which two lines of text occur every two bars of music. The texture here (at R60, for example) is freer rhythmically, at least, than that of the following movement, even if it is somewhat more lyrical than a conventional Verdian *parlante melodico*. It sounds as if the Romantic lyricism is trying to break through but is temporarily unable—a musical metaphor, perhaps, for Angelica's pent-up emotion that needs to find release. This release—both musical and emotional—happens in short order: the verse meter shifts audibly at "Ora che sei un angelo del cielo" to the much longer line of lyric *endecasillabo*—or, more broadly, to the heightened, rhymed *scena* verse (mixed lines of *endecasillabo* and *settenario*) typical of Puccini's lyric movements—now organized in three quatrains plus a distich and now set musically in a clearly Romantic, fully-realized lyric style. The coincidence here of multiple, salient structural strategies creates the strongest, clearest, most expressive formal articulation in the entire work. The verse meter changes; the harmonic language changes, so that it now includes typically Puccinian, Romantic-style progressions and the music sounds considerably more kinetic (compare the highly static, chromatic A-minor material of the "Senza mamma" movement); and the second rotational cycle begins, reintroducing a prominent theme heard earlier at a key dramatic moment in the work ("Da gran signori," R36.1). This theme, as Hepokoski has noted, appears here at a noticeably slower tempo, which creates the enormously expressive effect of a gradual emergence (rather than a bursting forth) of the lyric, Romantic style, as well as, it seems, a very slow, gradual, immensely satisfying release of the tension that by this point in the work has reached an almost unbearable thickness.

Another audible shift in the verse meter at the interlude for Genovieffa and the returning sisters ("Sorella, o buona sorella"—"Sarete contenta, sorella" in the libretto), now to an extremely unusual *novenario*,[21] marks the dividing point in the double cycle (moving now from child focus to grace focus), and the music returns here to a more recitative texture. Finally, as if Angelica had been so filled with pent-up emotion and anxiety that not all of it could possibly have been released in the "Ora che sei," she embarks on the expansively orchestrated "La grazia è discesa, dal cielo," the final lyric movement in the scene and some of the most clearly Romantic music in the entire opera. Note the formal articulation in the libretto here is in the *distribution* of text (i.e., in the shift of text back to Angelica) rather than in any change in the verse meter: Angelica continues the *novenari* of the previous movement, now in two quatrains and with a final line ("Lodiamo la Vergine santa"—"Let us praise the Virgin") for Angelica and chorus together, in a transcendent conclusion for the scene.

TABLE 4.3. Text in *Suor Angelica,* scene and aria for Angelica

part 1 (≈*scena*)

1	Angelica	4	Senza mamma,
2		6	bimbo, tu sei morto!
3		4	Le tue labbra,
4		6	senza i baci mei,
5		4	scoloriron
6		4	fredde, fredde!
7		4	E chiudesti,
8		6	bimbo, gli occhi belli!
9		4	Non potendo
10		4	carezzarmi,
11		4	le manine
12		6	componesti in croce!
13		5	E tu sei morto
14		5	senza sapere
15		5	quanto t'amava
16		5	questa tua mamma!

part 2 (≈*adagio*)

17		11	Ora che sei un angelo del cielo,
18		11	ora tu puoi vederla la tua mamma!
19		11	Tu puoi scendere giù pel firmamento
20		11	ed aleggiare intorno a me ... ti sento ...
21		11	Sei qui ... sei qui ... mi baci ... m'accarezzi ...
22		11	ah! dimmi quando anch'io potrò vederti?
23		7	Quando potrò baciarti! ...
24		11	Oh! dolce fine di ogni mio dolore!
25		11	Quando in cielo con te potrò salire? ...
26		7	Quando potrò morire? ...
27		7	Quando potrò morire? ...
28		11	Dillo alla mamma, creatura bella,
29		11	con un leggiero scintillar di stella ...
30		7	parlarmi, amore, amore! ...

part 3 (≈*tempo di mezzo*)

31	Sisters[1]	9	Sarete contenta, sorella,[2]
32		9	la Vergine ha accolto la prece.
33		9	Sarete contenta, sorella,
34		9	la Vergine ha fatto la grazia.

part 4 (≈*cabaletta*)

35	Angelica	9	La grazia è discesa, dal cielo
36		9	già tutta già tutta m'accende,
37		9	risplende! Risplende! Risplende!
38		9	Già vedo, sorelle, la meta . . .
39		9	Sorelle, son lieta! Son lieta!
40		9	Cantiamo! Già in cielo si canta . . .
41		9	Lodiamo la Vergine santa!
42	*Tutte*	9	Lodiamo la Vergine santa!

Notes
1. Forzano used "Sisters" ("Le suore") throughout the libretto to designate lines for an unspecified sister or sisters, perhaps, but not necessarily, the entire chorus (for which he used "Tutte"). Puccini set lines 31–32 for Genovieffa alone, lines 33–34 for the whole chorus.
2. Score: "Sorella, o buona sorella."

These four distinct parts produce a clear analog to the conventional schema, the *solita forma* for a scene and aria: a *scena* ("Senza mamma"), an *adagio* ("Ora che sei"), a *tempo di mezzo* ("Sorella, o buona sorella") for Genovieffa and the sisters, and a *cabaletta* ("La grazia è discesa"). (As such, it may well be appropriate to call the piece "Ora che sei"—consistent with the common practice of naming arias with the first line in the *adagio* movement—rather than the more common "Senza mamma.") As in *Tabarro*, the formal reference here is just that—a schematic *reference*, the parts of which fulfill the formal functions of, even if not all the precise musical, textual, and dramaturgical characteristics of, the conventional multi-part design—certainly not a perfectly conventional iteration of the *solita forma*. The most obvious differences lie in the internal designs of the lyric movements. The *adagio* is in two parts—one in F major (R61) and a second in A minor (R61.17)—and makes no reference to a conventional lyric form; and the "La grazia è discesa" movement—unlike *Tabarro's* "È ben altro il mio sogno," which was a real *cabaletta* even in its formal design—is rather a *cabaletta*-function in the sense that it comprises the concluding lyric movement of a four-part, double musical-dramatic cycle; otherwise this is not a conventional *cabaletta* at all (even its tempo is slow, which is atypical). This is not surprising, of course, since, as noted, *cabalette* were well out of date by Puccini's time; the fact that "È ben altro il mio sogno" adheres to a variation on the conventional *cabaletta* design is far more surprising than the fact that "La grazia è discesa" departs from it.

Even the *scena,* less lyrical though it is, is more tightly organized than its typical nineteenth-century counterpart, with four, four-bar phrases organized in smaller two-bar units and with a thematic scheme that resembles an expanded version of the lyric prototype with a coda (i.e., A A B A, B A, C C: see example 4.4). The characteristic two-eighth-note pickup figure that proliferates here (second beat of R60.2, for example) results from the prevalence of *quaternari* and their *accento comune* on the third syllable. This rhythmic feature becomes even more salient because the musical setting gives the impression that lines 2, 4, 8, and 12—all non-*quaternario* meters—are joined to their immediately preceding *quaternario* line to make, in every case, a single line of *decasillabo* with an accent on the third syllable. The verse meter changes, as does, therefore, the musical motive, at line 13: this is *quinario* verse, set with the climactic, upward-leaping motive C.

The movements nevertheless exhibit conventional features, even with respect to their internal designs. Both the *adagio* and the *cabaletta,* for example, have static codas in the tonic key, typical of their nineteenth-century counterparts (the *adagio's* is at R62, "Dillo alla mamma," which follows a weak, typically Puccinian cadence—i.e., one with no dominant—in A minor; the *cabaletta's* is the modally inflected music immediately following the climactic, long-awaited cadence in C four bars before R66).[22] The textures are also treated conventionally: the *adagio* and the *cabaletta* are fully lyrical, while the *scena* and the *tempo di mezzo*—again, perhaps not declamatory in the traditional sense—both exhibit decidedly less lyricism with more pitch repetition in the vocal lines and considerably more metric freedom.

The scene and duet for Angelica and the Princess is stylistically less fully Romantic—it exhibits fewer of the musical signatures Puccini

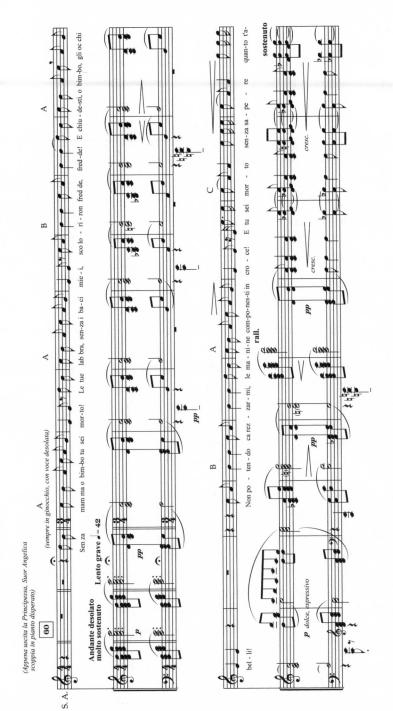

EXAMPLE 4.4. *Suor Angelica*, "Senza mamma," organization of the *scena* movement.

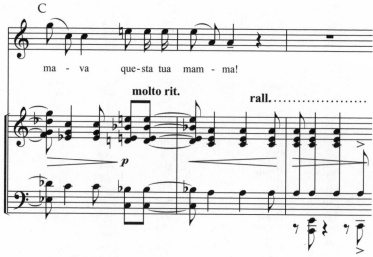

ma - va   que-sta tua   mam - ma!

EXAMPLE 4.4. *continued*

invokes to signal a shift to the lyric mode—and, as a result, also less formally conventional. Generically speaking, this makes some sense, as the piece belongs—like the second Giorgetta-Luigi duet and the Giorgetta-Michele duet in *Il tabarro*—in the category of the dialogue duet, implying that it should involve dramatic activity outside normal, acceptable parameters and thus also involve an attendant formal design outside normative schemata.[23] But, as in many dialogue duets, the scene initially implies that it will engage with the formal prototype for a conventional duet: the Princess enters, the Abbess exits, and Angelica remains; two characters are left together on stage in a situation ripe for musical conflict. And, at the opening at least, the music proceeds as the drama implies it should, with kinetic dialogue establishing the scene's premise: the Princess needs Angelica to relinquish her claim to her family's estate in advance of her sister's marriage. The Princess begins with a declamatory opening (in C♯ minor, R44.2) in which she presents the document for Angelica's consideration; Angelica follows (now in E, R46.2) with an attempt—still declamatory and orchestrated now with harp and tremolo strings to lend it an ancient flavor—to find human compassion in the Princess, a segment in which she declaims her "È luogo di clemenza . . . / è luogo di pieta" ("[This] is a place of mercy, a place of pity") over a litany refrain (in the subdominant A, R46.5). The Princess squelches the move, actually cutting Angelica off by breaking into and finishing the *endecasillabo* line with a cadence of her own (back in E, R46.10);[24] Angelica responds to the news of her sister's impending marriage with a lyrical expansion (now in G♭, R47), which sounds like it could be the first static movement (the *adagio*, perhaps) in the duet until it degenerates into modality (R47.5) and moves toward a chromatic modulation (to G at R48), suppressing the potential stylistic shift; and finally, an extremely agitated confrontation with more declamatory dialogue (ending in A♭) leads to the Princess's "Nel silenzio di quei raccoglimenti" (R50.4, in C♯).

The succession of episodes here clearly implies a multi-sectional *tempo d'attacco*, while the Princess's subsequent "Nel silenzio" moves toward a tonal stability and metric regularity that just as clearly implies the onset of an *adagio* movement. In the latter the dialogue becomes static and reflective—consistent with an *adagio*—as the Princess recounts her meditations in the silence of the family chapel, in which she enters into spiritual communion with Angelica's dead mother to lament Angelica's sin. But another lyric movement ("Tutto ho offerto alla Vergine") follows, now for Angelica and now much longer, much more agitated, and not exactly "static": Angelica demands information on her son. The latter movement is less clearly part of a putative *adagio*. The lyric statements for Angelica and the Princess in direct succession, however, as discussed in connection with "Hai ben ragione" and "È ben altro il mio sogno" in *Il tabarro*, do suggest a form in dialogue with the *adagio* of a conventional duet, which normally opens with parallel statements (*proposta* and *risposta*—usually also comprising parallel stanzas in the verse) for the two characters before moving to a coda with *a due* singing. Here again we should understand Puccini's setting of the scene as but a formal analog and not a precise iteration of a conventional design. The two statements are much longer and more formally independent than would be expected in a conventional *proposta-risposta;* they have nothing at all in common with regard to key, musical meter, or thematic content (although the latter is not a requirement, as duets often open with parallel dissimilar statements);[25] and even the verse meter offers no clarification: the entire scene is in the typically loose, rhymed *scena* verse, and thus any formal groupings or demarcations at all are of Puccini's own making, articulated solely in the music.

The strategy is highly expressive. Angelica's statement, in fact, sounds like an independent lyric movement that opens with a *recitative* of its own ("Tutto ho offerto," R52) but then departs from any sense of normalcy. A reference to the litany refrain (R52.3–5, in C: "Ma v'è un'offerta") gives way to two groups of two bars each ("alla Madre, soave della Madri" and "non posso offrire di scordar") that, while sounding like they may be the point of departure for a metrically regular, lyric movement, collapse at "mio figlio" ("my son") into a frenzied, hysterical outburst (R53, marked *gridato*—"shouted"). This leads in turn to music (R53.3) in which both Angelica and the orchestra seem stuck: Angelica is unable to get past the words "Figlio mio," and the orchestra likewise is unable to move away from a violent, chromatic motive that repeats, relentlessly, no fewer than sixteen times—mostly at the same pitch, no less, with only the sixth and seventh repetitions shifted up three half steps (R53.8–9, at Angelica's anguished "che ho veduto e baciato una sola volta"—"[my son,] whom I have seen and kissed only once"). The whole texture begins to disintegrate at the seventeenth repetition (three bars before R54) and the music simply comes to a complete stop shortly thereafter (the fermata at R54). Angelica allows herself one final, excruciatingly chromatic outburst (R54.2–7), threatening her aunt with eternal damnation, before concluding the monologue with a litany refrain, now horribly deformed by the preceding chaos (the motive is mapped onto a whole-tone collection; see R55.4–7). The scene is totally unable to continue in a normal fashion: any reference to the Romantic style has been violently suppressed, as has any reference to a conventional formal arrangement. The Princess delivers the news of the child's death in seven cold, brutal measures (R55.10–R56); Angelica utters two more words ("È morto?"—"He's dead?") and manages a feeble cry (a *grido lamentoso*, R56.5) before the scene comes completely apart in a wordless pantomime in which Angelica signs the document and the Princess leaves.

As with *Tabarro*, *Angelica* is another classic example of Puccini's use of conventional formal schemata for expressive effect. Again, it may be possible to experience the work's emotional force, especially the cruel desperation in the Angelica-Princess scene, without the interpretive framework provided by Puccini's underlying formal strategies—this music is certainly powerful enough on its own terms—but the opera achieves a matchless emotional height when one hears everything from the Princess's entrance on as an intensifying, highly expressive dialogue with normative formal prototypes. Perhaps one of the most interesting interpretive outcomes of such an analysis is what it implies with regard to Angelica's deteriorating mental condition—an aspect of the piece that has received some attention in recent secondary literature.[26] In my view, Puccini locates Angelica's psychological plunge *musically* more clearly, and earlier, than Forzano locates it *dramatically*. That is, my reading suggests that her descent into irrationality, though certainly not her actual hallucination (which comes later, after she drinks the poison), begins toward the end of the "Tutto ho offerto" monologue, most likely at the obsessive "Figlio mio" music, in which the Princess scene comes completely unraveled. This is a somewhat different—again, earlier—location than in other published interpretations: Girardi and Hepokoski, for example, both have proposed that Angelica's departure from reality (Hepokoski: her "hallucinatory self-deception") begins at the onset of her lyric "Ora che sei un angelo del cielo" (R61)—at the start, in Hepokoski's terms, of the definitive second cycle in the rotational form. But in my analysis this is too late: we should understand all of "Senza mamma" as delivered from a state of total mental detachment from reality, where the detachment results directly from Puccini's suppression of musical-formal normalcy in the preceding Angelica-Princess scene, as well as his expressive reversion, at "Senza mamma" itself, to a rhetorically marked, conventional musical style and concomitant expressive reference to a conventional musical-dramatic form. Unlike in *Tabarro*—in which the discursive shift was in the middle of the work and represented an unattainable ideal from which the characters had no choice but to retreat—the shift in Angelica occurs toward the work's end and functions as a springboard for the transcendent ending. Only the self-poisoning and hallucination remain, and, as if to refuse to let the music descend from the emotional heights it worked so arduously to achieve, Puccini recapitulates, one last time and quickly now, the full four-module rotational scheme—including the fully Romantic "La grazia è discesa, dal cielo" telos music (R81), now at a miraculously surreal pianissimo and with the hymn text "O gloriosa virginum." This is clearly Angelica's demise: just as Puccini musically located her mental break with reality, so too did he musically convey her hallucinatory death and departure from the world.

FIVE

Humor and Filmic Effects in the Structure of *Gianni Schicchi*

In some ways *Gianni Schicchi* is the most musically conventional of the three *Trittico* panels, but in other important ways this concluding opera is also the most complex, least conventional among the three. Its conventionality results from its comprising no fewer than five closed set pieces (see table 5.1)—as many as were in *Tabarro* (three) and *Angelica* (two) combined. But its unconventionality stems from its achieving, very much like *Turandot* after it, a near-complete integration of conventional formal strategies with the newer, episodic organizational approach: whereas *Tabarro* and *Angelica* both had episodic introductions and conclusions but interiors comprising expressive references to formal conventions, in *Schicchi* the episodic strategy more audibly permeates the entire work. This is largely a result of the way Puccini uses stylistic plurality in *Schicchi*, a strategy somewhat different from that in the previous two pieces: *Tabarro* and *Angelica* each shifted decisively to the Romantic, lyric style only once, but *Schicchi*, again like *Turandot*, makes multiple shifts toward the Romantic style, none necessarily linked to a coincident shift in the underlying formal approach. This causes the Romantic style in *Schicchi* to be relegated to a position we can understand as lying *outside* the normative formal space of the work—a position from which it interrupts larger, overarching formal processes and engenders multiple levels of expressive meaning almost every time it appears.

That *Schicchi* should be conventional in many respects proves consistent both with the *Trittico*'s backward progression in time (i.e., toward a more traditional age) and with *Schicchi*'s underlying themes of old social establishments and family aristocracies. What begins as a bargain between the aristocratic Donatis—Zita (*La Vecchia*), cousin of the wealthy, deceased patriarch Buoso and the oldest of the surviving family; Rinuccio, her nephew; Gherardo (Buoso's nephew), his wife Nella, and young son Gherardino; Buoso's cousin Simone (former mayor of Fucecchio, a small township in the Florence city-state); Simone's son Marco and his wife Ciesca; and Betto, Buoso's unfortunate brother in law from Signa (another town in Florence)—and social upstart Gianni Schicchi evolves into a morality tale on the risks of unrestrained greed, complete with intrigue and a romantic subplot (the budding love of Rinuccio and Lauretta, Schicchi's daughter). At least three of its five closed set pieces refer audibly to conventional schema (see table 5.1); almost all, furthermore, are much simpler than those in the previous operas: only two suggest a complete, four-part arrangement with a double kinetic-static cycle, and even in one of these the reference is oblique at best. The other three consist of only one or two kinetic, declamatory movements (perhaps a *recitative,* or even a *recitative* plus a *tempo d'attacco*) followed by a single lyric movement. Two of the latter, moreover, involve only one character, and as such may be categorized generically as "*recitative* and aria": one for Rinuccio ("Avete torto," R28.2, and "Firenze è come un albero fiorito," R30; the latter was discussed in chapter 2) and another for Schicchi ("Prima un avvertimento," R62.18, and "Addio Firenze," R64).

Both of these latter two, furthermore, exhibit similarities on global and local formal levels. Globally, each engages with the conventional *romanza* genre; in each the *recitative* is in a *parlante* texture (more *parlante armonico* in "Avete torto," more *parlante melodico* in "Prima un avvertimento"), with a character presenting a premise (the Donatis have Schicchi all wrong; the punishment for forging a will is physical maiming); in each the aria involves, as might be expected, that same character's reflecting on the subject of the recitative; and each romanticizes Florence (Rinuccio avers that there is room in Florence for Schicchi; Schicchi warns that failure means banishment from Florence for the Donatis, the same fate suffered by the Ghibellines).[1] Locally, each aria is delineated structurally by a shift from the *recitative*'s rhymed *scena* verse (mostly *quinari* in "Avete torto," mostly *settenari* in "Prima un avvertimento") to more regular *endecasillabi*—although Schicchi's *terzina* in "Addio" is metrically very loose: the second line is a *dodecasillabo,* and even the

TABLE 5.1. Formal organization in *Gianni Schicchi*

	Large formal function	Small formal function	Personnel	Keys
R0	PART 1 INTRODUCTION	orchestra		B♭
1	Buoso's will (mourning motive):	mourning and rumor	relatives	
7	search		orchestra	
10		[interruption: discovery; "Addio, speranza bella" theme]	[Rinuccio]	
11.11		resumption: anticipation	relatives	
14		reading and reaction	orchestra	
16		concertato conclusion	relatives	a, A♭
24	Schicchi:	introduction of Schicchi (name only)	relatives	
28.2		Scene and aria: *recitative*	Rinuccio	
30		aria		B♭
35.3	PART 2 SCENE AND QUARTET	part 1 (*recitative*)	Schicchi	
36		part 2	Schicchi/Zita, Rinuccio/Lauretta	C, A♭
38		part 3 (*recitative*)	Schicchi	
38.8		part 4	Schicchi/Zita, Rinuccio/Lauretta	
38.20		[interruption: "Addio, speranza bella"]		D♭

38.28		resumption		A♭
40		[interruption: "O mio babbino caro"]	Lauretta	c
41	SCENE AND ARIA	part 1 (≈*scena*)	Schicchi	F
42.4		[interruption: "Addio, speranza bella"]	[Rinuccio, Lauretta]	A♭
42.8		resumption	Schicchi	D♭
43.3		[interruption: "Addio, speranza bella]	[Rinuccio, Lauretta]	c
43.11		resumption	Schicchi	
44			Schicchi + relatives	
45			+ Spinelloccio	
48			(exit Spinelloccio)	
49		part 2 (≈*primo tempo*)		D, c#
50.9		part 3 (≈*tempo di mezzo*)		c#
51		part 4 (*cabaletta*-function)		c
52		coda	relatives	
53	SCENE AND TRIO	part 1 (≈*scena*)	Schicchi + relatives	d
60.6		part 2 (≈*tempo d'attacco*)	Zita, Nella, Ciesca (+ Schicchi, relatives)	
61.2		part 3 (≈*adagio*)		C

TABLE 5.1. *continued*

	Large formal function	Small formal function	Personnel	Keys
62.18	SCENE AND ARIA	*recitative*	Schicchi	
64		aria	+ relatives (coda)	G
66	FINALE	notary	notary, witnesses, Schicchi, relatives	C
71		invocation and dictation		
80		aftermath	Schicchi, relatives (exit notary, witnesses)	
84		lovers ("Addio, speranza bella" theme)	Rinuccio, Lauretta	G♭
85		*licenza*	Schicchi	

first is set in the music as if it were also, with *dialefe* at "Firenze, addio" (see R64.2). Each is based on a series of three, four-bar phrases (two lines of text per four measures of music in the first and last parts of Rinuccio's aria; one line of text for the same amount of music in Schicchi's, which has only one part and thus is much shorter); each has a coda (at the entrance of Schicchi and Lauretta immediately following Rinuccio's closing cadence in "Firenze"; at the chorus of relatives repeating Schicchi's music verbatim in "Addio"); and each exhibits characteristics of Tuscan folk music (among them *endecasillabo* verse, latent modality, and idiosyncratic rhythmic-melodic features—including, for example, the melisma on "Firenze" in Schicchi's aria).[2]

The scene and trio for the three women, Zita, Nella, and Ciesca, comprises only an oblique reference to a conventional prototype. It opens when the concertato coda to Schicchi's first aria ("Schicchi!") abruptly breaks off at Simone's "O Gianni, ora pensiamo" (R53), a formal demarcation at which the texture reverts to recitative dialogue and the dramatic focus shifts abruptly, from the relatives' elation in the wake of Schicchi's explaining his plan to a more detail-oriented discussion of exactly how to divide up Buoso's estate.[3] This is an extended, multipartite, active, mostly rhythmically irregular section for the relatives and Schicchi and thus exhibits features consistent with a traditional *scena*. But nothing about it necessarily suggests that it should be the opening of a scene specifically for the three women, and thus it links formally to the following two trio movements only in the loosest sense, perhaps as an active *recitative* that sets up a series of movements in *tempo giusto*. It includes, incidentally, the interlude in which we hear the death knell for the captain's Moor, one of many elements of the story Forzano borrowed directly from the *commedia dell'arte* (in which a Spanish captain and his Moor are stock characters).

The first of the two subsequent *tempo giusto* movements may loosely resemble a multipartite *tempo d'attacco* (beginning at "Ecco la cappellina!," pickup to R60.6), while the second is apparently an *adagio* (the *a tre*, at R61.2). The former is perhaps best thought of as analogous to a *tempo d'attacco* because of its change to a more predictable (if not completely regular) verse structure—mostly *settenari* now, with occasional, comically juxtaposed *trisillabo* and *endecasillabo*—and a regular orchestral accompaniment. All the characters continue to participate, but the

TABLE 5.2. *Gianni Schicchi, adagio* for the three women (R61.2)

a. Text (libretto)

Part 1		Nella			Ciesca			Zita	
	a3								
1	7	Spogliati, bambolino,	a	7	Fa' presto, bambolino,	a	7	È bello! Portentoso!	a
2	7	ché ti mettiamo a letto,	a	7	ché devi andare a letto,	a	7	chi vuoi che non s'inganni?	d
3	7	e non aver dispetto	a	7	se va bene il giuochetto	a	7	é Gianni che fa Buoso	a
4	7	se cambi il camicino!	a	7	ti diamo un confortino!	a	7	o Buoso che fa Gianni?	d
5	7	Si spiuma il canarino,	a	7	L'uovo divien pulcino,	a	7	Un testamento è odioso?	a
6	7	la volpe cambia pelo,	a	7	il fior diventa frutto	a	7	Un camicion maestoso,	a
7	7	il ragno ragnatelo,	a	7	e i frati mangian tutto,	a	7	il viso dormiglioso,	a
8	7	il cane cambia cuccia,	b	7	ma il frate impoverisce,	c	7	il naso poderoso,	a
9	11	la serpe cambia buccia...		11	la Ciesca s'arricchisce...		11	l'accento lamentoso...	a

Part 2			
	a3		
(9)		...e il buon Gianni[1]	d
10	4	cambia panni,	d
11	4	cambia viso,	a
12	4	muso e naso,	a
13	4	cambia accento	a

14		5	e testamento	a
15		7	per poterci servir!...	e

Part 3

16	Schicchi	7	Vi servirò a dovere!...		c
17		7	Contenti vi farò!		a
18	Women	11	O Gianni Schicchi, nostro salvator!		f
19		7	È preciso?	Men	Perfetto!	a
20	Tutti	5	A letto! A letto!		a

b. Puccini's treatment of the text in part 2 (R62).

8	e il buon Gianni cambia panni,		d
7	per poterci servir!...		e
8	cambia viso, muso e naso,		a
7	per poterci servir!...		e
8	cambia accento [e] testamento		a
7	per poterci servir!...		e

Note

1. Beginning with the second half of the *endecasillabo* line 9 Forzano is not specific with regard to assigning particular lines to particular characters. Puccini divides the next six and a half lines (through line 15) among all three, ingeniously using line 15 ("per poterci servir!...") as a refrain (see section b of the present table).

focus begins to crystallize around Zita, Nella, and Ciesca, occupied here with dressing Schicchi as Buoso; as such, the material can be regarded as kinetic—also consistent with a *tempo d'attacco*. The latter is perhaps best regarded as analogous to an *adagio* because of the shift in verse meter, now to a parallel series of regular, rhyming *settenari* for each woman *a tre*; and, more generally, the slower, lyrical, reflective setting in three parts of "O Gianni Schicchi, nostro salvator!" ("O Gianni Schicchi, our savior!"). The movement's verse (table 5.2a) delineates three subdivisions, which Puccini respects in the music. Part 1 is the parallel *settenari a tre*, where each woman sings two quatrains (lines 1–8) plus one piece (the *maggiore* segment—a *settenario*) of an *endecasillabo* (line 9—interesting because Forzano himself seems to have made a formal demarcation not only in the middle of a stanza but in the middle of a line); the quatrains for Nella and Ciesca are identically rhymed (line 8 contrasts with lines 1–7) while Zita's rhyme scheme differs—one of many examples in the piece illustrating Zita's differentiation from the other relatives, the whole group of which is treated throughout as a chorus rather than as distinct, individual characters. Part 2 comprises the *minore* segment of line 9 plus lines 10–15, the latter arranged as a *sestina* of four *quaternari* followed by a *quinario* and a *settenario*. In his setting, though, Puccini seems to treat the text as three groups of two lines each (see table 5.2b), where each group sounds like an *ottonario* (two of the original *quaternari* combined, albeit still divided among two different characters; he even drops the "e" in R62.5 as if it were elided with the "o" at the end of "accento," which it would be if the line were really an *ottonario*) plus a *settenario tronco* (the original line 15, "per poterci server!"). This makes the *settenario* sound like a refrain, expands the passage's textual and musical breadth, and lends a striking regularity to the music—which has a lulling, calming effect, eminently appropriate for the women's serenade to Schicchi just before he pulls off the hoax. Part 3 begins at the re-entrance of Schicchi; here, again, Puccini expands Forzano's verse, inserting a *quinario tronco* after each of the first two lines ("Bravo, così" after line 16, "Proprio così" after line 17; see R62.7–9), which, together with his truncating the last syllable of line 16 (the score has "dover" instead of the libretto's "dovere"), yields a rather unusual sequence of four consecutive *tronco* lines. This produces a somewhat abrupt, decidedly comic sound in the declamation: every line now ends on a beat, whereas the normative line ending is off the beat. This, in turn, may have been the inspiration for the conspicuously comical, mock-pathetic tone in this music (Carner, for one, describes the women's forthcoming "O Gianni Schicchi, nostro salvator!" as "deliciously parodistic").[4]

At the same time, that *Schicchi* should in other respects be the most complex and least conventional of the three *Trittico* panels proves consistent with the work's emphasis on the increasing irrelevance of the old social order in enlightened, renascent, turn-of-the-fourteenth-century Florence in favor of a newer, younger generation of Florentines like Schicchi, Lauretta, and the pedigreed but enlightened Rinuccio. According to Girardi, in Schicchi himself Puccini and Forzano probably intended to represent the vital bourgeois class so important to life in their own contemporary Italy—a social upstart of whom the old social order would have naturally been afraid.[5] The story is much older, of course, originating, as has been explained in numerous sources, in Canto 30 of the *Inferno*, the first volume of the *Divine Comedy* of Dante Alighieri (1265–1321)—which Puccini knew well. According to Dante, Schicchi—a real member of the prominent Cavalcanti family and a well-known mimic who died around 1280—is one of the residents of Hell, condemned there for a crime in which, upon a request by a Donati heir (Simone) for him to impersonate a deceased Donati patriarch (Buoso) and forge a more favorable will, he craftily willed himself some of the most valuable items in the Donati estate (including "la donna della torma"—"the queen of the herd," or the most beautiful mule in Tuscany).[6] In their retelling, Puccini and Forzano appear to take the bourgeois point of view (although this is a more complex issue to which I will return at the end of the chapter). Their sympathies seem to lie with Schicchi, Lauretta, and Rinuccio, all three of whom struggle together against a hypocritical, oppressive, bigoted aristocracy in a search for freedom and relief from the stifling world of class and power (and here there are echoes of *Suor Angelica*, specifically in Angelica's own similar struggle against the aristocratic social stratum embodied in her aunt, the *Principessa*). As such, Puccini sets Rinuccio and Lauretta with the music of sincerity—music in the Romantic style—while generally the Donati family remains mired throughout in comical, stylistically non-Romantic music of insincerity.[7]

As in *Tabarro* and *Angelica*, *Schicchi*'s series of set pieces are framed by an episodic introduction and finale. The finale includes five episodes:

the notary's arrival, with Schicchi now dressed as Buoso and in Buoso's bed (in the same linens from which the dead Buoso has just been removed, as many have noted),[8] ready to carry out the prank; Schicchi's dictating the will; the aftermath, in which Schicchi forcibly orders the relatives out of the house (now his house, not theirs); the final episode for the lovers, Rinuccio and Lauretta, with the last statement of the definitively Romantic "Addio, speranza bella" theme (more on this presently); and the *licenza,* the standard device in Italian theater in which a character steps out from behind the fourth wall to address the audience directly at the end of a work. The *licenza,* notably, is not unfamiliar in opera: it also appears in, for example, *Don Giovanni, Così fan tutte,* and *Falstaff.* Interesting in this context is Girardi's observation that whereas traditional *licenze* include commentary on the work just witnessed, Schicchi's explicitly hands over powers of interpretation to the audience, in a gesture emphasizing the artificiality of what just transpired: "se stasera vi siete divertiti, / concedetemi voi . . . / l'attenuante!" ("If you have been entertained tonight, allow me extenuating circumstances!": i.e., "grant me a pardon from the fate to which Dante condemned me").[9]

The introduction is not only episodic, but also establishes—as in *Tabarro* and *Angelica*—the work's prevailing musical *tinta.* And here this means establishing rhythmic fluidity, and especially metric ambiguity, as thematized, expressive elements in the work's non-Romantic music. This becomes apparent in one of the work's central themes: the "mourning motive," used here as an ostinato theme, incessantly repeated, that controls nearly the first fifteen minutes of the opera. As written (see example 5.1, Ro.8) the theme starts on an upbeat, such that what is really an appoggiatura (an accented—located on the beat—downward-resolving upper neighbor) becomes metrically displaced, backward, by one eighth note (example 5.2 shows a hypothetical normative version of the theme). But the displacement is initially *in the notation only:* we hear the appoggiatura as a downbeat, and indeed cannot yet hear the motive as metrically displaced because we have no other, normative point of reference clearly establishing the location of any other downbeat, or even any larger, regular metric groupings.[10] The opera's first seven measures are themselves essentially ametric (example 5.1, Ro.1–7); we hear duply grouped events (pairs of accented eighths), especially in Ro.3–7, but no *meter* here because of the undifferentiated rhythmic values and evenly distributed accents. At the relatives' entrance at R1, their scattered comments ("Povero Buoso," "Povero cugino," etc.) coincide with the notated downbeats but, importantly, not with the ostinato, a misalignment that produces a highly comical effect: the ostinato continues to sound *normal,* while the relatives sound *abnormal* (i.e., metrically displaced) and, as a result, even more bumbling and amusing than they already are. Moreover, when one of the main motives associated with Schicchi (Carner's "Schicchi the clever impersonator") appears in the piece's sixteenth bar (see example 5.1), one must either accept this motive as highly syncopated or reorient oneself metrically; the latter is *very* challenging. Thus the ostinato, again, sounds normal, while the Schicchi motive sounds abnormal; in reality—that is, *on the notated page* and thus, apparently, in Puccini and Forzano's bourgeois view of the story, as opposed to the Donati family's aristocratic view—the truth is exactly opposite: Schicchi is the normal one, while the relatives are deviant.

As mentioned, *Schicchi*'s unconventionality also stems from its achieving a near-complete integration of the conventional melodramatic approach to form and the unconventional, episodic approach. As a result, the episodic strategy pervades large sections of the work, and the more frequent shifts toward the marked, Romantic style often function as formal interruptions within larger, mostly unconventional formal procedures. Good examples include the Romantic music for Rinuccio at "Zia, l'ho trovato io" (R10); for Rinuccio and Lauretta at "Addio, speranza bella" (R38.20); for Lauretta at "O mio babbino caro" (R40); for Rinuccio and Lauretta again, still on the text "Addio, speranza bella" (at R42.4 and 43.3); and finally for Rinuccio and Lauretta's concluding "Lauretta mia" (R85). Each functions to create a structural rupture in the form, and all but one, moreover, uses some variation of the same music, which I will call the "Addio, speranza bella" theme (the version at R43.3 is definitive): a lyric, expansive, characteristically Puccinian Romantic melody with a distinctive appoggiatura on every downbeat and the hallmark *violinata* orchestration. The only case in the whole opera, in fact, of Romantic-style music *not* functioning as a disruption in a larger, episodic formal unit is Rinuccio's *recitative* and aria discussed earlier ("Avete torto" and "Firenze"), and even this, while still a self-contained set piece, functions formally on a lower hierarchical level: it concludes part two (the "Schicchi" part) of the bipartite introduction.

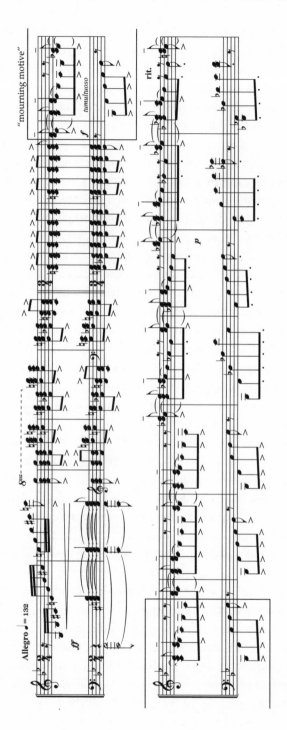

EXAMPLE 5.1. *Gianni Schicchi*, opening.

EXAMPLE 5.2. *Gianni Schicchi,* hypothetical normative version of the mourning motive (compare example 5.1, R0.8).

Perhaps the two best examples of Romantic interruptions both occur near the beginning of the second large part of this two-part opera, in the scene and quartet for Schicchi, Zita, Rinuccio, and Lauretta, and in the first scene and aria for Schicchi—specifically in the latter's long and complex *scena.*[11] The scene and quartet ensemble is not conventional—or, perhaps, is only conventional in the most generic possible sense, in that it comprises an extended block of the opera that revolves around a dramatic confrontation among four characters. It proceeds, as a conventional ensemble would, in four main parts (parts 1–4 in table 5.1), but even so there is certainly no clear reference to the *solita forma.* In concept, this is similar to the second and third duets in *Il tabarro,* each of which was a conventional set piece in the broadest sense—each was a closed, self-contained confrontation between two characters—but neither of which seemed to refer directly to melodramatic formal prototypes. The piece comprises a *recitative* for Schicchi ("Ah! . . . Andato??," R35.3), a concerted movement ("Sicuro! Ai frati!," R36), another very short *recitative* for Schicchi ("Brava la vecchia! Brava!," R38), and a final *concertato* (R38.8—to which Schicchi's "Vecchia taccagna!" is a pickup). The only way of inferring a reference here to the conventional four-part, double cycle of kinesis-stasis would be to hear parts 1 and 3 as kinetic and parts 2 and 4 as static. But this is untenable, because while parts 1 and 3 certainly *are* kinetic, so are 2 and 4—a feature befitting the accelerated structural rhythms, perhaps, of a comic opera. In part 2, Zita uses the excuse that the Donatis have been disinherited to order Schicchi to take his daughter and leave the house—she wants no part of Rinuccio's plans to marry Lauretta. Part 4 is similarly active, beginning with some rather comic name-calling on Schicchi's part (Zita is a "vecchia taccagna," "stillina," "sordida," "spilorcia," and "gretta"—an "old, stingy, sordid, avaricious, petty miser") and moving to an equally comic ensemble in which characters pair off by generation and continue to either argue (Schicchi-Zita) or swoon over one another (Rinuccio-Lauretta). The more important formal-dramatic principle at work here seems to be that of the confrontation unfolding essentially in *one* large part, not two smaller cycles: a concertato (part 2), preceded by one *recitative* (1) and interrupted by another (part 3) before continuing (4) where it left off.

The Romantic-style interruptions are in the "Vecchia taccagna" section (part 4). Here minor-mode, chaotic, decidedly non-Romantic music associated with the ongoing argument between Schicchi and Zita is interrupted twice (R38.20 and R40) by lyric, stylistically Romantic music identified with Rinuccio and Lauretta (in the first instance both sing the "Addio, speranza bella" theme; the second time Lauretta alone sings the "O mio babbino caro"). The music for both interruptions has, among other attributes, a similar rocking quality in its rhythmic and motivic profile (a result of the appoggiaturas on every downbeat in the "Addio" theme and the pastorale rhythm in "O mio babbino") that creates a sharp contrast with the aggressive, perpetual rhythmic motion of the main ensemble music. The styles' close proximity and stark contrast create not only tropological significance (the old aristocratic establishment as an immovable object that gradually, reluctantly yields to the force of the up-and-coming, enlightened, younger generation) but also an environment in which the interludes are easily heard not exactly as interruptions, but rather as parallel musical strands sounding not opposite or in alternation with the Schicchi-Zita music, but rather *simultaneously with it* (see example 5.3). That is, each block can be heard as constantly present. When the Rinuccio-Lauretta music first appears, the Schicchi-Zita music continues, even though we cannot hear it, and vice-versa: the Rinuccio-Lauretta music continues under the Schicchi-Zita music (and in fact had always been present, from the beginning of the scene), even though it is not heard. The effect is similar to multiple shots in a film: the action is continuous, but we can see only part of it—wherever the camera happens to be focused—at any given moment.[12]

Debussy's music has recently been described in these same terms. Rebecca Leydon has observed that certain "modes of continuation" (i.e., processes by which events in a series—such as different shots in a film—

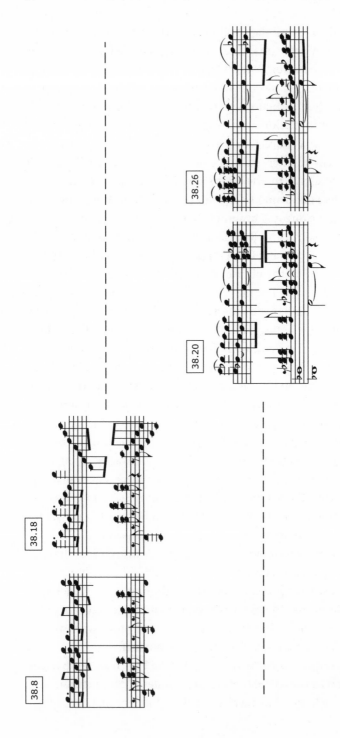

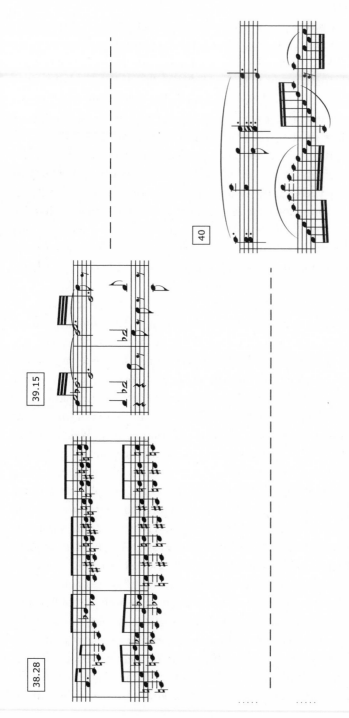

EXAMPLE 5.3. Stylistic contrast in the *Gianni Schicchi* quartet.

are linked together) common in early cinematography can provide a framework for understanding structural discontinuity in Debussy's music, which, like Puccini's, became gradually more discontinuous later in his career.[13] In this scene in *Gianni Schicchi*, Puccini uses a *direct cut*, or an immediate shift to a different view of the same action. Other modes of continuation with musical corollaries include the *cut-in* (an instant shift to a close-up shot), the *matting* (placing one image on the film with another to create two different images seen on screen at once), and the *dissolve* (when one image shifts gradually to another such that both are momentarily visible at the same time). According to Leydon, different modes of continuation have different temporal implications: a dissolve, for example, may imply a temporal *meanwhile* (and in some cases even a change in location), while a direct cut may imply that various views of the same action are occurring simultaneously. The latter clearly describes what happens in our scene in *Schicchi*.

Edward T. Cone has also famously observed the same kinds of effects in Stravinsky's music (without remarking on their filmic qualities), in which the texture and ultimately the large form each depend on juxtapositions of contrasting blocks of musical material. Cone, in a passage that applies as well to Puccini as it does to Stravinsky, describes what in film would be called a direct cut: "Although heard in alternation, each line [block of material] continues to exert its influence even when silent. As a result, the effect is analogous to polyphonic strands of a melody: the successive time segments are as it were counterpointed one against the other." Cone calls this an *interlock,* or a return of one thematic block following its interruption by another. This is but one phase of a three-phase process Cone describes as also comprising *stratification,* or the differentiation among blocks of material and their attendant separation in musical space (e.g., in *Schicchi*, Puccini's assigning one block of material to Schicchi and Zita and another, contrasting block to Rinuccio and Lauretta), and *synthesis,* or the joining in time and space of one or more of the divergent strands (which seems not to have been part of Puccini's strategies, at least not in this part of the *Schicchi* quartet).[14]

Thus the direct cut audible at each of the scene's Romantic interruptions implies that the chaotic, non-Romantic ensemble music will eventually resume and the scene will continue. That this happens after the first ("Addio") but not the second interruption ("O mio babbino") makes the whole ensemble sound, strangely enough, as if it ends abruptly, even though the last music we hear in the set piece is not the ensemble music per se but rather Romantic-style music for Lauretta. The sense of abruptness arises partly because the ensemble's perpetual motion was sharply interrupted at Schicchi's "Vien! vien! vien!," which sets up Lauretta's interlude, and partly because Schicchi embarks on a *recitative* of his own immediately after Lauretta sings "O mio babbino." Schicchi's ensuing recitative clearly does not belong to the preceding ensemble—there is no sign at all in the music that it should be heard as such, as it retains none of the ensemble's characteristics—and thus must be regarded as the beginning of a new formal unit.

Schicchi controls the next seven and a half minutes of the opera, all of it subsumed in a scene and aria (see table 5.1) that makes a rather loose but still audible reference to the *solita forma*. Here again, conventionality and unconventionality are more integrated in *Schicchi* than in the previous two *Trittico* works. A reference to the conventional prototype does not necessarily cue a reference to the Romantic style, and vice versa—a move to the Romantic style in the music is not necessarily supported with a coincident shift in the formal strategy. Music, drama, and text all unfold in a large action-narration cycle divided into four parts (parts 1–4 in table 5.1). The action component is a long, recitative block mainly for Schicchi but in which the others participate as well—formally consistent with a *scena*. Here Schicchi paces the room trying to think of a way to get the Donatis out of their predicament; apparently reaches a solution and sends Lauretta (too innocent to hear her father engage in such trickery) out to the terrace; begins to implement the plan without fully explaining it to the Donatis; and finally impersonates the deceased Buoso, whom no one outside the house knows has died, in order to dispose of Buoso's doctor Spinelloccio—the stock Bolognese Dottore Balanzone from the *commedia dell'arte*—who unexpectedly knocks at Buoso's door and enters the room in the middle of the action. This last episode is an interruption of its own, in which Spinelloccio's static, oscillating, dissonant harmonies (along with new articulation markings and a very high register for the strings) contrast sharply with the surrounding *scena* music for Schicchi and indicate Spinelloccio's position outside the normative temporal and dramatic space of the scene. A return to musical normalcy (vocally, orchestrationally, harmonically, and melodically) at Schicchi's

"Era uguale la voce?" (R48) suggests a resumption of Schicchi's *scena*, which now wraps up in short order with his first declaring victory, then realizing that no one understands what he is proposing to do.

This is the impetus for the rest of the scene, in which Schicchi narrates his plan to the dim-witted relatives. The scene unfolds in three sections: the outer two are in *tempo giusto* (first, an allegro at R49, "Si corre dal notaio"; second, an andante moderato e sostenuto at R51, at "In testa / la cappellina"), analogous to the two lyric movements in a conventional multi-movement aria; the middle is in a freer, more recitative mode (complete with a variation of the original mourning motive in Schicchi's vocal line) and thus suggests, at least texturally, the formal function of a *tempo di mezzo*.[15] Table 5.1 marks the first *tempo giusto* movement *primo tempo* rather than the standard *adagio* because of the obvious inconsistency in the tempo implications; "Si corre dal notaio" is not even close to being a slow movement or even a cantabile, let alone adagio.[16] The last movement is likewise not a *cabaletta* but more properly one of Ashbrook's *cabaletta*-functions—a movement functioning formally as the last lyric piece in a four-part scheme but not necessarily exhibiting the internal formal or dramaturgical properties specific to a conventional *cabaletta*. The movement meets the standard for a *cabaletta*-function in that its tempo is differentiated from the other movements—even while it is *slower,* not faster, and thus opposite of the norm—and its emotional intensity is heightened in order to produce a dramatic climax, one so intense, in fact, that the scene requires an emotional release in a coda for the relatives, at "Schicchi!" (R52).

Even the verse here articulates a four-part form. The entire *scena,* from "Datemi il testamento" to "Ah! . . . che zucconi" and including the scene with Spinelloccio, is in rhymed *scena* verse, the loose mixture of *quinari, settenari,* and *endecasillabi* (and occasionally other meters as well) typical, as mentioned, in Puccini's libretto. A clear, audible change occurs at "Si corre dal notaio" (part 2, functionally the *primo tempo;* the text is given in table 5.3), now to more consistent *settenari,* with two *endecasillabi* (lines 6 and 7) grouped in two quatrains. A shift to *quinari* at line 9 articulates another formal unit, now part 3 (functionally the *tempo di mezzo*), organized in one quatrain with two *quinari* and two *settenari;* and another very audible metric shift marks the final formal unit (*cabaletta*-function) at line 13. This opens with four lines of short

TABLE 5.3. *Gianni Schicchi,* parts 2–4 of Schicchi's recitative and aria

Part 2 (≈*primo tempo*)

1	Schicchi	7	Si corre dal notaio:
2		7	"Messer notaio, presto!
3		7	Via da Buoso Donati!
4		7	C'è un gran peggioramento!
5		7	Vuol fare testamento!
6		11	Portate su con voi le pergamene,
7		11	presto, messere, presto, se no è tardi! ..."
8		7	Ed il notaio viene.

Part 3 (≈*tempo di mezzo*)

9	5	Entra: la stanza
10	5	è semioscura,
11	7	dentro il letto intravede
12	7	di Buoso la figura!

Part 4 (*cabaletta*-function)

13	3	In testa
14	5	la cappellina!
15	3	al viso
16	5	la pezzolina!
17	11	Fra cappellina e pezzolina un naso
18	11	che par quello di Buoso e invece è il mio ...
19	11	perché al posto di Buoso ci son io!
20	11	Io, lo Schicchi, con altra voce e forma!
21	11	"Io falsifico in me Buoso Donati
22	11	testando e dando al testamento norma!"
23	11	O gente! Questa matta bizzaria
24	11	che mi zampilla dalla fantasia
25	11	è tale da sfidar l'eternità!

meters—two *trisillabo-quinario* pairs that facilitate Schicchi's *canto spezzato*—before continuing with nine lines (two quatrains plus a line) of *endecasillabo* set very freely in the music. The initial short meters in lines 13–16 cause the subsequent *endecasillabo* (beginning at line 17) to sound like it breaks off a highly regular verse structure; the characterization—wherein Schicchi is heard as unable to do anything as straightforward as maintain metric regularity in the verse—is extremely comical.

We find also in Schicchi's long *scena* exactly the same formal feature as in the last movement of the preceding quartet: an episodic organizational strategy creeping into what is otherwise a single movement in a larger, coherent set piece. Here, as before, music in the Romantic style interrupts non-Romantic music; the effect is again filmic, and we hear (i.e., *see*) direct cuts from one shot to another, with different views of the same ongoing action (see example 5.4). Following Schicchi's "Datemi il testamento"—which, as mentioned, initiates the scene—are two cycles of the same sequence of events: Schicchi paces the room, deliberating on the Donatis' situation; Schicchi offers an estimation of what can be done (apparently nothing, or so he thinks at first); and Rinuccio and Lauretta interrupt. Each cycle (R41 and 42.8) begins with the motive from R0.16, associated with Schicchi (Carner: "Schicchi the clever impersonator") and comprising the same arpeggiated figure from before but now transformed into a comical march that accompanies Schicchi's nervous pacing. Note that this motive, as Girardi has observed, bears a resemblance to a second Schicchi motive, the one for Schicchi's name (first heard at R25.7); Carner and Girardi both, moreover, identify three "Schicchi" motives in all, where the third is the "Motteggiatore! . . . Beffeggiatore! . . ." ("Mocker! . . . Joker! . . .") motive first introduced in Rinuccio's "Avete torto" *recitative* (see R28.9)—where the fanfare-like vitality of the latter, according to Girardi, represents Schicchi's spirit as an embodiment of the new generation of Florentines.[17]

In both cycles, Schicchi ends the marching music with an abrupt, decisive "Niente da fare!" ("Nothing to be done!," at R42.3 and R43.2), at which time the music immediately shifts stylistic gears to the "Addio speranza bella" theme—which, by now, we must hear as humorous by virtue of its constant use as a comic interruption of the main action sequence. Moreover, to accentuate the comic effect in what is one of the most amusing sequences in the opera, the scene accelerates as it unfolds,

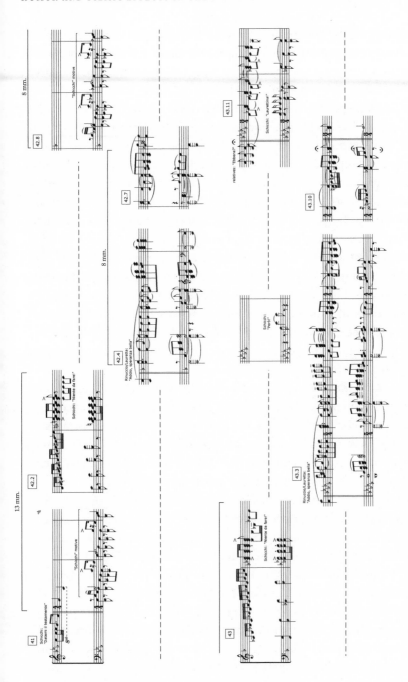

EXAMPLE 5.4. *Gianni Schicchi*, stylistic contrast in Schicchi's *recitative* (R41).

an effect owing to a gradual temporal compression that comes from Puccini's manipulating the length of, and spatial relationship between, the two stylistic blocks. The first marching block lasts thirteen measures before being interrupted with eight bars of "Addio speranza bella." At the first juxtaposition (R42.4) the blocks remain separated in the musical space—"Addio" begins immediately after Schicchi's "fare!"—but at the next juxtaposition (back to the marching music, R42.8) the blocks are pressed together in time so as to overlap by two beats: one shot *dissolves* into another. This marching block lasts eight bars and thus is noticeably shorter than the first, so that the next "Addio" interruption seems to appear prematurely (pickup to R43.3). The music of the latter, moreover, features a spatial juxtaposition at Schicchi's "Però!," which is a short glimpse of Schicchi's own music and not part of the continuing "Addio, speranza bella." As such, it is another device that compresses time: that is, there is no room here to insert a full episode of Schicchi's music and still maintain the action's pace, so Schicchi simply sings on top of Rinuccio and Lauretta and we momentarily hear (see) both shots at once—a good musical example of the cinematographic technique known as *matting*.

In both the scene and quartet and the scene and aria, the contrast between Romantic and non-Romantic styles serves both the comedy and the characterization. In each, the Romantic music—three episodes of "Addio, speranza bella" and one of "O mio babbino caro"—lies outside the normative formal-temporal space. Every time it appears, it interrupts the main action sequence in such a way that it sounds formally subordinate to the non-Romantic music, which sounds formally primary. The hierarchical opposition reinforces the sense that the Romantic style is non-normative and thus marked: as a result, each Romantic interlude not only shifts the work's discursive level but each is, furthermore, *diegetic* (now in the more traditional, filmic sense of the word), not only in the sense of its dissociation from the main formal space but also in the sense that we hear it as originating from within the dramatic space on the stage. That is, we hear Rinuccio and Lauretta sing, but everyone else on stage *also* hears their music *as sung music*—not, as is more common in opera, as spoken text that only we the audience hear as sung. Carolyn Abbate and Gary Tomlinson have both described this kind of (diegetic) music as "phenomenal": music *openly declared* that the characters on stage also hear as music, even though here this is not made explicit in the score like it is in many other examples they cite (Abbate names the "Bell Song" in Delibes' *Lakmé,* for instance). The opposite would be Tomlinson's "noumenal" music, that to which on-stage characters are deaf—or hear "problematically, if at all."[18] The end result, in *Schicchi,* is that "Addio, speranza bella" and, more generally, the Romantic style itself and all its manifestations in the piece, become comical, and thus we must understand Puccini as having *used* the formal structure to make the piece more humorous. Every time the style appears, it sounds so completely out of place, so unexpected, and so sharply disengaged with the music around it that we have no choice but to laugh at it.[19]

On the surface, this use of the Romantic style seems to make *Schicchi* fundamentally different from *Tabarro* and *Angelica.* Neither of the latter are comical, and likewise *Schicchi* seems so much more positive and optimistic than the other two that a comparison is challenging. But a reading—such as what Hepokoski has advocated[20]—that bears in mind the theatrical context of *Schicchi* as a work following directly from *Tabarro* and *Angelica,* on the same night, for the same audience, in the same theater, forces us to consider some similarities. At the most general level the stylistic plurality achieves the same effect in all three works, especially once one is prepared by the experience of *Tabarro:* in each, the Romantic style is reserved, or withheld, such that when it does emerge, the discourse changes markedly. One hears *the style* more than one hears *the music* or *the drama;* that is to say, one's attention is directed away from the characters and actions on stage and onto technical-stylistic features of the music. In each work, furthermore, the effect of the Romantic music's *disengagement* from the opera's normative formal and stylistic space metaphorically underscores the characters' own disengagement either from normal society (as for the hopeless, pathetic Giorgetta and Luigi) or from a normal state of mind (as for the delusional, and in many ways equally pathetic, Angelica). In *Schicchi* the focus is on Rinuccio and Lauretta, two young, vital, open-minded characters just as disengaged from their surroundings as are these other three. Their detachment is from society, in their case the old societal

EXAMPLE 5.5. *Gianni Schicchi,* transformation of "Addio, speranza bella" to "Lauretta mia." (a) pickup to R42.4; (b) R84.

b) R84:

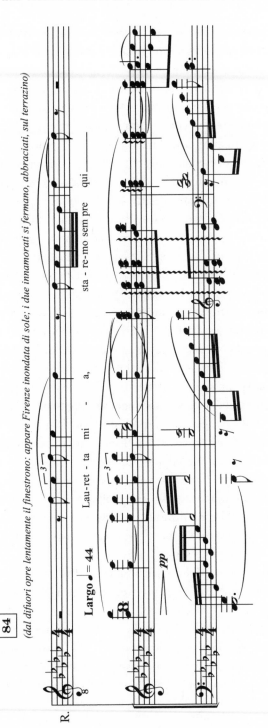

EXAMPLE 5.5. *continued*

norms of Renaissance Florence, such that they represent a kind of changing of the guard that arouses fear in the older, established generation embodied by the aristocratic Donatis.

There may even be similarity in these works' underlying messages. This is not obvious on the surface, where *Schicchi,* again, seems filled with hope and optimism: Schicchi triumphs, the old guard is put in its place, Rinuccio and Lauretta will marry and live happily ever after, and even the hopeless (albeit comically so) "Addio, speranza bella" becomes, at the end, the sanguine "Lauretta mia" (R84), text sung to the same musical theme and thus apparently a sentimental happy ending for the two lovers. But because of the way Puccini strategically uses this theme throughout the opera—almost always as a comic interruption of the main action sequence—it is, by the end, troped so as to be fully *ironized*—even as it remains the embodiment in the piece of the Romantic style and all its supposed sincerity. What the theme apparently signifies is no longer actually what it means, and any expressive interpretation depends on recognizing that the meaning cannot be taken literally (Hatten: *irony* is "a higher-order trope inaugurated by the contradiction between what is claimed [or observed, or done] and a context that cannot support its reality [or appropriateness])."[21] By the end of *Schicchi,* the "Addio, speranza bella" theme is no longer sentimental but comical, no longer sincere but disingenuous, and indeed no longer genuinely optimistic but rather transformed into nothing more than a façade for an ironic pessimism that parallels that of *Tabarro* and *Angelica*—operas in both of which the central characters are hopeless victims of circumstance with no way out and no future. This explains the theme's text— "Addio, speranza bella" ("Farewell, beautiful hope")—apparently the real message in *Schicchi,* a message far more cynical and suspicious than the musical surface would seem to allow. The bourgeois, ultimately, cannot triumph against the immovable forces of heritage and societal pressures.

This message is audible even at the work's opening (see example 5.1). As mentioned, when Schicchi's motive appears over the relatives' ostinato mourning motive, Schicchi's is the one that sounds metrically abnormal while the relatives' sounds normal—even though visually, in the score, the situation is exactly opposite. Schicchi's theme aligns with the written meter (the motive's sixth note falls on a downbeat, for example), while the mourning motive is highly syncopated. But the latter metrically overpowers the former, as it were; the immobility of the old societal norms is simply too strong, the Schicchi theme is unable to overcome the relatives' metric displacement, and the message we *hear* is not the same as what appears on the printed page.

The same message is cleverly disguised in the "Addio, speranza bella" theme and its treatment at the work's end. Consider that the theme is perfectly designed to accommodate its text, "Addio, speranza bella / dolce mirragio," a *settenario* followed by a *quinario* (as at R42.4; see example 5.5a): three initial notes in which the first is a pickup naturally accommodate "Addio" (the word has three syllables—Ad-di-o—if read with *dieresis* between "di" and "o"; the accent is on the second syllable), and the setting naturally emphasizes the sentimental "farewell" to Florence as we know it. Five more notes follow (for "speranza bella"), the fourth of which falls on a downbeat and thus naturally accommodates the line's *accento comune* ("*bel*-la"). The next five notes begin with an ecstatic upward leap to the third scale degree that reverts immediately to a stepwise descent, and the fourth of these falls on the next downbeat and accommodates the next *accento comune* ("mi-*rag*-gio"). But at the end (R84; see example 5.5b) the situation is quite different: here the theme lacks its characteristic pickup note (the first note is the downbeat at R84); its text is now "Lauretta mia / staremo sempre qui," a *quinario* followed by a *settenario tronco,* exactly the reverse of the original text's metric sequence. The *quinario* joins the music late—the theme's first three notes sound in the orchestra before Rinuccio enters—momentarily giving the impression that Rinuccio has nothing to say; and the following *settenario tronco* must now be declaimed over music clearly designed for a *quinario piano,* thus sounding hurried and completely unnatural.

Oddly, then, at ostensibly the happiest moment in the work, with past and future merging in the present, the music leaves us with a strange, ironic, subtly nihilistic sense of complete detachment and disjunction. Text and music, characters and language, style and substance do not—cannot—agree. Perhaps the message of *Schicchi* is not optimistic at all; perhaps the comedy is really a façade for something far more serious, pessimistic, and hopeless.

SIX

Puccini's Solution: Integrating the Conventional and Unconventional

Turandot is a fitting end for Puccini's career. The subject is eminently amenable to the directions in which he was moving, especially toward a solution to the formal problem posed in the *Trittico:* how to achieve a near-total integration of conventionality with unconventionality— that is, an approach that arranges kinetic and static movements into set pieces analogous to conventional melodramatic prototypes and one that simultaneously deploys a series of shorter episodes articulated according to a complex array of musical styles. Puccini seems to have turned to the subject of Turandot on the suggestion of Veronese journalist and playwright Renato Simoni, then working in Milan as editor of *La Lettura* and drama critic for *Il corriere della sera*.[1] Simoni had extensive knowledge of both the eighteenth-century Venetian writer of fantastic plays, Carlo Gozzi (on whom he had written a play, *Carlo Gozzi*, in 1903), and China (where he had at one time worked as the *Corriere's* Asian correspondent). He suggested in March 1920 that Puccini read Andrea Maffei's Italian translation of Friedrich Schiller's German version of Gozzi's *Turandot*, which Gozzi himself derived from "The Story of Prince Calaf and the Princess of China" in *Les Mille et un Jours,* a 1710 French translation by François Pétis de la Croix of the ancient Persian collection *1001 Days* (the Persian counterpart to the Arabian *1001 Nights*). Schiller's play had recently been given in a well-known Max Reinhardt production in Berlin, in October 1911, and the story had a well-established history of musical settings: numerous composers in the nineteenth and early twentieth centuries (including Carl Maria von Weber in 1813) had written incidental music for Schiller's *Turandot*, and operas on the subject had been written by—among many other, more obscure examples—Antonio Bazzini (*Turanda*, 1867, on a libretto by Antonio Gazzoletti derived mainly from Maffei) and Feruccio Busoni (*Turandot*, 1917, on his own libretto based on Gozzi's original).[2]

In some ways the tale is well-suited for an opera with a largely conventional underlying structure. The tale is ancient: Turandot has origins in mythological marriage resisters as diverse as the part-woman, part-lion Sphinx and the mythic hunter-athlete Atalanta, and in stories of riddling princesses from the oral and written traditions of a wide variety of cultures, including ancient Greece (in a millennia-old Cretan fairy tale), Persia (in both the *1001 Days* and "The Story of Turandocht's Riddles," one of the *Seven Stories of the Seven Princesses* by twelfth-century poet Muhammad Elyās edn-e Yusof Nezāmi), and India (where perhaps the oldest riddling princess exists in the form of the goddess Kali, who wears male heads like a string of pearls around her neck).

But in other ways the story is ripe for a highly unconventional operatic setting.[3] The tale manifests societal tendencies, current in both Puccini's era and Gozzi's own, toward a fear of "dangerous" women: women of intellectual prowess and influence, women interested in subverting traditional social hierarchies, and women branded "deviant" for undermining male authority and taking pleasure in the destruction of men. Such women, especially those of intellectual curiosity and emerging cultural authority, were a reality in Gozzi's Italy and even in his own family, into which the playwright, poet, and entrepreneur Luisa Bergalli had married by way of Gozzi's older brother Gasparo. Gozzi is known to have harbored fears toward such women and to have been interested in reasserting the order of the social status quo. More than a century later, the same kinds of fears are discernible in the anti-feminist movements that were gaining currency in fin-de-siècle Italy and elsewhere across Europe. Misogynistic views of women as threats to the societal order—reactions to the rapidly growing feminist movement that, in Italy, originates in 1880s Milan—are evident in work of pre-fascist Italian writers Giovanni Papini and Filippo Tommaso Marinetti (especially in the latter's famous *Fondazione e Manifesto del Futurismo* of 1909, in which he glorifies contempt for women), criminologists Cesare Lombroso and Guglielmo Ferrero (who together in 1893 published an empirical analysis of criminal women's physical features), anthropologist Paolo Mantegazza (who in the 1890s promoted theories of women's natural intellectual inferiority), and Austrian philosopher Otto Weininger (whose 1903 *Geschlect und Charakter* urged the liberation of men from predatory women). And this is not even to mention the polemics of Torrefranca himself, whose writing exhibits a modernist, anti-feminist bent and who, in branding Puccini "effeminate," meant to associate him with the lowest members of contemporary society. Given such an intellectual climate, it should not be surprising that "dangerous" women would find homes in contemporary literature, visual arts, and opera: examples from the latter include, among others, Strauss's *Salome* and *Elektra;* Massenet's *Herodiade, Thaïs,* and *Sapho;* Saint-Saëns's *Delilah;* and even Puccini's own *Tosca.*

The Puccini-Adami-Simoni treatment of the Turandot tale reveals in several ways the influence of these modern cultural currents. First, the three collaborators had been uncertain from the beginning about how to handle the problem of the dénouement (Turandot's conversion from man-hating decapitator to possessor of what Puccini wanted to be an intense passion: "Simplify it with the number of acts and work it [*Turandot*] to make it slim and effective, and above all to heighten the amorous passion of Turandot, which she has smothered under the ashes of her great pride for so long").[4] When Puccini suggested to the others that Calaf initiate Turandot's thaw with a kiss (a metaphor for sex, and not present in Gozzi's original), he introduced into the story the "physical subjugation of the unruly woman" theme pervasive in contemporary thought. Second, the team retained from Gozzi's original the Venetian masks of the *commedia dell'arte* (in which players wore masks, or half-masks, because they represented character *types* rather than individuals per se), but Truffaldino (in Gozzi, master of the eunuchs), Brighella (master of the pages), Pantalone (the emperor's secretary), and Tartaglia (the chancellor) became Puccini's rather bizarre, fully Chinese ministers to the emperor: Ping, the *Gran cancelliere,* head of the government and, as such, the only low voice among the three and the one with the most well-developed, individualized role; Pang, the *provveditore* or the financial administrator; and Pong, the emperor's head chef.[5] Collectively the masks became not only Shakespearean commentators outside the action proper (Gozzi also used them this way) but also emphasized—in their trio in the first scene of Act II, for example—Turandot's identity as the deviant feminine destroyer of men, national identity, and culture.

Third, Puccini and his librettists added to the story the Princess Lou-Ling narrative (part of Turandot's Act II entrance aria, "In questa Reggia"), also not present in Gozzi and a tale that (as Carner has observed) resembles the myth, known widely in Puccini's day, of the Amazon Queen Tanais: she was forced to marry a king who invaded her homeland, then murdered him on their wedding night. The story reinforces the modern view of the deviant woman as hopelessly irrational. And finally—and perhaps most significantly—they introduced Liù, a character with no precedent in any other version of the Turandot story and one apparently of Puccini's own invention (though she bears some similarity to Adelma, one of Turandot's slaves in Gozzi's original). Liù functions as a role model of sorts for the deviant Turandot and inspires her (in the torture and death scene in Act III) to recognize, eventually, the all-conquering power of love.[6]

Turandot is one of the largest of all Puccini's works, a grand opera in the truest sense: an enormous, late-Romantic, Germanic orchestra with large percussion forces and an on-stage band (complete with saxophones and the ever-present gong—the latter used dramatically more than musically) supports a cast of two sopranos (Turandot and Liù), four tenors (*primo tenore* Calaf, a Tatar prince whose identity remains unknown until the end; the aged Emperor Altoum; and, as noted, Pang and Pong), two baritones (Ping and the mandarin—i.e., a public official—who proclaims Turandot's law at the opera's opening and again in its third act), a bass (Timur, the rather pathetic father of Calaf and an exiled central-Asian king), and two essentially non-speaking roles, a Persian Prince (Turandot's latest victim; he cries out once, just before his beheading) and an executioner (named Pu-Tin-Pao and completely silent). The piece also includes Puccini's largest and most active chorus, cast as a Pekingese crowd of onlookers but also including servants of the executioner, attendants to Turandot, a group of phantoms (spirits of dead suitors), imperial guards and soldiers, banner bearers, priests, sages, mandarins, and other of the emperor's dignitaries (all of which make for an elaborate, well-populated set and one of the most visually captivating of Puccini's works).

Structurally, as mentioned, the closest model for *Turandot* is *Schicchi*—one of Puccini's more intimate operas—specifically its tendency to integrate an episodic formal design with one based on older, conventional models. The relationship between these two approaches becomes the central issue in *Turandot*: here Puccini achieved, perhaps more so than in any other work, their near-complete integration, such that the entire opera exhibits an episodic design but also exhibits features of the older organizational strategies, as if the episodes have been lowered onto a conventional foundation and both approaches adjusted into a meaningful, expressive interaction. This mixture of formal approaches mirrors Puccini's larger concern with mixing genres: whereas *Il trittico* assembles the three theatrical modes—tragic, pastoral, and comic—*Turandot* blends them. Similar to *Gianni Schicchi* and in contrast to *Il tabarro* and *Suor Angelica*, references to conventional formal models in *Turandot* are not reserved for sections of the work exhibiting the conventional Romantic musical style; rather, they permeate the entire work, sometimes audibly but sometimes not. And, as in *Schicchi*, in *Turandot* changes in musical style demarcate smaller formal episodes; that the entire work is now episodically organized naturally creates more complexity, as does the fact that the issue of musical style per se is more complex in *Turandot* than in *Schicchi*—and, indeed, than in any other of Puccini's works.

In all of the *Trittico*, musical style could be meaningfully accounted for with a binary opposition: the music was either Romantic or non-Romantic. The Romantic style was always cued with similar musical features, whereas the non-Romantic style varied but comprised, generally, one main trait in all three *Trittico* works: musical monotony, usually the result of incessant repetition in some or another of the musical dimensions. In *Turandot* the same binary opposition is present—the styles are Romantic or non-Romantic—but Puccini also employed in this piece a more nuanced approach to the non-Romantic music. This is a unique feature of the piece that allowed him to *use* styles structurally and expressively in a more complex way than in any previous opera; that is, the styles in *Turandot*—Romantic and non-Romantic alike—are so strongly asserted and the contrasts among them so apparent that they naturally produce independent, autonomous formal units—*episodes*—on all levels of the structure, global to local. In this sense, the styles in this opera function similarly to more traditional operatic formal delineators such as keys, themes, tempos, textures, verse meters, and the like—as if the styles create their own melodramatic form, complete with their own formal functions and expressive implications. This is not a new premise in Puccini studies: that style assumes a structural role in *Turandot* is a central point in Ashbrook and Powers' 1991 book and in Johanne Cassar's 2000 musical-semiotic study of the work.[7]

This increased stylistic-formal complexity also gives rise to the issue—less crucial in the *Trittico* analyses but much more pressing now—of how to categorize the styles in *Turandot;* numerous precedents for how to address the problem exist in published literature on the work. Ashbrook and Powers find "four colors" in the piece: "Chinese," "dissonant," "middle-Eastern," and "romantic diatonic," the last of these also the "Puccinian norm."[8] Cassar finds seven stylistic "isotopies" (recurring musical-stylistic patterns), including the "macabre," "lyrique," "la nuit," "héroïque," "grotesque," "pouvoir," and "nocturne."[9] Carner, one of the earliest to point to the importance of stylistic plurality in the work, names the "lyric-sentimental," the "heroic-grandiose," the "comic-grotesque," and the exotic.[10] And Girardi, while less systematic than some others in inventorying discrete styles, likewise finds that comic, heroic, tragic, pathetic, and exotic colors are of critical importance.[11]

My own taxonomy follows suit. I hear three primary styles in the work: Romantic, Dissonant, and Exotic. The latter includes stylistic variation, some of which seems significant enough that it warrants three Exotic subcategories: Chinese, Primitive, and Persian. Note that this kind of taxonomy is consistent with how I viewed Puccini's stylistic plurality in *Il trittico,* insofar as the styles still fall into an essentially binary opposition of Romantic versus non-Romantic. But the additional detail reflects two important features of *Turandot's* musical language: first, the non-Romantic music I am calling Dissonant seems to grow out of Puccini's effort to not only subvert the Romantic style but also to invoke some of the features characteristic of contemporary German and, especially, French music; second, the work's exotic setting seems to have demanded from Puccini its own, separate musical color, not just a specifically Chinese exoticism but also one for the middle-eastern (or Persian) and another for the primitive elements in the plot—where the latter is sometimes naïve and innocent (as in the music for Liù) but sometimes also brutal and violent (as in the music for the executioners) in a way that recalls other primitivist work from around the same period (Stravinsky's *Le Sacre du Printemps* among them).

Moreover, the stylistic-formal complexity in *Turandot* also presents some analytical difficulties not encountered in *Il trittico*. The notion of categorizing the work's styles may suggest, perhaps, a rather formulaic, inflexible reading of the music that I would like to avoid. Rather, I wish to view the stylistic categories as dynamic and evolving, ones with which listeners can be in constant dialogue as the work unfolds. Certainly one may hear *Turandot* differently from one performance to the next, and one's own categorization of styles may change; the categories are thus not necessarily rigid containers in which slices of the work are stored.

Some theoretical apparatus will make this clearer.[12] Strictly speaking, the styles themselves are not simply *styles* or *colors* but *style types:*[13] that is, large stylistic categories distinguished by specific *style tokens,* themselves compositional procedures such as motives, rhythms, harmonic progressions, metric features, and the like. In fact we have encountered many tokens already in the discussion (chapter 2) of Puccini's Romantic style, which is a style type with tokens including non-functional dominants, *violinata* orchestrations, and metric elasticity. Listeners use style tokens to recognize and build a larger understanding of style types in a dialectical process similar to that used in the cognitive dialogue with formal schemata and their features. Tokens are understood as defining a type; once this is understood, the appearance of one or more of these tokens signals the appearance of the type—even if *all* a type's tokens never appear at once and a prototype of any given type remains an abstraction. This is a process by which listeners acquire stylistic competency at all levels, from the specific ("the French Baroque style of the early eighteenth century") to the general (the "minimalist style"). Listeners *learn* a style by making generalizations from the tokens in specific works, then interpret other works, known or unknown, based on their emerging stylistic literacy.

The same dialectic proves useful in understanding the structural role of styles in *Turandot*. The *style* versus *style type* distinction is more than semantic, and it suggests a view of the work rather different from what has until now been widely accepted. Style types in *Turandot* are differentiated from one another at a high level of the musical structure as discrete, autonomous entities with organizational and expressive functions. Thus, the music is discontinuous or disjunct at the highest conceptual level. Nearly every other writer who has engaged the topic has suggested a somewhat different perspective. Ashbrook and Powers are a case in point, as their own terminology reveals: they define the contrasts in *Turandot* as contrasts in *tinte* (*colors;* i.e., "The Four Colors"),[14] which implies—even though, as I noted earlier (n. 7), their sense of a *tinta* may be close to my own sense of a *style*—that they still understand the work's disjunctions at a level structurally subordinate to that of true *style types*. According to such a view, style remains uniform, perhaps colored at various times with contrasting compositional strategies but coherent and unified nevertheless at the broadest level. Puccini thus remains similar to almost every opera composer since the birth of the genre, from Monteverdi to Mozart to Verdi, in that distinctions among musical colors have aided characterization, atmosphere, and dramatic expression. But my view, in which the disjunctions exist at a higher structural level, yields a picture of a composer doing something fundamentally different, taking the traditional notion of *tinta* and moving it to a new level of structural consequence in the service of fragmenting the musical language—creating, in effect, the same kind of *patchwork* or *collage* effect found in the contemporary theatrical music of Stravinsky, Debussy, and Strauss.[15]

The very notion of *categorization* itself can also be problematic, especially in an opera and even in music analysis more generally, in that it tends (as I suggested before) to imply a rather rigid or formulaic reading inconsistent with the dynamic nature of both the music itself and the act of interpreting it. But in fact the categories I have in mind are much more fluid, along the lines of those described by recent work in prototype theory, as discussed in chapter 1. This work underlines the fact—which as analysts we know intuitively—that categorizing every measure of music in *Turandot* would be not only cumbersome but also theoretically impossible.[16] In any category, some members will be better examples of the category than others; categories themselves have no fixed definitional boundaries but rather come closer to what in other fields (mathematics among them) are known as *fuzzy sets,* which expand and contract dynamically so as to include or exclude various members at their boundaries. Whether an object (a passage of music, for example) is a member of a category is thus a graded judgment: some necessarily will have more or less membership than others, where the *most* representative examples are the *prototypes.* Practically speaking, then, understanding style types in *Turandot* requires only that one be familiar with a few prototypical examples, not every possible example in the score; from there one can build an understanding—an evolving, dynamic understanding—of the work's complexly pluralistic musical language.

Among the non-Romantic styles in *Turandot,* the two most important—in the sense that they make an important contribution to the work's *tinta* and play a significant role in the piece structurally—are the Dissonant and the Chinese Exotic.[17] Regarding the former, Puccini's language is often thought to be more dissonant in *Turandot* than in any of his previous operas, an aspect of the work often taken as direct evidence of a concern on his part for musical modernism, a concern that he is otherwise thought to have lacked. The opera's distinctive opening, for example, with its well-known, much-discussed polychord (two triads with roots a half step apart; see R0.5ff) is often given as an example of an inclination on Puccini's part toward an advanced musical language, where *advanced* means *non-tonal* and in line with contemporary musical developments, especially those from Germany and Austria—locales in which polytonality had become an important tool for musical modernists.[18]

But describing this music as atonal or even polytonal is probably something of an exaggeration: *Turandot* is dissonant, certainly; as a result, the harmonic language is probably as complex as in any other of Puccini's works, and in the piece Puccini seems to have made an overt effort to make the non-Romantic music audibly more dissonant than in any of his other operas. But in reality neither the dissonance in *Turandot* nor the overall harmonic complexity *exceeds* that in some of his other operas, most especially those of *Il trittico,* in which numerous non-Romantic passages exhibit rather obvious, modernistic dissonances consistent with contemporary European musical trends (Schicchi's "Niente! Niente! Niente!" right before "O mio babbino caro"—see R40—is a good example, as is the impressionistic dissonance at the coach's arrival in *Angelica*—see R34—and in the organ-grinder's waltz in *Tabarro*—see R13).[19] Moreover, most of the dissonance in *Turandot* never manages to assume tonal-*structural* status; that is, most of it is used as a highly coloristic effect but still within a larger, conventionally tonal or modal context.

Prototypical cues for the Dissonant-style music include a foregrounding of dissonant intervals in the harmony and melody, especially half steps, tritones, major sevenths, and minor ninths; an angularity in the melodic lines that contrasts sharply with the smooth contours of the Romantic melodies; and a heightened importance in the harmony of overtly dissonant, non-functional sonorities.[20] The last of these is often the most important. The opening episode, mentioned previously, in which a mandarin reads a decree ("Popolo di Pekino") that efficiently summarizes the premise for the entire opera, is a good example. The polychord appears throughout, on, variously, bass D (see R0.5), C (R2.5), and B♭ (R1.3);[21] the chord is highly dissonant, but the dissonance, again, is an *effect* more than a structural element, one that functions here— consistent with the music in most other of Puccini's introductory episodes—to establish a characteristic *tinta*. And, in fact, the music is not even strictly polytonal: the tonality may be ambiguous, but most of this music seems to be in D minor, if we take the D-minor triads in the bass at the beginning and end as referential (see R0.5 and R2.8; the bass C at R2.9 is a large passing tone on its way to B♭ at R3).[22] Even the piece's first five notes (the "execution motive"—a good example of a Puccinian *motivo di prima intenzione*)[23] reflect the same kinds of strategies. This angular and decidedly non-lyrical line is distinctive anyway because of the full orchestration in octaves, but the tritone between the second and third notes elevates the *tinta*'s dissonance and reinforces a general sense of tonal ambiguity. The effect is compounded because the first four of these five notes are members of a whole-tone scale but all five together are diatonic, in F♯ minor (where E♯ is a raised leading tone and the falling fifth, C♯–F♯, points to F♯ as a local, short-lived tonic).[24]

Each Exotic style—Chinese, Primitive, and Persian—has its own characteristic token: pentatonicism for the Chinese Exotic, open fifths for the Primitive, and augmented seconds for the Persian.[25] The pentatonicism in the Chinese Exotic is mainly melodic but influences the harmony as well. The children's chorus in Act I ("Là sui monti dell'Est," R19), the first section of the Act I trio for the three ministers ("Fermo! Che fai?," R28), and the emperor's march in Act II ("Diecimila anni," R32.9) are all typical: each has an exclusively pentatonic melody, with only occasional neighboring and passing tones lying outside the prevailing collection. The children's chorus melody (example 6.1), for instance, is an authentic Chinese folk tune known as "Mo-li-hua" and uses the collection $E\flat$-F-G-$B\flat$-C, of which the $A\flat$ at R20.5 is not a member but also clearly subordinate: it falls in the weakest part of the measure as an incomplete upper neighbor to the G on the second beat, itself an upper neighbor to the F on beat 1.

Sometimes the pentatonic music is more complex, as at R28.7 in the ministers' trio melody. Here is a G not easily explained as tonally subordinate (the note is an important member—the leading tone—of the supporting dominant harmony) but also not a member of the prevailing pentatonic collection, $A\flat$-$B\flat$-C-$E\flat$-F. As Ashbrook and Powers have observed, the notion of modulating pentatonic scales, or *exchange-tone metabole*, is useful here: this describes a change of pentatonic collection wherein four notes remain constant but one *exchanges* places with another (the change is "based on a technique of modulation—'metabole' would be a better word—that shifts from one pentatonic module into another through the conversion of an accessory tone into a principal one; the Chinese technical term is *biàn yin*, 'exchange tone'").[26] Here $A\flat$ in the original scale trades places with G to temporarily make a new scale, $E\flat$-F-G-$B\flat$-C (the same thing happens again at R29.15, where C exchanges places with a $D\flat$ to make the new collection $D\flat$-$E\flat$-F-$A\flat$-$B\flat$). The procedure is idiomatic in Asian music, and whether Puccini employed it consciously or not, it does lend a certain degree of authenticity to his treatment of pitch material in the style. And while it was likely *not* a conscious compositional decision—there is no evidence to suggest Puccini would have been this intimately familiar with the technical details of Chinese music—the feature is probably authentic nevertheless. As has been noted by numerous writers, this tune, along with "Mo-li-hua" and most of Puccini's Chinese melodies in the piece, comes from one of two authentic Chinese sources: a Chinese music box belonging to Puccini's friend, the Baron Fassini, who had acquired the box in his travels as an

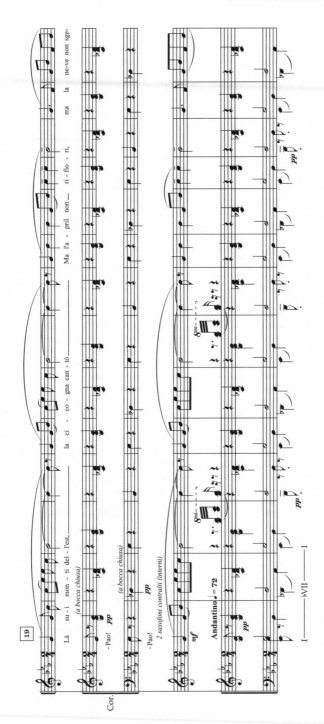

EXAMPLE 6.1. *Turandot* I, children's chorus ("Là sui monti dell'Est").

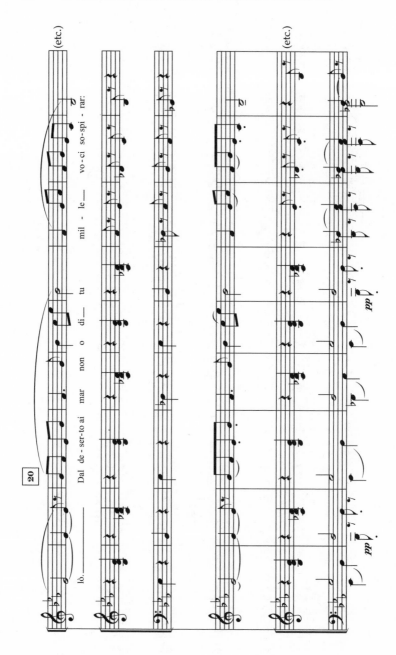

EXAMPLE 6.1. *continued*

Italian diplomat in the Far East; or a late-nineteenth-century, Shanghai-published volume of *Chinese Music* by J. A. van Aalst.[27]

Even the odd sense of metric instability in the ministers' trio (see the rapidly changing meters) is authentic, to an extent: where the tune pauses on the music box for an unspecific duration, Puccini elongates the meter by shifting from $\frac{2}{4}$ to $\frac{3}{4}$ (at the words "fai," "vuoi," and "questa"), such that for at least the first eight bars of the tune, the meter sounds as if it should be $\frac{5}{4}$.[28] But this irregularity also allows Puccini to both accommodate the text—three quatrains of *settenari* and an odd *decasillabo tronco* at the end, all treated very loosely in a mostly syllabic, prose-like text setting (table 6.1 gives the text as it appears in the libretto side by side with Puccini's setting)—and characterize well the three comic, bumbling masks of the *commedia dell'arte*.

Pentatonicism's influence is also evident in Puccini's Chinese Exotic harmony. The bass line in the children's chorus, for example, oscillates between E♭, D♭, E♭, and B♭, a characteristic group (set class [025], with a whole step and a minor third) that in early twentieth-century music often stands in for a complete pentatonic collection (which, interestingly, in the case of this bass line could not be the same E♭-F-G-B♭-C collection that appears in the melody). This gives rise to a subtonic triad (♭VII) functioning as a substitute dominant in a progression I-♭VII-I (first three measures of example 6.1; Puccini might just as easily have written I-V-I or even the modal I-v-I) and lending an especially exotic flavor to an already distant, exotic text ("Là sui monti dell'Est / la cicogna canto"— "There on the mountains of the East the lark sang") sung by children and accompanied by offstage saxophones.

Puccini invokes the Primitive Exotic style mainly with open fifths, but also with modal melodies and orchestrations emphasizing percussion. In Liù's short interlude, "Nulla sono," in Act I (R8), a drone fifth, B♭-F—embellished toward the end with a colorful neighboring chord (see R8.8, 10, and 12) and with exotic, chromatic, descending parallel motion (R8.13–14) in the trumpets and celeste—supports an Aeolian melody in B♭. But this melody's expressive power is also somewhat more nuanced, in that segments of it (for example, R8.1–2 and 5–6) clearly exhibit a strong pentatonic flavor. This is a good example of a phenomenon I earlier called *stylistic integration*. Important in *Turandot*, this is when the principal style in a passage (here the Primitive Exotic) is inflected

TABLE 6.1. *Turandot* I, ministers' trio text

Libretto:				Puccini's setting:	
					Ministers *a tre*
1 Ministers	7	—Fermo! / —Che fai? / —T'arresta!		a	Fermo! Che fai? T'arresta!
2	7	—Chi sei? / —Che vuoi? / —Va' via!		a	Chi sei, che fai, che vuoi? Va' via!
3	7	—Pazzo! La porta è questa		a	va' la porta è questa
4	7	della gran beccheria.		a	della gran beccheria!
				a	Pazzo, va'via!
5	7	—Qui si strozza! / —Si sgozza!		a	Ping: Qui si strozza! Si sgozza!
6	7	—Si trivella! / —Si spella!		a	Pong and Pang: Si trivella! Si spella!
7	7	—Si uncina e scapitozza!		a	Ping: Si uncina e scapitozza!
					Pong and Pang: va'via!
8	7	—Si sega e si sbudella!		a	Ping: Si sega e si sbudella!
					Pong and Pang: va'via!

9	—Sollecito, precipite,
10	—al tuo paese torna!
11	—Ti cerca là uno stipite
12	—per romperti le corna!
13	—Ma qui no!
	—Ma qui no!
	—Ma qui no!

		Ping	Sollecito, precipite,
7	b	Pong and Pang	va' via!
7	a	a tre	al tuo paese torna!
7	b	Ping	in cerca d'uno stipite
			per romperti le corna!
7	a	Pong and Pang	Che vuoi? Chi sei? Va'via!
10	c	Ping	Ma qui no!
		a tre	Ma qui no!
		a tre	Pazzo, va'via! Va'via!

with style tokens borrowed from another, apparently incompatible type (Chinese Exotic) so as to produce a new, emergent meaning, or trope. I have borrowed the concept from Hatten's work, in which *thematic integration* describes the process of "bringing together previously opposed thematic material into a single context," whether for purposes of development, climax, or culminating closure.[29] It conveniently explains situations in which, for example, the melody seems to be in one style and the harmony in another, or the orchestration suggests a style different from that of the large-scale tonal structure. The phenomenon's presence stems directly from the plurality of the musical language, in that it seems only natural for Puccini to assimilate elements from various styles into a single location for expressive purposes. Here, Puccini's troping on Primitive and Chinese Exotic styles functions to characterize Liù as primitively innocent and pathetic, but it simultaneously underscores her heritage as a Chinese slave—which, in light of her intense attraction to her Tatar master Calaf (already evident, even this early in the opera), forms one of the central motivating dramatic conflicts for the work.

Similar Primitive Exotic features likewise appear in the executioner's chorus immediately following "Nulla sono," which comprises two alternating sections, one in $F_\sharp$ (R10.2) and another in $B_\flat$ (R11). Rhythmic ostinatos on open fifths sound throughout, either in $F_\sharp$ or $B_\flat$ and always in the timpani and low strings (sometimes in low winds as well). Almost the entire battery of percussion assumes an important role in what is surely one of Puccini's most colorful orchestrations: timpani, triangle, snare drum, gongs (tam tams), Chinese gongs, glockenspiel, xylophone, bass xylophone, celeste, and harp all are important. And the melodies are modal, or at least make reference to modality: the $F_\sharp$ sections suggest the Phrygian mode, while the $B_\flat$ music suggests the Lydian mode.

The Persian Exotic plays a smaller role in the work and appears only twice: once for the Prince of Persia's cortège in Act I, a scene that follows the Prince's unsuccessful attempt to solve Turandot's riddles and precedes his beheading (the latter is at R21: the hapless Prince is allowed almost no text at all, save for a final "Turandot!" just before the executioner's sword drops; the sword, apparently along with a rolling head—as in, notably, Strauss's *Salome*—are both gruesomely illustrated in the music at R27, some of Puccini's most vivid text painting), and again for the "temptations" scene in Act III (R8.5), just after Calaf's "Nessun dorma." The former is by far the longer and more involved example: this is a concerted funeral march in four strains for chorus and Calaf, with a short Chinese Exotic interlude (R23.5–13)—in which Turandot appears for the first time and gives the order (without speaking) to execute the Persian Prince—between strains three and four. Augmented seconds saturate the melody (see, for example, the constant reiteration of the G♭-A interval in the measures following R21) and even have some bearing on the harmony, in which the fully-diminished seventh chord acquires gradually more importance as the march develops (see, for example, the parallel diminished seventh chords in R22.4–5).

Ashbrook and Powers' *Turandot* analysis is compelling: they show the work taking a decidedly traditional turn in its organizational strategies and incorporating the *ottocento* principles of kinetic-static cycles combined into coherent set pieces. Clearly the opera does exhibit aspects of conventionality that suggest a regression in Puccini's approach coincident with the later years of his career. But I also find that the work's well-developed stylistic plurality makes it hard to hear it as a conventional number opera, and that the immediate experience of the piece seems to be controlled more by its rapidly changing stylistic language—which produces a series of formal episodes with their own structural and expressive functions—than by a series of kinetic or static movements.[30] This is true even though, of course, one's experience with the work's form may be dynamic and evolving, different from one hearing to the next. It should come as no surprise, then, that various commentators have understood the work differently. Some—Carner, Stoïanova, and Cassar among them—take its episodic qualities as primary, while others—Ashbrook and Powers—take the piece as fundamentally conventional, even while it exhibits a distinctive stylistic plurality. This suggests that the work's interest resides above all in the intersection of the two approaches: the most important aspect of the work's form may well be its multivalency. That is to say, similar to his strategy in *Angelica*, in *Turandot* Puccini superimposed multiple formal approaches—one old, one new; one conventional, one unconventional—on top of one another. Sometimes they coincide, but sometimes they conflict. Girardi has perhaps expressed this view best in suggesting that instead of adopting conventional forms wholesale or rejecting them completely, Puccini instead sought in *Turandot* to find a solution to the problem of integrating the two, a "connection between the 'apparatus' of *melodramma* and the more advanced European theater experiments of his time"; that he accomplished this in "the juxtaposition of episodes, each complete in itself"; and that we would do well to move beyond "the fictitious opposition between symphonic structure and 'number' opera," thereby initiating a "new and more fertile period of discussion of Puccini's last masterpiece."[31]

Such a view ultimately heightens the structural significance and expressive potential of both the conventional and unconventional approaches. It does not, however, diminish the importance of one while increasing the importance of the other. Interpreting structure in *Turandot* is not a zero-gum game, in other words: the stylistically articulated episodes expand the expressive potential of the embedded formal prototypes, while at the same time the embedded references to prototypical forms are critical for understanding the musical meaning of stylistic discontinuities. The newer formal strategies become in some sense a commentary on the conventions, in that they shed new light, from different angles, on the work's more traditional features; the presence of the older formal models compels us to interpret the work's less conventional aspects—the episodes and their large formal functions, their expressive and narrative meanings, and their implications for understanding dramaturgical proportion and pacing—in ways that might never have been possible, or necessary, had the conventions been completely abandoned.

The beginning of the first act is a good example of how contrasting styles articulate an episodic form. The Dissonant style opens, setting the ominous tone that prevails for much of the work. The mood changes markedly (R4) when the recognition scene brings a shift to the Romantic style; except for a brief Dissonant excursion (R6.12), Romantic music continues until the Primitive Exotic style first appears, at Liù's "Nulla sono" (R8). Some form of Exoticism then controls the next several minutes of the act: "Nulla sono" and the executioner's chorus (R9) use the Primitive Exotic style; the moonrise chorus (R17), children's chorus (R19), and Turandot's appearance (R23.5) use the Chinese Exotic; and the Prince of Persia's funeral march (R21) uses the Persian Exotic. This all suggests that the music through the interlude for Timur and Calaf

("Figlio! Che fai?," R25) comprises three large formal sections, each articulated by a shift from one style to another: one section, all Dissonant, lasts from the beginning through the recognition scene (R4); a second, mainly Romantic, extends from there to "Nulla sono" (R8); and a third, mainly Exotic, extends from "Nulla sono" through "Figlio! Che fai?"

Table 6.2 maps this process for the entire act. The episodes (fourth column) are demarcated at their beginnings and ends by audible shifts from one style to another; as mentioned, three occur before R25, beginning, respectively, at R0, R4, and R8. Eight more follow, for a total of eleven in the act. The table's fifth column shows smaller formal functions—smaller subdivisions within the larger episodes, or *subepisodes*, perhaps. Most of these are marked by some kind of change in one or more musical parameters—motive, key, rhythmic qualities, meter, orchestration, texture, verse structure, personnel—and sometimes, but not always, by a formally subordinate change of style. An important formal shift occurs at R9, for example—here to a chorus following Liù's short solo—but the style remains Exotic and thus this is music subsumed within the third episode. A similar shift occurs in the fourth episode, at R26.11, where a move to the Chinese Exotic style is so short it seems like an interruption more than a true shift to a new formal episode. The sixth column shows even lower-level formal subdivisions, often internal sections of individual movements, as in, for example, the A B A B A scheme in the executioner's chorus (R10.2) or the four strains in the funeral march for the Prince of Persia (R21)—both in the long third episode. Occasionally these subdivisions also involve momentary, subordinate shifts away from the prevailing style, as, for example, in episode 6 (on which more follows).

Some of the episodes are not as easily categorized as the table suggests: several exhibit stylistic integration, an expressive strategy discussed earlier. Episode 4, for example, is mainly Romantic, especially in its melody and orchestration (the latter exhibits the *violinata*), but incorporates Exotic and Dissonant elements as well (see example 6.2). The Exoticism is thematic, in a fleeting appearance of the "Mo-li-hua" theme in the horns near the episode's opening (R25.3); the Dissonance is harmonic, in a rising, sequential, gradually accelerating whole-tone progression (in which each statement lasts a fewer number of beats than the previous one) used to slowly drive up the musical tension. Again, as

TABLE 6.2. *Turandot,* formal organization in Act I

Large formal function	Set pieces and movements[1]		Episode		Small formal functions		Personnel		Keys
EXPOSITION	R0	A introduction	1 Dissonant		mandarin's decree		mandarin, chorus		f#, d
	R4	recognition	2 Romantic		recognition		chorus, Liù, Timur, Calaf		f#, g, ab
	6.12			Dissonant			chorus		a
	7	interlude					Timur: "Perduta la battaglia"		e, G
	8						Liù: "Nulla sono"		Bb
	9	chorus	3 Exotic Primitive (+ Chinese Exotic)		executioner's chorus	Introduction	chorus		
	10.2					A			F#
	11					B			Bb
	12.4					A			F#
	13.4					B			Bb
	14.4					A			F#
	17	B moonrise		Chinese	moonrise chorus				D, Eb

	Measure					Scene	Strain/Letter	Text	Key
EXPOSITION	19	chorus				children's chorus			$E\flat$
	21	cortège			Persian	Prince of Persia's cortège	strain 1		
	21.11						strain 2		
	22						strain 3		
	23.5				Chinese	Turandot's appearance			
	23.14				Persian		strain 4	Timur, Calaf: "Figlio! Che fai?"	
INTERLUDE (PRINCE OF PERSIA'S EXECUTION)	25	interlude		4	Romantic (+Dissonant, +Chinese Exotic)				
					Exotic	Chinese			
	26.11				Exotic	Chinese			
	26.13			5	Dissonant				
DEVELOPMENT (MINISTERS)	28	ministers	C	6	Exotic Chinese	ministers' trio	A	ministers: "Fermo! Che fai?"	$A\flat$
	30.2				Dissonant		B	+ Calaf	
	30.7				Romantic				
	31				Dissonant				
	31.5				Romantic				
	31.11				Dissonant				
	32				Exotic Chinese		A		
	33.20				Dissonant		B		

TABLE 6.2. *continued*

Large formal function		Set pieces and movements¹	Episode		Small formal functions		Personnel	Keys
			Exotic	Chinese		A		
	34							f♯
	35	interlude a	7	Dissonant	chorus of servants		Turandot's servants	
	36	interlude b	8	Exotic Chinese	ministers' trio (cont.)	A (cont.)	ministers	f♯ b
	38	spirits	9	Dissonant	chorus of spirits		spirits of dead suitors	a
DEVELOPMENT (MINISTERS)	39	conclusion	10	Dissonant	ministers' trio (cont.)	B	ministers	
	40.2			Romantic				A♭
	40.14			Dissonant				

CONCLUSION (STRIKING OF THE GONG)

41.4	D	transition	11	Romantic			
42		aria		(+ Chinese Exotic)	aria	Timur: "O figlio, vuoi dunque"[2]	e, e♭
43		aria			aria	Liù: "Signore, ascolta"	G♭
						Calaf: "Non piangere, Liù"	e♭
46		concertato			finale	Liù, Timur, Calaf, ministers, chorus	D
48				Exotic Chinese			e♭
48.5				Romantic			

Notes

1. After Ashbrook and Powers, *Puccini's "Turandot,"* 15–23 and 166.
2. Libretto: "Crudele! Vuoi dunque ch'io solo"; score: "O figlio, vuoi dunque ch'io solo."

in most other instances of the device, the integration here is expressive. The Romantic style is the natural choice for Timur, a minor character but one who easily invites sympathy as he struggles with a son's irrationality; the Chinese Exotic "Mo-li-hua" theme, associated with Turandot throughout the opera, here literally indicates in music the presence of Turandot's "scent" (Calaf: "Non senti? Il suo profumo è nell'aria! è nell'anima!"—"Don't you feel it? Her scent is in the air and in my soul!"); and the added Dissonance—gradually heightened by the increasingly chromatic harmony and the composed-out acceleration—destabilizes the structure and underscores the rising intensity of the disagreement between Timur and Calaf.[32]

Most of the rest of the act, like its opening, is clearly organized. At the end of episode 4, the music makes a sharp turn toward the Dissonant style (R26.13), at the moment of the Persian Prince's execution, and Dissonance governs the music—now in episode 5—until the three ministers make their sudden, unexpected entrance and the style veers sharply again, this time toward the Chinese Exotic. Episodes 7, 9, and 10 are all Dissonant. Episode 9, the chorus of spirits, is especially interesting in that a *violinata* orchestration suggests integrated Romanticism, perhaps a nod to the lost chivalry of Turandot's executed suitors; episode 10 has a short, contrasting Romantic interlude in the middle. Meanwhile, episode 8 is Chinese Exotic and episode 11 is a Romantic conclusion for the act, interrupted with a short, contrasting Chinese Exotic block just before the end, just after Calaf finally strikes the gong.

Only episode 6 is articulated somewhat differently. This is part of a larger (unconventionally organized) set piece, the first trio for the ministers, and rather than employing a single style for its duration as most other episodes do, it gathers several styles into a coherent formal pattern that unifies what otherwise sounds like a series of short, rapidly shifting, and rather incoherent subsections. The form here, as mentioned, is a simple, rondo-like A B A B A (compare the second Giorgetta-Luigi duet in *Il tabarro*), where the A sections are stylistically Exotic (Chinese) and the B sections are both Dissonant and Romantic. Episodes organized as such are less common in *Turandot,* and this one may seem rather unremarkable, given that the trio naturally forms an independent unit in the structure: a highly organized, extended confrontation between Calaf and the ministers, the latter seeing as their duty the protection of

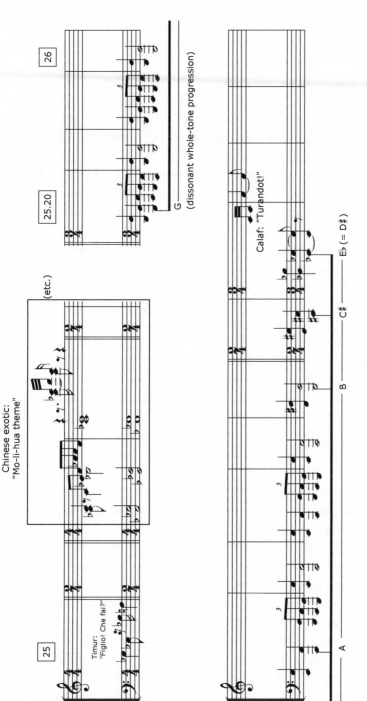

EXAMPLE 6.2. Sketch of *Turandot* I, R25. Integrated exoticism and dissonance in the Romantic episode 4.

naïve, would-be suitors from certain execution. But the opera's structure is so multivalent that stylistic and conventional formal boundaries do not always coincide; that multiple formal strategies *are* apparently in synch here creates a heightened sense of stability in the structure that contrasts markedly with both the instability of this music on a local level (especially in its metric irregularity, discussed earlier) and the tension in the plot—not only in the Calaf-ministers' confrontation but also in the ministers' rather morbid text (see table 6.1): "la porta è questa / della gran beccheria! . . . Qui si strozza! Si sgozza! . . . Si trivella! Si spella!" ("this is the gate to the great butcher shop . . . Here they strangle you, impale you, cut your throat, and skin you"). But the formal stability eventually breaks down: the chorus of servants and chorus of spirits (R35 and 38, respectively) each function to interrupt the trio and overpower any emerging sense of conventionality, such that toward its end the trio degenerates from a single, continuous set piece into a series of four independent episodes: the servants (episode 7, Dissonant), followed again by a resumption of the ministers' trio (episode 8), then the spirits (episode 9, Dissonant), followed again by more trio (episode 10)—as if the ministers simply must have the last word. At the largest level the effect here is identical to the filmic juxtapositions in *Gianni Schicchi*, although in *Schicchi* the effect is more immediately audible because the juxtapositions are in such close proximity. Here in *Turandot* the technique implies that the trio never really stops, but rather that we simply cut directly from one shot to another in order to show concurrent facets of the action on stage. Indeed, the notably abrupt onset of Timur's stylistic Romanticism in episode 11 makes it sound as if the ministers' trio never ends; this is as frustrating for a listener as are the ministers' repeated attempts to curb Calaf's irrational infatuation with Turandot. Episode 11, incidentally, also features another expressive example of stylistic integration: Liù's "Signore ascolta," like her earlier, "Nulla sono," integrates pentatonic melodic segments (and thus the Chinese Exotic style) into a stylistic canvas that remains fundamentally Romantic—again symbolizing a certain innocence and pathos in the Chinese slave girl.

This kind of formal multivalency—which here takes the form of a conflict, or better, a *dialogue*—between an episodic form and a more conventional form clearly has implications for how we understand expressive meaning in the opera and for how we experience the work as a piece of theater. In this spirit, table 6.2 includes a summary (in the third column) of the work's conventional formal features as explained by Ashbrook and Powers. The column shows the formal units articulated by alternating blocks of kinesis and stasis, usually grouped into four-movement set pieces, each with two kinetic-static pairs. These pairs are analogous to the conventional double musical-dramatic cycles of the *solita forma,* even if they only rarely make explicit reference to the conventional internal movements of the Italian melodrama (the *scena, tempo d'attacco, adagio, tempo di mezzo,* and *cabaletta*).[33]

The conventional units and the episodic units sometimes correlate closely and sometimes do not. The interest, again, is in the interaction of the two strategies. In Act I, for example, the closest correspondence is at the end, where Ashbrook and Powers' last number (D, the finale) corresponds exactly with my last episode (11). This is not surprising: Puccini's original conception of the whole opera was in two acts, not three, and Act I comprised everything we now know as Act I plus the second scene of Act II, minus the Act I concertato finale ("Ah! Per l'ultima volta!") and Turandot's "In questa Reggia" (and its concluding "Gli enigma sono tre" *a due*). The Act I arias for Liù and Calaf ("Signore, ascolta" and "Non piangere, Liù") were also in reverse order. He later reversed the order of the Act I arias and added the concertato, and thus there is evidence that he conceived of the first act's entire closing segment (beginning at the transitional music for Timur, "O figlio, vuoi dunque") as a single musical-formal unit.[34] This is the only such one-to-one correspondence of episodes and numbers in the act, and indeed the only one in the entire opera; in all other instances, episodes outnumber conventional set pieces. The beginning of number C, for example, aligns with the beginning of episode 6, but, as noted earlier, the piece comprises all of episode 6 plus four more complete episodes (7–10). The first two numbers (A, the sunset, and B, the moonrise) also comprise, together, five episodes (1–5). Some episodes correspond, predictably, to the smaller, movement-level divisions in the conventional form: the onset of the second movement ("recognition") in number A, for example, coincides with the shift to episode 2 (at R4), and the last movement in number B (the interlude before the ministers' trio) coincides with the start of episode 4 (at R25). But this is certainly not the rule, and in fact the tendency is for episodes and numbers to be out of phase. Number B begins right in the middle of my episode 3, for example; movement-level divisions are present at R7, 9, 19, and 21, none of which correlate with an episodic boundary; and the beginnings of episodes 3 and 5 align with no boundary on any level of the conventional form.

Broadly speaking, the shifting styles move more quickly than the slower-churning *solita forma* units; this means the music seems to have a larger number of higher-level formal divisions, and that these divisions occur more frequently, than a purely conventional reading of the structure might suggest. Episodes 6–10, for example, comprise a segment of the act unified dramatically and even unified *formally*—in the sense of there being a coherent formal patterning at work—but not unified *musically,* in terms of its musical language or musical style. Episode 2 exhibits similar qualities: this is strongly marked by a shift to purely Romantic music right after an extended section of the rather extreme (for Puccini) dissonance and tonal ambiguity in the mandarin's decree, and it marks the first appearance in the opera of the Romantic style (indeed, the *Turandot* opening famously defies the expectations of any listener anticipating the "normal" Puccinian lyric style or even a normal Puccinian orchestral opening). This episode makes the appearance of the Romantic style at R4 all the more striking and, indeed, satisfying, and we hear the change as something more structurally significant—the moment is more strongly initiatory—than what is implied by the lower-level shift of movements within a larger, unified set piece. And episode 4 is conspicuous for similar reasons: the shift here back to the Romantic style following a long section of Exotic music makes this interlude for Timur and Calaf striking and creates a strong formal articulation—one accentuated by the fact that this music sounds similar to the earlier interlude for Timur, at "Perduta la battaglia," R7 in episode 2).

In this regard, consider also the beginnings of episodes 3 and 5: neither correlates with a formal division on any level in the conventional reading. The nearest conventional boundaries around the beginning of episode 3 are at Timur's "Perduta la battaglia" (R7, the third movement in number A and as such a kinetic interlude between two static choral movements) and at the executioner's chorus (R9, the final choral movement). But the styles suggest something different, specifically that the principal division here is at R8. Timur's "Perduta" (R7) connects backward to the recognition scene (R4) because its style is the same—both are Romantic—while Liù's music looks forward for the same reason: both "Nulla sono" (R8) and the executioner's chorus (R9) are Primitive Exotic. Thus the stylistic shift at R8 is a conspicuous formal joint; this is, indeed, the first time in the work we hear the Exotic style, and this is the opening block of a long stretch of the act devoted exclusively to that style.

Such a view of the work, furthermore, has important implications for how to account for the experience it yields in the theater. Perhaps the effect of the formal multivalency is clearest in this respect: the misalignment of episodes and conventional numbers broadens the distance between the audience and the events on stage; it forces listeners to confront not only a musical structure exposed by conspicuously shifting styles but also clear, audible disagreements between the stylistic blocks and the conventional *solita forma* prototypes. This produces an effect similar to that of the generic juxtaposition fundamental to the aesthetics of the *Trittico*: some of the listener's intellectual energy must be expended to deal with the technical means with which the piece is constructed, leaving less attention for plot, dramatic development, and characters—the latter traditionally seen as essential elements in the operatic experience.[35]

This effect and its expressivity obviously depend in part on both a listener's ability to *recognize* in the piece the presence at least of analogues to conventional forms, and that same listener's *expectations* that such forms may play an important role in the work. In order for a stylistic shift, for example, to be perceived as formally out of place, one must first be aware that there may be other kinds of formal schemata operating beneath the surface, and that these schemata have their own set of implications for how the musical setting should be shaped. We hear novelty when the setting does not proceed as expected—when a major shift of style, perhaps, occurs where a conventional schema implies there should be no formal boundary. As noted in chapter 3, however, this dependency is not absolute: the effect may be stronger for listeners who notice the underlying conventionality of the forms, but it will not be altogether absent for those who either have no knowledge or pay no attention to this facet of the piece. And, again, explaining how a contemporary audience may have heard this music—and what that audience's expectations may have been—is very different from explaining ways of hearing this music today, given everything we know not only about Puccini but also about Verdi, Donizetti, Bellini, and Rossini. Hearing the formal conventionality in

Turandot may be easier today, in fact, than it was in Puccini's day; in any case, listeners familiar with the earlier repertoire will hear Puccini very differently from those not fluent with it.

Not only the misalignments but also the *alignments* among various formal strategies can enhance the theatrical effect. This may seem counterintuitive, but consider that those moments in which the organizational strategies move into agreement are *necessary* in order to make the other moments—in which the strategies conflict—stand out as unusual. That is to say, there are enough instances in *Turandot* of numbers and episodes being out of synch that we cannot help but notice those moments when a sharp stylistic discontinuity makes immediate sense because it supports a conventional formal juncture. The stylistic shifts we would not expect, and those not explainable by invoking traditional explanations related to plot or text setting, make those we *would* expect—those in agreement with broader, more traditional musical-dramatic outlines—all the more interesting and arresting. In either case, the music thrusts *structure* to the foreground of one's experience.

All this in turn has some bearing on the elusive subject of the opera's *pace.* One way of describing pace is to measure the time it takes (either in terms of clock time or in terms of numbers of some constant metric unit—beats, for example) for various segments of music and drama to unfold, then study the proportional relationships among these—as I have done elsewhere in print and here in chapter 3 with *Il tabarro,* and as Hepokoski has done in his study of *Suor Angelica.*[36] But another way is to observe the relative, internal pacing of the work's structural rhythms, without regard to absolute time. Musical change in any dimension suggests *progress* or *motion;* as the frequency of such changes increases or decreases, the perception is of a work's motion through time accelerating or decelerating. Just as a faster harmonic rhythm leads in traditional tonal music to a sense of an increase in rate of motion, more frequent structural junctures—frequent shifts in style (rapid *stylistic rhythm,* so to speak), or even a larger number of junctures in one formal dimension relative to the number in another—likewise can cause the music to sound as if it moves more quickly; a prolonged period with no structural demarcations, on the other hand, can slow the work's pace and make it seem more static.

In these terms, Act I is brilliantly paced: it moves more slowly at the beginning, accelerates somewhat at episode 4, accelerates further at episode 7, then decelerates toward the end of the act. The first three stylistic episodes are relatively long, especially with respect to the length of their underlying conventional units: there are more junctures before R25, in other words, in the conventional numbers than in the episodes. But beginning with episode 4 the episodes become noticeably shorter, so that the pace seems to accelerate; at R28 it broadens again, now because of the perceived formal unity in the ministers' trio. Indeed, in some sense the motion seems to stop when the ministers enter, a sensation wholly consistent with the effect of a surprise at the moment of their entrance followed by an extended period in which we can step back from the drama and absorb aspects of their characterization (not to mention, again, their roles *outside* the work's normative dramatic space, as *commedia dell'arte* imports). But as the trio's unity gradually dissolves, the pace gradually quickens. Episodes 7–10 occur in rapid succession—these are relatively short compared to the episodes that precede them—and this creates a noticeable acceleration that subsides only at Timur's "O figlio, vuoi dunque" (R41.4), the opening movement in the final number. Here we have a noticeable deceleration caused by the lack of major stylistic shifts in a relatively long segment of the act, and by the one-to-one correspondence of episode 11 and number D.

The act thus has a clear arch shape—slower in the beginning, faster in the middle, and slower again at the end—that very effectively creates a satisfying sense of proportionality and logic in the structure. It also encourages listeners to linger in the diegetic, discursively distant arias at the end, Liù's "Signore, ascolta" and Calaf's "Non piangere, Liù"—the most fully Romantic movements in the entire act (Calaf's aria especially; Liù's integrates elements borrowed from the Exotic style, in particular in its melodic pentatonicism). Global and local elements are thus consistent and support one another: the Romantic style has as one of its tendencies the undermining of forward motion (using, for example, non-functional dominants, as in "Non piangere, Liù"; see chapter 2), and here the structure supports this with a deceleration in the act's pace. This creates the perception that the structure allows the performers space to sing the arias and listeners space to hear them—for listeners to devote all their attention, that is, to the emergent voice-objects. In the end, disunity in the structure becomes unity in the theatrical effect: Puccini *uses* style and structure, in all their various forms, to skillfully manipulate his audience and deftly control the theatrical experience.

The structure also supports the larger dramaturgical organization. Act I unfolds in three stages: exposition, development, and conclusion, with an interlude between the exposition and development (refer to table 6.1). We might also say the act as a whole is goal-oriented, with action directed toward Calaf and his striking the gong to indicate a commitment to pursuing Turandot—the premise that sets the rest of the plot in motion. The first three episodes are expository in that they introduce all the characters and the plot's basic elements: the mandarin's decree concisely summarizes the state of affairs in Peking; the recognition scene, Timur's "Perduta la battaglia," and Liù's "Nulla sono" together introduce Calaf, Timur, Liù, and their relationships; and the executioner's chorus, moonrise chorus, children's chorus, and funeral march together render a rather bleak picture of Turandot, a failed suitor, and Turandot ordering an execution. These three episodes together function as a typically Puccinian introduction that establishes the opera's *tinta:* death, struggle, and a sense of hopelessness prevail, and in this way the work sets a tone strikingly similar to that of all three panels of *Il trittico.* Episodes 6–10 are developmental in that every event, from the ministers' warnings to the handmaidens' admonishments to the spirits' appearance, is an effort to dissuade Calaf from striking the gong, and episode 11 is conclusive: Timur and Liù issue final pleas ("O figlio, vuoi dunque" and "Signore, ascolta"), while Calaf resolutely denies them both ("Non piangere, Liù") and strikes the gong anyway.

Note in this regard an interesting musical indication of Calaf's decision to turn away from Timur and Liù at the end of the act. In the course of his revisions, Puccini transposed all the music from the middle of Timur's "O figlio, vuoi dunque" to the end of the act down a half step, thereby introducing an abrupt E–E♭ tonal shift in the middle of Timur's solo (see R41.7) and moving what was once a sequence of movements in G major ("Signore ascolta," R42) and E minor ("Non piangere, Liù," R43, and the final concertato, R46, with its reprise of the "Mo-li-hua" theme in E♭) to G♭ major and E♭ minor (with a "Mo-li-hua" reprise in D). Whether Puccini meant it or not, this musically reorients Calaf away from his father and his familial commitments—associated, as Powers has shown, throughout the act with E minor and related keys—and toward Turandot—associated throughout the opera with the key of E♭.[37]

The expository quality of episodes 1–3 is musical as well as dramatic: these episodes survey the work's complete stylistic vocabulary, introducing, in order, Dissonant (episode 1), Romantic (episode 2), and all three varieties of Exotic (episode 3) styles. Likewise, episodes 6–10 are also musically developmental, especially episode 6, which (unlike all the episodes before and after it) uses all three styles instead of just one. And even the goal-directedness is present in the music: at episodes 4 and 11, the music reverts to the Romantic style after having been away from it for some time, suggesting this style functions as a musical point of arrival correlating with Calaf himself—to whom, after all, the Romantic style *belongs*, in the sense that Calaf is the *primo tenore* and, as such, the character who uses the style most clearly and most often—as we would expect. Stylistically, episode 4 (Timur's "Figlio! Che fai?") sounds in many ways like a relief, palpable for listeners immersed for so long in the dissonance and exoticism so prevalent in the act's exposition. The style is conspicuous enough here that it sounds at first like episode 4 could be the Romantic goal toward which the act is directed and indeed that the act's conclusion may be near, but its near-immediate undercutting by a rapid succession of Exotic and Dissonant blocks undermines this impression and forces the act into continued development—as when the ministers intrude on the scene shortly afterward to try to divert Calaf. Only the return to Romanticism at episode 11 brings true closure: Liù and Timur each get fully Romantic, solo arias, and a large, concerted, Romantic finale concludes the act.

The first four episodes plus the last thus articulate the act's essential shape: motion toward the Romantic style, interrupted and then resumed later. The middle episodes (6–10, plus episode 5, which acts as a transitional, destabilizing block) interrupt the forward progress, lying in some sense outside the main dramatic scheme. Again, this is consistent with the dramatic function of the ministers, who, as noted, intrude abruptly and mysteriously into the story a little over halfway through the act (in an entrance described thus: "E si slancia contro il gong. Ma d'improvviso fra lui e il disco luminoso tre misteriose figure si frappongono"—"And he [Calaf] hurls himself toward the gong. But suddenly three mysterious figures insert themselves between him and the luminous disk"). This underscores the aesthetic principle mentioned earlier: the ministers are imports, literally foreign to the story, never fully integrated into the drama beyond adopting Chinese dress, mannerisms, and government appointments. They almost never directly effect plot development, never communicate directly with anyone other than themselves or Calaf, never take a personal interest in Calaf and his fate the way Timur and Liù do (they see Calaf only as yet another example of a irrational foreigner foolish enough to challenge Turandot), and almost always speak with a tone of mockery or irony that alienates them even further from the main action on stage. Indeed, Puccini himself wanted it this way, once suggesting to Adami "Don't overdo it with the Venetian masks—those have to be the *clowns* and philosophers who here and there toss in a *lazzo* or a point of view (well selected—even the moment), but they shouldn't be annoying or petulant" (emphasis original).[38]

Acts II and III proceed according to similar organizational strategies, which I will survey here in less detail. Act II (see table 6.3) comprises a dozen episodes and a half dozen conventional numbers, all in two scenes: another trio for the ministers (episodes 1 and 2), this time a *fuori-scena* and much longer than their Act I trio; and a ceremonial scene (episodes 3–12) that includes a court processional, Turandot's aria, the pivotal riddle scene, and a conclusion in which Calaf turns the tables and proposes his own riddle.

In the opening trio, the Dissonant episode 1 is introductory, while episode 2 is the longest in the opera but unified nevertheless by a consistent musical language: the whole episode is Exotic, mostly Chinese but also Primitive, where every instance of the latter recalls the Act I executioner's chorus. Only the short Romantic excursion at "L'anno del topo" (R6), on a theme borrowed from the Act I trio, provides relief, even though "Ho una casa nell'Honan" (R9) also introduces some change. Here, short Chinese Exotic blocks move through a sequence of abrupt, half-step tonal shifts from A to A♭ (R9.5; see example 6.3) and back to A (R9.8), and the oscillating, chromatically related sonorities (a D-major triad and a dominant seventh on E at R9, for example) likewise integrate a stylistic Dissonance that both increases the urgency of the ministers' longings and foreshadows a similar oscillation in the opening lyric movement of "In questa Reggia" (see also example 2.2).

TABLE 6.3. *Turandot*, formal organization in Act II

Large formal function	Set pieces and movements[1]		Episode			Small formal functions	Personnel		Keys
	A	R0				ministers's trio	ministers:	"Olà Pang! Olà Pong!"	
	scena								
	tempo d'attacco	1	1 Dissonant					"Io preparo le nozze!"	d
		6	2 Exotic	Chinese		(=Act I, R30.7)		"L'anno del Topo"	B♭
		6.15		Romantic				"al tredicesimo con quello"[2]	a
		7.5			Primitive	(executioner's chorus)			
	andantino	9		Chinese (+ Dissonant)				"Ho una casa nell'Honan"	D, A, A♭
		10.12							
		11.2							
		12.2							
	tempo di mezzo	13						"O mondo, o mondo"	B♭
		14						"Vi ricordate il principe"[3]	e♭

MINISTERS' TRIO

TABLE 6.3. *continued*

Large formal function	Set pieces and movements[1]		Episode		Small formal functions	Personnel		Keys
MINISTERS' TRIO	15.6			Primitive	(executioner's chorus)			
	16			Chinese				
	17.4			Primitive	(executioner's chorus)			
	18			Chinese			"Addio, amore!... Addio, razza!"	Eb
	21.3	*stretta*					"Non v'è in Cina"	G
CEREMONIAL SCENE	25	B transition	3 Dissonant			(exit ministers)		Ab
	28.9	processional	4 Exotic	Chinese	mandarins' march / sages' march	orchestra, chorus		Gb, A
	29.8				ministers' march			c#
	30			Dissonant				
	30.9				imperial hymn			Bb, B, C, Db
	32.9							Ab

CEREMONIAL SCENE

Measure		Section	No.	Style	Subsection	Characters	Text	Key
34	C	emperor						C
35		conclusion				Calaf, Emperor: "Un giuramento atroce"		B♭
39.2	D	mandarin	5	Dissonant	mandarin's decree	mandarin		d
40.4		chorus	6	Exotic · Chinese	children's chorus			D
42		aria	7	Romantic	scene and aria			D
43					*recitative*		Turandot: "In questa Reggia"	
44.3				(+ Dissonant)	aria		"Principessa Lo-u-ling"	f♯, d
47					coda	+ Calaf, *a2*:	"Mai nessun m'avrà"	G♭
47.15							"Gli enigmi sono tre"	
50	E	first riddle	8	Dissonant	riddle scene · riddle 1	Turandot, Calaf, chorus		d
54.3		second riddle			riddle 2			
59.2		third riddle			riddle 3			e♭

TABLE 6.3. *continued*

Large formal function	Set pieces and movements¹		Episode		Small formal functions	Personnel		Keys
	62.7		9	Exotic / Chinese		chorus		E♭
	63	coda		Romantic (+ Dissonant)		Turandot:	"Figlio del cielo!"	
	65.4			Exotic / Chinese		chorus		A♭, C
	65.9	F riddle	10	Dissonant	Calaf's riddle	Calaf:	"Tre enigmi mai proposto!"	d
CONCLUSION	65.15		11	Romantic			"Il mio nome non sai!"	D♭
	67.3	reaction	12	Exotic / Chinese		Emperor, chorus		
	68.3	conclusion						B♭

Notes

1. After Ashbrook and Powers, *Puccini's "Turandot,"* 24–31 and 166–67.
2. Libretto: "al tredicesimo / con questa che va sotto"; score: "al tredicesimo / con quello che va sotto."
3. Libretto: "Non ricordate il principe"; score: "Vi ricordate il principe."

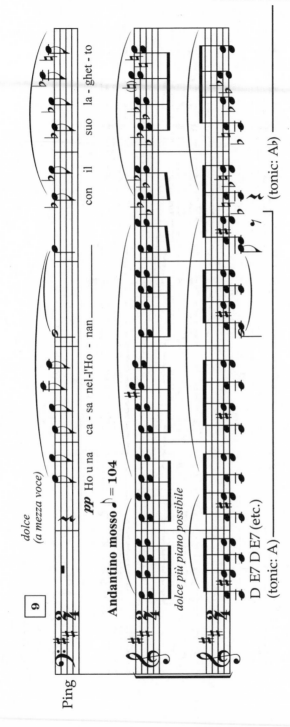

EXAMPLE 6.3. *Turandot* II, "Ho una casa nell'Honan."

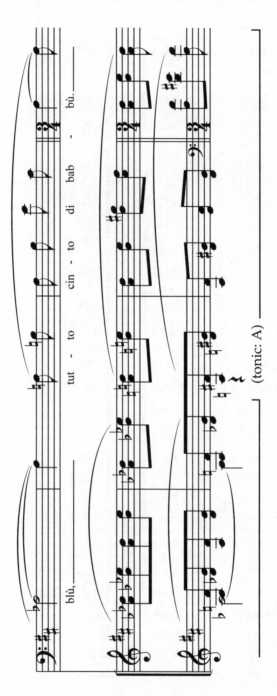

EXAMPLE 6.3. *continued*

Scene 2 begins with the grand processional, which follows a short, Dissonant, transitional episode (episode 3, at R25) in which the ministers—still in their *fuori-scena*—are interrupted by distant music for the forthcoming processional, very effectively introduced in off-stage trumpets, trombones, and snare drum so as to overlap (as indicated with the dotted lines in table 6.3) with the ministers' own Chinese Exotic music. The musical overlap is an example of the cinematographic technique known as the dissolve, which here implies not only the temporal *meanwhile* and the change of location that normally correlate with this technique, but also implies—now structurally speaking—that episode 3 has a double formal function, as both the end of the trio and the beginning of the ceremonial scene.[39] The processional comprises one large episode, mainly Chinese Exotic, opening with marches for the mandarins, sages, and ministers (the latter is Dissonant, using the same music heard shortly before, in episode 3) as well as the imperial hymn, the tune of which also comes from the Fassini music box (complete with a coda to which Puccini set the *endecasillabo* "Diecimila anni al nostro Imperatore"—"Ten thousand years to our emperor"—at R32.9). Episodes 5 and 6 follow and link the processional to Turandot's scene and aria, all of which comprises episode 7; note the abrupt appearance of the Dissonant-style music at R40.4, in another very sharp stylistic juxtaposition, the discontinuity of which, again, is characteristic of this opera's overall sound. The riddle scene follows in episodes 8 (Dissonant-style music for the riddles) and 9. The latter is a highly variegated episode comprising Chinese Exotic music for the crowd, elated in the wake of Calaf's shocking success with Turandot's riddles. This episode is followed by an extended interruption ("Figlio del cielo!" for Turandot, who now wants to renege; see example 6.4), Romantic in its melody and orchestration but with integrated Dissonance in its tonal structure, very similar to the "Figlio, che fai" music from Act I. The episode concludes with a short return, at R65.4, to more Chinese Exotic music for the chorus.[40] Episodes 10, 11, and 12 conclude the act with motion through all three styles in rapid succession, for, respectively, Calaf's riddle (Dissonant—note another especially abrupt juxtaposition with which this episode begins—at "Tre enigma hai proposto," R65.9, then a Romantic turn—with nothing less than the famous "Nessun dorma" theme—at "Il mio nome non sai," R65.15) and the reaction of the Emperor and the crowd (Chinese Exotic).

The rapidly changing styles make the end of this act some of the most disjunct music in the entire opera.

As in Act I, the intersection of episodes with conventional organizational features sheds light on the second act's structural rhythm and pace. The stylistic plurality again makes the music sound more discontinuous than the organization of underlying set pieces might suggest: Act II has twice as many episodes as conventional numbers, where my view of the latter again follows that of Ashbrook and Powers (third column in table 6.3). Seven episodes begin in the middle of a number; the beginnings of two of these (9 and 11) do not coincide with a conventional formal articulation at any level, even while these same two articulate important junctures in the highly discontinuous music toward the end of the act. On the other hand, the episodic and conventional forms occasionally coincide in interesting ways: in the opening number Puccini differentiates the *scena* from the four core *solita forma* movements by using one style for the *scena* (Dissonant—episode 1) and another for the rest of the piece (Exotic—episode 2; note here that the *stretta* replaces the *cabaletta* in an ensemble movement and serves the same closing, conclusive formal function). This suggests Puccini may have tended in *Turandot* toward delineating the conventional formal prototypes *stylistically* in addition to textually and musically. This is an important change from his strategy in *Il trittico*, in which the clearest conventional formal references were always stylistically Romantic, and it has the effect of musically unifying an underlying reference to a conventional organizational procedure. Even the onset of the closing lyric movement, a very strong (conventional) formal articulation, triggers no concomitant change of style.

The most interesting feature of Act II may be its pacing. The first four episodes are exceptional in this regard: they comprise about nineteen and a half minutes of music—close to half the act[41]—with very little significant shift in stylistic language. As mentioned, the only real contrast in episode 2 is in the Romantic "L'anno del topo"; episode 3 provides a brief Dissonant transition (the fact that this follows directly from, and contrasts sharply with, the *stretta* in the ministers' trio is perhaps supporting evidence that Puccini may well have been thinking of the whole trio in terms of a prototypical *solita forma* model); and episode 4 returns immediately to the Chinese Exotic and remains there

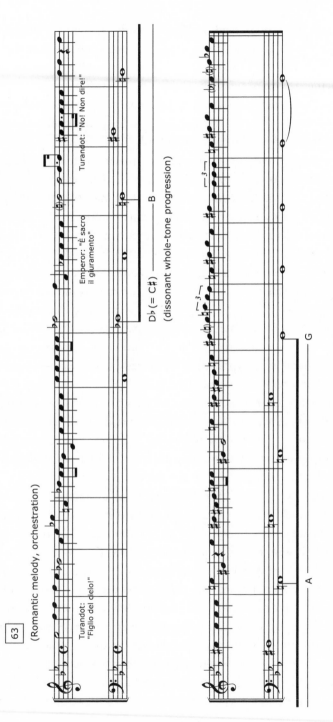

EXAMPLE 6.4. Sketch of *Turandot* II, R63. Integrated dissonance in the Romantic episode 9, at "Figlio del cielo."

throughout the processional (except in the short, eight-bar Dissonant march for the three ministers at R30). Even the Primitive contrasts in episode 2 are entirely subordinate: each is short, and each, rather than introducing new music, simply recalls the executioner's chorus from the first act. As such the second episode comprises by far the longest, most stylistically unified stretch of music in the entire opera. No other episode comes close: even the Exotic third episode in Act I, which lasts over thirteen minutes, contains more significant, extended blocks in one of the contrasting Exotic subtypes, either Chinese or Primitive. This episode's length accounts in large part for the sense that the pace of the second act's first half is very slow—much slower, in fact, than that of the rest of the work—and, in turn, it supports this music's large-scale dramatic function. Like the Act I ministers' trio before it, the Act II trio lies outside the opera's main dramatic trajectory. Likewise, the ministers, *commedia* imports that they are, lie outside the normative dramatic space, and their trio—as a *fuori-scena* (i.e., in front of the curtain)—lies outside, literally, the normative physical space on the stage. None of it develops the plot, in the sense that none of it adds information about the main characters beyond what we already know. Rather, both the trio and the processional essentially do nothing but make us *wait* for the ministers' strange series of laments, fantasies, and reveries to finish and for the court to assemble. None of this is surprising in the context of the scene's genesis: the *fuori-scena* was a late addition to the opera, added when the original long Act I was divided in two, which perhaps explains why it never fully integrates with the rest of the work.[42]

With the exception of the riddle scene (itself an extended Dissonant episode in which the pace also slackens) the rest of the act moves rapidly—at a pace consistent with that of the whole opera more generally, even if now it sounds *more* rapid because of its stark contrast with the sluggish trio-processional sequence. Episodes 5, 6, and the onset of 7 produce a marked acceleration, with three stylistic juxtapositions in quick succession, but the pace relaxes for Turandot's fully Romantic "In questa Reggia." This is Turandot's *aria di sortita*—her "entrance aria"—which, as many have noted, occurs no less than halfway through the second act of a three-act opera. But despite its decidedly unconventional location, the piece is otherwise conventional, and shares features with other of Puccini's entrance arias, as Greenwald has noted. Its semi-biographical tale within a tale (the Princess Lo-u-Ling narrative, discussed earlier), for example, makes it similar to the entrances of Mimi and Rodolfo in *La bohème* and Rinnucio in *Gianni Schicchi*. In fact, as indicated in table 6.3 and consistent with Greenwald's observation that this is indeed one of the most formal and conventional entrance arias in Puccini's entire oeuvre, the piece is a mostly traditional scene and aria.[43] Together with its preparatory episodes 5 and 6, "In questa Reggia" was also added by Puccini after he split the original long Act I. The fact that this music was not part of his original conception still shows, perhaps, in that the quickened pace here at episode 5 seems surprising and somewhat out of place—even if it does provide relief from the sluggishness of everything up to this point (and, incidentally, without these three episodes—5, 6, and 7—the act would comprise a sequence of trio-processional-riddle scene, which, because all three of these are paced so slowly, may have resulted in a seemingly interminable second act). The act also ends rather abruptly, which can be unsettling; at the very least it heightens noticeably the anticipation for the last act and the dénouement.

My comments regarding Act III will be limited to the music Puccini wrote himself. As is well known, he completed everything through the death of Liù and the final cortège, through R35, before his untimely death from throat cancer complications in November 1924. Upon Puccini's death, Casa Ricordi directors Clausetti and Renzo Valcarenghi,[44] together with Arturo Toscanini—all knowing the opera was nearly complete—commissioned the young Neapolitan composer Franco Alfano to study Puccini's unfinished materials and write a suitable finale. Alfano, in fact, produced not one, but two endings. Toscanini deemed the first, now known as "Alfano I," too lengthy and ordered Alfano to shorten it; the second (now "Alfano II") premiered, with the rest of *Turandot*, on or shortly after April 26, 1926, at La Scala in Milan (by most accounts Toscanini stopped the La Scala premiere, in dramatic fashion, at Liù's death, withholding a performance of Alfano's music; his motivations for doing so remain unclear).[45] Alfano II remains the most commonly performed ending, although there have recently been signs that this may change: American composer Janet Maguire has written an ending that she describes as based entirely on Puccini's own sketches, and Casa Ricordi recently commissioned a new finale, this time from Luciano Berio.

Berio's ending in particular has received an ever-increasing amount of attention, both among scholars and in opera houses, since its publication in 2001 and its premiere in Las Palmas (Gran Canaria, Spain) in January 2002.[46]

Puccini's failure to complete the piece has garnered a good deal of attention in print in the years since his death, and the issue of *why* he never finished the opera has been a source of fascination for many writers. Some have not been willing to accept the simplest explanation, that his health prevented it, and have attributed it instead to a failure of creativity or something fundamentally lacking in his psyche. Carner famously assessed that "Puccini's failure to complete this particular love duet [the final Turandot-Calaf confrontation] cannot be merely ascribed to the onset of his tragic illness; it seems to have sprung from something deep down in himself, from obstacles in his unconscious mind." Budden, in a more damning critique, opined that "Puccini's limitations as an artist were, in a sense, spiritual. . . . The wider issues, whether of politics or religion, lay outside his grasp. . . . Inevitably, when an element of transfiguration was required he was found wanting: a defect that prevented him from finishing *Suor Angelica* satisfactorily and *Turandot* at all."[47] Perhaps Puccini's own correspondence itself invites speculation on this subject: he acknowledged early in the work's genesis that a Calaf-Turandot confrontation in a duet late in the last act would be the crux of the dénouement, but that it was causing him some trouble: late in 1921, unsatisfied with one of Adami's early attempts at the piece, he wrote, "I think the real heart of the matter may be the [final] duet. And this duet as it is doesn't seem to me what's needed here."[48]

Others have suggested the real problem was in the work's dramaturgy, including Ashbrook and Powers, who place the blame—correctly, it seems—on decisions made by Puccini and his librettists rather than on any inherent psychological flaw in Puccini himself (although for a more detailed consideration of this problem, see the epilogue): "Their task [writing the last act] was not made any easier by the intensification of the Princess's cruelty they had themselves added in the cortège for the Prince of Persia and the grisly details of his decapitation, further highlighted by contrasts with the sympathetic and pathetic ingénue they had developed during the creation of Liù. We can only suppose that . . . the music would have made it all clear, even though in Puccini's case it was his own music . . . that had raised the greatest obstacles."[49] Carner has elsewhere touched on the same issue: "Had [Liù's] suicide actually been used to bring about Turandot's transformation, Puccini would not have been guilty of a serious flaw [making the love scene that follows the suicide seem superimposed] in the dramaturgy of the third act."[50]

In this context, Act III's most interesting feature is the way its formal organization contributes to the debate surrounding Puccini's inability to complete the piece. Specifically, the act shares several structural features with Act I and, most importantly perhaps, like Act I it implies structural completion—although here the completion occurs at the end of Liù's cortege, which, of course, is not and cannot be the end of the act. The act is in three large parts (see table 6.4), all of which are articulated, as in Act I, both musically-stylistically and dramatically. First is an exposition, focused on Calaf's (seemingly foolish) resolve to win over a resolute Turandot, in which all three styles appear in the same order (Dissonant, Romantic, Exotic) as in the exposition of Act I. Next is a development, focused on Liù and the attempts made to extract from her the name of the as-yet-unknown Calaf, in which—again as in Act I—all styles participate and the stylistic rhythm accelerates. Finally is a conclusion, the stylistically Romantic (as in Act I) suicide and cortège sequence.

The exposition comprises the first three episodes; episode 2 includes two alternating subsections, the pentatonicism of which weakly suggests the Chinese Exotic style, and episode 3 is wholly exotic—Persian at first, then Chinese. Calaf's frantic protest at the end of the ministers' temptations (of which they offer three: women, money, and power), "Alba, vieni! Quest'incubo dissolvi!" (Dawn, come! Dissolve this nightmare!"), to the stage direction "con crescente minacciosa disperazione" ("with growing, threatening desperation"), triggers the onset of the development. This is marked with a simultaneous musical turn toward the Romantic style (R12.6), now undercut and distorted with integrated Dissonance—specifically in the embedded whole-tone segment ($E\flat$-F-G-A-B) in the "Straniero, tu non sai" melody. Here the Romanticism sounds more plaintive than heroic, and as such entirely suitable for what becomes one of the ministers' last attempts to dissuade Calaf (an endeavor with which almost all their time has been occupied since the opera's first act). This kind of stylistic undercutting indeed characterizes more generally the rest of Puccini's music for the last act, in which we find the episodes

TABLE 6.4. *Turandot*, formal organization in Act III (through the end of Liù's cortège)

Large formal function		Set pieces and movements[1]	Episode	Small formal functions	Personnel	Keys
EXPOSITION: CALAF'S RESOLVE	R0	A introduction	1 Dissonant	heralds	heralds: "Così comanda Turandot"; chorus	f♯, A
	4	romanza	2 Romantic	romanza	Calaf: "Nessun dorma"	G, D
	6.5	transition		coda	+ ministers	
	7		Exotic Chinese			
	7.16		Exotic Chinese			
DEVELOPMENT; CONFRONTATION AND TORTURE	8.5	B temptation 1	3 Exotic Persian	temptations: women		g, d
	9	temptations 2, 3	Exotic Chinese	riches		
	11.9			glory		
	12.6		4 Romantic (+ Dissonant)		ministers: "Straniero, tu non sai"; chorus	G, D♭
	14		5 Exotic Chinese (+ Dissonant)	capture	chorus: "Non l'avrai!"; bounty hunters, Calaf, ministers	d, e♭, c♯
	16.6	enter Turandot		enter Turandot	"Principessa!... Divina!..."	G♭
	18.3		6 Romantic (+ Dissonant, + Chinese Exotic)	(recognition)	Turandot, Liù, Calaf	c, a♭
	20	C tempo d'attacco				e

DEVELOPMENT: CONFRONTATION AND TORTURE	21.9		7 Dissonant	persuasion	Turandot: "Sei pallido, o stranierol"; Liù, Timur, Calaf, ministers, chorus	e, G
	24	aria [adagio]	8 Romantic (+ Chinese Exotic)	aria	Liù: "Tanto amore, segreto"	F
	25.7	tempo di mezzo	9 Exotic Primitive	torture	Ping: "Sia messa alla tortura"; Liù, chorus	f♯
CONCLUSION: DEATH OF LIÙ	27	suicide and cortège (cabaletta-function)	10 Romantic (+ Persian Exotic)	aria (part 2)	Liù: "Tu che di gel sei cinta"	e♭
	29	coda		coda	orchestra, Calaf, Timur, Ping, chorus	

Note

1. After Ashbrook and Powers, *Puccini's "Turandot,"* 31–38 and 167.

EXAMPLE 6.5. *Turandot* III, embedded pentatonicism
in Liu's aria (Romantic-Exotic integration).

moving more quickly and the styles changing more often, but also the
styles themselves less clearly expressed: the Chinese Exotic episode 5, for
example, integrates Dissonance in its thoroughly chromatic harmonic
structure—in which the key shifts from the opening D minor to a relatively stable E♭ minor (R14.11); episode 6 begins with a clear expression
of the Romantic style (recalling the recognition music from Act I) but
breaks down in the wake of gradually increasing Dissonance (coincident
with the beginning of the torture sequence, at R20) and Chinese Exoticism (in the "Mo-li-hua" theme, which appears briefly at R21). Episodes
7 and 9 are clearer: 7 is fully Dissonant, suitable for the agonizing torture
scene, while 9 is fully Primitive Exotic and quotes the theme from the
Act I executioner's chorus. But episodes 8 and 10 are, again, somewhat
ambiguous: these are the two lyric movements of a four-movement aria
for Liù (more on this presently) and are generally Romantic, but here
again the style is undercut, now with integrated Exotic tokens in Liù's
melodies. The "Tanto amore, segreto" movement embeds pentatonicism (example 6.5) in a manner similar to Liù's earlier "Nulla sono" and
"Signore ascolta," both from Act I, while the concluding "Tu che di gel
sei cinta"—as Ashbrook and Powers have pointed out—derives straight
from one of the work's most Romantic themes (that of the last F♯-minor
section of Turandot's scene and aria from Act II; see example 6.6) but
also has an exotic quality stemming from its close relationship (especially in its rhythm and contour) to one of the work's prototypically
Persian Exotic melodies—that of the Prince of Persia's cortège in Act I.[51]

The act is also goal-oriented, another quality borrowed from Act I.
Puccini's music comprises three numbers (again, according to Ashbrook
and Powers), only the last of which makes a clear reference—one of the

EXAMPLE 6.6. Stylistic integration in *Turandot* III (after Ashbrook and Powers, *Puccini's "Turandot,"* 110, 114).

clearest in the whole piece, in fact—to a conventional formal prototype. This set piece is a four-movement aria complete with two kinetic movements and two static, lyric movements. One kinetic movement is a dialogic, recitative *tempo d'attacco,* and the other is a similarly recitative, agitated *tempo di mezzo* that introduces, via Liù's torture, the traditional irreversible change in the dramatic situation. The two static, lyric movements are both for Liù: the first loosely suggests a traditional *adagio* (its tempo is slow, but the form is through-composed), while the second (in which Liù throws herself on a soldier's sword), rather than adopting characteristics of a *cabaletta,* reverts back to the measured lyricism of the *adagio* (although we may hear some of Ashbrook's *cabaletta*-function here, in that the piece is tonally differentiated from the *adagio* and heightens the emotional intensity so as to produce a dramatic climax). The act thus becomes more conventional as it progresses: a set piece (C in table 6.4) with a structure audibly analogous to the conventional four-part model follows from two other decidedly less conventional numbers (A and B). And the same end-oriented process is evident in other important facets of the act—all of which, again, mirror Act I. Its pace, for example, begins slowly, accelerates in the middle, then decelerates toward the end, a process produced as much by the stylistic rhythm as by the relationship of styles to conventional numbers. Styles and numbers are somewhat out of phase at the beginning of the act, Three movements in number A comprise two stylistic episodes; three stylistic episodes and part of another support three more movements in number B. They go even more out of phase in the middle: the music toward the end of movement B is some of the most formally multivalent in the opera in that no style change supports the last movement of number B (Turandot's entrance), the Romantic shift (onset of episode 6) at R18.3 falls in the middle of the same movement, and the set piece for Liù begins at R20 but a supporting style change is delayed until R21.9. But they begin to move into agreement in the last part of the act, which stabilizes the form and creates a strong sense of conclusion by the end of Liù's cortège. The *adagio, tempo di mezzo,* and final lyric movement all correspond in a one-to-one fashion with the last three episodes (8–10)—more evidence that Puccini may have been thinking of delineating conventional formal prototypes stylistically.

The large, coherent, three-part design; the arch shape in the pacing; and the goal-directed quality of the third act all strongly suggest that the music from the opening of Act III through R35 forms one large, structurally complete unit; Act III *feels* complete at the end of Liù's cortège. The fact that the last act corresponds with the first on each count also helps, as Act I is, again, structurally coherent and complete. But this is clearly a problem, because in terms of plot, the act is only complete on a subsidiary level: the plot is complete with respect to Liù, but this is a subplot, a smaller thread within the larger—if less rational, less realistic, less human—world of Turandot, Calaf, the riddles, and Calaf's name. Thus the plot's main thread is still hanging—we have no idea yet what will happen to Calaf, Turandot, or even Timur[52]—even though the cortège closes with a finality worthy of the work's end (in the same key, no less, as the end of Act I). And whether it has anything to do with why Puccini never finished the opera—and given his considerable powers for making effective theatrical drama it seems we must award him the benefit of the doubt, that given good health he eventually would have resolved the problem—it surely has something to do with why the piece sounds so puzzling, so difficult, at the end of Liù's cortège. Indeed, this is one of the most paradoxical moments in all of Puccini: dramatically the work *must* continue, but musically—structurally—it *need not* continue.

Late Style and Puccini

Late style as an aesthetic category has been explored in various disciplines, including music, for some years now.[1] This book has attempted to locate a late style in Puccini's music, and to situate Puccini among the growing cadre of composers for whom a late style is recognized in their output. I intend here, as an epilogue, a speculative, contextualizing conclusion that seeks a way of accounting for both the long, gradual shift in Puccini's musical aesthetics over the course of his career and the gradual decline in productivity evident in his later years.

Much recent work on late style centers on a single, central problem: how to identify a composer's late style or late works. Two common solutions have appeared: one is temporal, the other purely musical. The temporal approach identifies a composer's late works first, then itemizes those works' style traits to form a definition of the late style; the purely musical approach first identifies generic style traits that may be understood very broadly as markers of late style, in any repertoire, then locates those traits in works of a given composer. The first approach hinges on chronology: late works are identified, for example, as all of a composer's works after a certain date, period, or event in that composer's life. This method entails, among other tasks, accounting biographically for why a composer's style should have undergone a major, final change after or during the date or period in question. The second approach hinges on the assumption that we can identify stylistic features marking "lateness"—independent of, among other factors, composer, era, style, or nationality—across a wide range of different music.

Both approaches are problematic—and thus the root of most difficulties associated with the notion of late style. The temporal approach is awkward because *late* has no absolute chronological definition: some have invoked a composer's age as a criterion (late works, for example, are those written during the last period of a composer's life), while others have tried to constrain the chronology more tightly by invoking composers' awareness of their own impending deaths (late works are, perhaps, those written after a composer knew death was imminent). But what qualifies as the last period of one's life? The last six months? The last year? Five years? The last ten percent of one's life span? Many composers never even reached an "old age": Mozart and Schubert, for example—both long recognized as having a late style—died just short of their 36th and 32nd birthdays, respectively, so what part of either of their lives, if any, was "late"? Some composers, moreover, began writing in what we now regard as their late style long before reaching any period we could reasonably take to be "late in life": Beethoven, Brahms, and Bach, for example, all adopted a late style at least ten years prior to their deaths—and Bach lived to age 70, Brahms to almost 64, and Beethoven to only 56. Even foreknowledge of death, while apparently a convenient restricting criterion, often provides no further clarity: many, of course, were never aware their deaths were near, and many others adopted their late styles long before being forced to confront their own mortality.

Furthermore, there simply is no way to generalize biographically what kinds of events may account for the development of a late style. Some composers, though certainly not all or even most, navigate some kind of rite of passage in their lives—an artistic, personal, or physical crisis, perhaps—and emerge with an enlightened, refined, or otherwise altered sense of their own artistic identities, and, therefore, a changed musical style.[2] Others find motivation in what Joseph Straus has recently called a sense of "authorial belatedness" with respect to their predecessors:[3] this is a self-consciousness triggered by a sense that the composer has lived too late in a historical era and that nothing new remains to be accomplished; a good nineteenth-century example is Brahms, who was known for some anxiety about composing in Beethoven's long shadow.[4]

Still others are shaped by having outlived their eras: they are usually seen as unwilling or unable to adapt musically or culturally to new stylistic trends, and their late styles are widely viewed as anachronistic and backward-looking. Bach—viewed as outdated by the time of his death— is a good example, as are Strauss (long regarded as having composed his most backward-looking music late in his life) and, of course, Puccini (more on him presently).[5]

The purely musical approach is problematic because, again, it assumes we can identify generic musical traits that mark stylistic "lateness." But it seems self-evident that late styles should exhibit different traits in music of different composers or different eras; surely something as complex as one's stylistic evolution or lifetime stylistic trajectory cannot be generalized and remains as unique as one's own fingerprint. Limiting the question to the output of one composer at a time likewise proves difficult: why should we assume a composer's late works will exhibit a consistent style? Nevertheless, many commentators have tried to itemize "late" style traits: Adorno, in a widely cited essay on Beethoven's late style, famously pointed to features such as extreme discontinuity, fragmentation, instability, and tension; Edward Said, in a posthumously published book on late style heavily influenced by Adorno, noted, among other qualities, a dramatization of irresolvable relationships.[6] Straus, in a recent attempt to inventory these and numerous other attempts to generically define stylistic lateness, found that most writers on the subject describe late style with language derived from one of six adjectival categories, including *introspective* (which comprises descriptors such as alienated, personal, intimate, and withdrawn), *austere* (impersonal, expressionless, or bare), *difficult* (complex, technically advanced, contrapuntal, and enigmatic), *compressed* (dense, concentrated, or economical), *fragmentary* (discontinuous, episodic, paratactic, or torn), and *retrospective* (anachronistic, nostalgic, or archaic).[7] The inventory, by Straus's own admission, reveals much about the problems with purely musical definitions of late style: some of the categories overlap, but, even more importantly, some are contradictory, and in fact it would be impossible for a single work to exhibit features from *each* category (and thus the question: with how many categories must a work engage before we consider it "late"?). Moreover, the list is *too* comprehensive: numerous of its members could describe almost any kind of music imaginable.

Accounting for what I have identified in this book as Puccini's late style using either definitional approach may be possible, but both are problematic in various ways. Consider first the temporal explanation: indeed, this has been invoked, even if only implicitly, by almost every Puccini biographer since his death. This is because Puccini's biography conveniently contains events that may have functioned as motivators for significant aesthetic and stylistic shifts, including, most notably perhaps, a prolonged personal and artistic rite of passage that began in February 1903 and culminated a year later in February 1904. He had a major car accident (his car went off a road in bad weather between Lucca and Viareggio) on February 25, 1903, which required at least eight months of convalescence at home in Torre del Lago and at a mountain resort, Boscolungo Abetone. The very next day (February 26, 1903), the husband of his companion Elvira Bonturi Gemignani died, initiating a ten-month period through which he had to wait before formally marrying Elvira (which he did in January 1904). In April 1903 Puccini hired a lawyer to handle his situation with a young woman, known to Puccini researchers only as Corinna, with whom he had apparently been carrying on an affair since 1901 and whom he was afraid would blackmail him for money once he broke off the relationship (the problem was settled out of court that November). Finally, on February 17, 1904, the first version of *Madama Butterfly* debuted at La Scala in Milan in what almost every commentator has called an utter fiasco—handing Puccini his first complete disaster at a premiere and sending him into what has been described as "suicidal despair."[8] After this his work habits and productivity changed noticeably: he embarked on a prolonged, sometimes futile search for a new libretto, considering over thirty subjects before finally settling on David Belasco's *The Girl of the Golden West,* which he had seen on stage in January 1907 during his first visit to New York City but which he did not confirm as the source of his next opera until February 1908. This was a full four years after the premiere of his last opera; before this he had never in his career been without a subject for more than a month.

By this definition all the works after *Butterfly*—*La fanciulla del West, La rondine, Il trittico,* and *Turandot*—would be Puccini's "late works" and their style his "late style"—which we would understand as having developed in response to the stress of and recovery from his lengthy, multifaceted crisis. This certainly seems reasonable: the change of aesthetics already noted as evident in his correspondence from around this time (including, for example, his acceptance by 1907 of the theatrical viability of juxtaposed operas in various genres) may well have resulted in part from his ordeal. But in other ways this formulation remains problematic: not least is the difficulty that the putative late works, while sharing some stylistic features, are quite different. *Fanciulla,* clearly a demarcation in Puccini's stylistic evolution and, as Girardi has noted, the first of Puccini's operas to fully exploit the idea of generic blending,[9] is also more of a self-conscious attempt to suppress lyric singing—what I have called here the Italian lyric style—than any of the others; indeed, this change was duly noted by the contemporary critics, including the *New York Times* reviewer the day after the premiere, who called it "a contradiction in terms of all conceptions of what the lyric drama could or should be" and noted that "it may be doubted whether any who knew the composer only though 'La Bohême' [sic] would recognize him in this, so far has he traveled in thirteen years."[10] Moreover, *La fanciulla* and especially *La rondine* make very different uses of their episodic formal designs than any of the three *Trittico* works or *Turandot,* and neither of the former can be described as employing a strategic use of *ottocento* formal structures in the same way as I have described in the latter. At best, then, the post-*Butterfly* operas could be regarded as exhibiting not necessarily a coherent late style but rather, perhaps, a *late transition* toward a particular expressive strategy—the *late style*—that finds its final, most thoroughly developed manifestation in Puccini's last four works.

Other temporal explanations prove even more troublesome in Puccini's case. There is no strong evidence that he was plagued by a sense of authorial belatedness, beyond some ambivalence about being considered a successor to Verdi (which affected him his whole career, not just in his later years, and thus may account for some aspects of his style but not necessarily his *late* style).[11] He seems, in fact, to have been more concerned with his contemporaries—his competitors in the opera marketplace, as he saw them—and expressed on numerous occasions, for example, a mild hostility toward Richard Strauss. Numerous letters to this effect appear between 1906 and 1909, right in the middle of his crisis period and also in the years in which Strauss's two great expressionist works debuted: Puccini saw *Salome* at its Austrian premiere in Graz on May 16, 1906,[12] and *Elektra* at its Italian premiere in Milan on

April 6, 1909. And, conversely, while the idea that Puccini outlived his era and thus produced stylistically anachronistic music has long been an important part of the standard Puccini narrative (even if contemporary reception of his music was quite different and much more nuanced, as Wilson has established), Puccini himself is well known to have at least outwardly expressed a concern for maintaining currency in contemporary European (and American, if *La fanciulla* is any indication) musical-theatrical currents. Girardi has compellingly shown that this is an aspect of Puccini's thinking overtly manifested in his music.

Furthermore, Puccini wrote none of his putative late works at an advanced age, and even his period of personal and artistic crisis did not occur late in life. He was only 45 at the *Butterfly* Milan premiere, and actuarial tables constructed from contemporary Italian census data indicate the average 45-year-old male at that time could have expected to live another twenty-five years, to age 69.[13] He was only 49 in May 1908 when he began work on *La fanciulla,* still sixteen and a half years from his death, and the same tables show that by that time he could have expected to live another twenty-four years, to age 73. Moreover, average Italian males who lived to be 66 by 1924—Puccini died a month short—lived an average of almost twelve more years, to age 78. Thus statistically speaking, Puccini never reached an age that could be considered "old," and his crisis occurred in mid-life, not late in life. Thus, his age is a dubious measurement for historical or stylistic lateness.

Puccini's awareness of his own imminent death as a motivator for stylistic change seems similarly untenable. All accounts of Puccini's last twelve months make clear that he had no direct knowledge of the extent or severity of his final illness: he first complained of severe throat pain late in 1923 but attributed it at that time to his smoking or to an incident earlier that year in which, while on a Bavarian vacation, a goose bone became lodged in his throat during a dinner. Both his personal physician and a Milan specialist, in March 1924, made no diagnosis of any serious problem beyond rheumatic inflammation. On the advice of his physician he underwent in late May of that year a short, unsuccessful throat treatment at Salsomaggiore, a resort near Parma, and in October he consulted a specialist in Viareggio and another in Florence, the latter finally finding the malignant tumor and diagnosing advanced, inoperable cancer—a diagnosis that was revealed to Puccini's son Antonio but not to Puccini himself. It might be asserted, on the other hand, that Puccini in fact always had some consciousness of his own mortality: references to what he perceived as his advanced age—and health problems he associated with it—begin to appear relatively early in his correspondence, around age 40, and, in his mid-sixties, after the onset of the cancer symptoms, his letters reflect a growing awareness that his health may have been irrevocably failing and his life approaching its end. It would be reasonable to assume that his musical style might have changed in response to the stress, but chronologically this might account for a late style in parts of *Turandot,* though not necessarily *Il trittico* (which had been completed by April 1918, well before the onset of any of his more serious problems) and certainly not *La fanciulla* (completed in August 1910) or *La rondine* (April 1916).

Perhaps a purely musical identification of Puccini's late style—to the extent such an identification of *any* late style is possible—may be more reasonable: his last four works do exhibit some characteristics from the six adjectival categories traditionally used to mark stylistic lateness. Certainly *Tabarro* is personal and alienated (especially in its characters utterly detached from mainstream society), *Suor Angelica* introspective and intimate, *Schicchi* austere and impersonal (in that most of its expression is feigned or ironic), and *Turandot* fragmentary, episodic, and among the most technically complex of Puccini's works, harmonically and structurally. All of *Il trittico,* furthermore, is compressed, dense, and economical—by definition, we might say: these are one-act operas, the only such forms in all of Puccini's output. And all three *Trittico* panels as well as *Turandot* are retrospective and nostalgic both dramatically (all either take place in the past or long for it, and in some cases—the *Turandot* ministers' scene, for example—do both) and technically (all engage, as discussed here, older and newer formal strategies in an expressive dialogue). But of course inconsistencies remain. Certainly *Turandot* could not, for example, be described as austere, introspective, or compressed (it is, as noted, Puccini's grand opera, on the grandest scale of any of his works); likewise *Il tiabarro* and *Angelica* are probably not the best examples of austerity (both have their share of highly emotional outbursts and colorful, lush orchestrations—typical in all Puccini's music). And other late-style descriptors apply just as well to Puccini's earlier works, or to his output as a whole, as to any of the works written chronologically late in his life: much of *La fanciulla* is austere, introspective, and very complex; and much of the dramatic action in both *Tosca* and (especially) *La bohème* is highly compressed—which, again, is typical of Puccini's work more generally and, in fact, typical of most post-Verdi Italian opera.

There may be, however, another way not yet considered of account-ing for Puccini's late style: a temporal, biographical approach that avoids some of the problems discussed previously and that may account for Puccini's musical-aesthetic shift as well as his decline in productivity. This is an approach that draws on recent research in the emerging field of disability studies, which asserts that a composer's *experience of living with a disability* may be a stronger impetus for stylistic evolution—and, indeed, for development of a late style—than any of the more traditional temporal-biographical criteria such as age, foreknowledge of death, rites of passage, authorial belatedness, or outliving a historical era—although certainly some of these may be closely related. In Puccini's case, such a view has the potential to justify his stylistic trajectory and perhaps even pinpoint which of his operas we should consider *late*. Which is to say, it is possible that Puccini's evolution as a composer was strongly influenced by a *disability* with which he struggled throughout his life, especially in his last twenty years: an apparent mental condition we could classify as instability at best and illness at worst, one manifested specifically in a disorder that might now be recognized and treated as *melancholia,* or simply *chronic depression.*

That said, what follows is not intended as a detailed analysis of Puc-cini's psychology, a study of which would move well beyond the scope of this book and require many more references than I have provided, not to mention interviews and oral histories. Moreover, this idea is not entirely new, but rather only a new way of framing one that has been present in the literature for years: Mosco Carner argued for a similar view of Puccini in his landmark biography, the first edition of which appeared in 1958. Carner's psychological analysis of Puccini was mostly Freudian and comprised these essential points: Puccini's father died when Puccini was very young (on January 23, 1864, just after Puccini turned five); after this Puccini formed a very close, affectionate connection to his mother, Albina Magi Puccini, a relationship he failed to sever at an early enough age and in fact failed to sever at all before his mother's death on July 17,

1884, when Puccini was 25 and living in Milan (emotional severance of a young male's relationship with his mother is an essential element in Freudian psychology; it prevents the boy from becoming too feminine and allows him to develop appropriate, culturally acceptable masculinity);[14] and this explains in part Puccini's problematic associations with women throughout his life, including his notoriously poor relationship with his eventual wife Elvira (even though, Carner says, Elvira "contributed a considerable share to this unhappiness")[15] and his serial extramarital affairs (he needed, according to Carner, an outlet in which to exert dominance that would counteract his unconscious dependence on his mother).

Recent psychology suggests the Freudian preoccupation with a male's severance of his maternal relationship may be out of date;[16] for some time now, Carner's analysis of Puccini has been regarded as outmoded and unverifiable. But some aspects of Carner's assessment seem to indicate he was more aware—more than many recent writers—of certain important, problematic facets of Puccini's personality, so much so that we may not want to be so quick to dismiss him as dated or speculative (even though this whole enterprise is necessarily somewhat speculative). I would like not necessarily to resuscitate Carner's analysis wholesale, but rather to revisit some of it in light of both the foregoing study of Puccini's last operas and recent work in late style and disability studies. In doing so I am proposing a certain way of understanding not only Puccini's life as a whole, but also, and especially, his last twenty years, his stylistic evolution, and his late style.

Puccini seems to have perceived his adolescence and young adulthood as difficult. His family was likely not well off financially in the wake of his father's death, and he was almost certainly aware of this fact at a young age. And his entering the conservatory in Milan in late 1880 almost surely caused him a good deal of anxiety: every Puccini biographer has noted his lifelong provinciality ("I'm continually thinking of my Torre del Lago!"),[17] and we have no reason to suspect his attitude toward leaving his Lucca home at age 22 would have been positive, especially given what was apparently a close relationship with his mother and five older sisters. His departure for Milan almost certainly also caused him and his family additional financial strain: he and his mother apparently went to great lengths to secure funding to support him during his Milan years, and much of his correspondence from throughout this period reflects an overt concern for his financial situation—which, though probably not dire, was certainly not comfortable or secure.[18]

Indeed, beginning in his early letters from Milan, there are almost constant references to his struggle with money and his fear of not having enough of it. Sometimes these letters make it seem as though nearly everything he did in those years was motivated by financial concerns. Comments such as "Hunger: I can't tolerate it. I'm eating poorly, but I'm filling myself up on minestrone, watered-down broth, and leftovers. The belly is satisfied," "At five I go to my frugal meal (and I emphasize frugal!)," and "Damn poverty!!!! Yesterday I went to hear *Carmen* for free" are all typical.[19] These early financial struggles may explain why he continued to exhibit elevated anxiety about his finances well into the more successful periods of his career—even well into the 1890s, after the successful *Manon Lescaut* (February 1893) and *La bohème* (February 1896). Typical is a comment to Giulio Ricordi (with whose firm he was then under contract) from 1898: "I beg you to send me *money immediately* because I'm broke. It disappears quickly in Paris, with nothing to show for it."[20] These early struggles to adjust to all facets of life outside Lucca may explain his exaggerated sensitivity—which seems trivial unless considered in the larger context of his possible depression—to the weather, especially bad weather: comments on this subject are even more frequent than references to his financial situation. Remarks such as "Today is a dreadful day—extremely boring weather" (from one of his earliest letters to his mother from Milan, in December 1880) and, from 1889, "The weather is horrible. Fog and a fine rain. Half of Milan has the flu" are both characteristically pessimistic.[21]

Add to this the fact that in the mid-1880s Puccini began living with Elvira (and one of her children—daughter Fosca—from her marriage to Narciso Gemignani; upon leaving Narciso she left behind a son, Renato), and that on December 6, 1886, their son Antonio was born, and we have additional stressors that may have contributed to ill emotional health. Elvira was initially Puccini's voice and piano student, and their personal relationship—after the initial courtship and earliest years of cohabitation—seems to have been deeply troubled. Some of the earliest letters in which Puccini tries to address Elvira's jealousy—a constant theme throughout their early association and later marriage, and a concern so troubling for Elvira that Carner called it pathological—date from 1890 and 1891, and all of these express deep distress and an unmistakable desperation.[22] A decade later, in the early 1900s, during one of Puccini's most artistically successful periods, their correspondence indicates that they endured extended periods of separation and a mutually pessimistic view of their union's durability.[23] Letters to this effect continue throughout their relationship, such as the often-cited, rather sensational example from August 1915: "Your suspicions lead you to the most undignified investigations. You invent women in order to give free play to your policeman's instinct. . . . You have never looked at these matters as do other women who are more reasonable—Good God!"[24]

Clearly the relationship was a source of almost constant anxiety for Puccini. This is true even though Elvira's suspicions about some of Puccini's private habits were justifiable: it is now well known that Puccini's extramarital affairs began at least as early as 1901, with the woman known as Corinna.[25] His subsequent liaisons are probably not all known to biographers but include a wealthy English banker's wife, Sybil Seligman, whom Puccini met in London in late 1904 (they apparently had a short-lived sexual relationship that turned platonic, and they managed to maintain a close friendship until Puccini's 1924 death); Blanka Lendvai (sister of his friend Ervin Lendvai), with whom Puccini was involved from 1909 to 1911; Josephine von Stängel (a German noblewoman he met in Viareggio sometime in 1911), from 1912 to 1917—at which time he ended his relationship with her (she was expelled from wartime Italy as a foreign alien) but not his desire for her, as is evident in a 1924 letter to his good friend Riccardo Schnabl fondly recalling one of their trysts;[26] German soprano Rose Ader, to whom, according to Girardi, Puccini's only known love letter dates from May 24, 1921, but with whom Carner suggests he was involved until 1923;[27] and Giulia Manfredi, starting sometime in the early 1920s (recent research suggests Puccini may have had a son by Giulia, also named Antonio, born in 1923; Giulia was a cousin of Doria Manfredi, with whom Puccini was suspected by Elvira, apparently incorrectly, of having an affair sometime between February 1903—when Doria was taken into employment in Puccini's Torre del Lago home shortly after the car accident that month—and October 1908, when she was expelled from the home by the jealous Elvira).[28] All of these liaisons can be accurately understood, as they are in most Puccini literature, as evidence of Puccini's masochistically inflicting pain and suffering on his own marriage—betrayals for which his wife had good reason to be disturbed. Clearly they had an enormous impact not only on his personal but also his professional life; Carner has suggested that the fallout from them (in particular from Elvira's false allegations in late 1908 and 1909 of an affair with Doria) was "the major if indeed not the sole factor responsible" for Puccini's waning productivity in the years during which he produced the late works.[29]

But it may be that we can also update our understanding of Puccini's serial affairs as byproducts of pain he was already suffering—as his own (unhealthy at best, pathological at worst) responses to an ongoing depression from which he suffered, a depression triggered by a number of his circumstances, including what he perceived as the miserable state of his personal life. There is ample evidence to support such an interpretation. Most contemporaries and most modern biographers have reflected on what they see as Puccini's generally oversensitive disposition. Girardi observes in Puccini a tendency to, at even a hint of personal challenge, "retreat into a fictitious world, to take shelter from the bad moments in life"—to withdraw, that is, into a private, depressed existence. Puccini was, Girardi says, more easily able—as are many successful artists—to absorb life's trials if he was intensively involved in his creative work.[30] Vincent Seligman, who personally observed Puccini from around age ten while in the company of his mother Sybil, remarks that "the most surprising thing" about Puccini's letters "is that, although they are the record of an unparalleled series of triumphs, they are most emphatically not the letters of a happy, nor even of a moderately contented, man."[31] Librettist Luigi Illica described him in 1893 (when Puccini turned 35) as "a clock-work which is rapidly wound up and as rapidly runs down." Carner suggests that Puccini seems to have gradually become more susceptible to mental fatigue and self-pitying moods, which became longer and more exhausting, and thus more likely to affect his creative work and productivity, as he got older;[32] Carner's hypothesis—probably correct—is that Puccini suffered from either an inherited susceptibility to depression ("congenital melancholia") or a chemical imbalance: "he grew increasingly prone to such labile moods. . . He was famous, wealthy and in a position to gratify every whim—which he did. Yet he found life an intolerable burden."[33] Even Puccini himself on numerous occasions explicitly acknowledged, and bemoaned, the problem of his own hypersensitivity and what he apparently recognized as abnormally depressed moods: "I make the great mistake of being too sensitive, and I suffer too when people don't understand me and misjudge me. Even my friends don't know what sort of man I am—it's a punishment that has been visited on me since the day of my birth"; and "I have always carried with me a large load of melancholy. I'm not right for doing so, but I'm made that way, as are all those men who have a heart and for whom a lesser degree of superficiality is lacking."[34]

This last letter also expresses a phobia Puccini seems to have lived with for most of his life, one often symptomatic of depression: an irrational fear of not gaining acceptance from, or of being abandoned by, others whose professional, personal, and emotional support he craved. He may well have always had these fears, but they emerge with some force during the convalescence period after his car accident. He wrote to Illica, for example, from Torre del Lago on November 24, 1903, "Write to me often. I'm here alone and sad! If only you knew about my suffering! I need a friend so much, and I don't have one, or if there is someone who cares for me, he doesn't understand me. My temperament is so different from everyone else's! Only I understand myself, and this gives me grief; but my pain is constant, and it gives me no peace."[35] These fears only intensified later: he wrote Adami in November 1921, "Why . . . why . . . 'don't you love me any more'? . . . why? Am I outdated? or of no value? Only *Madeira* is left for me. I've been sick. I'm always a little down. Not seeing your letters leaves me feeling even more down. Simoni [his lack of attention] truly buries me [i.e., wants to be rid of me]!"[36] In 1900 he wrote to Ricordi, "Neither from Illica nor from Giacosa have I ever had news . . . Therefore I am truly the forgotten one";[37] and in 1923 he composed some (mostly) *quinario* verse that opens "I am friendless / And alone / Even music / Saddens me. / When death comes / To call me / I shall find happy repose."[38] Moreover, in the middle of his crisis period he even found himself dealing with what he perceived as a lack of validation from one of his most trusted confidants, the always supportive Giulio Ricordi, who, in the wake of the disastrous *Butterfly* premiere in Milan, apparently began advising Puccini to consider writing something that would ensure critical success—something "stronger and more ambitious."[39]

This distressed Puccini—"He [Ricordi] now seems to have changed his mind on this [*Butterfly*], and seems to be changing his mind concerning all my work, calling everything I've done little sketches. This is really discouraging and disheartening for me"[40]—even though he seems to have later accepted it as a good idea, while continuing to worry about what to do. "The whole world is waiting on an opera from me, and there is really a need for one. Enough of *Bohème*, *Butterfly*, and company; I'm fed up with them too! But I'm very, very worried,"[41] he wrote. Interpreting these and similar sentiments as overblown expressions of Puccini's own frustration with librettists, publishers, or the opera-going public is easy; in fact, Puccini is often viewed as someone who had a compulsive need to control every aspect of his work, someone who routinely overreacted to a lack of sufficient attention or difference of opinion with his collaborators. But the consistency with which these kinds of attitudes appear in his correspondence may also reflect an intense fear of rejection and an attendant depression, both of which haunted him almost constantly—most especially when he encountered some kind of personal or professional obstacle.

Puccini, as mentioned, also exhibited a conspicuous fear of aging—or a preoccupation with death—even when he was relatively young. Oblique references to his age appear as early as 1898 (for example, in a letter to Ricordi from Paris on May 15: "I have too much nervous agitation and am without the tranquility I need. . . . I'm made like this and can't be changed at almost forty years old!"),[42] and his concern deepened as he grew older (he wrote to Sybil in November 1918, "I'm nearly sixty, dear friend! How unjust it is that one should grow old—it makes me simply furious, confound it!").[43] And for about the last fifteen years of his life, he exhibited a markedly elevated concern about his physical health. Beginning in the mid-1900s his correspondence is filled with complaints about ailments, real or perceived—including, among others that are verifiable, his diabetes. One of his first references to this dates from late August 1903, during his recovery from the car accident, in a letter from Boscolungo in which he mentions a urine test for glucose. Apparently the problem was evaluated incorrectly at first, but when the diagnosis was later rectified Puccini seems to have been upset about it and refers to it more frequently (typical is a letter of November 14, 1906: "I have had some very bad days. My accursed diabetes gives me a great deal of trouble"). And while some of his health worries may have been unwarranted and he may have often tended, as many have noted, toward hypochondria (remarks in his letters about influenza are so common that one assumes he probably used this word to describe common colds and perhaps many other discomforts), others are probably more justified than is usually acknowledged. He wrote, for example, in June 1921 to Adami, "I am in a diabolical mood. Perhaps I am not feeling too well? My work is at a standstill. I need encouragement from one who understands me. . . . I think I'm becoming neurasthenic."[44] Neurasthenia is a psychological affliction marked by fatigue, lassitude, easy fatigability, lack of motivation, and feelings of inadequacy, and indeed in all probability this letter expresses much more than an artist's routine frustration with slow progress on his work: Puccini very likely did suffer from a disorder of this kind.

Puccini's anxieties about his age and health naturally grew worse later, especially after he turned 60. On at least three occasions he expressed a desire to seek treatment for what commentators usually describe as senescence, although it may be that he was trying to treat either a fading sex drive or impotence. In the summer of 1920 (when he was 61) he considered seeing a specialist on aging and rejuvenation in Berlin; in March 1923 (age 63) he wrote to Sybil that he had "such a fear and such horror of old age!" and wanted to see a Viennese doctor (endocrinologist Eugen Steinach) known for performing experimental operations intended to sexually rejuvenate aged men; and in April 1924 he apparently considered consulting the Russian-born French surgeon Serge Voronoff, well known at the time for his attempts to retard aging (and perhaps increase libido) by grafting tissue from monkey testicles onto the testicles of human men.[45] Comments from the early 1920s, as noted, indicate that Puccini was aware his health really may have been failing—that he was racing against the clock to finish *Turandot,* for example. He wrote to Simoni in late December 1923 regarding the piece's ever-troublesome last act, "I've started orchestrating to save time; but I won't be content until this duet is finished. Do me the favor of dedicating yourself to this last work. Be good to me as you've always been; take some time from your busy schedule and devote it to this poor maestro who really wants to finish this 'magna' opera."[46] All this—advancing age and an adulthood of health concerns that only grew more serious—likely contributed to an ever-worsening depression that, as Carner has surmised, probably played a significant role in reducing his creative productivity and, more importantly, a shift in his musical-theatrical aesthetics. If Puccini was indeed affected by a depression that manifested itself early in his life but grew noticeably worse in the years immediately after his crisis period, it provides a plausible biographical explanation—much more plausible than the more common explanations of old age or final illness—for his gradual acceptance of contemporary Euro-American artistic aesthetics. Much of the secondary Puccini literature as well as primary source material supports such an analysis of his style change: Girardi, as noted, has shown that Puccini adapted his style to maintain aesthetic currency, and he traces Puccini's most significant style changes to the period following *Butterfly* (1905–1910); Puccini's correspondence, moreover, documents this same timing with specificity—as I have shown in chapter 3—and thus allows for a direct correlation between his style change and his possible developing depression. He considered an opera based on contrasting episodes from a single work—not quite the *Trittico* idea, but close—as early as March 1900, after a trying young adulthood but several years before any of his more serious personal crises. In September 1904—after enduring the stress of the car accident, the long convalescence, the diabetes diagnosis, the Corinna settlement, and the *Butterfly* fiasco—he became noticeably more comfortable with a trilogy on contrasting stories, but set aside the idea because he still had aesthetic concerns. Finally, by early 1907—still in the middle of a long (the longest of his life), anxiety-producing, fruitless search for a new subject, after seeing the successful premieres of Strauss's *Salome* and *Elektra,* after the death of librettist Giuseppe Giacosa (September 1, 1906), and after enduring the rejection of close confidant and supporter Giulio Ricordi—he completely accepted the idea and all its aesthetic implications in the form in which we know it today, even though it took him nearly nine more years (one premiere [*La fanciulla*] and one commission [*La rondine*] later) to begin the project. Work on *Il tabarro* began in October 1915, after, notably, Doria Manfredi died (she attempted suicide on January 23, 1909, and died five days later), he ended one love affair (Lendvai) and began another (Stängel), his sister Ramelde died (April 1912), Giulio Ricordi died (June 6, 1906), and Fausto Torrefranca published his infamous *Giacomo Puccini e l'opera internazionale* (December 1912)—which by all accounts (not surprisingly, given his typical reaction to criticism) sent Puccini into another prolonged period of overt depression.

Moreover, accepting that Puccini's mental state may have played a role in his stylistic evolution may even explain, at least in part, the precise nature of his late style per se. That is, the adjectives typically used to describe late styles—fragmented, tormented, complex, detached, withdrawn, uncommunicative—all are bodily metaphors that may describe just as well the mental or physical condition of an artist with a disability, including an acute mental depression.[47] That Puccini was tormented, withdrawn, and detached from reality is clear, and thus perhaps it should come as no surprise that his late works exhibit the same characteristics. *Il trittico* and *Turandot* are both grounded in the aesthetic of detachment: the stylistic plurality in each serves to deflect spectators' attention away from musical-dramatic concerns and toward the more structural-technical facets of the music. These works' expressive power lies in part in their ongoing dialogue between conventional and unconventional means of organization. Even Girardi's discussion of *La fanciulla del West*—not considered in this book but, as mentioned, often regarded as the first of Puccini's late works—is especially apropos. Puccini began in that work, he says, an experiment with more intimate, withdrawn forms of expression in which "the text was a vehicle for interiority" and the characters "went beyond the bounds of verisimilitude."[48] *Fanciulla*'s music remains completely detached from its characters and the actuality of their existence; its text, characters, and music are all fragmented, withdrawn, introverted, and unreconciled to reality—just as was Puccini himself. There was in this opera—and, we might say, in Puccini—a "detachment, felt and realized unconsciously," between work, feelings, and indeed reality itself; any reconciliation among the three was "artificial and unattainable."[49]

Whether (to invoke a well-known Oscar Wilde observation) "life imitates art" or vice versa, Puccini's musical style and his life are almost certainly inextricably linked, one motivating the other in a mutual relationship that ultimately made possible *Il trittico, Turandot,* and his late style.

NOTES

NOTE ON SCORES, LIBRETTOS, AND TRANSLATIONS

1. See Dieter Schickling, *Giacomo Puccini: Catalogue of the Works*, trans. Michael Kaye (Kassel: Bärenreiter, 2003), 18.

INTRODUCTION

1. Carolyn Abbate, *Unsung Voices: Opera and Musical Narrative in the Nineteenth Century* (Princeton, N.J.: Princeton University Press, 1991); Abbate, *In Search of Opera* (Princeton, N.J.: Princeton University Press, 2001); Gary Tomlinson, *Metaphysical Song: An Essay on Opera* (Princeton, N.J.: Princeton University Press, 1999); Lawrence Kramer, *Classical Music and Postmodern Knowledge* (Berkeley: University of California Press, 1995); Robert Hatten, *Musical Meaning in Beethoven: Markedness, Correlation, and Interpretation* (Bloomington: Indiana University Press, 1994); Hatten, *Interpreting Musical Gestures, Topics, and Tropes: Mozart, Beethoven, Schubert* (Bloomington: Indiana University Press, 2004); and Michel Poizat, *L'Opéra ou le cri de l'ange: Essai sur la jouissance de l'amateur d'opéra* (Paris: A. M. Métailié, 1986), in English as *The Angel's Cry: Beyond the Pleasure Principle in Opera*, trans. Arthur Denner (Ithaca, N.Y.: Cornell University Press, 1992).

2. On *Edgar*, see, for example, *Quaderni Pucciniani* 3 (1992) and *Quaderni Pucciniani* 4: *Lettere di Ferdinando Fontana a Giacomo Puccini, 1884–1919* (1992). Fontana was Puccini's librettist for both works.

3. Mosco Carner, *Puccini: A Critical Biography*, 3rd ed. (London: Duckworth, 1992; 1st ed. London: Duckworth, 1958), 180. All page references are to the 3rd edition.

4. On Puccini's crisis during this period, see Michele Girardi, *Puccini: His International Art*, trans. Laura Basini (Chicago: University of Chicago Press, 2000), 259–83 (originally in Italian as *Giacomo Puccini: L'arte internazionale di un musicista italiano* [Venice: Marsilio, 1995]); Carner, *Puccini*, 3rd ed., 158–202; Mary-Jane Phillips-Matz, *Puccini: A Biography* (Boston: Northeastern University Press, 2002),

147–55; and Julian Budden, *Puccini: His Life and Works* (Oxford: Oxford University Press, 2002), 240–43 and 274–91. On his interest in contemporary Italian literature, see Alexandra Wilson, "Modernism and the Machine Woman in Puccini's *Turandot*," *Music and Letters* 86, no. 3 (2005): 432–51 (esp. 441). On his off-and-on interest in Oscar Wilde, see Phillips-Matz, *Puccini*, 166, 223; and Marco Beghelli, "Quel 'Lago di Massaciuccoli tanto . . . povero d'ispirazione!' ," *Nuova Rivista Musical Italiana* 20 (1986): 605–25.

5. William Ashbrook and Harold Powers, *Puccini's "Turandot": The End of the Great Tradition* (Princeton: Princeton University Press, 1991); Jürgen Maehder, "*Turandot* and the Theatrical Aesthetics of the Twentieth Century," in William Weaver and Simonetta Puccini, eds., *The Puccini Companion* (New York: Norton, 1994), 265–78; Maehder, "Die Glorifizierung der toskanischen Stadt in der italienischen Oper des 20. Jahrhunderts," in *Mahagonny: Die Stadt als Sujet und Herausforderung des (Musik)theaters*, ed. Ulrich Müller (Salzburg: Müller-Speiser, 2000), 417–38.

6. Hatten, *Musical Meaning in Beethoven;* Hatten, "On Narrativity in Music: Expressive Genres and Levels of Discourse in Beethoven," *Indiana Theory Review* 12 (1991): 75–98; Hatten, *Interpreting Musical Gestures, Topics, and Tropes;* and Abbate, *Unsung Voices.*

7. William Rothstein, *Phrase Rhythm in Tonal Music* (New York: Schirmer, 1989); Carl Schachter, "Rhythm and Linear Analysis: A Preliminary Study," *The Music Forum* 4 (1976): 281–334; Schachter, "Rhythm and Linear Analysis: Durational Reduction," *The Music Forum* 5 (1980): 197–232; and Schachter, "Rhythm and Linear Analysis: Aspects of Meter," *The Music Forum* 6, no. 1 (1987): 1–59. All three Schachter articles have been reprinted in Carl Schachter, *Unfoldings: Essays in Schenkerian Theory and Analysis,* ed. Joseph N. Straus (New York: Oxford University Press, 1999), 17–53, 54–78, and 79–117, respectively.

8. For this point, see especially Harold Powers, "'La solita forma' and 'The Uses of Convention,'" *Acta Musicologica* 59, no. 1 (1987): 65–90; and Philip Gossett, "Verdi, Ghislanzoni, and *Aïda*: The Uses of Convention," *Critical Inquiry* 1, no. 2 (1974): 291–334. A slightly different, earlier version of the Powers piece appears under the same title in *Nuove prospettive nella ricerca verdiana: Atti del convegno internazionale in occasione della prima del "Rigoletto" in edizione critica, Vienna, 12–13 marzo 1983,* ed. Marcello Pavarani and Marisa Di Gregorio Casati, 74–105 (Parma: Instituto di studi verdiani-Ricordi, 1987).

9. David Rosen, "'La solita forma' in Puccini's Operas?" in *"L'insolita forma": Strutture e processi analitici per l'opera italiana nell'epoca di Puccini: Atti del Convegno internazionale di studi Lucca, 20–21 settembre 2001,* ed. Virgilio Bernardoni, Michele Girardi, and Arthur Groos, 179–99 (Lucca: Centro studi Giacomo Puccini, 2004); Girardi, *Puccini;* Ashbrook and Powers, *Puccini's "Turandot."*

1. STYLISTIC PLURALITY, NARRATIVE, LEVELS OF DISCOURSE, AND VOICE

1. On operatic music, see Carolyn Abbate, "Elektra's Voice: Music and Language in Strauss's Opera," in *Richard Strauss: Elektra,* ed. Derrick Puffett (Cambridge: Cambridge University Press, 1989), 107–27; Abbate, "Opera as Symphony, a Wagnerian Myth," in *Analyzing Opera: Verdi and Wagner,* ed. Carolyn Abbate and

Roger Parker (Berkeley: University of California Press, 1989), 92–124; Elliot Anto-koletz, "Bartok's *Bluebeard: The* Sources of its Modernism," *College Music Symposium* 30, no. 1 (1990): 75–95; Robert Hatten, "Pluralism of Theatrical Genre and Musical Style in Henze's *We Come to the River*"; Carolyn Abbate, *Unsung Voices;* Kim Kowalke, "Kurt Weill, Modernism, and Popular Culture: *Öffentlichkeit als Stil*," *Modernism/Modernity* 2, no. 1 (1995): 27–69; and Hatten, "Penderecki's Operas in the Context of Twentieth-Century Opera," in *Krzysztof Penderecki's Music in the Context of Twentieth-Century Theater,* ed. Teresa Malecka (Kraków: Akademia Muzyczna, 1999), 15–25. On symphonic music, see J. Peter Burkholder, "Uniformity and Diversity in the History of Musical Style," keynote address to the joint meeting of the American Musicological Society (South-Central Chapter) and the Georgia Association of Music Theorists, Morrow, Georgia, April 6, 2001; Peter Dickinson, "Style-Modulation: An Approach to Stylistic Pluralism," *The Musical Times* 130 (1989): 208–11; Lawrence Starr, *A Union of Diversities: Style in the Music of Charles Ives* (New York: Schirmer, 1992); Glenn Watkins, *Pyramids at the Louvre: Music, Culture, and Collage from Stravinsky to the Postmodernists* (Cambridge, Mass.: Belknap Press of Harvard University Press, 1994); and Jean-Paul Olive, *Musique et montage: essai sur le matériau musical au début du XXe siècle* (Paris: L'Harmattan, 1998).

2. Puccini's move toward stylistic pluralism is a central facet in Girardi's interpretation of Puccini's modernity; see his *Puccini,* esp. 259–327 and 365–487. The earliest source to call attention directly to this aspect of the late music is Ivanka Stoïanova, "Remarques sur l'actualité de *Turandot*," in *Esotismo e colore locale nell'opere di Puccini: Atti del I convegno internazionale sull'opera di Giacomo Puccini (Torre del Lago: Festival pucciniano 1983),* ed. Jürgen Maehder (Pisa: Giardini: 1985), 199–210; and the issue is central in the analyses of Ashbrook and Powers (*Puccini's "Turandot"*) and Johanne Cassar (*"Turandot de Puccini: Essai d'analyse sémiotique"* [Ph.D. diss., Université de Provence, 2000]). See also Maehder, *"Turandot* and the Theatrical Aesthetics of the Twentieth Century"; Leonardo Pinzauti, "Giacomo Puccini's *Trittico* and the Twentieth Century," in *The Puccini Companion,* 228–43 (New York: Norton, 1994); Budden, *Puccini,* 274–473; Carner, *Puccini,* 3rd ed., esp. 509–541; and Helen Greenwald, "Dramatic Exposition and Musical Structure in Puccini's Operas" (Ph.D. diss., City University of New York, 1991).

3. This is a central issue in much of the literature on the fundamentals of musical style. See, for example, Leonard Meyer, *Style and Music: Theory, History, Ideology* (Philadelphia: University of Pennsylvania Press, 1989), 38; Jan LaRue, *Guidelines for Style Analysis* (New York: Norton, 1970), ix; and Robert Pascall, "Style," *Grove Music Online,* ed. Laura Macy, http://www.grovemusic.com (accessed May 30, 2007).

4. In Leonard Meyer's hierarchical taxonomy of "laws," "rules," and "strategies," this formulation of "style" comes closest to his "strategies": the choices a composer makes from among the many options available within the governing, and more culturally and generically universal, laws and rules. See Meyer, *Style and Music,* 8–23. For a critique of Meyer, and for the importance of *symbolic competency* in any definition of style, see Robert Hatten, "Toward a Semiotic Model of Style in Music: Epistemological and Methodological Bases" (Ph.D. diss., Indiana University, 1982), esp. 87–128.

5. Starr, A Union of Diversities, 8; Meyer, Style and Music, 3.

6. Stoïanova, "Remarques sur l'actualité de *Turandot*," 202–203; Carner, *Puccini*, 3rd ed., 520; Girardi, *Puccini*, 447.

7. Carl Dahlhaus, "The Dramaturgy of Italian Opera," trans. Mary Whittall, in *Opera in Theory and Practice, Image and Myth*, part II [*Systems*], vol. VI of *The History of Italian Opera*, ed. Lorenzo Bianconi and Giorgio Pestelli (Chicago: University of Chicago Press, 2003), 73–150: 78 ("The musical-dramatic means available") and 81 ("The musical means at an opera composer's command").

8. The latter is a distinguishing feature of early twentieth-century modernist music theater; see Hatten, "Pluralism of Theatrical Genre and Musical Style," 292–311.

9. Compare the definition of *stylistic plurality* given on page 6.

10. Alexandra Wilson, *The Puccini Problem: Opera, Nationalism, and Modernity* (Cambridge: Cambridge University Press, 2007).

11. Puccini to D'Annunzio, November 11–15, 1912, in Eugenio Gara, ed., *Carteggi pucciniani* (Milan: Ricordi, 1958), letter 629: "Ma dammi una scena di grande amore. Sarà possibile? In questo soggetto? E soprattutto ogni atto abbia la sua grande emozione da lanciare al pubblico." Puccini to Adami, undated, in Giuseppe Adami, ed., *Giacomo Puccini: Epistolario* (Milan: A. Mondadori, 1928), letter 178: "Potrebbe anche darsi che conservando *con giudizio* le maschere si abbia un elemento nostrano il quale in mezzo a tanto manierismo (poiché è) cinese porterebbe una nota nostra e soprattutto sincera" (emphasis original). Puccini to Schnabl, October 8, 1922, *Carteggi pucciniani*, letter 842: "*Turandot* dorme: ci vuole una grande aria al secondo, bisogna innestarla e . . . trovarla."

12. Abramo Basevi, *Studio sulle opere di Giuseppe Verdi* (Florence: Tipografia Tofani, 1859), 191. For an English translation, see Robert Anthony Moreen, "Integration of Text Forms and Musical Forms in Verdi's early Operas" (Ph.D. diss., Princeton University, 1975), 31.

13. Harold Powers, "'La solita forma' and 'The Uses of Convention,'" 67. Other important sources include Philip Gossett, "Verdi, Ghislanzoni, and *Aïda*: The Uses of Convention"; David Lawton, "Tonality and Drama in Verdi's Early Operas" (Ph.D. diss.: University of California Berkeley, 1973); David Lawton and David Rosen, "Verdi's Non-Definitive Revisions: The Early Operas," in *Atti del III Congresso internazionale di studi verdiani, 12–17 giugno 1972*, ed. Maria Medici and Marcello Pavarani (Parma: Instituto di studi verdiani, 1974), 189–237; Moreen, "Integration of Text Forms and Musical Forms"; David Rosen, "Le quattro stesure del duetto Filippo-Posa," in *Atti del II Congresso internazionale di studi verdiani, 30 luglio–5 agosto 1969*, ed. Marcello Pavarani, 368–88 (Parma: Instituto di studi verdiani, 1971) (this and Lawton and Rosen's "Le quattro stesure" both refer directly to Basevi's model for the *solita forma*); and Peter Ross, "Studien zum Verhältnis von Libretto und Komposition in den Opern Verdis" (Inauguraldissertation: Bern, 1980). For more on the historical development of the form beginning around the time of Rossini, see, among others, Scott L. Balthazar, "Evolving Conventions in Italian Serious Opera: Scene Structure in the Works of Rossini, Bellini, Donizetti, and Verdi, 1810–1850" (Ph.D. diss., University of Pennsylvania, 1985); Philip Gossett, "The 'Candeur virginale' of *Tancredi*," *The Musical Times* 112 (1971): 326–29; and Gossett, "Gioachino Rossini and the Conventions of Composition," *Acta Musicologica* 42, no. 1 (1970): 48–58.

14. "Melodrama" (unitalicized) is the English equivalent for It. *melodramma*, which is a standard nineteenth-century Italian term for opera (and thus interchangeable with the common expression "*ottocento* opera"). In this context, it does not invoke either of its more common definitions: a popular English Victorian-era form of stage entertainment; or simply "words spoken over music." For a concise definition, see Julian Budden, "Melodramma (It.)," *Grove Music Online*, ed. Laura Macy, http://www.grovemusic.com (accessed July 12, 2009).

15. Basevi, *Studio sulle opere di Giuseppe Verdi*, 268: "può costruirsi una specie di catena fra i varj ordini di musica vocale, ponendo successivamente il *recitative semplice*, l'*obbligato*, il *parlante armonico*, il *melodico*, e finalmente l'*aria*." For an English translation, see Moreen, "Integration of Text Forms and Musical Forms," 28.

16. For a fuller discussion of genre theory in the context of Italian opera, see James Hepokoski, "Genre and Content in Mid-Century Verdi: 'Addio, del passato' (*La Traviata*, Act III)," *Cambridge Opera Journal* 1, no. 3 (1989): 249–76 (esp. 249–57). Carl Dahlhaus has long been concerned with these issues: especially relevant here (all cited by Hepokoski) are his "The Dramaturgy of Italian Opera"; "New Music and the Problem of Musical Genre," in Dahlhaus, *Schoenberg and the New Music: Essays*, trans. Derrick Puffett and Alfred Clayton, 32–44 (Cambridge: Cambridge University Press, 1987); "Was ist eine musikalische Gattung?," *Neue Zeitschrift für Musik* 135 (1974): 620–25; and "Zur Problematik der musikalischen Gattungen im 19. Jahrhundert," in *Gattungen der Musik in Einzeldarstellungen: Gedenkschrift Leo Schrade*, ed. Wulf Arlt, Ernst Lichtenhahn, and Hans Oesch (Bern: Francke, 1973), 840–95. For more on Dahlhaus's thinking on these issues, see Philip Gossett, "Carl Dahlhaus and the Ideal Type," *19th-Century Music* 13, no. 1 (1989): 49–56; and Jeffrey Kallberg, "The Rhetoric of Genre: Chopin's Nocturne in G minor," *19th-Century Music* 11 (1988): 238–61. An interesting article on Verdi that addresses related issues is Piero Weiss, "Verdi and the Fusion of Genres," *Journal of the American Musicological Society* 35 (1982): 138–56.

17. This is clarified in Moreen, "Integration of Text Forms and Musical Forms," 27ff.

18. "*Recitative*" (italicized) is an Italian noun referring to a structural unit (one of the *solita forma* movements, for which the term *scena* is equivalent); unitalicized "recitative" is an English adjective describing a texture. Note that often the word *scena* is used today to refer to an entire scene, even though in Verdi's own correspondence and contemporary criticism (and thus in a good deal of present-day opera analysis, including this book) the word refers only to the *recitative*.

19. On schema theory in music, see Robert O. Gjerdingen, *Music in the Galant Style* (Oxford: Oxford University Press: 2007) (11 for "packet of knowledge"); Gjerdingen, *A Classic Turn of Phrase* (Philadelphia: University of Pennsylvania Press, 1988). On schema theory more generally, see (cited in Gjerdingen, *A Classic Turn of Phrase*) David E. Rummelhart, "Schemata: The Building Blocks of Cognition," in *Theoretical Issues in Reading Comprehension: Perspectives from Cognitive Psychology, Linguistics, Artificial Intelligence, and Education*, ed. Rand J. Spiro, Bertram C. Bruce, and William F. Brewer (Hillsdale, N.J.: Lawrence Erlbaum Associates, 1980), 33–58.

20. *Music in the Galant Style*, 11.

21. On what follows, and for more on prototype and categorization theory, see George Lakoff, *Women, Fire, and Dangerous Things: What Categories Reveal about the Mind* (Chicago: University of Chicago Press, 1987), esp. 5–57. On aspects of schema theory that parallel Lakoff's prototype theory, see Gjerdingen, *Music in the Galant Style*, 10–16, and Gjerdingen, *A Classic Turn of Phrase*, 4–6.

22. Eleanor Rosch is the leading challenger of the traditional view of prototypes and categorization, and Lakoff's work draws heavily on hers. See, among others, Rosch, Carolyn B. Mervis, Wayne D. Gray, David M. Johnson, and Penny Boyes Braem, "Basic Objects in Natural Categories," *Cognitive Psychology* 8, no. 3 (1976): 382–439; Rosch and Mervis, "Family Resemblances: Studies in the Internal Structure of Categories," *Cognitive Psychology* 7, no. 4 (1975): 573–605; and Rosch and Barbara B. Lloyd, eds., *Cognition and Categorization* (Hillsdale, N.J.: Lawrence Erlbaum Associates, 1978).

23. I have in mind here Beethoven's overture to the incidental music for Kotzebue's *Die Ruinen von Athen*, op. 113; Hepokoski has discussed the movement in his unpublished "Sonata Theory and Dialogic Form," paper presented to the Sixth European Music Analysis Conference, October 12, 2007, Freiburg, Germany, and to the annual meeting of the Texas Society for Music Theory, February 22, 2008, San Marcos, Texas. I use the adjective *deformed* (v. *to deform*; n. *deformation*) here in the sense of an expressive alteration of a normative schema; the meaning is the same as in James Hepokoski and Warren Darcy, *Elements of Sonata Theory: Norms, Types, and Deformations in the Late Eighteenth-Century Sonata* (New York: Oxford University Press, 2006).

24. James Hepokoski, "Back and Forth from 'Egmont': Beethoven, Mozart, and the Nonresolving Recapitulation," *19th-Century Music* 25, no. 2/3 (2001–2002): 127–64 (135 for "the concept of 'form'" and "sets of tools for understanding"). The idea of music *in dialogue* with one or more prototypical features of any of its underlying normal schemata plays an important theoretical role in Hepokoski and Darcy, *Elements of Sonata Theory*. For similar approaches see also Hepokoski, "Genre and Content in Mid-Century Verdi"; "Fiery-Pulsed Libertine or Domestic Hero? Strauss's Don Juan Reinvestigated," in *Richard Strauss: New Perspectives on the Composer and His Work*, ed. Bryan Gilliam, 135–75 (Durham, N.C.: Duke University Press, 1992); and "Structure, Implication, and the End of *Suor Angelica*," in *Studi Pucciniani* 3 (2004): 241–264. For a nuanced consideration of the complex relationship between *structure* and *expression* in music, see Hatten, *Interpreting Musical Gestures, Topics, and Tropes*, 9–11.

25. The summary here draws on the sources cited in n. 13 and, from the Puccini literature, Harold Powers, "Form and Formula," in *Studi Pucciniani* 3 (2004): 11–49; and David Rosen, "'La solita forma' in Puccini's Operas?," 179–99.

26. This is because from about Verdi's middle period, the prototypical situation in Romantic Italian opera was the dramatic confrontation, and thus the duet became the prototypical scene type. For this reason, perhaps, duets in this repertoire almost always exhibit a more conventional formal organization—they typically hew more closely to the schema—than any of the other possible Italian formal genres. The aria underwent significant formal alteration even as early as middle Verdi, with its full four-movement form beginning to change as early as the 1850s and all but dying out by about 1870, whereas Verdi's use of the standardized form in his duets persisted the longest.

27. The terms "kinetic" and "static" are Gossett's; see "The 'Candeur virginale' of *Tancredi*."

28. For more details on Italian prosody, see chapter 2, n. 20.

29. "*Adagio*" (italicized) means the second of the four core *solita forma* movements. Unitalicized, "adagio" refers to a tempo.

30. On the points in this paragraph, see especially Perluigi Petrobelli's formulation of opera's "three main systems" and the nature of their relationships and interactions, in "Music in the Theater (apropos of *Aïda*, Act III)," in *Themes in Drama* vol. 3: *Drama, Dance, and Music*, ed. James Redmond (Cambridge: Cambridge University Press, 1981) (reprinted in Perluigi Petrobelli, *Music in the Theater: Essays on Verdi and Other Composers*, trans. Roger Parker, 113–126 [Princeton, N.J.: Princeton University Press, 1994]). See also Ross, "Studien zum Verhältnis von Libretto und Komposition."

31. Powers, "'La solita forma' and 'The Uses of Convention,'" is definitive on these points. On the issue of deformations of the *solita forma* in Italian opera, Verdi likely assumed his audience was familiar with the normal formal schemes, though actual contemporary evidence on Verdi's audience (or even Verdi's own thinking on this point) is scarce; see Powers, "'La solita forma' and 'The Uses of Convention,'" passim. On *solita forma* deformations as intentional, see David Rosen, "'La solita forma' in Puccini's Operas?," 181–84; on the issue of intentionality and its implications in analysis and criticism more generally, see the classic article by William K. Wimsatt and Monroe C. Beardsley, "The Intentional Fallacy," *Sewanee Review* 54 (1946): 468–88 (with numerous reprints).

32. *Italia umbertina* refers to the period (1878–1900) of King Umberto I of Italy, the strict conservative son of Vittorio Emanuele II. Umberto was unpopular among the growing number of Italian left-wing activists who opposed his hostility toward the spread of socialism, his favorable attitude toward the spread of colonialism, and his crackdowns on civil liberties. He was assassinated in 1900, the year after the landmark Bava Beccaris massacre in Milan, during which the general for whom the event is named used force to quell anti-colonialist political demonstrations related to the ongoing wars in North Africa.

33. The turn of phrase is Steven Huebner's: "[Puccini's] repertory repeatedly manifests an impetus to have the best of two worlds: on the one hand, the preservation of *cantabile* singing in closed structural units and, on the other, an obfuscation of those units for the sake of continuity that reflects local colour, provides a naturalistic unfolding of events, and produces psychological veracity." See his "Thematic Recall in Late Nineteenth-Century Opera," *Studi Pucciniani* 3 (2004): 104.

34. I have in mind the influence on Puccini of the Italian *partimenti* tradition: see Nicholas Baragwanath's forthcoming book, *Puccini and the Italian Traditions* (Bloomington: Indiana University Press).

35. Girardi, *Puccini*, is relevant on these points (especially the influence of French music on Puccini); I am indebted in much of this summary to his discussions of Puccini's early, non-operatic output and to his work on *Le villi* (1–19), *Manon Lescaut* (56–98), *La bohème* (99–144), *Tosca* (145–194), and *La fanciulla del West* (259–327). The discussions in Budden, *Puccini*, overlap in many places with those in Girardi; see Budden, 1–57 on Puccini's early output, 87–130 on *Manon Lescaut*, 131–80 on *La bohème*, 181–222 on *Tosca*, and 274–331 on *La fanciulla*. For more on the French influence in Puccini, see Nicolaisen, *Italian Opera in Transi-*

tion, 1871–1893 (Ann Arbor, Mich.: UMI Research Press, 1980), 67–69 and 187–239; Carner, *Puccini,* 3rd ed., passim (Debussy's influence in particular plays an important role in Carner's view of Puccini's music); and, on Puccini's fascination with French literature and culture more generally, Giuseppe Pintorno, "Les sources françaises des opéras de Giacomo Puccini" (Ph.D. diss., University of Milan, 1970).

36. For more on these aesthetic trends in contemporary European theater, see Jürgen Maehder, "Drammaturgia musicale e strutture narrative nel teatro musicale italiano della generazione dell'ottanta," in *Alfredo Casella e L'Europa: Atti del convegno internazionale di studi,* Siena, June 7–9, 2001 (*Chigiana* vol. 44), ed. Mila de Santis (Florence: Olschki, 2003), 223–48. For Brecht's often-cited use of the term *verfremdung,* see Brecht, *Brecht on Theatre,* trans. and ed. John Willett (New York: Hill and Wang, 1964), esp. 26–29, 53–57, 91–100, and 136–53 (on acting); 84–91 (on the use of music); and 29–31, 33–43, and 130–36 (on approaches to form and dramaturgy).

37. On these aspects of Puccini's late music, I have been influenced especially by Maehder, "*Turandot* and the Theatrical Aesthetics of the Twentieth Century"; Pinzauti, "Giacomo Puccini's *Trittico*"; Stoïanova, "Remarques sur l'actualité de *Turandot*"; and Girardi, *Puccini,* 365–487.

38. Notions of how we experience opera and music in general are important topics in recent, post-structuralist musicological and non-musicological literature, all of which draw on work in narrative theory, psychoanalytical theory, and linguistic semiotics. Sources for the ideas in what follows will be cited as needed; other important influences on my thinking include Guy Rosolato, "La voix: entre corps et langage," *Revue française de psychanalyse* 38 (1974): 75–95; Gary Tomlinson, *Metaphysical Song;* Carolyn Abbate, *In Search of Opera;* Roland Barthes, *Image–Music–Text,* trans. Stephen Heath (New York: Hill and Wang, 1977); Lucien Dällenbach, *The Mirror in the Text,* trans. Jeremy Whiteley and Emma Hughes (Chicago: University of Chicago Press, 1989); Jacques Derrida, *Of Grammatology,* trans. Gayatri Chakravorty Spivak (Baltimore: Johns Hopkins University Press, 1976); and Derrida, *Positions,* trans. Alan Bass (Chicago: University of Chicago Press, 1981).

39. Carolyn Abbate, *Unsung Voices,* 10. For more on narrative pragmatics in a non-musical context, and on the field of narrative linguistics more generally, see Steven Cohan and Linda M. Shires, *Telling Stories: A Theoretical Analysis of Narrative Fiction* (New York: Routledge, 1988); Michael Toolan, *Narrative: A Critical Linguistic Introduction,* 2nd ed. (New York: Routledge: 2001); and W. J. T. Mitchell, ed., *On Narrative* (Chicago: University of Chicago Press, 1981). All are cited in Stephen McClatchie, "Towards a Post-Modern Wagner," review of Carolyn Abbate, *Unsung Voices,* in *Wagner* 13, no. 3 (1992): 108–121, which provides not only a succinct introduction to narrative and other theories important in Abbate's work, but also a clear, penetrating discussion of *Unsung Voices.* For an alternative, wide-ranging approach to musical narrative that appeared after this manuscript was complete, see Byron Almén, *A Theory of Musical Narrative* (Bloomington: Indiana University Press, 2008).

40. Abbate, *Unsung Voices,* 27.

41. Abbate, *Unsung Voices,* 19.

42. Hatten frames the issue structurally in terms of semiotics rather than narrative theory; see *Musical Meaning in Beethoven,* 174–202. See also Hatten, "On Nar-

rativity in Music"; and Hatten, *Interpreting Musical Gestures, Topics, and Tropes,* 35–52. For a clear, concise explanation of how Hatten's "levels of discourse" overlap with Abbate's "narrating voices," see Hatten, *Musical Meaning in Beethoven,* 315 n. 13.

43. Many others have described the phenomenon of multiple voices in literature: see, among others, Roland Barthes, *S/Z,* trans. Richard Miller, preface by Richard Howard (New York: Hill and Wang, 1974) (originally in French as *S/Z* [Paris: Editions de Seuil, 1970]), in which, in a structuralist analysis of an Honoré de Balzac short story, he enumerates five "codes" (or "means of signification") and five "voices," each intrinsic to the text and all of which together frame the space in which the text derives its meaning; and Mikhail Bakhtin, *The Dialogic Imagination: Four Essays,* ed. Michael Holquist, trans. Caryl Emerson and Michael Holquist (Austin: University of Texas Press, 1981), in which he describes the novel as "multiform in style," "variform in speech and voice," as including "several heterogeneous stylistic unities," and as comprising a "system of languages that mutually and ideologically interanimate one another." On Barthes, Bakhtin, and their relevance in Abbate's theory of narrative pragmatics, see also McClatchie, "Towards a Post-Modern Wagner," 114–15, and Christopher Wintle, "Wotan's Rhetoric of Anguish," review of Carolyn Abbate, *Unsung Voices, Journal of the Royal Musical Association* 118, no. 1 (1993): 121–22.

44. On diegesis in music, see Abbate, *Unsung Voices,* xi–xii.

45. On *musica in scena,* see Girardi, "Per un inventario della musica in scena nel teatro verdiano," *Studi verdiani* 6 (1990): 99–145 (esp. 106–107); Carl Dahlhaus, "The Dramaturgy of Italian Opera"; and Girardi, *Puccini,* 10.

46. Abbate, *Unsung Voices,* 12.

47. Wilson, *The Puccini Problem,* 185–220.

48. Abbate, *Unsung Voices,* 10. The notion of the singing voice as a sonic object with the capacity to drown out words, characters, and even music itself is from Michel Poizat, *The Angel's Cry,* as is Abbate's reference to the "presence of the performer." Other commentators have invoked the same ideas to explain the way listeners experience opera; see, for example, Anne C. Shreffler, "The Coloratura's Voice: Another Look at Zerbinetta's Aria from *Ariadne auf Naxos,*" in *Richard Strauss und die Moderne: Bericht über das International Symposium München, 21. bis 23. Juli 1999,* ed. Bernd Edelmann, Birgit Lodes, and Reinhold Schlötterer (Berlin: Henschel, 2001), 361–90.

49. Abbate, Unsung Voices, 10.

50. On oppositions as a source of meaning (and the oft-cited formulation that "meaning is difference"), see Ferdinand de Saussure, *Course in General Linguistics,* ed. Charles Bally and Albert Sechehaye, trans. Wade Baskin (New York: McGraw-Hill, 1966) (originally in French as *Cours de linguistique générale,* ed. Charles Bally and Albert Sechehaye, avec la collaboration de Albert Riedlinger [Paris: Payot, 1916]). Saussure's binary oppositions also play an important role in the semiotics of Charles Sanders Peirce; see Peirce, *Collected Papers of Charles Sanders Peirce,* vols. 1–6 ed. Charles Hartshorne and Paul Weiss, vols. 7–8 ed. Arthur W. Burks (Cambridge: Harvard University Press, 1931–1960). Peirce's *Collected Papers* is being superseded by a chronological edition of Peirce's output, produced by the Peirce Edition Project at Indiana University–Purdue University at Indianapolis (see *The*

Essential Peirce: Selected Philosophical Writings, ed. Nathan Houser and Christian Kloesel [Bloomington: Indiana University Press, 1992–]). On markedness theory, see Michael Shapiro, *Asymmetry: An Inquiry into the Linguistic Structure of Poetry* (Amsterdam: North-Holland, 1976); Shapiro, *The Sense of Grammar* (Bloomington: Indiana University Press, 1983); and Edwin L. Battistella, *Markedness: The Evaluative Superstructure of Language* (New York: State University of New York Press, 1990). Markedness originates in the phonology theory (the theory of how sounds function in a language) of Nicolai Trubetzkoi, *Principles of Phonology,* trans. Christine A. M. Baltaxe (Berkeley: University of California Press, 1969) (originally in German as *Grundzüge der Phonologie* [Prague: Travaux du Cercle Linguistique de Prague, 1939]); and Roman Jakobson and Morris Halle, *Fundamentals of Language* (The Hague: Mouton, 1956). For applications of all these theoretical constructs, especially markedness theory, in music analysis, see Hatten, *Musical Meaning in Beethoven;* and Hatten, *Interpreting Musical Gestures, Topics, and Tropes.*

2. THE ROMANTIC STYLE IN LATE PUCCINI

1. Commentary on Puccini's melodic style is ubiquitous in the literature; for a more detailed consideration of his melodic and orchestrational approach across his entire output, see especially Mosco Carner, *Puccini,* 3rd ed., 318–25.

2. Girardi, *Puccini,* comments throughout on Puccini's stylistic relationship specifically to Massenet; on this topic see also Huebner, "Thematic Recall in Late Nineteenth-Century Opera."

3. "R" stands for "rehearsal number." "Rm.n" reads "the nth measure of rehearsal number m," where the measure at the rehearsal number is measure 1. Measures before the first rehearsal number will be designated "Ro.n" (thus "Ro" is the first measure in the score, "Ro.2" is the second, etc.). All references are to the full orchestral scores; see the Note on Scores, Librettos, and Translations in this volume. In *Turandot,* rehearsal numbers start over in each act, but for the sake of concision I have not indicated the act number in the orthography referring to measure numbers. The act in question will be clear from the text.

4. The pastorale is one of three dance topics in compound duple meter; the others are the gigue, which is faster, lighter, and typically includes dotted rhythms, and the siciliano, which is slower and more rustic. See Wye Jamison Allanbrook, *Rhythmic Gesture in Mozart: "Le Nozze di Figaro" and "Don Giovanni"* (Chicago: University of Chicago Press, 1983), 40–45; and Raymond Monelle, *The Musical Topic: Hunt, Military, and Pastoral* (Bloomington: Indiana University Press, 2006), 185–271.

The term "topic" (Gr. *topos*) is from rhetorical theory and has been borrowed by numerous authors to explain how music signifies; in musical contexts the word refers to characteristic styles or figures that have strong associations—because of their familiarity—with particular expressive meanings and thus serve as subjects in the musical discourse. The seminal source on topic theory in music is Leonard G. Ratner, *Classic Music: Expression, Form, and Style* (New York: Schirmer, 1980). See also Allanbrook, *Rhythmic Gesture in Mozart;* Fritz Noske, *The Signifier and the Signified: Studies in the Operas of Mozart and Verdi,* reprint (New York: Oxford

University Press, 1990); V. Kofi Agawu, *Playing with Signs: A Semiotic Interpretation of Classic Music* (Princeton: Princeton University Press, 1991); Elaine Sisman, *Mozart: The "Jupiter" Symphony, no. 41 in C major, K. 551* (Cambridge: Cambridge University Press, 1993); Hatten, *Musical Meaning in Beethoven;* Raymond Monelle, *The Sense of Music: Semiotic Essays,* with a foreword by Robert S. Hatten (Princeton, N.J.: Princeton University Press, 2000); Hatten, *Interpreting Musical Gestures, Topics, and Tropes;* and Monelle, *The Musical Topic.*

5. On the *violinata* in music of the *giovane scuola,* see Adriana Guarnieri Corazzol, "Opera and Verismo: Regressive Points of View and the Artifice of Alienation," trans. Roger Parker, *Cambridge Opera Journal* 5, no. 1 (1993): 39–53 (originally in Italian as "Opera e verismo: Regressione del punto di vista e artificio dello straniamento," in *Ruggero Leoncavallo nel suo tempo: Primo convegno internazionale di studi su Ruggero Leoncavallo,* ed. Lorenza Guiot and Jürgen Maehder, 13–31 [Milan: Sonzogno, 1993]). Ashbrook and Powers, *Puccini's "Turandot,"* 94, also mention Puccini's use of the technique.

6. "To trope" in music is to bring together "two otherwise incompatible style types in a single location to produce a unique expressive meaning from their collision or fusion" (Hatten, *Interpreting Musical Gestures, Topics, and Tropes,* 68). That is, novel interactions of apparently incongruous musical elements (conflicting style types, genres, formal functions, etc.) in close proximity, either simultaneously or successively, produce a new, emergent meaning, or emergent trope, that goes beyond the expressive meaning of each individual element on its own terms. For more see Hatten, *Musical Meaning in Beethoven,* 166–72; and Hatten, *Interpreting Musical Gestures, Topics, and Tropes,* 68–89. This meaning of *trope* draws on the sense of the word common in language and literature, in which a *trope* (Gr. *tropos:* "to turn") is a word or expression used in a figurative rather than a literal sense (also known as a figure of speech). It can also refer to a recurring, or overused, theme or device (in this sense otherwise known as a cliché). It should not be confused with several other possible musical meanings. In medieval sacred music, a *trope* is an addition—either textual, musical, or both—to an existing plainchant (see Hatten, *Musical Meaning in Beethoven,* 314, n. 4); medieval music theorists used the word to mean what we now call "mode" (Boethius, for example, used the Latin *modus, tonus,* and *tropus* interchangeably; see Calvin M. Bower, "The Modes of Boethius," *Journal of Musicology* 3, no. 3 [1984]: 253, 259); and Josef Hauer—clearly borrowing this latter sense of the word—used it to describe a pair of unordered hexachords (of which he identified a total of forty-four) in his version of the twelve-tone compositional method (see John R. Covach, "The Music and Theories of Josef Matthias Hauer" [Ph.D. diss., University of Michigan, 1990]).

7. Note that "Firenze è come un albero fiorito" was originally a half step lower and appears as such in the first Italian edition of the piano-vocal score (Milan: Ricordi, 1918; © 1918; plate no. 117000; Schickling 84.E.1). Beginning with the second (1919) edition, the aria is in B♭ (all the music from R28 through R35 is a half step higher than in the original). See Greenwald, "Dramatic Exposition and Musical Structure in Puccini's Operas," 120; and Schickling, 363.

8. The term "hypermeasure" was introduced in Edward T. Cone, *Musical Form and Musical Performance* (New York: Norton, 1968). For more, and for more on durational reductions, see Rothstein, *Phrase Rhythm in Tonal Music;* Schachter,

"Rhythm and Linear Analysis: A Preliminary Study"; Schachter, "Rhythm and Linear Analysis: Durational Reduction"; and Schachter, "Rhythm and Linear Analysis: Aspects of Meter."

9. "Se in lontano giorno / io t'ho sorriso / per quel sorriso, dolce mia fanciulla . . . / . . . Dell'esilio addolcisci a lui le strade." For *Turandot* translations I have relied primarily on William Weaver's, printed in Nicholas John, ed., *Giacomo Puccini: "Turandot,"* English National Opera Guide no. 27, 68–109 (London: John Calder, 1984).

10. James Hepokoski has described these same kinds of non-functional harmony and voice leading with the terms "non-progression" and "non-voice-leading" and the attendant effects as producing a state of "tonal vertigo"; see his "Structure, Implication, and the End of *Suor Angelica.*" Incidentally, the V-IV-I cadence is most likely a musical corollary for transcendence; this is the same cadence, with the same meaning, used by Wagner at the end of Isolde's Liebestod in *Tristan und Isolde,* by Strauss at the end of the symphonic poem *Don Juan,* and by Strauss again at the end of "Frühling," the first of the *Vier Letzte Lieder* (I am grateful to my student Adam Hudlow for calling my attention to the latter).

11. See chapter 3 for more details on *Il tabarro*'s formal organization, including details on individual set pieces and consideration of the work's embedded references to conventional *ottocento* formal prototypes.

12. On the lyric prototype see Friedrich Lippmann, *Vincenzo Bellini und die Italienische Opera Seria seiner Zeit: Studien über Libretto, Arienform, und Melodik,* Analecta Musicologica 6 (Köln: Bohlau, 1969); Julian Budden, *The Operas of Verdi,* vol. 1: *From Oberto to Rigoletto,* rev. ed. (New York: Clarendon Press, 1992); Gary Tomlinson, "Verdi After Budden," *19th-Century Music* 5 (1981): 170–81; Joseph Kerman, "Lyric Form and Flexibility in Simon Boccanegra," *Studi Verdiani* 1 (1982): 47–62; Scott L. Balthazar, "Evolving Conventions in Italian Serious Opera," 42–71, 221–31; Balthazar, "Rossini and the Development of the Mid-Century Lyric Form," *Journal of the American Musicological Society* 41, no. 1 (1988): 102–25; and Roger Parker, "'Insolite Forme,' or Basevi's Garden Path," in *Leonora's Last Act: Essays in Verdian Discourse,* 42–60 (Princeton, N.J.: Princeton University Press, 1997). Parker finds (50) a description of exactly the same formal schema in Basevi, *Studio sulle opere di Giuseppe Verdi,* 24.

13. For *Il trittico* translations I have relied largely on Kenneth Chalmers' translations, printed in the 1999 Antonio Pappano recording on EMI Classics (7243 5 56587 2 2).

14. Some forms of these arpeggiations are known in the parlance of Schenkerian analysis as an *initial arpeggiation* (Gr. *Anstieg*).

15. What I will observe here in Puccini's music is similar to what Frank Samarotto has observed in music of late Beethoven and others and described, in much more theoretical detail, as "temporal plasticity"; see his "A Theory of Temporal Plasticity in Tonal Music: An Extension of the Schenkerian Approach to Rhythm with Special Reference to Beethoven's Late Music" (Ph.D. diss., City University of New York, 1999). Like Samarotto and many others, I regard *meter* as absolute—a periodic, temporal constant—and various deformations (expansions and contractions) as strictly *rhythmic* phenomena that occur within the fixed metric frame and that do not threaten the integrity of the meter itself. See Samarotto, "A Theory of

Temporal Plasticity," esp. 13–39 and 63–80. For theoretical foundations, see, among others, Fred Lerdahl and Ray Jackendoff, *A Generative Theory of Tonal Music* (Cambridge, Mass.: MIT Press, 1983); Schachter, "Rhythm and Linear Analysis: Aspects of Meter"; and Rothstein, *Phrase Rhythm in Tonal Music.* For a different point of view, see Christopher F. Hasty, *Meter as Rhythm* (New York: Oxford University Press, 1997).

16. Luigi Ricci, *Puccini interprete di se stesso* (Milan: Ricordi, 1954), trans. and annotated in Harry Nicholas Dunstan, "Performance Practices in the Music of Giacomo Puccini as Observed by Luigi Ricci" (Ph.D. diss., Catholic University of America, 1989) (see 1–3 on Puccini's tempo preferences). Ricci was a contemporary vocal coach, accompanist, and conductor in Rome who worked directly with Puccini on productions of Puccini's operas (Dunstan, "Performance Practices in the Music of Giacomo Puccini," viii–xi).

17. According to Ricci, Puccini is known to have disliked fermatas of exaggerated length—"no notes of a long agony"; see Dunstan, "Performance Practices in the Music of Giacomo Puccini," 4.

18. Mosco Carner, *Puccini*, 3rd ed., 505 has written that Puccini's well-known marking for this aria, "*ad uso di stornello toscano*" (R30), refers not so much to the music but to the text, specifically the lyric *endecasillabo* verse—i.e., verse with eleven syllables per line, common in popular music of Tuscany and elsewhere but until late in the nineteenth century common in opera only in *recitatives.* This raises the question of what to make of the use of the same lyric *endecasillabo* in, for example, Luigi's "Hai ben ragione." That this piece lacks both the rhythmic character of "Firenze" and the specific *stornello* (or any other) designation may say more about either the rather ordinary status of lyric *endecasillabo* verse by the 1910s or about Puccini's assimilation of Tuscan folk music than about the accuracy of Carner's claim. See also Paolo Fabbri, "Istituti metrici e formali," in *Teorie e technice, immagini e fantasmi,* vol. VI of *Storia dell'opera italiana,* ed. Lorenzo Bianconi and Giorgio Pestelli, 163–233 (Turin, EDT: 1988) (in English as "Metrical and Formal Organization," in *Opera in Theory and Practice, Image and Myth,* 151–219), who observes that lyric *endecasillabo* verse was used even in the mid-nineteenth century to lend a literary, chivalrous, or popular quality. For more on Tuscan folk music, see Francesco Balilla Pratella, *Le Arti e le tradizioni popolare d'Italia: primo documentario per la storia dell'etnofonia in Italia* (Udine: Editrice IDEA, 1941); and Eugenia Levi, *Fiorita di canti tradizionali del popolo italiano,* 2nd ed. (Firenze: Bemporad, 1926) (both cited in Carner, *Puccini,* 3rd ed., 504). For more on Italian prosody, see n. 20.

19. "Structure, Implication, and the End of *Suor Angelica,*" 251–56. This is the "telos music" in Hepokoski's teleologically oriented rotational form. See the discussion of formal design in *Suor Angelica* in chapter 3.

20. On the metric qualities of the *novenario* meter, see Moreen, "Integration of Text Forms and Musical Forms," 16—where he also speculates that the similarity between the *novenario* and *decasillabo* may be the reason *novenario* is so uncommon in Verdi's libretti. For *novenario* in Boito's *Mefistofele,* see, for example, Faust's "Dai campi, dai prati, che inonda" from Act I and the well known Faust-Margherita duet from Act III, "Lontano, lontano, lontano." The *Mefistofele* libretto, Boito's own, was printed with a *Prologo in teatro* and extensive annotations by Boito himself,

including commentary on the metric innovations. The original, with the *Prologo*, is reprinted in Boito, *Tutti gli scritti*, ed. Piero Nardi (Milan: Mondadori, 1942), 95–179. For more on the subject, see William Ashbrook, "Boito and the 1868 *Mefistofele* Libretto as a Reform Text," in *Reading Opera*, ed. Arthur Groos and Roger Parker, 268–87 (Princeton, N.J.: Princeton University Press, 1988); and Jay Nicolaisen, "The First *Mefistofele*," *19th-Century Music* 1, no. 3 (1978): 221–32.

Some knowledge of Italian prosody and prosodic terminology is also necessary here. The normative form of a line of Italian poetry has an accent on the penultimate syllable; this accent is the *accento comune*, and a line exhibiting this property has a *piano* ending. Two other line endings are possible: the *tronco*, in which the *accento comune* falls on the last syllable; and the *sdrucciolo*, in which the *accento comune* falls on the antepenultimate syllable. Verse meters are defined according to the numbers of syllables per line in the poetry: common options include *quinario* (five syllables per line), *senario* (six), *settenario* (seven), *ottonario* (eight), *decasillabo* (ten), and *endecasillabo* (eleven). Numbers of syllables per line are always counted as if the line has a *piano* ending (with one syllable following the *accento comune*): thus *tronco* lines appear to be missing a syllable and *sdrucciolo* lines appear to have one extra. For a more detailed summary of principles of Italian poetry as they relate to opera, see Robert Anthony Moreen, "Integration of Text Forms and Musical Forms," 9–26; a more extensive discussion (with historical context and a comprehensive bibliography) is in Paolo Fabbri, "Metrical and Formal Organization," 151–219. Two standard texts on Italian prosody (cited by Moreen) are also helpful: Alberto del Monte, *Retorica, stilistica, versificazione* (Torino: Loescher, 1968); and Bruno Migliorini and Fredi Chiapelli, *Elementi di stilistica e di versificazione italiana* (Firenze: Le Monier, 1960). An interesting German source on the subject is W. Theodor Elwert, *Italienische Metrik* (Munich: M. Huebner, 1968).

21. Hepokoski: "The music throws itself brutally onto the third chord [of the third cycle], stilling its ongoing measured tread, as if martyring itself for four long bars on this minor-mode mediant. Indeed, the four bars, *forte-piano* followed by a *diminuendo molto*, are sustained even longer by a fermata, and into their decaying stasis breaks the now-meaningless clatter of the cloister, the nightly signal to retire into one's private cell" ("Structure, Implication, and the End of *Suor Angelica*," 253).

22. In some ways Puccini's metric deformations are reversions to an older, *primo ottocento* practice. Scott L. Balthazar, "Evolving Conventions in Italian Serious Opera," 48, has found that Rossini's music "distorts the upper levels of the metric hierarchy" at the ends of phrases (although typically just *before* the cadence rather than just *after* it, as is more common in Puccini) more often than does the music of Bellini, Donizetti, and Verdi—each of whom tend toward a more absolute metric regularity in their lyric movements. A comparison of a typically Verdian example such as Abigaille's slow movement "Anch'io dischiuso un giorno" from *Nabucco* Act II—which maintains strict four-bar groupings so that not a single hypermeter is expanded or contracted—with one of Puccini's most regular lyric movements, "Firenze è come un albero fiorito," is instructive: even the latter, as regular as it is on the phrase level, contains one metric expansion (the $\frac{2}{4}$ measure at 30.9) among the first three phrases.

23. The best way to hear (or feel) the effect depicted in the durational reduction—and it must be emphasized that the effect is meant to be *heard*, not *seen*—is

to listen to the music and conduct, marking beats one through four in every measure at the location indicated by the Arabic numerals in example 2.8. The sensation of accelerating to keep up with the truncated measures and "waiting" on the expanded measures becomes real because the conducting requires a physical, tactile response to the music.

24. James Hepokoski, *Giuseppe Verdi: "Otello"* (Cambridge: Cambridge University Press, 1987), 139–40.

25. The following draws on work of Jürgen Maehder and Peter Ross: see Maehder, "The Origins of Italian *Literaturoper: Guglielmo Ratcliff, La Figlia di Iorio, Parisina,* and *Francesca da Rimini,*" in *Reading Opera,* ed. Arthur Groos and Roger Parker, 92–128 (Princeton, N.J.: Princeton University Press, 1988); and Ross, "Der Librettoovers im Übergang vom späten Ottocento zum frühen Novecento," in *Tendenze della musica teatrale italiana all'inizio del Novecento: Atti del 40 convegno internazionale "Ruggero Leoncavallo nel suo tempo,"* Locarno, Biblioteca Cantonale, *23–24 maggio 1998,* ed. Lorenza Guiot and Jürgen Maehder, 19–54 (Milan: Sonzogno: 2005).

26. See Maehder, "The Origins of Italian *Literaturoper,*" 92, 128.

27. For a more in-depth discussion of duple or quadruple hypermeter as the norm in tonal music and triple hypermeter as the exception, see Rothstein, *Phrase Rhythm in Tonal Music,* esp. 33–40; and Schachter, "Rhythm and Linear Analysis: Aspects of Meter." Any non-duple groupings are almost always perceived as modified duple groups—a phenomenon from which German music theorist Hugo Riemann (1849–1919) even went so far as to warn composers that they could never escape (Rothstein, *Phrase Rhythm in Tonal Music,* 33).

28. On the *cavatina* and the *romanza,* see Martin Chusid, "The Organization of Scenes with Arias: Verdi's Cavatinas and Romanzas," in *Atti del Io Congresso internazionale di studi verdiani, 31 July–02 August 1966,* 59–66 (Parma: Instituto di studi verdiani, 1969); see also Hepokoski, "Genre and Content in Mid-Century Verdi," 265. Note that Chusid's article is pioneering in that it engages the topic of the *solita forma* before much of the seminal, detailed work on the topic (such as Moreen's dissertation) had appeared in print. Thus Chusid employs terminology somewhat differently than we are used to seeing today, which can lead to confusion if one is not mindful of the problem. The word "aria" in his title, for example, refers to what we think of today as a single, lyric "movement" (either the *adagio* or the *cabaletta*) embedded in a full, four-movement *solita forma*—where the latter is referred to in his title with the "scene." Today the entire piece (Chusid's "scene") would be called the "aria."

3. EXPRESSIVE USES OF CONVENTION IN *IL TABARRO*

1. *Puccini,* 3rd ed., 473.

2. Certainly other readings are possible, including one that views each of the panels as unified by the same nihilistic sense of hopelessness. See Hepokoski, "Structure, Implication, and the End of *Suor Angelica,*" 259–62, and chapter 5.

3. On Puccini's inspiration for *Il trittico,* see, among many others, Carner, *Puccini,* 3rd ed., 473; Girardi, *Puccini,* 365–79; Mike Ashman, "Divided They Fall," *Op-*

era 49, no. 4 (1998): 389–93; and Budden, *Puccini*, 370–80. On Puccini's interest in French sources, see Helen Greenwald, "Puccini, *Il tabarro*, and the Dilemma of Operatic Transposition," *Journal of the American Musicological Society* 51, no. 3 (1998): 521–58 (esp. 529); Guarnieri Corazzol, "Opera and Verismo"; Ashman, "Divided They Fall," 390–91; and Pintorno, "Les sources françaises des opéras de Giacomo Puccini."

4. *Tinta* (pl. *tinte*) refers to a work's characteristic color, atmosphere, or ambience, something along the lines of, as Powers has pointed out, the French notion of *couleur* or *couleur locale* (often rendered with the Italian *colore locale* in Puccini studies—and I use the terms interchangeably); see Powers, "'La solita forma' and 'The Uses of Convention,'" 65–67. The word seems to originate in Basevi, *Studio sulle opere di Giuseppe Verdi*, 114–16. See also Budden, *The Operas of Verdi, vol. 2: From Il Trovatore to La Forza del destino*, rev. ed. (New York: Clarendon Press, 1992), 53–54; and Gilles de Van, "La notion de *tinta*: mémoire confuse et affinities thématiques dans les opéras de Verdi," *Revue de musicologie* 76 (1990): 187–98. In the Puccini literature, *tinta* has also been used to mean approximately what I call "style": see Ashbrook and Powers, *Puccini's "Turandot"*; see also chapter 4, n. 7.

5. September 24, 1904, *Carteggi pucciniani*, letter 395: "Insisto per i tre colori." On Puccini's first mention of joining contrasting works in a single evening, see Maehder, "*Turandot* and the Theatrical Aesthetics of the Twentieth Century," 272; Girardi, *Puccini*, 263–64; Carner, *Puccini*, 3rd ed., 163–64; and Ashbrook, *The Operas of Puccini* (Ithaca, N.Y.: Cornell University Press, 1985 [orig. 1968]), 170.

6. *Carteggi pucciniani*, letter 501 (cited in Girardi, *Puccini*, 372): "sono sempre in angustie per il libretto. Non farò più *La femme et le pantin*. Mi è sorta un'idea: tempo fa avevo pensato di fare tre bozzetti differenti (3 atti) da Gorki, presi dai *Vagaboni* e dai *Racconti della steppa*; avevo scelto la *Zattera* e i 26 per uno: mi mancava un terzo drammatico, forte, come finale di serata, e non mi riuscì trovarlo in tutte le cose gorkiane."

7. See Girardi, *Puccini*, 118–26 (on *La bohème*) and 203 (on *Madama Butterfly*). For a discussion of similar filmic effects *in Il trittico*, see chapter 5.

8. What follows draws on Girardi, *Puccini*, 372–74.

9. On aspects of unity in *Il trittico*, see Marcelo Conati, "*Il tabarro* ovvera la 'solita' insolita forma," in *Studi Pucciniani 3* (2004): 265–81; Girardi, *Puccini*, 370–77; Carner, *Puccini*, 3rd ed., 473; and Ashman, "Divided They Fall."

10. Girardi, *Puccini*, 375–76; Conati, "*Il tabarro* ovvera la 'solita' insolita forma"; and Karl Georg Maria Berg, *Giacomo Puccinis Opern: Musik und Dramaturgie* (Kassel: Bärenretier Hochschulschriften, 1991), 56–57.

11. *Carteggi pucciniani*, letter 501 (cited in Girardi, *Puccini*, 372): "poi ci ripensai e non trovai pratica la cosa: tre cose differenti, che poi sarebbero state eseguite dai medisimi artisti toglieva l'illusione e nuoceva alla verità rappresentativa. E allora smisi l'idea." On Puccini's interest around 1900 in the Daudet novels, see Girardi, *Puccini*, 200.

12. Puccini to Clausetti, April 8, 1918, *Carteggi pucciniani*, letter 718: "Per il tabarro, oltre il Galeffi ci vuole una donna a sè, che può fare *Schicchi* anche; me per *Schicchi* occorre una donnina ingenua di figura piccola e voce fresca, senza drammaticità, etc. La Dalla Rizza, che non sarebbe l'ideale per S. A., può benissimo fare la Lauretta di G. S."

13. *Carteggi pucciniani*, letter 501: "Ora ci ripenso, non ai bozzetti ma a Gorki, che credo trovisi ancora a Capri."

14. Guarnieri Corazzol, "Opera and Verismo," 39-46; Greenwald, "Puccini, *Il tabarro*, and the Dilemma of Operatic Transposition," 525-27; and Maehder, "*Turandot* and the Theatrical Aesthetics of the Twentieth Century," 269-70.

15. On this point specifically, see Maehder, "*Turandot* and the Theatrical Aesthetics of the Twentieth Century," 272. For a fuller discussion, see chapter 1.

16. Paris: Ondet and Titerbo, 1911. The play premiered on September 1, 1910, at the Théâtre Marigny in Paris; Puccini probably saw a production in May 1912. See Schickling, *Catalogue of the Works*, 346.

17. Carner, *Puccini*, 3rd ed., 473-76; Girardi, *Puccini*, 379-80.

18. Guarnieri Corazzol, "Opera and Verismo." On the *verismo* genre and the problems of its identity, see especially Andreas Giger, "Verismo: Origin, Corruption, and Redemption of an Operatic Term," *Journal of the American Musicological Society* 60, no. 2 (2007): 271-315; Matteo Sansone, "Verismo: From Literature to Opera" (Ph.D. diss., University of Edinburgh, 1987); and Sansone, "The Verismo of Ruggero Leoncavallo: A Source Study of *Pagliacci*," *Music and Letters* 70 (1989): 342-62.

19. Girardi's (*Puccini*, 379-96) terms for the three themes are "River," "Adultery," and "Cloak"; Greenwald ("Puccini, *Il tabarro*, and the Dilemma of Operatic Transposition") uses "River," "Fate," and "Cloak"; Carner (*Puccini*, 3rd ed., 476-86) uses "River," "Love," and "Cloak."

20. "Nel fondo il profilo della vecchia Parigi e principalmente la mole maestosa di Notre Dame staccano sul cielo di un rosso meraviglioso" ("In the distance the outline of old Paris, and mainly the majestic edifice of Notre Dame, stands out against a wondrously red sky").

21. On creating stasis as a strategy central to *Il tabarro*, see Greenwald, "Puccini, *Il tabarro*, and the Dilemma of Operatic Transposition," esp. 532-38.

22. On the structural and dramatic significance of this half-step shift, see Greenwald, "Puccini, *Il tabarro*, and the Dilemma of Operatic Transposition," 545ff.

23. Carner, *Puccini*, 3rd ed., 485.

24. Nicolaisen, *Italian Opera in Transition*, 15. Historical examples include, among many others, Barnaba's "O monument" in *La Gioconda*, Iago's Credo in *Otello*, and almost every example of an extended lyrical episode in *Falstaff*; Michele's monologue is in the same tradition.

25. "Nulla! . . . Silenzio! . . ." replaced Michele's original monologue, "Scorri, fiume eterno!," for the first time in a performance probably on January 22, 1922 in Rome (Schickling, *Catalogue of the Works*, 348). Puccini had earlier shown some dissatisfaction with "Scorri, fiume," and by the time the second Italian edition of the piano-vocal score was printed (1919; plate no. 117000; Schickling 84.E.2) the monologue had been shortened by nine bars. He apparently decided to eliminate it completely in favor of a new piece in November 1921; see *Carteggi pucciniani*, letter 819; and *Epistolario*, letters 195 (November 1, 1917) and 197 (November 17). According to Schickling, the first score that contains "Nulla! . . . Silenzio! . . ." is a single surviving copy, in the Bibliothèque nationale de France in Paris, of the second French edition of the piano-vocal score (copyright 1921; printed by Ricordi in Paris in 1922 at the earliest). The third Italian edition (plate no. 117404, 1924, Schickling

85.E.3) has the new monologue, as does the second Italian edition of the full score (plate no. 120480, 1927, Schickling 85.E.3B). For notes on the *Tabarro* editions, see Schickling, *Catalogue of the Works,* 341–46.

26. Greenwald ("Puccini, *Il tabarro,* and the Dilemma of Operatic Transposition," esp. 533ff.) has made the same point. On the transposition of the second Giorgetta-Luigi duet, see ibid., 542; and Budden, "Puccini's Transpositions," *Studi Pucciniani* 1 (1998): 13–15; and n. 59.

27. Corazzol, "Opera and Verismo," 42. For the term *musica di conversazione* in connection with *Il tabarro,* see Conati, *"Il tabarro* ovvera la 'solita' insolita forma," 273.

28. This was a late addition to the opera, inserted into the autograph full score in February 1917 and probably composed that same month (the score—Schickling 85.B.1—had been completed on November 25, 1916). See Schickling, *Catalogue of the Works,* 340 and 347.

29. See Moreen, "Integration of Text Forms and Musical Forms," 27ff. (and chapter 1, n. 17); and Paolo Fabbri, "Metrical and Formal Organization," 151–219.

30. Jürgen Maehder, "The Origins of Italian *Literaturoper,*" has discussed what he views as the general decline, evident just after the turn of the twentieth century, of Italian libretto-writing, especially with regard to librettists' use of conventional Italian verse and metric structures.

31. James Hepokoski, *Giuseppe Verdi: "Otello,"* 139–40. For more on the complications of poetic meters in this period, see also Maehder, "The Origins of Italian *Literaturoper,*" esp. 113–116; and Ross, "Der Librettoovers im Übergang vom späten Ottocento." I am grateful also to Peter Ross for sharing, in detailed personal correspondence with me, his expertise on this and numerous other issues related to Italian verse.

32. On the problem of locating the *tempo d'attacco,* see Moreen, "Integration of Text Forms and Musical Forms," 252–93; and Rosen, "'La solita forma' in Puccini's Operas?," 185ff. Also the statement that *versi sciolti* normally do not return after the *scena* is somewhat of an overgeneralization: Moreen 252–93 discusses this in more detail and provides examples from Verdi of *versi sciolti* in both *tempi d'attacco* and *tempi di mezzo.* The essential point, however, is that these are deformations of the normative schemata, invoked for dramatic or expressive effect, not norms in themselves.

33. On the use of lyric *endecasillabo* verse, see chapter 2, n. 18. Fabbri's observation ("Metrical and Formal Organization," 203) that lyric *endecasillabi* have a literary, chivalrous, and popular quality seems to apply well to Luigi's *adagio.* Moreen, "Integration of Text Forms and Musical Forms," 132–39, provides a table (1.1) listing precedents in Verdi's works through *Aïda.*

34. See Moreen, "Integration of Text Forms and Musical Forms," 210–51.

35. On this kind of "inward" discursive shift as stylistically idiomatic in late nineteenth-century Italian opera, see Guarnieri Corazzol, "Opera and Verismo," 39–46.

36. Numerous recent authors have discussed Frugola's "mechanical" characteristics, her unique position in *Il tabarro*'s dramatic space, and her similarity to other characters in Puccini: see Girardi, *Puccini,* 390; Carner, *Puccini,* 3rd ed., 483; and, for a more extensive discussion, Conati, *"Il tabarro* ovvera la 'solita' insolita forma," 278ff. The most detailed discussions of the theatrical aesthetic from which Frugola originates—a discussion that never mentions Frugola herself but focuses instead on

characters from *Turandot*—are Wilson, *The Puccini Problem*, 193–220; and Wilson, "Modernism and the Machine Woman." On masking actors as an alienation device, see W. Anthony Sheppard, *Revealing Masks: Exotic Influences and Ritualized Performance in Modernist Music Theater* (Berkeley: University of California Press, 2001). The idea of replacing live actors with puppets is Edward Gordon Craig's; see Wilson, "Modernism and the Machine Woman," 440; Sheppard, *Revealing Masks*, 28ff.; and Craig, "The Actor and the Übermarionette," *The Mask* 1, no. 2 (1908) and "Some Evil Tendencies of the Modern Theater," *The Mask* 1, no. 8 (1908) (both cited in Wilson, *The Puccini Problem*, 288). On the synthesis of actors with machines, see, among others, Filippo Tommaso Marinetti, *Teoria e invenzione futurista* (Milan: Mandadori, 1968), and Marinetti, *Let's Murder the Moonshine: Selected Writings*, trans. R. W. Flint and Arthur A. Coppotelli (Los Angeles: Sun and Moon Classics, 1991). For a discussion of these aesthetic trends in Italian theater and opera, especially in work of Mascagni, Malipiero, Illica, and Pirandello, see Maehder, "Drammaturgia musicale e strutture narrative."

37. Girardi, *Puccini*, 377 has noted Puccini's use of the river theme to mark large formal articulations.

38. See Powers, "'La solita forma' and 'The Uses of Convention,'" 68: the Italian verb *"attaccare,"* from which the *"attacco"* in *tempo d'attacco* derives, means both "to attack" and "to attach." The *tempo d'attacco* does both, functioning as a "beginning" (an "attack") as well as an "attachment," or "conjunction," between free *versi sciolti* and strict *versi lirici*.

39. On conventional multisectional *tempi d'attacco*, see Moreen, "Integration of Text Forms and Musical Forms," 210–51; for a discussion of this issue and the problems it can pose in analyses of conventional forms in Puccini, see Rosen, "'La solita forma' in Puccini's Operas?," 186–87.

40. Carner, *Puccini*, 3rd ed., 476; Girardi, *Puccini*, 380. The overtly political nature of Luigi's text, which Puccini and Adami added in their adaptation of Gold, runs counter to the normal image of Puccini as apolitical. For more on the politics of *Il tabarro* (especially its populism), see Aldo Nicastro, "Reminiscenza e populismo nella poetica di Puccini: Appunti sul *tabarro*," *Nuovo rivista musicale italiana* 2, no. 6 (1968): 1092–1104.

41. Ashman, "Divided They Fall," 390 has observed Puccini's practice of delaying for longer and longer periods the entrances of major characters.

42. See Balthazar, "Evolving Conventions in Italian Serious Opera," 486–88; and Rosen, "'La solita forma' in Puccini's Operas?," 185–89.

43. See chapter 2 for a detailed discussion of the movement's Romantic stylistic features.

44. Adami most likely intended another ten- (not eleven-) line block here; the Ricordi first edition splits "Balli all'aperto" and "e intimità amorose!? . . ." into two lines (71 and 72), which is probably a misprint. Combining these ("Balli all'aperto" and "e intimità amorose!? . . .") produces a single *endecasillabo* line 71 and an organization (quatrain plus quatrain plus distich) that parallels both previous ten-line blocks. Every other edition of this libretto I have seen prints this text in a single line; see, for example, Enrico Maria Ferrando, ed., *Tutti i libretti di Puccini* (Milan: Garzanti, 1984), 439.

45. William Ashbrook, "Whatever Happened to the Cabaletta?," *Opera Quarterly* 12, no. 3 (1996): 35–44 (originally published as "Whatever Happened to the

Cabaletta? Intensity, Brevity, and the Transformation of the Cabaletta from Form to Function," in *Letteratura, musica e teatro al tempo di Ruggero Leoncavallo: Atti del 20 convegno internazionale, "Ruggero Leoncavallo nel suo tempo," Locarno, Biblioteca Cantonale, 7-9 October 1993*, ed. Lorenza Guiot and Jürgen Maehder, 83-87 [Milan: Sonzogno, 1995]).

46. David Rosen, "'La solita forma' in Puccini's Operas?," 190-99, has explored a similar formal problem in the love duet at the end of *La bohème* Act I; Girardi, *Puccini*, 124-25, has concurred that a similar formal strategy may be at work in the same scene.

47. The unusual form is not completely out of character for an *adagio* movement written after the 1880s; according to Nicolaisen, *Italian Opera in Transition*, 45, these movements began around that time to take on more unconventional shapes, to merge more smoothly into and out of surrounding material, or even to fail to fully develop or finish. At least the first two of these features describe "Hai ben ragione" well.

48. The following discussion draws directly on Ashbrook and Powers, *Puccini's "Turandot"*; Linda Fairtile, "Giacomo Puccini's Operatic Revisions as Manifestations of his Compositional Priorities" (Ph.D. diss., New York University, 1996); Philip Gossett, "The Case for Puccini," review of Girardi, *Puccini*; Budden, *Puccini*; and Phillips-Matz, *Puccini, New York Review of Books* (March 27, 2003): 38–42; Greenwald, "Dramatic Exposition and Musical Structure in Puccini's Operas"; Huebner, "Thematic Recall in Late Nineteenth-Century Opera"; Nicolaisen, *Italian Opera in Transition*; Powers, "Form and Formula"; Rosen, "'La solita forma' in Puccini's Operas?"; and Wilson, *The Puccini Problem*.

49. Powers, "Form and Formula," 28 ("free-floating remnants").

50. Basevi, *Studio sulle opere di Giuseppe Verdi*; the correspondence of Muzio has been published in Luigi Agostino Garibaldi, *Giuseppe Verdi nelle lettere di Emanuele Muzio ad Antonio Barezzi* (Milan: Fratelli Treves, 1931).

51. The discussion that follows draws on Parker, "'Insolite Forme,' or Basevi's Garden Path."

52. On these aspects of Puccini's audience, see Rosen, "'La solita forma' in Puccini's Operas?," esp. 179–84; and Nicolaisen, *Italian Opera in Transition*, 45ff.

53. Wilson, *The Puccini Problem*, esp. 193–220.

54. Rosen, "'La solita forma' in Puccini's Operas?," 181–83.

55. For an example of the former, see Ashbrook and Powers, *Puccini's "Turandot,"* which is convincing because of the flexibility with which they treat the conventional *solita forma* models. Good examples of the latter are harder to find, which speaks perhaps to a general recognition by scholars that Puccini was engaging to some degree with the older, *ottocento* prototypes. Skeptics exist, however. Powers himself, ironically, became one late in his career; see his "Form and Formula." Philip Gossett is another ("The Case for Puccini," 40: "the reign of fixed musical forms for arias, duets, and ensembles that had dominated Italian opera was over, and composers sought new ways of providing continuity"), as is David Rosen ("'La solita forma' in Puccini's Operas?," esp. 199: "I find it difficult to persuade myself that this [an engagement with the *solita forma*] is a useful way of hearing and analyzing this duet [*La bohème* Act I]").

56. Greenwald, "Dramatic Exposition and Musical Structure in Puccini's Operas," 107–14. The second half is often related tonally to the first by falling fifth. See

also Greenwald, "Puccini, *Il tabarro,* and the Dilemma of Operatic Transposition," 539–40; and Carner, *Puccini,* 3rd ed., 316. Guarnieri Corazzol has observed that the practice originates in the late nineteenth century ("Opera and Verismo," 40–41).

57. This is the underlying premise in Ashbrook and Powers, *Puccini's "Turandot,"* in which the authors assert that *Turandot* is not only a number opera in the Rossinian-Verdian mold, but that it *became* one over the course of its long and complicated genesis (see 3–38, esp. 13: "For all its occasionally fluid structure, and sometimes decadently up-to-date texture, moreover, *Turandot* is a "number" opera in the Great Tradition of Italian Romantic melodrama—or, rather, during the course of its long genesis it gradually became one").

58. Paolo Fabbri, "Metrical and Formal Organization," 151–219, passim. On the structural importance of the duet in nineteenth-century opera having solidified by Verdi's middle period but having deteriorated by the 1890s, see esp. Nicolaisen, *Italian Opera in Transition,* 15ff; see also Powers, "'La solita forma' and the 'Uses of Convention,'" 68–70.

59. Indeed, Greenwald has observed that the entire second duet was originally a half step lower, so that it opened in C minor, the same key as "Hai ben ragione"; the transposition to C♯ adds variety to an otherwise monochromatic tonal structure, also tonally effecting a "scene change" and encapsulating the "hidden violence" of the love affair in, specifically, its tritone relation to an implied tonic G at the opening, its half-step relation to the C-minor close of the opera, and its augmented-second relation to the B♭ of the earlier *cabaletta.* See Greenwald, "Puccini, *Il tabarro,* and the Dilemma of Operatic Transposition," 542ff.

60. Good examples of the genre include Donizetti's Rustighello-Astolfo duet from *Lucrezia Borgia,* Verdi's Rigoletto-Sparafucile duet from *Rigoletto* (famously used by Basevi in *Studio sulle opere di Giuseppe Verdi* as an example of a duet not adhering to "la solita forma dei duetti"), Verdi's Paolo-Fiesco duet from *Simon Boccanegra,* and Verdi's Philip-Grand Inquisitor scene in *Don Carlos.*

"Dialogue duet" is Harold Powers' term referring to a duet in a single poetic meter and composed in a *parlante* texture; obviously the first part of this definition does not apply either in general to Puccini or in particular to *Il tabarro,* wherein both dialogue duets comprise (as is common in Puccini) a series of smaller formal episodes in various, loosely organized poetic meters. "Duologue" is a variation of the same term introduced (very much *en passant*) by Roger Parker to describe those dialogue duets (as in Puccini) in which two characters engage in an illicit exchange and, rather than being musically differentiated from one another as would be common in a traditional duet, remain absorbed into the larger "atmosphere" of the work. See Powers, "By Design: The Architecture of *Simon Boccanegra,*" *Opera News* 49, no. 7 (December 22, 1984): 16–21, cont. 42–43; Powers, "*Simon Boccanegra* I.10–12: A Generic-Genetic Analysis of the Council-Chamber Scene," *19th-Century Music* 13, no. 2 (1989): 101–28; Parker, "Analysis: Act I in Perspective," in Mosco Carner, ed., *Giacomo Puccini: "Tosca,"* 117–42 (Cambridge: Cambridge University Press, 1985); William Ashbrook, *Donizetti and His Operas* (Cambridge: Cambridge University Press, 1982), 350; and Gary Tomlinson, "Opera and *Drame:* Hugo, Donizetti, and Verdi," in *Music and Drama,* Studies in the History of Music, vol. 2, 171–92 (New York: Broude, 1988). Others using the term include James Hepokoski, "Genre and Content in Mid-Century Verdi," 254 n. 18; Helen Greenwald, "Verdi's Patriarch and Puccini's Matriarch: Through the Looking-Glass and What Puccini

Found There," *19th-Century Music* 17, no. 3 (1994): 220–36 (esp. 228ff.); and Greenwald, "Puccini, *Il tabarro,* and the Dilemma of Operatic Transposition," 540–41.

61. Girardi, *Puccini,* 385 (see also his diagram of the whole opera, 385–86).

62. In the 1999 Antonio Pappano recording on EMI Classics (7243 5 56587 2 2).

63. Allan W. Atlas has also found in Puccini a propensity for golden section proportions. See "Stealing a Kiss at the Golden Section: Pacing and Proportion in the Act I Love Duet of *La bohème,*" *Acta Musicologica* 75, no. 2 (2003): 269–91. The golden section is a proportion such that, given a length divided into two segments, one longer (X) than the other (Y), the ratio of the longer segment to the shorter (X:Y) is the same as the ratio of the whole to the longer segment ([X+Y]:X). Atlas provides a helpful introductory discussion of the golden section and its properties; for more on this proportion, especially its relevance in music, see Jonathan D. Kramer, *The Time of Music: New Meanings, New Temporalities, New Listening Strategies* (New York: Schirmer, 1988), esp. 303–21; and Roy Howat, *Debussy in Proportion: A Musical Analysis* (Cambridge: Cambridge University Press, 1983). All three have extensive bibliographies on the golden section, Fibonacci series, and other subjects related to time and proportion.

64. I am not claiming that the golden section proportions were intentional on Puccini's part, nor am I even claiming (more generally) that Puccini may have had any awareness of them or their expressive implications; either assertion seems to me completely implausible. But ultimately such questions are irrelevant: that the proportions are present is fact; as such, they have the power to influence our hearing and interpretation of the music. On this point I agree with Atlas, "Stealing a Kiss at the Golden Section," 279–80.

4. FORMAL MULTIVALENCE IN *SUOR ANGELICA*

1. Hepokoski, "Structure, Implication, and the End of *Suor Angelica,*" 240.

2. On Forzano's idea for *Suor Angelica* as original, see his own comments in *Come li ho conosciuti* (Turin: Edizioni della radio, 1957), 13, a passage—cited in Girardi, *Puccini,* 366 and Greenwald, "Verdi's Patriarch and Puccini's Matriarch," 222—in which Forzano claims to have refused to collaborate with Puccini on *Il tabarro* because he was interested only in inventing his own subjects.

3. Among many authors citing similarities with Massenet's *Le jongleur* are Girardi, *Puccini,* 396; Carner, *Puccini,* 3rd ed., 487; Greenwald, "Verdi's Patriarch and Puccini's Matriarch," 223; Ashbrook, *The Operas of Puccini,* 180; as well as contemporary critics: Greenwald cites a review in *The New York Herald* (December 15, 1918: 13) by Reginald de Koven from the day after *Il trittico*'s premiere at New York's Metropolitan Opera that compares the two works directly. Carner (487) also notes the similarity to Puccini's own *Madama Butterfly:* both center on a woman character driven to suicide by a mother's innate love for her child (in both cases a child she does not know); both depict the woman in a scene of extreme psychological duress; and in both the woman addresses the child directly just before her death. James Hepokoski, "Structure, Implication, and the End of *Suor Angelica,*" 240, has also commented on the *Butterfly* connection, specifically with regard to Puccini's

own (musical) strategies, in which a falsely "pure" world is disrupted occasionally, and violently, by ruthless bursts of reality.

4. The Rodenbach comparison is Claudio Casini's, *Giacomo Puccini* (Turin: Unione Tipografico Editrice Torinese, 1978); the Manzoni connection is from Casini (398) and Riccardo Allorto, "Suor Angelica nella unità del Trittico," *Musica d'Oggi* 2 (1959): 198–204 (201) (both cited in Greenwald, "Verdi's Patriarch and Puccini's Matriarch," 223). Greenwald herself has also pointed out similarities with the Chabrier and Debussy pieces ("Verdi's Patriarch and Puccini's Matriarch," 223).

5. Girardi, *Puccini*, 366ff.

6. For more on this subject see Greenwald, "Verdi's Patriarch and Puccini's Matriarch," esp. 226–28; and Marcelo Conati, "*Il tabarro* ovvera la 'solita' insolita forma," 271ff.

7. Hepokoski, "Structure, Implication, and the End of *Suor Angelica*," 241.

8. I use the term *colore locale* interchangeably with *tinta;* see chapter 3, n. 4.

9. Hepokoski, "Structure, Implication, and the End of *Suor Angelica*," 241.

10. Angelica's quotation (R69.3) was a later addition to the score, part of the music Puccini recomposed, in order to link R69 and R75, after deciding to omit for the January 29, 1922 Milan premiere Angelica's highly dissonant "aria dei fiori" (beginning "Amici fiori, voi mi compensate" and formerly occupying R70 to R74—rehearsal numbers that are still omitted in the score; the first printed score to exhibit the cut is the third Italian piano-vocal edition: Milan: Ricordi, 1927; © 1918, 1919; plate no. 117406; Schickling 87.E.3). The entire "wasps" episode (from R24 to 29) is an optional cut that Puccini first indicated as such in 1919; the episode was probably omitted in every performance of the piece until the 1922 Milan production. The cut makes sense only if the "aria dei fiori" is performed, because the two sections duplicate dramatic information (Angelica's expertise with flowers and herbs). A score for the "aria dei fiori" is available in Alfredo Mandelli, "Il recupero dell' 'Aria dei fiori' in *Suor Angelica*," *Quaderni Pucciniani* 5 (1996): 161–71. For more on this issue see Fedele D'Amico, "Una ignorata pagina maliperiana di *Suor Angelica*," *Rassaegna Musicale Curci* 19, no. 1 (1966): 7–13; Hepokoski, "Structure, Implication, and the End of *Suor Angelica*," 256–57; Girardi, *Puccini*, 408–414; *Carteggi pucciniani*, letter 741 (January 25, 1919); and Schickling, *Catalogue of the Works*, 355 and 360. Girardi discusses the dramatic implications of both cuts and critiques D'Amico on numerous points, including that Puccini could not possibly have known Malipiero's *Le sette canzoni*—the second of which D'Amico proposes as a model for the "aria dei fiori"—because Malipiero wrote the work a year after the *Trittico* premiere and debuted it even later, in 1925; and that D'Amico's claim—based on oral evidence—that the "aria dei fiori" probably *was* performed at the Milan premiere (i.e., together with the "wasps" episode) is unrealistic, given Puccini's own indication (Simonetta Puccini, ed., *Giacomo Puccini: Lettere a Riccardo Schnabl* [Milan: Emme Edizioni, 1981], letter 92; cited in Girardi, *Puccini*, 413) that the wasps episode would be reinstated at that performance.

11. "Soave Signor mio," originally in E♭ minor, was transposed by Puccini to G minor sometime in 1918, before the printing of the first (October 1918) Italian edition of the piano-vocal score (Schickling 84.E.1). He transposed the monologue back to E♭ minor in 1919, by the time of the second piano-vocal edition (Schickling

87.E.2). See Schickling, *Catalogue of the Works,* 352–55; and Budden, "Puccini's Transpositions," 15–17.

12. Puccini called the last of these three sections (the one I marked "C") a "ritornello all'entrata della principessa" ("ritornello for the entrance of the Princess") in an October 11, 1918 letter to Tito Ricordi , *Carteggi pucciniani,* letter 734.

13. I am using the generic "monologue" here, as before (in reference to Michele's monologue in *Il tabarro*), to mean a tightly organized piece that cannot properly be called an aria (see chapter 3, n. 24). "I desideri" is so short, however, the common term "arietta" may also be appropriate. Carner, *Puccini,* 3rd ed., 492, and Hepokoski, "Structure, Implication, and the end of *Suor Angelica,*" 242, n. 1, have each called it an "aria" (though both have noted its brevity).

14. "Structure, Implication, and the End of *Suor Angelica,*" 242, n. 1.

15. Hepokoski, "Structure, Implication, and the End of *Suor Angelica,*" has pointed to this aspect of large-scale formal organization in *Angelica* in particular. For an extended discussion of formal multivalence see James Webster, "The Analysis of Mozart's Arias," in *Mozart Studies,* ed. Cliff Eisen (New York: Oxford University Press, 1991), 101–99. See also Webster, "To Understand Verdi and Wagner We Must Understand Mozart," *19th-Century Music* 11, no. 2 (1987): 175–93; and Webster, "Mozart's Operas and the Myth of Musical Unity," *Cambridge Opera Journal* 2, no. 3 (1990): 197–218. In the same spirit, Carolyn Abbate, "Opera as Symphony, A Wagnerian Myth," in *Analyzing Opera: Verdi and Wagner,* 92–124 (Berkeley: University of California Press, 1989), has suggested that anomalies in an opera's musical design (stylistic incongruities or other discontinuities, for example) may not be always explainable simply as a correspondence between music and text. On multivalence in Puccini, see especially Allan W. Atlas, "Crossed Stars and Crossed Tonal Areas in Puccini's *Madama Butterfly,*" *19th-Century Music* 14, no. 2 (1990): 186–96; Atlas, "Multivalence, Ambiguity, and Non-Ambiguity: Puccini and the Polemicists," *Journal of the Royal Musical Association* 188, no. 1 (1993): 73–93; Atlas, "Puccini's *Tosca:* a New Point of View," in *Studies in the History of Music* v. 3, "The Creative Process," 247–73 (New York: Broude, 1992); and Roger Parker and Allan W. Atlas, "Dialogue: A Key for Chi? Tonal Areas in Puccini," *19th-Century Music* 15, no. 3 (1992): 229–34.

16. For "an ordered arrangement of diverse thematic modules," see James Hepokoski, "Back and Forth from 'Egmont': Beethoven, Mozart, and the Nonresolving Recapitulation," *19th-Century Music* 25, no. 2/3 (2001–2002): 127–64 (128).

17. For a full discussion of *Suor Angelica*'s rotational form and its expressive implications, see Hepokoski, "Structure, Implication, and the End of *Suor Angelica.*" Rotational form is an important part of "sonata theory" as developed by Hepokoski and Darcy, *Elements of Sonata Theory;* see also Hepokoski, "Back and Forth from 'Egmont'"; Hepokoski, "Beyond the Sonata Principle," *Journal of the American Musicological Society* 55 (2002): 91–154; and Darcy, "Bruckner's Sonata Deformations," in *Bruckner Studies,* ed. Timothy L. Jackson and Paul Hawkshaw (Cambridge: Cambridge University Press, 1997), 256–77. For more on the theory of rotational form outside the context of sonata theory, see Hepokoski, *Sibelius: Symphony no. 5* (Cambridge: Cambridge University Press, 1993), 23–26 and 58–84; Hepokoski, "The Essence of Sibelius: Creation Myths and Rotational Cycles in *Luonnotar,*" in *The Sibelius Companion,* ed. Glenda Dawn Goss, 121–46 (Westport, Conn.: Greenwood, 1996); Hepokoski, "Rotations, Sketches, and the Sixth Symphony," in *Sibelius Stud-*

ies, ed. Timothy L. Jackson and Veijo Murtomäki, 322–51 (Cambridge: Cambridge University Press, 2001); and Darcy, "Rotational Form, Teleological Genesis, and Fantasy-Projection in the Slow Movement of Mahler's Sixth Symphony," *19th-Century Music* 25, no. 1 (2001): 49–74. On rotational form in opera, see also Darcy, "The Metaphysics of Annihilation: Wagner, Schopenhauer, and the Ending of the *Ring,*" *Music Theory Spectrum* 16, no. 1 (1994): 1–40; and Andrew Davis and Howard Pollack, "Rotational Form in the Opening Scene of Gershwin's *Porgy and Bess,*" *Journal of the American Musicological Society* 60, no. 2 (2007): 373–414.

18. See n. 10.

19. Greenwald—in a tonal-motivic reading of the opera—takes R42 to be the beginning of the second part of a three-part work (part 3 begins at R60, Angelica's "Senza mamma"). See "Dramatic Exposition and Musical Structure in Puccini's Operas," 107–14.

20. Hepokoski, "Structure, Implication, and the End of *Suor Angelica,*" 249–50.

21. "Sorella, o buona sorella" is a *novenario* with *dialefe* between "Sorella" and "o."

22. Codas are defining features of both lyric movements in the *solita forma*; see Moreen, "Integration of Text Forms and Musical Forms," 157–205 and 305–307.

23. Helen Greenwald, "Verdi's Patriarch and Puccini's Matriarch," has made the argument that not only is the Angelica-Princess scene a dialogue duet in the manner of the Philip-Grand Inquisitor scene from Verdi's *Don Carlos,* but that Puccini actually went so far as to *recast* Verdi's scene, so that the two are nothing less than mirror images of one another.

24. Splitting an *endecasillabo* into its two constituent parts (normally a *settenari* and a *quinari*) and distributing those parts among two characters is not uncommon, of course, but here it clearly has the effect of an interruption. The same device appears again five lines later, where the Princess begins ("anderà sposa.") and Angelica finishes ("Sposa?!") a line of *settenario.*

25. Balthazar, "Evolving Conventions in Italian Serious Opera," 24ff.

26. Girardi, *Puccini,* 408; and Hepokoski, "Structure, Implication, and the End of *Suor Angelica,*" 250, and 257, n. 10.

5. HUMOR AND FILMIC EFFECTS IN THE STRUCTURE OF *GIANNI SCHICCHI*

1. The reference at the end of Schicchi's aria to "e vo randagio come un Ghibellino" ("and go wandering off like a Ghibelline") is to the long-running political struggle in Europe between the popes and the Holy Roman Emperors that reached a head in the early thirteenth century, a few decades before Dante's birth in 1265. Influential families in most European cities found themselves on one side of the conflict or another; those who supported the popes were known as Guelfs (after a powerful Bavarian family), while those aligned with the emperors were known as Ghibellines (after a German castle owned by the emperors). A civil war between Florentine Guelfs and Ghibellines erupted in 1215 and resulted, decades later, in the expulsion of Ghibellines from Florence. Dante's family was Guelf; the Donatis (from whom Dante's wife Gemma was descended) were Ghibelline. See Ronald L.

Martinez and Robert M. Durling's "Introduction" to Dante Alighieri, *The Divine Comedy of Dante Alighieri*, vol. 1, *Inferno*, ed. and trans. Robert M. Durling (New York: Oxford University Press, 1996), 3–24. For family names, general cultural life, maps, and other information on Dante's Florence, a convenient reference is Christopher Kleinheinz, ed., *Medieval Italy: An Encyclopedia*, 2 vols. (New York: Routledge, 2004).

2. On Tuscan folk music, see also chapter 2, n. 18. Carner (*Puccini*, 3rd ed., 503–504) has discussed the Tuscan folk qualities in Schicchi's "Addio, Firenze." Girardi (*Puccini*, 420–21) has observed the relationship of the "Firenze" melisma to the ostinato theme from the introduction and has noted the dramatic implications—Schicchi has now assumed control of the relatives—of this theme's increasing importance as a unifying device in this part of the piece; it appears again, for example, in the scene in which Schicchi dictates the will, as a device that holds the relatives' protests in check by reminding them of the possible gruesome consequences of their actions.

Both Girardi and Carner, incidentally, seem to struggle with how to generically categorize the set pieces for both Rinuccio and Schicchi: Girardi simply uses the term "solo" ("Rinuccio's solo," "Schicchi's solo": 422 and 424, respectively) to describe both, in an apparent effort to avoid all the implications of "scene and aria"; Carner (502ff.) describes the piece for Rinuccio as "an aria in two parts" and the one for Schicchi as "more properly a song" (again in two parts).

3. My reading of the form here departs from Girardi's (*Puccini*, 420ff.), who takes all the music from R52 to 60.6 as one formal unit, which he calls the "second concertato" (the first was at R16, "Dunque era vero!").

4. Carner, *Puccini*, 3rd ed., 507.

5. On Forzano's sources for *Schicchi*, see Girardi, *Puccini*, 415ff. Forzano's primary source apparently was a nineteenth-century transcription of an anonymous fourteenth-century commentary on the *Divine Comedy* containing many of Forzano's plot details (and spelling the main character's name "Gianni Sticchi").

6. *Inferno*, canto 30, lines 31–45: "E l'Aretin, che rimase, tremando / mi disse: 'Quel folletto è Gianni Schicchi, / e va rabbioso altrui così conciando.' // 'Oh,' diss' io lui, 'se l'altro non ti ficchi / li denti a dosso, non ti sia fatica / a dir chi è, pria che di qui si spicchi.' // Ed elli a me: 'Quell' è l'anima antica / di Mirra scellerata, che divenne / al padre, fuor del dritto amore, amica. // Questa a peccar con esso così venne, / falsificando sé in altrui forma, / come l'altro che là sen va, sostenne, // per guadagnar la donna de la torma, / falsificare in sé Buoso Donati, / testando e dando al testamento norma.'" ("And the Aretine who remained, trembling, told me: 'That goblin is Gianni Schicchi, and in his rage he goes treating others so.' 'Oh,' I said to him, 'so may the other not set his teeth in you, let it not be a labor to tell me who he is, before he disappears.' And he said to me: 'That is the ancient soul of wicked Myrrha [mother of Adonis], who became, beyond right love, her father's lover. She came to sin with him by counterfeiting herself in another's shape, just as the other who goes off there, to gain the queen of the herd [i.e., the best mule in Tuscany] dared to counterfeit in himself Buoso Donati, making a will and giving it legal form [i.e., executing it before a notary and witnesses].'") See Alighieri, *The Divine Comedy of Dante Alighieri*, vol. 1, *Inferno*, 467 and 473–74.

7. On Puccini's music as at once "sincere" and "insincere," see chapter 1, n. 47.

8. Girardi, *Puccini*, 415; Carner, *Puccini*, 3rd ed., 498.

9. Girardi, *Puccini*, 434.

10. Girardi, *Puccini*, 505–506, has observed that the mourning motive parodies Puccini's typical music for death scenes—which often include "lugubrious" open fifths, a "drooping" melody, and "woeful" appoggiaturas—such that it represents here the relatives' "feigned grief.". The metric displacement, he says, adds to the comic effect.

11. That *Schicchi* divides so clearly into two parts makes it consistent with Puccini's practice of dividing his one-acts and first acts into "ambience" and "character" halves; see chapter 3, n. 56. Greenwald ("Dramatic Exposition and Musical Structure in Puccini's Operas," 107–114) puts the division close to where I have placed it, at R34 (I prefer it at R35.3; R34 is a long, dramatically active orchestral coda—one that introduces two key characters, Schicchi and Lauretta—to Rinuccio's "Firenze è come un albero fiorito"). Girardi (*Puccini*, 420) likewise finds a formal division at R35.3 and, incidentally, another at R67.10, where Schicchi impersonates Buoso and dictates the will; thus he views the work as tripartite at the largest level, with each part demarcated by a reappearance of the opening ostinato (the "mourning motive") that "restarts" action abruptly interrupted.

12. On Puccini's music as filmic, see Girardi, *Puccini*, 118–26; Greenwald, "Dramatic Exposition and Musical Structure in Puccini's Operas," 14; and Jürgen Leukel, "Puccinis kinematographische Technik," *Neue Zeitschrift für Musik* 143, no. 6–7 (1982): 24–26. On sectional discontinuities similar to those encountered here in *Schicchi* as sources of expressive meaning, see Hatten, "The Expressive Role of Disjunction: A Semiotic Approach to Form and Meaning in Bruckner's Fourth and Fifth Symphonies," in *Perspectives on Anton Bruckner,* ed. Paul Hawkshaw, Crawford Howie, and Timothy L. Jackson, 145–84 (Aldershot, UK: Ashgate, 2001).

13. Rebecca Leydon, "Debussy's Late Style and the Devices of the Early Cinema," *Music Theory Spectrum* 23, no. 2 (2001): 217–41. See also Anthony Newcomb, "Schumann and Late Eighteenth-Century Narrative Strategies," *19th-Century Music* 11 (1987): 164–74, for "modes of continuation" applied in a musical context.

14. Edward T. Cone, "Stravinsky: The Progress of a Method," *Perspectives of Mew Music* 1, no. 1 (1962): 18–26 (19 for "Although heard in alternation") (reprinted in Benjamin Boretz and Edward T. Cone, eds., *Perspectives on Schoenberg and Stravinsky,* 155–94 [Princeton, N.J.: Princeton University Press, 1968]).

15. Girardi, *Puccini*, 424, has noted the transformation of the mourning motive here, while Carner, *Puccini*, 3rd ed., 503–504, has noted the similarity of the line to Schicchi's "warning" in "Addio, Firenze."

16. Balthazar, "Evolving Conventions in Italian Serious Opera," uses the term *primo tempo* (literally "first movement") to refer to the opening lyric movement of aria forms for the same reason: to avoid the confusion that may arise from using *adagio*, which has, of course, a specific tempo meaning ("slow") but also a more generic structural meaning ("slow movement"—i.e., in any slow tempo).

17. Carner, *Puccini*, 3rd ed., 502ff; Girardi, *Puccini*, 422.

18. Abbate, *Unsung Voices*, especially 3ff., 134–35, and 148; Tomlinson, *Metaphysical Song*, 85ff.

19. This seems an appropriate place to note that I find baffling Carner's remark that "There is little profit in discussing the musico-dramatic structure of *Gianni*

Schicchi in detail." Carner apparently arrived at this conclusion because he found the score too complex and episodic ("The scenes succeed each other with such rapidity and the changes of mood are so numerous and mercurial") and its textures too numerous and rapidly shifting ("*parlando, arioso*, solo pieces, and dramatic ensembles alternate as if by sleight-of-hand, Puccini coping with the succession of scenes in so elastic and fluent a manner that the ear is often unable to follow"). See *Puccini*, 3rd ed., 508.

20. Hepokoski, "Structure, Implication, and the End of *Suor Angelica*," 259–62.

21. Hatten provides a full theoretical discussion of the concept, with citations. Hatten, *Musical Meaning in Beethoven*, 172.

6. PUCCINI'S SOLUTION

1. For more detail on what follows, see Lo, *"Turandot" auf der Opernbühne*; Carner, *Puccini*, 3rd ed., 509–41; Girardi, *Puccini*, 435–87; Ashbrook and Powers, *Puccini's "Turandot*," 43–76; Wilson, *The Puccini Problem*, 185–220; Wilson, "Modernism and the Machine Woman"; and Patricia Juliana Smith, "The (D)evolution of Turandot, Lesbian Monster," in *En Travesti: Women, Gender, Subversion, Opera*, ed. Corinne E. Blackmer and Patricia Juliana Smith, 242–84 (New York: Columbia University Press, 1995).

2. For more on other *Turandot* settings, see Lo, *"Turandot" auf der Opernbühne*, 133–287. For a modern edition of Gozzi's original, see Carlo Gozzi, *Five Tales for the Theater*, ed. and trans. Albert Bermel and Ted Emery (Chicago: University of Chicago Press, 1989), 125–86.

3. On what follows, including Gozzi, contemporary societal views of women, and the politics of Torrefranca and others, see especially Wilson, *The Puccini Problem*, esp. 125–40 and 201–10; Smith, "The (D)evolution of Turandot, Lesbian Monster," 254–58; and Ashbrook and Powers, *Puccini's "Turandot*," 46–47.

4. Puccini to Simoni, March 18, 1920, *Carteggi pucciniani*, letter 766: "Semplificarlo per il numero degli atti e lavorarlo per renderlo snello, efficace e soprattutto esaltare la passion amorosa di Turandot che per tanto tempo ha soffocato sotto la cenere del suo grande orgoglio" (cited in Ashbrook and Powers, *Puccini's "Turandot*," 60–61).

5. For more on the masks and their role in the work, see Kii-Ming Lo, "Ping, Pong, Pang: Die Gestalten der Commedia dell'arte in Busonis und Puccinis *Turandot*-Opern," in *Die lustige Person auf der Bühne: Gesammelte Vorträge des Salzburger Symposions 1993*, ed. Peter Csobádi, Gernot Gruber, Jürgen Kühnel, Ulrich Müller, Oswald Panagl, and Franz Viktor Spechtler (Anif/Salzburg: Müller-Speiser, 1994), 311–23. See also Ashbrook and Powers, *Puccini's "Turandot*," chapter 2; Lo, "Giacomo Puccini's *Turandot* in Two Acts: The Draft of the First Version of the Libretto," in *Giacomo Puccini: L'uomo, il musicista, il panorama europeo: Atti del convegno internazionale di studi su Giacomo Puccini nel 700 anniversario della morte, Lucca, 25–29 novembre 1994*, ed. Gabriella Biagi Ravenni and Carolyn Gianturco (Lucca: Libreria Musicale Italiana, 1997), 239–58; and Olga Visentini, "Movenze dell'esotismo: 'il caso Gozzi,'" in *Esotismo e colore locale nell'opere di Puccini*, 37–51. *Turandot* librettist Giuseppe Adami was also a playwright who had experience with

commedia dell'arte characters; see Ashbrook and Powers, *Puccini's "Turandot,"* esp. 59–62.

6. For another view of *Turandot,* this time as a large, unified political allegory in which the crowd represents the rioting socialist and fascist revolutionaries in post–World War I Italy, Turandot the revolutionary populace that takes advantage of a weak central government, Altoum Vittorio Emanuele III, the ministers ineffectual politicians, and Calaf the political strongman who emerges to restore order (but not necessarily Mussolini himself), see Richard M. Berrong's speculative *"Turandot* as Political Fable," *Opera Quarterly* 11, no. 3 (1995): 65–75.

7. "In *Turandot* far more than in any of Puccini's other operas, *tinta* is structural: it emerges from a web of interlocking resemblances and contrasts based on tempo or pacing, on instrumental and/or harmonic color, on melodic or rhythmic *topoi* and types, on the texture of accompaniment patterns, and so on." Note that in their book, Ashbrook and Powers consistently use the term *"tinta"* to mean approximately the same thing as what I am calling "style," rather than (as is more traditional, but also more limited in scope) color, atmosphere, and ambience. Ashbrook and Powers, *Puccini's "Turandot,"* 94. Also, I am grateful to Dr. Cassar for providing me with a copy of her unpublished dissertation. Johanne Cassar, *"Turandot* de Puccini: Essai d'analyse sémiotique" (Ph.D. diss., Université de Provence, 2000).

8. Ashbrook and Powers, *Puccini's "Turandot,"* 89–114.

9. Cassar, *"Turandot* de Puccini," 102–126. "Isotopie" is a term from semiotic theory; see Eero Tarasti, *A Theory of Musical Semiotics* (Bloomington: Indiana University Press, 1994) and A. J. Greimas, *Du sens II: Essais sémiotiques* (Paris: Seuil, 1979). Greimas borrowed the term from the physical sciences and defines it as a "set of semantic categories whose redundancy guarantees the analyzability of any text or sign complex" (86–87, 112–20; cited in Tarasti, 6). In music, isotopies are essentially referential categories available for use in the analysis of (among other things) formal organization, text structure, and expressive meaning.

10. Carner, *Puccini,* 3rd ed., 520.

11. Girardi, *Puccini,* 435–87.

12. What follows draws directly on Robert Hatten's work on musical style, especially *Musical Meaning in Beethoven* and *Interpreting Musical Gestures, Topics, and Tropes.*

13. For the sake of brevity and concision, I will use the terms "style" and "style type" interchangeably throughout the text.

14. Ashbrook and Powers, *Puccini's "Turandot,"* 89–114.

15. See also Stoïanova, "Remarques sur l'actualité de *Turandot,*" 202–203. Stoïanova uses the visual image of a work organized in "boxes" or "sonorous panels," which recalls—in a way different from how I invoked it in chapter 5—Edward T. Cone's "Stravinsky: The Progress of a Method."

16. For what follows, see Lakoff, *Women, Fire, and Dangerous Things,* 5–57; see also 27ff.

17. Capitalized "Romantic," "Dissonant," and "Exotic" refer to specific style types; lowercase versions ("dissonant," "exotic") are generic adjectives.

18. Carner, for one (*Puccini,* 3rd ed., 525–28), calls *Turandot* Puccini's "most advanced" work and points for support to the polytonal, heterophonic, polyrhythmic, and generally Stravinskian textures in the Act I choruses; the dissonance of the

moonrise and spirit episodes in Act I (he compares these to *Pierrot Lunaire*); and the innovative orchestrational effects unprecedented in Puccini's work to date.

19. Girardi, *Puccini*, cites numerous other examples in his discussions of *La fanciulla del West, La rondine, Il trittico*, and *Turandot;* Girardi's book is the most comprehensive source to date on Puccini as a contemporary European composer in touch with the modernistic musical trends of the time.

20. Ashbrook and Powers, *Puccini's "Turandot,"* 100–107, have likewise noted Puccini's reliance on unprepared and unresolved tritones, augmented triads, and harmonic, non-functional whole and half steps (and their complements, major and minor sevenths).

21. Recall that rehearsal numbers in *Turandot* start over in each act; the act in question will be clear from the text. See chapter 2, n. 3.

22. Ashbrook and Powers, *Puccini's "Turandot,"* 16, hear this music in F♯ minor and thus as unified tonally with the opening "execution motive" (i.e., the piece's first five notes).

23. Carner, *Puccini*, 3rd ed., 314; and Deborah Burton, "A Journey of Discovery: Puccini's "motivo di prima intenzione" and Its Applications in *Manon Lescaut, La fanciulla del West* and *Suor Angelica*," *Studi Musicali* 30, no. 2 (2001): 473–99.

24. The opening five-note motive in *Turandot* has received a good deal of attention in print. Ashbrook and Powers, *Puccini's "Turandot,"* 89–90, have also observed its rapid but gradual progression from chromaticism to diatonicism and, like many others, associate it more generally with "execution." Carner, "The Score," in *Puccini: "Turandot,"* English National Opera Guide no. 27, notes its whole-tone roots but not its underlying diatonicism; he calls it "the main 'Turandot' motive which is the motto of the opera." Cassar, "*Turandot* de Puccini," 106, says it has "tonalité indefinite" and identifies it as the "Classème de l'exécution." And Girardi, *Puccini*, 470–73, links it to "Turandot's cruelty" (see also his "*Turandot:* Il futuro interrotto del melodrama italiano," *Rivista italiana di musicologia* 17 (1982): 175–76. Associating the motive with negative qualities of Turandot herself dates to contemporary reviews of the piece: see, for example, Andrea della Corte's review for *La Stampa*, excerpted in *Carteggi pucciniani*, 564. Some have even noted the motive's similarity to the theme for Iago's "Credo" in Verdi's *Otello*, among them Carner, "The Score," 22; Ashbrook and Powers, *Puccini's "Turandot,"* 175, n. 3; and Deborah Burton, "Dawn at Dusk: The Past and Future Meet in Puccini's Last Opera," program notes for *Turandot* at the Forbidden City, Beijing, September 1998.

25. See also Ashbrook and Powers, *Puccini's "Turandot,"* 98–100 (on the Chinese Exotic) and 107–11 (on what I am calling the Persian and Primitive Exotics).

26. Ashbrook and Powers, *Puccini's "Turandot,"* 100.

27. *Chinese Music* (Shanghai: Statistical Department of the Inspectorate General, 1884). For more on van Aalst—a Belgian working in the Chinese government and well known for chronicling Chinese music—see Han Koo-huang, "J. A. van Aalst and his *Chinese Music*," *Asian Music* 19, no. 2 (1988): 127–30. Regarding the music box, William Weaver located this in Rome in the 1970s, still in the possession of Fassini's family. See Ashbrook and Powers, *Puccini's "Turandot,"* 94–98; and Kii-Ming Lo, "Giacomo Puccini's *Turandot* in Two Acts." Giuseppe Adami describes hearing the music box for the first time at Fassini's home in his *Il romanzo della vita di Giacomo Puccini* (Milan: Rizzoli, 1942), 229 (Ashbrook and Powers translate

the relevant passage in *Puccini's "Turandot,"* 64). Mosco Carner, *Puccini,* 3rd ed., 523, cites as Puccini's source for the authentic tunes John Barrow, *Travels in China* (London: T. Cadell and W. Davies, 1804), which Ashbrook and Powers view as unlikely, especially in light of Weaver's discovery of the Fassini music box.

28. Ashbrook and Powers, *Puccini's "Turandot,"* 95.

29. Hatten, Musical Meaning in Beethoven, 170.

30. The analysis that follows descends from both Ashbrook and Powers, and from work of a long line of scholars who have recognized the importance of the opera's episodic quality. The earliest study to explore *Turandot* as an episodic design based on juxtapositions of independent musical units is Ivanka Stoïanova, "Remarques sur l'actualité de *Turandot.*" See also Fedele D'Amico, "L'opera insolita," *Quaderni Pucciniani* 2 (1985): 67–77. Ashbrook and Powers, *Puccini's "Turandot,"* note *Turandot's* juxtaposition of motives, tonal levels, and "musical colorations" (or *tinta*—see n. 7); Janet Maguire, "Puccini's Version of the Duet and Final Scene of *Turandot," The Musical Quarterly* 74, no. 3 (1990): 319–59, contrasts Puccini's approach, in which musical ideas tend to remain temporally independent, with Wagner's, in which ideas flow directly from one to another with no pause in between (see 345); Helen Greenwald, "Dramatic Exposition and Musical Structure in Puccini's Operas," 14, compares the effect of juxtaposed and deeply contrasting styles at the opening of *La fanciulla del West* to the effect that accrues from successive "shots" in a film; Leonardo Pinzauti, "Giacomo Puccini's *Trittico,*" 242, remarks on the prevailing musical style in *Gianni Schicchi* being continually interrupted for deeply contrasting arias or other episodes; Mosco Carner, *Puccini,* 3rd ed., 317, characterizes Puccini's music as a "mosaic," in which continuity stems not from connections among themes but from juxtapositions of "small melodic squares," and suggests the style has origins in the opera buffa of Pergolesi, Mozart, and Rossini; Fairtile, "Giacomo Puccini's Operatic Revisions as Manifestations of his Compositional Priorities," refers to the "dizzying variety of episodic content" (176) in *La bohème* and describes Puccini's approach as one in which scenes and arias are built from "smaller segments with their own keys, tempo markings, and often musical motives" (227).

31. Girardi, *Puccini,* 459 ("the connection between") and 460 ("the fictitious opposition").

32. Ashbrook and Powers, *Puccini's "Turandot,"* 90–94, have also discussed the music from R25.20 through the ministers' trio.

33. Ashbrook and Powers, *Puccini's "Turandot,"* 15–38 and 166–67. Girardi, *Puccini,* also takes Ashbrook and Powers' analysis as a point of reference (see, for example, 458 and 464).

34. For more on the genesis of the work and the original two-act version, see Kii-Ming Lo, "Giacomo Puccini's *Turandot* in Two Acts"; Lo, *"Turandot" auf der Opernbühne,* 289–346; and Ashbrook and Powers, *Puccini's "Turandot,"* 59–88.

35. Maehder has made the same point, in *"Turandot* and the Theatrical Aesthetics of the Twentieth Century" and "Drammaturgia musicale e strutture narrative."

36. Hepokoski, "Structure, Implication, and the End of *Suor Angelica*"; Davis and Pollack, "Rotational Form in the Opening Scene of Gershwin's *Porgy and Bess.*"

37. Harold Powers, "One Halfstep at a Time: Tonal Transposition and 'Split Association' in Italian Opera," *Cambridge Opera Journal* 7, no. 2 (1995): 135–64; a por-

tion was reprinted as "Dal padre alla principessa: reorientamento tonale nel finale primo della *Turandot*," trans. Giorgio Biancorosso, in *Giacomo Puccini: L'uomo, il musicista, il panorama europeo,* 259–80. See also Ashbrook and Powers, *Puccini's "Turandot,"* 102–107; Lo, "Giacomo Puccini's *Turandot* in Two Acts"; and, on Puccini's dividing the original two acts into three and the addition of the concertato to conclude Act I, n. 34.

38. Puccini to Adami, undated, *Epistolario,* letter 177 (cited in Ashbrook and Powers, *Puccini's "Turandot,"* 61): "Non abusate coi mascherotti veneziani—quelli debbono essere i *buffoncelli* e i filosofi che qui e lí buttano un lazzo o un parere (ben scelto, anche il momento) ma non siano degli importuni, dei petulanti." Incidentally, Ashbrook and Powers see the masks as more integrated into the plot, noting their "double function . . . as both participants and commentators, . . . dramatically occupying a middle ground between the heroic plane of Turandot and the unknown Prince on the one hand and the completely exotic background of Altoum's court and Peking on the other" (*Puccini's "Turandot,"* 62).

39. On the dissolve in music, see Leydon, "Debussy's Late Style and the Devices of the Early Cinema," esp. 223–26; and chapter 5, n. 13. See also Leukel, "Puccinis kinematographische Technik," 26, for a comparison of this moment with a similar moment near the end of *La bohème* Act II, at the end of Musetta's waltz.

40. For a detailed discussion of the riddle scene as a "highly stylized dialogue duet," see Ashbrook and Powers, *Puccini's "Turandot,"* 116–31. On dialogue duets, see chapter 3, n. 60.

41. The percentage is near fifty on most recordings; on the 1965 Nilsson-Corelli production conducted by Francesco Molinari-Pradelli (EMI 7 69327 2), for example, the time is 19' 25", about 49% of an act lasting just over 40 minutes.

42. See Lo, "Giacomo Puccini's *Turandot* in Two Acts."

43. Greenwald, "Dramatic Exposition and Musical Structure in Puccini's Operas," 139. On the "tale within a tale" as a device in contemporary opera, see also Robert Hatten, "Pluralism of Theatrical Genre and Musical Style," 307.

44. Clausetti and Valcarenghi had taken over the storied firm upon the retirement of Tito Ricordi—with whom Puccini always had a strained relationship—in 1919, following Tito's eight-year directorial tenure.

45. Ashbrook and Powers, *Puccini's "Turandot,"* 3, for example, cite for this story William Weaver, *The Golden Century of Italian Opera: From Rossini to Puccini* (London: Thames and Hudson: 1980), 242: "as he reached the conclusion of Liù's death scene, Toscanini laid down his baton and said, in effect (he has been quoted variously): 'The opera ends here, because at this point the Maestro died. Death was stronger than art.'"

46. The definitive source on Alfano's contribution, important enough to have warranted publication in three languages, is Jürgen Maehder's "Studien zum Fragmentcharakter von Giacomo Puccini's *Turandot,"* *Analecta Musicologica* 22 (1984): 297–379; translations include "Studi sul carratere di framento della *Turandot* di Giacomo Puccini," *Quaderni Pucciniani* 2 (1985), 79–163; and "Puccini's *Turandot:* A Fragment," in *Puccini: "Turandot,"* English National Opera Guide no. 27, 35–53 (the latter is an abridgement, with all Maehder's original charts and the sketch facsimiles). Other sources on the ending include Ashbrook and Powers, *Puccini's*

"*Turandot*," 33-41 and 132-140; Girardi, *Puccini*, 478-87; Janet Maguire, "Puccini's Version of the Duet and Final Scene of *Turandot*"; Roger Parker, "Berio's *Turandot*: Once More the Great Tradition," in Parker, *Remaking the Song: Operatic Visions and Revisions from Handel to Berio* (Berkeley: University of California Press, 2006), 90-120; Marco Uvietta, "'È l'ora della prova': un finale Puccini-Berio per Turandot," *Studi Musicali* 31 (2002): 395-479 (in English as "'È l'ora della prova': Berio's Finale for Puccini's *Turandot*," *Cambridge Opera Journal* 16, no. 2 [2004]: 187-238); Andrew Porter, "Solving The Enigmas," *Opera*, June 2002: 668-72; and Linda Fairtile, "Duetto a tre: Franco Alfano's Completion of *Turandot*," *Cambridge Opera Journal* 16, no. 2 (2004): 163-85.

47. Carner, *Puccini*, 3rd ed., 250; Budden, "Puccini, Giacomo," in *The New Grove Dictionary of Opera*, vol. 3, ed. Stanley Sadie (New York: Grove's Dictionaries of Music, 1992), 1171. I should observe that I find Budden's remark on *Angelica*'s ending just as baffling as Carner's on the structure of *Gianni Schicchi*; see chapter 5, n. 19.

48. *Epistolario*, letter 196: "Penso che il grande nocciòlo sia il duetto. E questo duetto cosí com'è non mi pare sia quello che ci vuole." Cited in Girardi, *Puccini*, 449; and Ashbrook and Powers, *Puccini's "Turandot*," 179.

49. Ashbrook and Powers, *Puccini's "Turandot*," 132.

50. Carner, "The Genesis of the Opera," in *Puccini: "Turandot*," English National Opera Guide no. 27, 12.

51. Ashbrook and Powers, *Puccini's "Turandot*," 99-100 have discussed the "Tanto amore, segreto" theme in more detail (also noting its integration of Italian and exotic qualities), as has Harold Powers in "Form and Formula," 43-47, the latter a detailed discussion of Puccini's musical treatment of the verse (which he set to music he had already composed). On the "Tu che di gel sei cinta" theme, see ibid., 110, 114.

52. Carner, *Puccini*, 3rd ed., 520, also notes the problem of Timur's disappearance from the libretto.

EPILOGUE

1. Among many others, see Theodor Adorno, "Late Style in Beethoven," in Adorno, *Essays on Music*, ed. Richard Leppert, trans. Susan Gillespie (Berkeley: University of California Press, 2002) (originally in German, from 1937, as "Spätstil Beethovens," *Gesammelte Schriften*, vol. 17, *Musikalische Schriften IV: Moments musiceaux. Neu gesdruckte Aufsätze 1928-1962*, 13-17 [Frankfurt am Main: Suhrkamp, 1982]); Edward T. Cone, "Schubert's Promissory Note: An Exercise in Musical Hermeneutics," *19th-Century Music* 5 (1982): 233-41; Anthony Barone, "Richard Wagner's 'Parsifal' and the Theory of Late Style," *Cambridge Opera Journal* 7 (1995): 37-54; Joseph N. Straus, *Stravinsky's Late Music* (Cambridge: Cambridge University Press, 2001); Edward Said, *On Late Style: Music and Literature Against the Grain*, foreword by Mariam C. Said, introduction by Michael Wood (New York: Pantheon, 2006); Laura Tunbridge, *Schumann's Late Style* (Cambridge: Cambridge University Press, 2007); Straus, "Disability and Late Style in Music," *Journal of Musicology* 25,

no. 1 (2008): 3–45; and Marianne Wheeldon, *Debussy's Late Style* (Bloomington: Indiana University Press, 2009).

2. Mary Ann Smart, "'Dernières Pensées': Questions of Late Style in Early Nineteenth-Century Italian Opera," conference paper delivered to "Rethinking Late Style: Art, Literature, Music, Film," London, November 16–17, 2007.

3. Straus, "Disability and Late Style in Music," 4–5.

4. Ibid., 5. This is the "anxiety of influence" effect; see Joseph Straus, *Remaking the Past: Musical Modernism and the Influence of the Tonal Tradition* (Cambridge: Harvard University Press, 1990).

5. For example, Bryan Gilliam, "Between Resignation and Hope: The Late Works of Richard Strauss," in *Late Thoughts: Reflections on Artists and Composers at Work,* ed. Karen Painter and Thoman Crow (Los Angeles: Getty Research Institute, 2006), 167–80. For a dissenting opinion on the late Strauss as a conservative, see Leon Botstein, "The Enigmas of Richard Strauss: A Revisionist View," in *Richard Strauss and His World,* ed. Bryan Gilliam (Princeton, N.J.: Princeton University Press, 1992), 3–32. On Brahms, see also Margaret Notley, *Lateness and Brahms: Music and Culture in the Twilight of Viennese Classicism* (Oxford: Oxford University Press, 2007).

6. In his introduction to Said, *On Late Style,* Michael Wood describes this as "a devotion to the truth of unreconciled relations" (xvii).

7. Straus, "Disability and Late Style in Music," 8–11.

8. Carner, *Puccini,* 3rd ed., 180 for "suicidal despair," 142–43 on the Corinna affair. For more on Puccini's crisis, see the introduction, n. 4.

9. Girardi, *Puccini,* 327.

10. *New York Times,* December 11, 1910, 2; cited in Girardi, *Puccini,* 280.

11. Among others, see Greenwald, "Verdi's Patriarch and Puccini's Matriarch," 235.

12. For a convenient, thorough, chronological list of Puccini's sojourns, travels, and visits to theatres, see Schickling, *Catalogue of the Works,* 425–53.

13. I consulted data compiled by the Human Mortality Database, a joint project of the University of California, Berkeley and the Max Planck Institute for Demographic Research, Rostock, Germany; see www.mortality.org or www.humanmortality.de (accessed March 24, 2009). Mortality tables were constructed using census data published by Italy's state statistical office, the Istituto Nazionale di Statistica (ISTAT), formerly the Istituto Centrale di Statistica (see www.istat.it); the first Italian census was in 1861, following unification, and decennial censuses have been conducted at mostly regular intervals since.

14. See Sigmund Freud, "Female Sexuality" (1931), reprinted in *Women and Analysis: Dialogues on Psychoanalytic Views of Femininity,* comp. Jean Strouse, 39–56 (New York: Grossman, 1974).

15. Carner, *Puccini,* 3rd ed., 302.

16. Among others: Jane Swigart, *The Myth of the Bad Mother: The Emotional Realities of Mothering* (New York: Doubleday, 1991); and R. William Betcher and William S. Pollack, *In A Time of Fallen Heroes: The Recreation of Masculinity* (New York: Atheneum, 1993).

17. Puccini to Giulio Ricordi, c. 1895, *Epistolario,* letter 49: "Penso al mio Torre del Lago continuamente!"

18. See especially Carner, *Puccini*, 3rd ed., 16–36; Budden, *Puccini*, 1–36; and Phillips-Matz, *Puccini*, 3–38.

19. Puccini to Albina Magi Puccini, c. 1880, *Epistolario*, letter 1: "La fame non la 'pato.' Mangio maletto, ma mi riempio di minestrone, 'brodo lungo' . . . e . . . 'seguitate.' La pancia è soddisfatta"; Puccini to Albina Magi Puccini, c. 1880, *Epistolario*, letter 2: "Alle cinque vado al pasto frugale (ma molto di quel frugale!)"; and, from the same letter: "Maledetta la miseria!!!! Ieri 'di scapaccione' sono stato a sentire la *Carmen*."

20. *Epistolario*, letter 54: "Pregola mandarmi *subito fondi* perché sono alla fine. Volano a Parigi e senza far niente!"

21. *Epistolario*, letter 1: "Oggi è giornata pessima, tempo noiosissimo"; *Epistolario*, letter 24: "Tempo orribile. Nebbia e pioggia fina. Mezza Milano è influenzata."

22. See Carner, *Puccini*, 3rd ed., 192–94 on the Puccini-Elvira relationship. George R. Marek, *Puccini* (New York: Simon and Schuster, 1951), on whom Carner relied heavily, cites (75–105) numerous relevant letters, most of them unsourced and without the original Italian.

23. Marek, *Puccini*, 92–93; cited in Carner, *Puccini*, 3rd ed., 194.

24. Marek, *Puccini*, 87. Cited in Carner, *Puccini*, 3rd ed., 192.

25. Carner, *Puccini*, 3rd ed., 142–43; see also 217–18 on Puccini's affairs.

26. August 17, 1924, *Lettere a Riccardo Schnabl*, letter 135 (also cited in Carner, *Puccini*, 3rd ed., 218): "Elvira e tutti ti salutano; Il Marienbad hotel ricordami primo rendez vous con Josi! bei tempi" ("Elvira and everyone send you their greetings. The Mariendbad hotel [from where Puccini wrote the letter, in Marianske Lazne, Czech Republic] reminds me of the first rendez-vous with Josi! Beautiful times").

27. Girardi, *Puccini*, 436; Carner, *Puccini*, 3rd ed., 218.

28. On the much-discussed Doria Manfredi episode, see Carner, *Puccini*, 3rd ed., 195–202; Girardi, *Puccini*, 269–73; Phillips-Matz, *Puccini*, 190–98; and Budden, *Puccini*, 297–300. On Giulia Manfredi, see Michele Girardi, ed., "Il figlio segreto di Giacomo Puccini," exhibit organized at Torre del Lago, 2008, for the Centro studi Giacomo Puccini, Lucca; see http://www.puccini.it/bollettinoValigia.htm (accessed March 31, 2009). See also, among other pieces in the international press, Anthony Tommasini, "Puccini at 150, Still Capable of Revelations," *New York Times*, August 17, 2008, AR16; Paolo Benvenuti's film on the subject premiered at the August 2008 Venice film festival. I am grateful also to Gabriela Biagi Ravenni for summarizing for me her research on the Manfredi situation.

29. Carner, *Puccini*, 3rd ed., 202. He also surmises here that at least two of Puccini's operatic characters represent Doria Manfredi (the tragic Angelica and Liù) and that at least two others represent Elvira (the tormentors Turandot and the Zia Principessa).

30. Girardi, *Puccini*, 159.

31. Vincent Seligman, *Puccini Among Friends* (New York: Macmillan, 1938), 5. All Seligman's letters are printed without the original Italian.

32. Carner, *Puccini*, 3rd ed., 181–82 (181 for the uncredited Illica citation).

33. Ibid., 184 ("congenital melancholia") and 181 ("labile moods").

34. Seligman, *Puccini Among Friends*, 77 ("I make the great mistake"). Puccini to Adami, November 10, 1920, *Epistolario*, letter 184 ("I have always carried"): "Ho

sempre portato con me un gran sacco di melanconia. Non ne ho ragione, ma cosí son fatto e cosí sono fatti gli uomini che hanno cuore e cui manca una piú piccola dose di fatuità." Both are cited in Carner, *Puccini*, 3rd ed., 181–82.

35. *Carteggi Pucciniani*, letter 332 (cited in Carner, *Puccini*, 3rd ed., 183): "scrivimi spesso. Sono qui solo e triste! Tu sapessi le sofferenze mie! Avrei tanto bisogno d'un amico, e non ne ho, o se c'é qualcuno che mi vuol bene non mi capisce. Sono un temperamento molto diverso da tanti! Solo io mi comprendo e mi addoloro; ma è continuo dolore il mio, non mi dà pace."

36. *Epistolario*, letter 197: "Perché . . . perché . . . 'non m'ami piú'? . . . perché? Sono scaduto . . . decaduto? . . . Non mi resta che *Madera*. Sono stato male. Sono sempre un po' giú. Il non vedere vostre lettere mi strapiomba piú in basso. Simoni poi mi sotterra addirittura!" Emphasis original. The quotation ("non m'ami piú . . .?") is from *Manon Lescaut*, Act II; Madera is the location to which Emperor Charles Hapsburg of Austria was exiled in October 1921; see Giuseppe Adami, *Letters of Giacomo Puccini: Mainly Connected with the Composition and Production of his Operas*, trans. and ed. Ena Makin (New York: AMS Press, 1971) (English translation of Adami, ed., *Giacomo Puccini: Epistolario*), 281, nn. 1 and 2.

37. Puccini to Giulio Ricordi, August 16, 1900, *Epistolario*, letter 68: "Né da Illica né da Giacosa ho avuto mai notizie . . . Sicché sono proprio il vero dimenticato." Carner, *Puccini*, 3rd ed., 180 has likewise observed Puccini's "morbid vulnerability" to any kind of criticism.

38. Arnaldo Fraccaroli, *Giacomo Puccini si confida e racconta* (Milan: Ricordi, 1957), 269 (cited in Carner, *Puccini*, 3rd ed., 183): "Non ho un amico / mi sento solo / anche la musica / triste mi fa. / Quando la morte / verrà a trovarmi / sarò felice a capo do riposarmi." The translation is Carner's.

39. Adami, *Epistolario*, 288, n. 1: "Giulio Ricordi pensava che a Giacomo convenisse ora un soggetto più ambizioso e forte dei soliti" ("Giulio Ricordi thought it was time for Giacomo to try a more ambitious and stronger subject than the usual ones").

40. Puccini to Illica, March 3, 1905, *Carteggi pucciniani*, letter 407: "Che ora cambi parere, e lo cambi per tutta l'opera mia, chiamando bozzetti tutto ciò che ho fatto, è davvero sconsolante e avvilente per me." See also Phillips-Matz, *Puccini*, 47ff on Puccini's relationship with Ricordi during this period.

41. Puccini to Tito Ricordi, February 18, 1907, *Carteggi pucciniani*, letter 500: "Tutto il mondo aspetta da me l'opera e ce n'è bisogno proprio. Ora basta colla Bohème, Butter[fly] e compagnia; anch'io ne ho sopra i capelli! ma sono tanto, ma tanto impensierito."

42. *Epistolario*, letter 53: "sono troppo eccitato di nervi e senza la tranquillità che mi è necessaria. . . . son fatto cosí e non mi si cambia a quasi 40 anni!"

43. Seligman, *Puccini Among Friends*, 282–83 (cited in Girardi, *Puccini*, 435).

44. *Epistolario*, letter 191: "Ho un umore diabolico. Forse mi sento poco bene? Sono arenato al lavoro. Ho bisogno d'incoraggiamento da chi mi capisce. . . . Credo che divento nevrastenico."

45. See Carner, *Puccini*, 3rd ed., 182 on the Berlin surgeon and Voronoff. For more on Voronoff see David Hamilton, *The Monkey Gland Affair* (London: Chatto and Windus, 1986). On Puccini's desire to see a specialist in Vienna, see Seligman,

Puccini Among Friends, 344 (Carner, *Puccini,* 3rd ed., 182 identifies the doctor as probably Steinach).

46. December 22, 1923, *Carteggi pucciniani,* letter 877 (also cited in Girardi, *Puccini,* 437): "Mi son messo a strumentare per guadagnar tempo; ma non ho l'animo tranquillo fino a che questo duetto non sia fatto. Fammi il piacere di metterti a questo ultimo lavoro. Si buono per me come sei sempre stato; strappa qualche ora al tuo grande da fare e dedicalo a questo povero maestro che ha urgenza di finire questa 'magna' opera."

47. The point is from Straus, "Disability and Late Style in Music."

48. Girardi, *Puccini,* 282-83.

49. Ibid., 284.

BIBLIOGRAPHY

This is not meant to be a complete Puccini bibliography; such a listing may easily be many times the length of this one. Rather, I have included sources relevant to issues discussed in the book. Many items listed here appear in footnotes; many do not. It may well be impossible to document every source that has influenced my thinking on these issues; any omissions are inadvertent, and I regret them.

van Aalst, J. A. *Chinese Music.* Shanghai: Statistical Department of the Inspectorate General, 1884.

Abbate, Carolyn. "Elektra's Voice: Music and Language in Strauss's Opera." In *Richard Strauss: Elektra,* edited by Derrick Puffett, 107–27. Cambridge: Cambridge University Press, 1989.

———. "Immortal Voices, Mortal Forms." In *Analytical Strategies and Musical Interpretation: Essays on Nineteenth- and Twentieth-Century Music,* edited by Craig Ayrey and Mark Everist, 288–300. Cambridge: Cambridge University Press, 1996.

———. *In Search of Opera.* Princeton, N.J.: Princeton University Press, 2001.

———. "Opera as Symphony, a Wagnerian Myth." In *Analyzing Opera: Verdi and Wagner,* edited by Carolyn Abbate and Roger Parker, 92–124. Berkeley: University of California Press, 1989.

———. *Unsung Voices: Opera and Musical Narrative in the Nineteenth Century.* Princeton, N.J.: Princeton University Press, 1991.

———. "Ventriloquism." In *Meaning in the Visual Arts: Views from the Outside,* edited by Irving Lavin, 305–11. Princeton: Institute for Advanced Study, 1995.

Abbate, Carolyn, and Roger Parker. "Introduction: On Analyzing Opera." In *Analyzing Opera: Verdi and Wagner,* 1–24. Berkeley: University of California Press, 1989.

Abel, Sam. *Opera in the Flesh: Sexuality in Opera Performance.* Boulder, Colo.: Westview Press, 1996.

Adami, Giuseppe, ed. *Giacomo Puccini: Epistolario.* Milan: A. Mondadori, 1928. In English as *Letters of Giacomo Puccini: Mainly Connected with the Composition and Production of his Operas*, translated and edited by Ena Makin. New York: AMS Press, 1971.

———. *Il romanzo della vita di Giacomo Puccini*. Milan: Rizzoli, 1942.

———. *Il tabarro (da "La Houppelande" di Didier Gold) [libretto]*. In *Il tabarro, Suor Angelica, Gianni Schicchi*. Milan: Ricordi, 1918.

Adami, Giuseppe, and Renato Simoni. *Turandot: Dramma lirico in tre atti e cinque quadri*. Milan: Ricordi, 1926.

Adorno, Theodor. "Late Style in Beethoven." In Theodor Adorno, *Essays on Music*, 564–68, edited by Richard Leppert, translated by Susan Gillespie. Berkeley: University of California Press, 2002. Originally in German as "Spätstil Beethovens" (1937), in *Gesammelte Schriften*, vol. 17, *Musikalische Schriften IV: Moments musiceaux. Neu gesdruckte Aufsätze 1928–1962*, 13–17. Frankfurt am Main: Suhrkamp, 1982.

Agawu, V. Kofi. *Playing with Signs: A Semiotic Interpretation of Classic Music*. Princeton, N.J.: Princeton University Press, 1991.

Alighieri, Dante. *The Divine Comedy of Dante Alighieri*, vol. 1, *Inferno*. Edited and translated by Robert M. Durling. Introduction by Ronald L. Martinez and Robert M. Durling. New York: Oxford University Press, 1996.

Alinovi, Margherita, ed. "Lettere di Giacomo Puccini." *Quaderni pucciniani 5* (1996): 187–274.

Allanbrook, Wye Jamison. *Rhythmic Gesture in Mozart: "Le Nozze di Figaro" and "Don Giovanni."* Chicago: University of Chicago Press, 1983.

Allorto, Riccardo. "Suor Angelica nella unità del trittico." *Musica d'Oggi* 2 (1959): 198–204.

Almén, Byron. *A Theory of Musical Narrative*. Bloomington: Indiana University Press, 2008.

Antokoletz, Elliot. "Bartok's *Bluebeard*: The Sources of its Modernism." *College Music Symposium* 30, no. 1 (1990): 75–95.

Arblaster, Anthony. *Viva La Libertà! Politics in Opera*. London: Verso, 1992.

Arrighi, Gino. "La corrispondenza di Giacomo Puccini con Maria Bianca Ginori Lisci." In *Critica pucciniana*. Lucca: Comitato nazionale per le onoranze a Giacomo Puccini nel cinquantenario della morte, 1976.

———. "Venti missive a Giacomo Puccini dal dicembre '83 al settembre '91." *Quaderni pucciniani* 2 (1985): 191–216.

Ashbrook, William. "Boito and the 1868 *Mefistofele* Libretto as a Reform Text." In *Reading Opera*, 268–87, edited by Arthur Groos and Roger Parker. Princeton, N.J.: Princeton University Press, 1988.

———. *Donizetti and His Operas*. Cambridge: Cambridge University Press, 1982.

———. *The Operas of Puccini*. New York: Oxford University Press, 1968.

———. Review of DiGaetani, *Puccini the Thinker*. *Music and Letters* 69, no. 4 (1988): 546–47.

———. "Whatever Happened to the Cabaletta?" *Opera Quarterly* 12, no. 3 (1996): 35–44. Originally "Whatever Happened to the Cabaletta? Intensity, Brevity, and the Transformation of the Cabaletta from Form to Function." In *Letteratura, musica e teatro al tempo di Ruggero Leoncavallo: Atti del 20 convegno internazionale, "Ruggero Leoncavallo nel suo tempo," Locarno, Biblioteca Cantonale, 7–9 October 1993*, edited by Lorenza Guiot and Jürgen Maehder, 83–87. Milan: Sonzogno, 1995.

Ashbrook, William, and Harold Powers. *Puccini's "Turandot": The End of the Great Tradition.* Princeton, N.J.: Princeton University Press, 1991.

Ashman, Mike. "Divided They Fall." *Opera* 49, no. 4 (1998): 389–93.

Atlas, Allan W. "Belasco and Puccini: Old Dog Tray and the Zuni Indians." *Musical Quarterly* 75, no. 3 (1991): 362–98.

———. "Crossed Stars and Crossed Tonal Areas in Puccini's *Madama Butterfly*." *19th-century Music* 14, no. 2 (1990): 186–96.

———. "Lontano–Tornare–Redenzione: Verbal Leitmotives and Their Musical Resonance in Puccini's *La fanciulla del West*." *Studi Musicali* 21, no. 2 (1992): 359–98.

———. "Mimi's Death: Mourning in Puccini and Leoncavallo." *Journal of Musicology* 14, no. 1 (1996): 52–79.

———. "Multivalence, Ambiguity, and Non-Ambiguity: Puccini and the Polemicists." *Journal of the Royal Musical Association* 188, no. 1 (1993): 73–93.

———. "Newly Discovered Sketches for Puccini's *Turandot* at the Pierpont Morgan Library." *Cambridge Opera Journal* 3, no. 2 (1991): 173–93.

———. "Puccini's *Tosca*: A New Point of View." In *Studies in the History of Music,* vol. 3, *The Creative Process,* 247–73. New York: Broude, 1992.

———. "Stealing a Kiss at the Golden Section: Pacing and Proportion in the Act I Love Duet of Puccini's *La bohème*." *Acta Musicologica* 75 (2003): 269–91.

Bakhtin, Mikhail M. *The Dialogic Imagination: Four Essays.* Edited by Michael Holquist. Translated by Caryl Emerson and Michael Holquist. Austin: University of Texas Press, 1981.

Balthazar, Scott L. "Aspects of Form in the Ottocento Libretto." *Cambridge Opera Journal* 7, no. 1 (1995): 23–35.

———. "Evolving Conventions in Italian Serious Opera: Scene Structure in the Works of Rossini, Bellini, Donizetti, and Verdi, 1810–1850." Ph.D. diss., University of Pennsylvania, 1985.

———. "Plot and Tonal Design as Compositional Constraints in *Il Trovatore*." *Current Musicology* 60/61 (1996): 51–78.

———. "Rossini and the Development of the Mid-Century Lyric Form." *Journal of the American Musicological Society* 41, no. 1 (1988): 102–25.

Barone, Anthony. "Richard Wagner's 'Parsifal' and the Theory of Late Style." *Cambridge Opera Journal* 7 (1995): 37–54.

Barrow, John. *Travels in China.* London: T. Cadell and W. Davies, 1804.

Barthes, Roland. *Image–Music–Text.* Translated by Stephen Heath. New York: Hill and Wang, 1977.

———. *S/Z.* Translated by Richard Miller. Preface by Richard Howard. New York: Hill and Wang, 1974. Originally in French as *S/Z.* Paris: Editions du Seuil, 1970.

Basevi, Abramo. *Studio sulle opere di Giuseppe Verdi.* Florence: Tipografia Tofani, 1859.

Batisti, Alberto. "'Con man furtiva?': Due probabili matrici debussyane nel *trittico* di Giacomo Puccini." In *Studi e fantasie: saggi, versi, musica e testimonianze in onore di Leonardo Pinzauti,* edited by Daniele Spini, 17–30. Antella: Passigli Editori, 1996.

Battistella, Edwin L. *Markedness: The Evaluative Superstructure of Language.* New York: State University of New York Press, 1990.

Baxter, Robert. Review of Girardi, *Puccini. Opera Quarterly* 18, no. 3 (2002): 454–57.

———. Review of Phillips-Matz, *Puccini: A Biography* and Budden, *Puccini: His Life and Works. Opera Quarterly* 19, no. 4 (2003): 785–94.

Beghelli, Marco. "Quel 'Lago di Massaciuccoli tanto . . . povero d'ispirazione!': D'Annunzio–Puccini: Lettere di un accordo mai nato." *Nuova rivista musicale italiana* 20, no. 4 (1986): 605–25.

Benco, Silvio. "Giacomo Puccini e un suo critico." *Il mondo artistico* 46, nos. 36–37 (August 21, 1912): 1–3.

Berg, Karl Georg Maria. *Giacomo Puccinis Opern: Musik und Dramaturgie.* Kassel: Bärenreiter Hochschulschriften, 1991.

———. *La maschere e la favola nell'opera italiana del primo novecento.* Venezia: Fondazione Levi, 1986.

Bernardoni, Virgilio, ed. *Puccini.* Bolgna: Società editrice il Mulino, 1996.

Berrong, Richard M. "*Turandot* as Political Fable." *Opera Quarterly* 11 (1995): 65–75.

Betcher, R. William, and William S. Pollack. *In A Time of Fallen Heroes: The Recreation of Masculinity.* New York: Atheneum, 1993.

Bianchi, Michele. "Il 'caso trittico': vitalità della morte e declino della vita." In *Giacomo Puccini: L'uomo, il musicista, il panorama europeo: Atti del convegno internazionale di studi su Giacomo Puccini nel 700 anniversario della morte, Lucca, 25–29 novembre 1994,* edited by Gabriella Biagi Ravenni and Carolyn Gianturco, 215–30. Lucca: Libreria Musicale Italiana, 1997.

Boito, Arrigo. *Tutti gli scritti.* Edited by Piero Nardi. Milan: Mondadori, 1942.

Boretz, Benjamin, and Edward T. Cone, eds. *Perspectives on Schoenberg and Stravinsky.* Princeton, N.J.: Princeton University Press, 1968.

Botstein, Leon. "The Enigmas of Richard Strauss: A Revisionist View." In *Richard Strauss and His World,* 3–32, edited by Bryan Gilliam. Princeton, N.J.: Princeton University Press, 1992.

Bower, Calvin M. "The Modes of Boethius." *Journal of Musicology* 3, no. 3 (1984): 252–63.

Brecht, Bertolt. *Brecht on Theatre: The Development of an Aesthetic.* Edited and translated by John Willett. New York: Hill and Wang, 1964.

Budden, Julian. "The Genesis and Literary Source of Puccini's First Opera." *Cambridge Opera Journal* 1, no. 1 (1989): 79–85.

———. "Melodramma (It.)." *Grove Music Online.* Edited by Laura Macy. http://www.grovemusic.com (accessed July 12, 2009).

———. *The Operas of Verdi.* Rev. ed. 3 vols. New York: Clarendon Press, 1992.

———. "Puccini, Giacomo." In *The New Grove Dictionary of Opera,* edited by Stanley Sadie, vol. 3, 1171. New York: Grove's Dictionaries of Music, 1992.

———. *Puccini: His Life and Works.* New York: Oxford University Press, 2002.

———. "Puccini's Transpositions." *Studi Pucciniani* 1 (1998): 7–17.

———. "Wagnerian Tendencies in Italian Opera." In *Music and Theater: Essays in Honour of Winton Dean,* 299–332. Cambridge: Cambridge University Press, 1987.

Burke, Richard. Review of Phillips-Matz, *Puccini: A Biography* and Budden, *Puccini: His Life and Works. Opera News* 67, no. 4 (2002): 89.

Burkholder, J. Peter. "Brahms and Twentieth Century Classical Music." *19th-Century Music* 8, no. 1 (1984): 75–83.

———. "Ives and the Nineteenth-Century European Tradition." In *Charles Ives and the Classical Tradition,* edited by Geoffrey Block and J. Peter Burkholder, 11–33. New Haven, Conn.: Yale University Press, 1996.

———. "Museum Pieces: The Historicist Mainstream in Music of the Last Hundred Years." *Journal of Musicology* 2 (1983): 115–34.

———. "Uniformity and Diversity in the History of Musical Style." Keynote address to the joint meeting of the American Musicological Society (South-Central chapter) and the Georgia Association of Music Theorists. Morrow, Georgia, April 6, 2001.

Burton, Deborah. "Dawn at Dusk: The Past and Future Meet in Puccini's Last Opera." Program notes for *Turandot* at the Forbidden City, Beijing, September 1998.

———. "A Journey of Discovery: Puccini's 'motivo di prima intenzione' and Its Applications in *Manon Lescaut, La fanciulla del West* and *Suor Angelica*." *Studi Musicali* 30, no. 2 (2001): 473–99.

Burton, Deborah, Susan Vandiver Nicassio, and Agostino Ziino, eds. *Tosca's Prism: Three Moments of Western Cultural History.* Boston: Northeastern University Press, 2004.

Busnelli, Maria, ed. "Carteggio Giacomo Puccini–Domenico Alaleona (1919–1924)." *Quaderni Pucciniani* 2 (1985): 217–30.

Campana, Alessandra. "La maledizione di Fausto." Review of Girardi, *Puccini. Cambridge Opera Journal* 12, no. 3 (2001): 261–66.

Caplin, William E. *Classical Form: A Theory of Formal Functions for the Instrumental Music of Haydn, Mozart, and Beethoven.* New York: Oxford University Press, 1998.

Carner, Mosco. "Esotismo e Colore Locale nell'Opera di Puccini." In *Esotismo e colore locale nell'opera di Puccini: Atti del I convegno internazionale sull'opera di Puccini a Torre del Lago,* edited by Jürgen Maehder, 13–34. Pisa: Giardini, 1985.

———. "The Genesis of the Opera." In *Giacomo Puccini: "Turandot."* English National Opera Guide no. 27, edited by Nicholas John, 7–18. London: John Calder, 1984.

———, ed. *Giacomo Puccini: "Tosca."* Cambridge Opera Handbooks series. Cambridge: Cambridge University Press, 1985.

———. *Puccini: A Critical Biography.* 3rd ed. London: Duckworth, 1992. First published 1958 by Duckworth.

———. "The Score." In *Giacomo Puccini: "Turandot."* English National Opera Guide no. 27, edited by Nicholas John, 19–34. London: John Calder, 1984.

Carr, Maureen A. *Multiple Masks: Neoclassicism in Stravinsky's Works on Greek Subjects.* Lincoln: University of Nebraska Press, 2002.

Casali, Patrick Vincent. "The Pronunciation of Turandot: Puccini's Last Enigma." *Opera Quarterly* 13, no. 4 (1997): 77–91.

Casini, Claudio. *Giacomo Puccini.* Turin: Unione Tipografico Editrice Torinese, 1978.

Cassar, Johanne. "*Turandot* de Puccini: Essai d'analyse sémiotique." Ph.D. diss., Université de Provence, 2000.

Cecchini, Riccardo, ed. *Giacomo Puccini: Lettere inedite ad Alfredo Vandini.* Lucca: Edizioni V. Press, 1994.

Cecchini, Riccardo, ed. *Trenta lettere inedite di Giacomo Puccini.* Lucca: Edizioni V. Press, 1992.

Cesari, Francesco. "Autoimpresito e riciclaggio in Puccini: il caso di Edgar." In *Giacomo Puccini: L'uomo, il musicista, il panorama europeo: Atti del convegno internazionale di studi su Giacomo Puccini nel 700 anniversario della morte, Lucca, 25–29 novembre 1994,* edited by Gabriella Biagi Ravenni and Carolyn Gianturco, 425–52. Lucca: Libreria Musicale Italiana, 1997.

———. "Genesi di *Edgar.*" In *Ottocento e oltre: Scritti in onore di Raoul Meloncelli,* edited by Francesco Izzo and Johannes Streicher, 451–69. Rome: Pantheon, 1993.

Cesari, Gaetano, and Alessandro Luzio, eds. *I copialettere di Giuseppe Verdi.* Bologna: Forni, 1968.

Chalmers, Kenneth. English translation of *Il trittico.* Liner notes, *Il trittico,* EMI Classics 7243 5 56587 2 2, cond. Antonio Pappano.

Chusid, Martin. "The Organization of Scenes with Arias: Verdi's Cavatinas and Romanzas." In *Atti del 10 congresso internazionale di studi verdiani,* 59–66. Parma: Instituto di studi verdiani, 1969.

Clark, Caryl. Review of Abbate, *Unsung Voices. Journal of Musicological Research* 14, nos. 1–2 (1994): 83–93.

Cohan, Steven, and Linda M. Shires. *Telling Stories: A Theoretical Analysis of Narrative Fiction.* New York: Routledge, 1988.

Conati, Marcelo. "Il tabarro ovvera la 'solita' insolita forma." In *Studi Pucciniani 3: "L'insolita forma": Strutture e processi analitici per l'opera italiana mell'epoca di Puccini: Atti del Convegno internazionale di studi Lucca, 20–21 settembre 2001,* edited by Virgilio Bernardoni, Michele Girardi, and Arthur Groos, 265–81. Lucca: Centro studi Giacomo Puccini, 2004.

Cone, Edward T. *Musical Form and Musical Performance.* New York: Norton, 1968.

———. "Schubert's Promissory Note: An Exercise in Musical Hermeneutics." *19th-Century Music* 5 (1982): 233–41.

———. "Stravinsky: The Progress of a Method." *Perspectives of New Music* 1, no. 1 (1962): 18–26.

Corse, Sandra. "Mi Chiamano Mimi: The Role of Women in Puccini's Operas." *Opera Quarterly* 1, no. 1 (1983): 93–106.

Covach, John R. "The Music and Theories of Josef Matthias Hauer." Ph.D. diss., University of Michigan, 1990.

Craig, Edward Gordon. "The Actor and the Übermarionette." *The Mask* 1, no. 2 (1908).

———. "Some Evil Tendencies of the Modern Theater." *The Mask* 1, no. 8 (1908).

D'Amico, Fedele. *L'albero del bene e del male: Naturalismo e decadentismo in Puccini.* Edited by Jacopo Pellegrini. Preface by Enzo Siciliano. Lucca: Maria Pacini Fazzi, 2000.

———. "Una ignorata pagina maliperiana di *Suor Angelica.*" *Rassaegna Musicale Curci* 19, no. 1 (1966): 7–13.

———. "L'opera insolita." *Quaderni Pucciniani* 2 (1985): 67–77.

Dahlhaus, Carl. "The Dramaturgy of Italian Opera." Translated by Mary Whittall. In *Opera in Theory and Practice, Image and Myth,* part 2 [*Systems*], vol. 6 of *The History of Italian Opera,* edited by Lorenzo Bianconi and Giorgio Pestelli, 73–150. Chicago: University of Chicago Press, 2003.

———. "New Music and the Problem of Musical Genre." In Carl Dahlhaus, *Schoenberg and the New Music: Essays,* 32–44. Translated by Derrick Puffett and Alfred Clayton. Cambridge: Cambridge University Press, 1987.

———. *Nineteenth-Century Music.* Translated by J. Bradford Robinson. Berkeley: University of California Press, 1989. Originally in German as *Die Musik des 19. Jahrhunderts,* Neues Handbuch der Musikwissenschaft, vol. 6. Wiesbaden: Academische Verlagsgesellschaft Athenaion, 1980.

———. "Was ist eine musikalische Gattung?" *Neue Zeitschrift für Musik* 135 (1974): 620–25.

———. "Zur Problematik der musikalischen Gattungen im 19. Jahrhundert." In *Gattungen der Musik in Einzeldarstellungen: Gedenkschrift Leo Schrade,* edited by Wulf Arlt, Ernst Lichtenhahn, and Hans Oesch, 840–95. Bern: Francke, 1973.

Dällenbach, Lucien. *The Mirror in the Text.* Translated by Jeremy Whiteley and Emma Hughes. Chicago: University of Chicago Press, 1989.

Darcy, Warren. "Bruckner's Sonata Deformations." In *Bruckner Studies,* edited by Timothy L. Jackson and Paul Hawkshaw, 256–77. Cambridge: Cambridge University Press, 1997.

———. "The Metaphysics of Annihilation: Wagner, Schopenhauer, and the Ending of the *Ring.*" *Music Theory Spectrum* 16, no. 1 (1994): 1–40.

———. "Rotational Form, Teleological Genesis, and Fantasy-Projection in the Slow Movement of Mahler's Sixth Symphony." *19th-Century Music* 25, no. 1 (2001): 49–74.

Davis, Andrew, and Howard Pollack. "Rotational Form in the Opening Scene of Gershwin's *Porgy and Bess.*" *Journal of the American Musicological Society* 60, no. 2 (2007): 373–414.

Della Seta, Fabrizio. "'O cieli azzuri': Exoticism and Dramatic Discourse in *Aïda.*" *Cambridge Opera Journal* 3, no. 1 (1991): 49–62.

———. "Some Difficulties in the Historiography of Italian Opera." *Cambridge Opera Journal* 10, no. 1 (1998): 3–13.

Derrida, Jacques. *Of Grammatology.* Translated by Gayatri Chakravorty Spivak. Baltimore: Johns Hopkins University Press, 1976.

———. *Positions.* Translated by Alan Bass. Chicago: University of Chicago Press, 1981.

Dickinson, Peter. "Style-Modulation: An Approach to Stylistic Pluralism." *The Musical Times* 130 (1989): 208–11.

Drabkin, William. "Characters, Key Relations, and Tonal Structure in *Il Trovatore.*" *Music Analysis* 1 (1983): 143–53.

———. "The Musical Language of *La bohème.*" In *Giacomo Puccini: "La bohème,"* edited by Arthur Groos and Roger Parker, 80–101. Cambridge Opera Handbooks series. Cambridge: Cambridge University Press: 1986.

Duncan, Michelle. "The Operatic Scandal of the Singing Body: Voice, Presence, Performativity." *Cambridge Opera Journal* 16, no. 3 (2004): 283–306.

Dunstan, Harry Nicholas. "Performance Practices in the Music of Giacomo Puccini as Observed by Luigi Ricci." Ph.D. diss., Catholic University of America, 1989.

Elphinstone, Michael. "*Le villi, Edgar,* and the 'Symphonic Element.'" In *The Puccini Companion,* edited by William Weaver and Simonetta Puccini, 61–110. New York: Norton, 1994.

Elwert, W. Theodor. *Italienische Metrik.* Munich: M. Huebner, 1968.

Fabbri, Paolo. "Istituti metrici e formali." In *Teorie e technice, immagini e fantasmi,* vol. 6 of *Storia dell'opera italiana,* edited by Lorenzo Bianconi and Giorgio Pestelli, 163–233. Turin, EDT: 1988. In English as "Metrical and Formal Organization." In *Opera in Theory and Practice, Image and Myth,* part 2 [*Systems*], vol. 6 of *The History of Italian Opera,* edited by Lorenzo Bianconi and Giorgio Pestelli, translated by Kenneth Chalmers, 151–219. Chicago: University of Chicago Press, 2003.

Fairtile, Linda B. "'Duetto a tre': Franco Alfano's Completion of *Turandot.*" *Cambridge Opera Journal* 16 (2004): 163–85.

———. *Giacomo Puccini: A Guide to Research.* New York: Garland, 1999.

———. "Giacomo Puccini's Operatic Revisions as Manifestations of his Compositional Priorities." Ph.D. diss., New York University, 1996.

Felman, Shoshana. *The Literary Speech Act: Don Juan with J. L. Austin, or Seduction in Two Languages.* Translated by Catherine Porter. Ithaca, N.Y.: Cornell University Press, 1983. Originally in French as *Le Scandale du corps parlant.* Paris: Editions du Seuil, 1980.

Ferrando, Enrico Maria, ed. *Tutti i libretti di Puccini.* Milan: Garzanti, 1984.

Ferraro, Giuseppe, and Annunziato Pugliese, eds. *Fausto Torrefranca: l'uomo, il suo tempo, la sua opera: Atti del Convegno internazionale di studi, Vibo Valentia, 15–17 dicembre 1983.* Vibo Valentia: Istituto di bibliografia musicale calabrese, 1993.

Ferrero, Lorenzo. "Turandot: Über den Verismus hinaus." In *Über Musiktheater: Eine Festschrift gewidmet Arthur Schnerle anlässlich seines 65. Geburstages,* 88–93. München: Ricordi, 1992.

Fodor, Jerry. "Not Entirely Nice." Review of Girardi, *Puccini. London Review of Books* 22, no. 21 (November 2, 2000): 32.

Forzano, Giovacchino. *Come li ho conosciuti.* Turin: Edizioni della radio, 1957.

———. Gianni Schicchi [libretto]. In *Il tabarro, Suor Angelica, Gianni Schicchi.* Milan: Ricordi, 1918.

———. Suor Angelica [libretto]. In *Il tabarro, Suor Angelica, Gianni Schicchi.* Milan: Ricordi, 1918.

Fraccaroli, Arnaldo. *Giacomo Puccini si confida e racconta.* Milan: Ricordi, 1957.

Freud, Sigmund. "Female Sexuality" (1931). In *Women and Analysis: Dialogues on Psychoanalytic Views of Femininity,* 39–56. Compiled by Jean Strouse. New York: Grossman, 1974.

Frisch, Walter. *German Modernism: Music and the Arts.* Berkeley: University of California Press, 2005.

Furman, Nelly. "Opera, or the Staging of the Voice." Review of Marie-France Castarède, *La voix et ses sortileges;* Michel Poizat, *L'Opera ou le cri de l'ange: Essai sor la jouissance de l'amateur d'opéra;* and Phillipe-Joseph Salazar, *Idéologies de l'opéra. Cambridge Opera Journal* 3, no. 3 (1991): 303–306.

Gara, Eugenio, ed. *Carteggi Pucciniani*. Milan: Ricordi, 1958.

Garibaldi, Luigi Agostino. *Giuseppe Verdi nelle lettere di Emanuele Muzio ad Antonio Barezzi*. Milan: Fratelli Treves, 1931.

Giger, Andreas. "Verismo: Origin, Corruption, and Redemption of an Operatic Term." *Journal of the American Musicological Society* 60, no. 2 (2007): 271–315.

Gilliam, Bryan. "Between Resignation and Hope: The Late Works of Richard Strauss." In *Late Thoughts: Reflections on Artists and Composers at Work*, edited by Karen Painter and Thoman Crow, 167–80. Los Angeles: Getty Research Institute, 2006.

Girardi, Michele, ed. "Il figlio segreto di Giacomo Puccini." Exhibit organized at Torre del Lago, 2008, for the Centro studi Giacomo Puccini, Lucca. http://www.puccini.it/bollettinoValigia.htm.

———. "Per un inventario della musica in scena nel teatro veridano." *Studi verdiani* 6 (1990): 99–145.

———. *Puccini: His International Art*. Translated by Laura Basini. Chicago: University of Chicago Press, 2000. Originally in Italian as *Giacomo Puccini: L'arte internazionale di un musicista italiano*. Venezia: Marsilio, 1995.

———. "*Turandot*: Il futuro interotto del melodrama italiano." *Rivista italiana di musicologia* 17 (1982): 155–81.

Gjerdingen, Robert O. *A Classic Turn of Phrase*. Philadelphia: University of Pennsylvania Press, 1988.

———. *Music in the Galant Style*. Oxford: Oxford University Press, 2007.

Goehring, Edmund J. *Three Modes of Perception in Mozart: The Philosophical, Pastoral, and Comic in "Così fan tutte."* Cambridge: Cambridge University Press, 2004.

Gold, Didier. *La Houppelande*. Paris: Ondet, 1910.

Gossett, Philip. "The 'Candeur virginale' of *Tancredi*." *The Musical Times* 112 (1971): 326–29.

———. "Carl Dahlhaus and the Ideal Type." *19th-Century Music* 13, no. 1 (1989): 49–56.

———. "The Case for Puccini." Review of Girardi, *Puccini*; Budden, *Puccini*; and Phillips-Matz, *Puccini*. *New York Review of Books* (March 27, 2003): 38–42.

———. "Gioachino Rossini and the Conventions of Composition." *Acta Musicologica* 42, no. 1 (1970): 48–58.

———. "Verdi, Ghislanzoni, and *Aïda*: The Uses of Convention." *Critical Inquiry* 1 (1974–75): 291–334.

Gozzi, Carlo. *Five Tales for the Theater*. Edited and translated by Albert Bermel and Ted Emery. Chicago: University of Chicago Press, 1989.

Greene, David B. *Listening to Strauss Operas: The Audience's Multiple Standpoints*. New York: Gordon and Breach, 1991.

Greenwald, Helen M. "Dramatic Exposition and Musical Structure in Puccini's Operas." Ph.D. diss., City University of New York, 1991.

———. "Picturing Cio-Cio-San: House, Screen, and Ceremony in Puccini's *Madama Butterfly*." *Cambridge Opera Journal* 12, no. 3 (2001): 237–59.

———. "Puccini, *Il tabarro*, and the Dilemma of Operatic Transposition." *Journal of the American Musicological Society* 51, no. 3 (1998): 521–58.

———. "Recent Puccini Research." *Acta Musicologica* 65, no. 1 (1993): 23–50.

———. Review of Girardi, *L'arte internazionale di un musicista italiano. Notes: Quarterly Journal of the Music Library Association* 53, no. 3 (1997): 803–804.

———. "Verdi's Patriarch and Puccini's Matriarch: Through the Looking-Glass and What Puccini Found There." *19th-Century Music* 17, no. 3 (1994): 220–36.

Greimas, A. J. *Du sens II: Essais sémiotiques.* Paris: Seuil, 1979.

Groos, Arthur, and Roger Parker, eds. *Giacomo Puccini: "La bohème."* Cambridge Opera Handbooks series. Cambridge: Cambridge University Press: 1986.

———. "Three Early Critics and the Brothers Mann: Aspects of the *La bohème* Reception." In *Giacomo Puccini: La bohème,* edited by Arthur Groos and Roger Parker, 129–41. Cambridge: Cambridge University Press, 1986.

Grout, Donald Jay. *A Short History of Opera.* 2nd ed. 2 vols. New York: Columbia University Press, 1965.

Guarnieri Corazzol, Adriana. "Opera and Verismo: Regressive Points of View and the Artifice of Alienation." Translated by Roger Parker. *Cambridge Opera Journal* 5, no. 1 (1993): 39–53. Originally in Italian as "Opera e verismo: Regressione del punto di vista e artificio dello straniamento." In *Ruggero Leoncavallo nel suo tempo: Primo convegno internazionale di studi su Ruggero Leoncavallo,* edited by Lorenza Guiot and Jürgen Maehder, 13–31. Milan: Sonzogno, 1993.

Hamilton, David. *The Monkey Gland Affair.* London: Chatto and Windus, 1986.

Hasty, Christopher F. *Meter as Rhythm.* New York: Oxford University Press, 1997.

Hatten, Robert S. "The Expressive Role of Disjunction: A Semiotic Approach to Form and Meaning in Bruckner's Fourth and Fifth Symphonies." In *Perspectives on Anton Bruckner,* edited by Paul Hawkshaw, Crawford Howie, and Timothy L. Jackson, 145–84 (Aldershot, UK: Ashgate, 2001).

———. *Interpreting Musical Gestures, Topics, and Tropes: Mozart, Beethoven, Schubert.* Bloomington: Indiana University Press, 2004.

———. *Musical Meaning in Beethoven: Markedness, Correlation, and Interpretation.* Bloomington: Indiana University Press, 1994.

———. "On Narrativity in Music: Expressive Genres and Levels of Discourse in Beethoven." *Indiana Theory Review* 12 (1991): 75–98.

———. "The Place of Intertextuality in Music Studies." *American Journal of Semiotics* 3, no. 4 (1985): 69–82.

———. "Pluralism of Theatrical Genre and Musical Style in Henze's *We Come to the River.*" *Perspectives of New Music* 28, no. 2 (1990): 292–311.

———. "Toward a Semiotic Model of Style in Music: Epistemological and Methodological Bases." Ph.D. diss., Indiana University, 1982.

Hepokoski, James. "Back and Forth from 'Egmont': Beethoven, Mozart, and the Nonresolving Recapitulation." *19th-Century Music* 25, no. 2/3 (2001–2002): 127–64.

———. "Beyond the Sonata Principle." *Journal of the American Musicological Society* 55 (2002): 91–154.

———. "The Essence of Sibelius: Creation Myths and Rotational Cycles in *Luonnotar.*" In *The Sibelius Companion,* edited by Glenda Dawn Goss, 121–46. Westport, Conn.: Greenwood, 1996.

———. "Fiery-Pulsed Libertine or Domestic Hero? Strauss's Don Juan Reinvestigated." In *Richard Strauss: New Perspectives on the Composer and His Work,* edited by Bryan Gilliam, 135–75. Durham, N.C.: Duke University Press, 1992.

——. "Genre and Content in Mid-Century Verdi: 'Addio, del passato' (*La Traviata*, Act III)." *Cambridge Opera Journal* 1, no. 3 (1989): 249–76.

——. *Giuseppe Verdi: "Otello."* Cambridge Opera Handbooks series. Cambridge: Cambridge University Press, 1987.

——. "Rotations, Sketches, and the Sixth Symphony." In *Sibelius Studies,* edited by Timothy L. Jackson and Veijo Murtomäki, 322–51. Cambridge: Cambridge University Press, 2001.

——. *Sibelius: Symphony no. 5.* Cambridge: Cambridge University Press, 1993.

——. "Sonata Theory and Dialogic Form." Lecture to the Sixth European Music Analysis Conference, October 12, 2007, Freiburg, Germany; and to the annual meeting of the Texas Society for Music Theory, February 22, 2008, San Marcos, Texas.

——. "Structure, Implication, and the End of Suor Angelica." *Studi Pucciniani 3: "L'insolita forma": Strutture e processi analitici per l'opera italiana mell'epoca di Puccini: Atti del Convegno internazionale di studi Lucca, 20–21 settembre 2001.* Edited by Virgilio Bernardoni, Michele Girardi, and Arthur Groos, 241–64. Lucca: Centro studi Giacomo Puccini, 2004.

Hepokoski, James, and Warren Darcy. *Elements of Sonata Theory: Norms, Types, and Deformations in the Late Eighteenth-Century Sonata.* New York: Oxford University Press, 2006.

Hopkinson, Cecil. *A Bibliography of the Works of Giacomo Puccini, 1858–1924.* New York: Broude, 1968.

Huebner, Steven. "Thematic Recall in Late Nineteenth-Century Opera." *Studi Pucciniani 3: "L'insolita forma": Strutture e processi analitici per l'opera italiana mell'epoca di Puccini: Atti del Convegno internazionale di studi Lucca, 20–21 settembre 2001.* Edited by Virgilio Bernardoni, Michele Girardi, and Arthur Groos, 77–104. Lucca: Centro studi Giacomo Puccini, 2004.

Human Mortality Database. University of California, Berkeley; Max Planck Institute for Demographic Research, Rostock, Germany. www.mortality.org or www.humanmortality.de.

Hutcheon, Linda, and Michael Hutcheon. Review of *En Travesti: Women, Gender, Subversion, Opera. Cambridge Opera Journal* 8, no. 3 (1996): 285–90.

Ingarden, Roman. *The Work of Music and the Problem of Its Identity.* Translated by Adam Czerniawski. Edited by Jean G. Harrell. Berkeley: University of California Press, 1986.

Ives, Charles. *Essays Before A Sonata and Other Writings.* Edited by Howard Boatwright. New York: Norton, 1962.

Jakobson, Roman, and Morris Halle. *Fundamentals of Language.* The Hague: Mouton, 1956.

John, Nicholas, ed. *Giacomo Puccini: "Turandot."* English National Opera Guide no. 27. London: John Calder, 1984.

Kallberg, Jeffrey. "The Rhetoric of Genre: Chopin's Nocturne in G minor." *19th-Century Music* 11 (1988): 238–61.

Kaye, Michael. *The Unknown Puccini: A Historical Perspective on the Songs, Including Little-Known Music from "Edgar" and "La Rondine," with Complete Music for Voice and Piano.* Oxford: Oxford University Press, 1987.

Kerman, Joseph. "Lyric Form and Flexibility in *Simon Boccanegra.*" *Studi Verdiani* 1 (1982): 47–62.

———. *Opera as Drama.* New and revised ed. Berkeley: University of California Press, 1988.

Kimbell, David R. B. *Verdi in the Age of Italian Romanticism.* Cambridge: Cambridge University Press, 1981.

Klein, Michael. *Intertextuality in Western Art Music.* Bloomington: Indiana University Press, 2005.

Kleinheinz, Christopher. *Medieval Italy: An Encyclopedia.* 2 vols. New York: Routledge, 2004.

Koo-huang, Han. "J. A. van Aalst and his *Chinese Music.*" *Asian Music* 19, no. 2 (1988): 127–30.

Korfmacher, Peter. *Exotismus in Giacomo Puccinis "Turandot."* Cologne: Dohr, 1993.

de Koven, Reginald. Review of Puccini, *Il trittico. The New York Herald,* December 15, 1918: 13.

Kowalke, Kim. "Kurt Weill, Modernism, and Popular Culture: *Öffentlichkeit als Stil.*" *Modernism/Modernity* 2, no. 1 (1995): 27–69.

Kramer, Lawrence. *Classical Music and Postmodern Knowledge.* Berkeley: University of California Press, 1995.

———. "Song and Story." Review of Abbate, *Unsung Voices. 19th-Century Music* 15, no. 3 (1992): 235–39.

Kreuzer, Gundula. "Voices from Beyond: Verdi's *Don Carlos* and the Modern Stage." *Cambridge Opera Journal* 18, no. 2 (2006): 151–79.

Kristeva, Julia. *Desire in Language: A Semiotic Approach to Literature and Art.* Edited by Leon S. Roudiez. Translated by Thomas Gora, Alice Jardin, and Leon S. Roudiez. New York: Columbia University Press, 1980.

———. *The Kristeva Reader.* Edited by Toril Moi. New York: Columbia University Press, 1986.

———. *Revolution in Poetic Language.* Translated by Margaret Waller. New York: Columbia University Press, 1989.

Lagaly, Klaus. "Hindemiths Einakter-Triptychon und Puccinis 'Il trittico': Analogien und Unterschiede." *Experiment und Erbe: Studien zum Frühwerk Paul Hindemiths.* Schriftenreihe der Musikhochschule des Saarlandes, vol. 2. Edited by Julius Berger and Klaus Velten. Saarbrücken: PFAU-Verlag, 1993.

Lakoff, George. *Women, Fire, and Dangerous Things: What Categories Reveal about the Mind.* Chicago: University of Chicago Press, 1987.

LaRue, Jan. *Guidelines for Style Analysis.* New York: Norton, 1970.

Lawton, David, and David Rosen. "Verdi's Non-Definitive Revisions: The Early Operas." In *Atti del III Congresso internazionale di studi verdiani, 12–17 giugno 1972,* edited by Maria Medici and Marcello Pavarani, 189–237. Parma: Instituto di studi verdiani, 1974.

Lawton, David. "Tonality and Drama in Verdi's Early Operas." Ph.D. diss., University of California, Berkeley, 1973.

Lehrdahl, Fred, and Ray Jackendoff. *A Generative Theory of Tonal Music.* Cambridge, Mass.: MIT Press, 1983.

Leukel, Jürgen. "Puccinis kinematographische Technik." *Neue Zeitschrift für Musik* 143, no. 6–7 (1982): 24–26.

———. *Studien zu Puccinis "Il trittico": Il tabarro–Suor Angelica–Gianni Schicchi.* München-Salzburg: Musikverlag Emil Katzbichler, 1983.

Levi, Eugenia. *Fiorita di canti tradizionali del popolo italiano*. 2nd ed. Firenze: Bemporad, 1926.

Leydon, Rebecca. "Debussy's Late Style and the Devices of the Early Cinema." *Music Theory Spectrum* 23, no. 2 (2001): 217–41.

Liao, Ping-Hui. "Of Writing Words for Music which is Already Made: *Madama Butterfly, Turandot,* and Orientalism." *Cultural Critique* 16 (1990): 31–59.

Lindenberger, Herbert. Review of Abbate, *Unsung Voices. Notes: Quarterly Journal of the Music Library Association* 49, no. 1 (1992): 152–54.

Lippmann, Friedrich. *Vincenzo Bellini und die Italienische Opera Seria seiner Zeit: Studien über Libretto, Arienform, und Melodik. Analecta Musicologica* 6. Köln: Bohlau, 1969.

Lo, Kii-Ming. "Giacomo Puccini's Turandot in Two Acts: The Draft of the First Version of the Libretto." In *Giacomo Puccini: L'uomo, il musicista, il panorama europeo: Atti del convegno internazionale di studi su Giacomo Puccini nel 700 anniversario della morte, Lucca, 25–29 novembre 1994,* edited by Gabriella Biagi Ravenni and Carolyn Gianturco, 239–58. Lucca: Libreria Musicale Italiana, 1997.

———. "Ping, Pong, Pang: Die Gestalten der Commedia dell'arte in Busonis und Puccinis *Turandot*-Opern." In *Die lustige Person auf der Bühne: Gesammelte Vorträge des Salzburger Symposions 1993,* edited by Peter Csobáldi, Gernot Gruber, Jürgen Kühnel, Ulrich Müller, Oswald Panagl, and Franz Viktor Spechtler, 311–23. Anif/Salzburg: Müller-Speiser, 1994.

———. *Turandot auf der Opernbühne.* Frankfurt: Peter Lang, 1996.

Maclean, Marie. *Narrative as Performance.* New York: Routledge, 1988.

Maehder, Jürgen. "Drammaturgia musicale e strutture narrative nel teatro musicale italiano della generazione dell'ottanta." In *Alfredo Casella e L'Europa: Atti del convegno internazionale di studi, Siena, 7–9 June 2001 (Chigiana* vol. 44), ed. Mila de Santis, 223–48. Florence: Olschki, 2003.

———. "Erscheinungsformen des Wagnérism in der italienischen Oper des Fin de siècle." In *Von Wagner zum Wagnérisme: Musik, Literatur, Kunst, Politik,* ed. Annegret Fauser and Manuela Schwartz, 575–621. Leipzig: Leipziger Universitätsverlag, 1999.

———. "Giacomo Puccinis *Turandot* und ihre Wandlungen: Die Ergänzungsversuche des III. *Turandot*-Aktes." In *Zibaldone: Zeitschrift für italienische Kultur und Gegenwart* vol. 35, ed. Thomas Bremer and Titus Heydenreich, 50–77. Tübingen: Stauffenburg, 2003.

———. "Die Glorifizierung der toskanischen Stadt in der italienischen Oper des 20. Jahrhunderts." In *Mahagonny: Die Stadt als Sujet und Herausforderung des (Musik)theaters,* ed. Ulrich Müller, 417–38. Salzburg: Müller-Speiser, 2000.

———. "Die italienische Oper des Fin de siecle als Spiegel politischer Stromungen im umbertinischen Italien." In *Der schöne Abglanz: Stationen der Operngeschichte, Hamburg Beitrage zur Öffentlichen Wissenschaft,* no. 9, ed. Udo Bermbach and Wulf Konold, 181–210. Berlin: Reimer, 1992.

———. "Il libretto patriottico nell'Italia della fine del secolo e la raffigurazione dell'Antichità e del Rinascimento nel libretto prefascista italiano." In *Atti del XIV congresso della Societa Internazionale di Musicologia, Bologna, 1987: Trasmissione e recezione delle forme di cultura musicale,* vol. 3, ed. Angelo Pompilio, 451–66. Torino: Edizioni di Torino, 1990.

———. "Nichtlineare Dramaturgie: Zur Erzahlhaltung im Musiktheater der Zwan-ziger Jahre." In *Alban Bergs "Wozzeck" und die Zwanziger Jahre*, ed. Peter Csobádi and Joachim Herz, 437–57. Salzburg: Müller-Speiser, 1999.

———. "The Origins of Italian *Literaturoper: Guglielmo Ratcliff, La Figlia di Iorio, Parisina*, and *Francesca da Rimini*." In *Reading Opera*, edited by Arthur Groos and Roger Parker, 92–128. Princeton, N.J.: Princeton University Press, 1988.

———. "Studien zum Fragmentcharakter von Giacomo Puccini's *Turandot*." *Analecta Musicologica* 22 (1984): 297–379. In Italian as "Studi sul carratere di framento della *Turandot* di Giacomo Puccini." *Quaderni Pucciniani* 2 (1985), 79–163. In English and abridged as "Puccini's *Turandot*: A Fragment." In *Giacomo Puccini: "Turandot*," 35–53. English National Opera Guide no. 27. Edited by Nicholas John. London: John Calder, 1984.

———. "*Turandot* and the Theatrical Aesthetics of the Twentieth Century." In *The Puccini Companion*, ed. William Weaver and Simonetta Puccini, 265–78. New York: Norton, 1994.

Maguire, Janet. "Puccini's Version of the Duet and Final Scene of *Turandot*." *Musical Quarterly* 74 (1990): 319–59.

Mandelli, Alfredo. "Il recupero dell' 'Aria dei fiori' in *Suor Angelica*." *Quaderni Pucciniani* 5 (1996): 161–71.

Marchetti, Arnaldo, ed. *Puccini com'era*. Milan: Curci, 1973.

Marchetti, Leopoldo, ed. *Puccini nelle immagini*. Milan: Maestri arti grafiche, 1968.

Marek, George R. *Puccini*. New York: Simon and Schuster, 1951.

Mariani, Renato. "Inevitabilità di Liù." In *Verismo in musica e altri studi*, edited by Cesare Orselli, 58–63. Firenze: Olschki, 1976.

Marinetti, Filippo Tommaso. *Let's Murder the Moonshine: Selected Writings*. Translated by R. W. Flint and Arthur A. Coppotelli. Los Angeles: Sun and Moon Classics, 1991.

———. *Teoria e invenzione futurista*. Milan: Mandadori, 1968.

McClatchie, Stephen. "Towards a Post-Modern Wagner." Review of Abbate, *Unsung Voices. Wagner* 13, no. 3 (1992): 108–21.

McCreless, Patrick. "Roland Barthes's *S/Z* from a Musical Point of View." *In Theory Only* 10, no. 7 (1988): 1–29.

Meyer, Leonard. *Style and Music: Theory, History, Ideology*. Philadelphia: University of Pennsylvania Press, 1989.

Migliorini, Bruno, and Fredi Chiapelli. *Elementi di stilistica e di versificazione italiana*. Firenze: Le Monier, 1960.

Mitchell, W. J. T., ed. *On Narrative*. Chicago: University of Chicago Press, 1981.

Monelle, Raymond. *The Musical Topic: Hunt, Military, and Pastoral*. Bloomington: Indiana University Press, 2006.

———. *The Sense of Music: Semiotic Essays*. With a foreword by Robert S. Hatten. Princeton, N.J.: Princeton University Press, 2000.

del Monte, Alberto. *Retorica, stilistica, versificazione*. Torino: Loescher, 1968.

Moreen, Robert Anthony. "Integration of Text Forms and Musical Forms in Verdi's Early Operas." Ph.D. diss., Princeton University, 1975.

Morgan, Robert P. Review of Abbate, *Unsung Voices. The Journal of Modern History* 64, no. 3 (1992): 576–81.

———. "Schenker and the Twentieth Century: A Modernist Perspective." In *Music in the Mirror: Reflections on the History of Music Theory and Literature for the 21st Century*, edited by Andreas Giger and Thomas J. Mathiesen, 247–74. Lincoln: University of Nebraska Press, 2002.

Newcomb, Anthony. "Schumann and Late Eighteenth-Century Narrative Strategies." *19th-Century Music* 11 (1987): 164–74.

Nicastro, Aldo. "Reminiscenza e populismo nella poetica di Puccini: Appunti sul *tabarro*." *Nuovo rivista musicale italiana* 2, no. 6 (1968): 1092–1104.

Niccolai, Michela. "'La scena ha dunque importanza massima': La *mise en scène* del *tabarro*." *Hortus musicus* 12 (2002): 40–42.

Nicolaisen, Jay. "The First *Mefistofele*." *19th-Century Music* 1, no. 3 (1978): 221–32.

———. *Italian Opera in Transition, 1871–1893*. Ann Arbor, Mich.: UMI Research Press, 1980.

Noske, Fritz. *The Signifier and the Signified: Studies in the Operas of Mozart and Verdi*. Reprint. New York: Oxford University Press, 1990.

Notley, Margaret. *Lateness and Brahms: Music and Culture in the Twilight of Viennese Classicism*. Oxford: Oxford University Press, 2007.

Ojetti, Ugo. *Cose Viste*. Milan: Frateeli Treves, 1924. In English as *As They Seemed to Me*. Translated by Henry Faust. Introduction by Gabriele D'Annunzio. Freeport, N.Y.: Books for Libraries Press, 1927.

Olive, Jean-Paul. *Musique et montage: essai sur le matériau musical au début du XXe siècle*. Paris: L'Harmattan, 1998.

Osborne, Charles. Review of Girardi, *Puccini*. *Opera* 53, no. 3 (2002): 363.

Paduano, Guido. "'Dubita di Dio': Drammaturgia delle villi." *Studi Pucciniani* 3: *"L'insolita forma": Strutture e processi analitici per l'opera italiana mell'epoca di Puccini: Atti del Convegno internazionale di studi Lucca, 20–21 settembre 2001*. Edited by Virgilio Bernardoni, Michele Girardi, and Arthur Groos, 227–40. Lucca: Centro studi Giacomo Puccini, 2004.

Parker, Roger. "Analysis: Act I in Perspective." In *Giacomo Puccini: "Tosca,"* ed. Mosco Carner, 117–42. Cambridge Opera Handbooks series. Cambridge: Cambridge University Press, 1985.

———. "Berio's *Turandot*: Once More the Great Tradition." In Roger Parker, *Remaking the Song: Operatic Visions and Revisions from Handel to Berio*, 90–120. Berkeley: University of California Press, 2006.

———. "'Insolite Forme,' or Basevi's Garden Path." In Roger Parker, *Leonora's Last Act: Essays in Verdian Discourse*, 42–60. Princeton, N.J.: Princeton University Press, 1997.

———. *Leonora's Last Act: Essays in Verdian Discourse*. Princeton, N.J.: Princeton University Press, 1997.

———. "Levels of Motivic Definition in Verdi's *Ernani*." *19th-Century Music* 6 (1982): 141–50.

———. "Phillipe and Posa Act II: The Shock of the New." *Cambridge Opera Journal* 14, nos. 1–2 (2002): 133–47.

———. *Remaking the Song: Operatic Visions and Revisions from Handel to Berio*. Berkeley: University of California Press, 2006.

———. "Round Table II: Literary Studies: Caught Up in the Web of Words." *Acta Musicologica* 69, no. 1 (1997): 10–15.

Parker, Roger, and Allan W. Atlas. "Dialogue: A Key for Chi? Tonal Areas in Puccini." *19th-Century Music* 15, no. 3 (1992): 229–34.

Pascall, Robert. "Style." *Grove Music Online.* Edited by Laura Macy. http://www.grovemusic.com (accessed May 30, 2007).

Peirce, Charles Sanders. *Collected Papers of Charles Sanders Peirce.* 8 vols. Cambridge: Harvard University Press, 1931–1960.

———. *The Essential Peirce: Selected Philosophical Writings.* Edited by Nathan Houser and Christian Kloesel. 2 vols. Bloomington: Indiana University Press, 1992–1998.

Petrobelli, Perluigi. "More on the Three 'Systems': The First Act of *La Forza del Destino.*" In *Music in the Theater: Essays on Verdi and Other Composers,* 127–40. Translated by Roger Parker. Princeton, N.J.: Princeton University Press, 1994.

———. "Music in the Theater (Apropos of *Aïda* Act III)." In *Music in the Theater: Essays on Verdi and Other Composers,* translated by Roger Parker, 113–26. Princeton, N.J.: Princeton University Press, 1994. Originally in *Themes in Drama,* vol. 3: *Drama, Dance, and Music.* Edited by James Redmond. Cambridge: Cambridge University Press, 1981.

———. "Verdi's Musical Thought: An Example from *Macbeth.*" In *Music in the Theater: Essays on Verdi and Other Composers,* 141–52, translated by Roger Parker. Princeton, N.J.: Princeton University Press, 1994.

Phillips-Matz, Mary Jane. *Puccini: A Biography.* Boston: Northeastern University Press, 2002.

Pintorno, Giuseppe. "Les sources francaises des operas de Giacomo Puccini." Ph.D. diss., University of Milan, 1970.

———, ed. *Puccini: 276 lettere inedite: il fondo dell'Accademia d'arte a Montecatini Terme.* Milan: Nuove edizioni, 1974.

———, ed. "Puccini e Giovannetti." *Quaderni pucciniani* 1 (1982): 47–76.

Pinzauti, Leonardo. "Giacomo Puccini's *trittico* and the Twentieth Century." In *The Puccini Companion,* edited by William Weaver and Simonetta Puccini, 228–43. New York: Norton, 1994.

———. "Memoria di Fausto Torrefranca." *L'approdo musicale, quaderni di musica.* Rome: Edizioni Rai Radiotelevisione, 1965.

Poizat, Michel. "'The Blue Note' and 'The Objectified Voice and the Vocal Object.'" *Cambridge Opera Journal* 3, no. 3 (1991): 195–211.

———. *L'Opéra ou le cri de l'ange: Essai sur la jouissance de l'amateur d'opéra.* Paris: A. M. Métailié, 1986. In English as *The Angel's Cry: Beyond the Pleasure Principle in Opera.* Translated by Arthur Denner. Ithaca, N.Y.: Cornell University Press, 1992.

Porter, Andrew. "Solving the Enigmas." *Opera* (June 2002): 668–72.

Powers, Harold. "By Design: The Architecture of *Simon Boccanegra.*" *Opera News* 49, no. 7 (December 22, 1984): 16–21, 42–43.

———. "Dal padre alla principessa: reorientamento tonale nel Finale primo della Turandot." In *Giacomo Puccini: L'uomo, il musicista, il panorama europeo: Atti del convegno internazionale di studi su Giacomo Puccini nel 700 anniversario della morte, Lucca, 25–29 novembre 1994,* ed. Gabriella Biagi Ravenni and Carolyn Gianturco, translated by Giorgio Biancorosso, 259–80. Lucca: Libreria Musicale Italiana, 1997.

———. "Form and Formula." *Studi Pucciniani 3: "L'insolita forma": Strutture e processi analitici per l'opera italiana mell'epoca di Puccini: Atti del Convegno internazionale di studi Lucca, 20–21 settembre 2001.* Edited by Virgilio Bernardoni, Michele Girardi, and Arthur Groos, 11–49. Lucca: Centro studi Giacomo Puccini, 2004.

———. "One Halfstep at a Time: Tonal Transposition and 'Split Association' in Italian Opera." *Cambridge Opera Journal* 7 (1995): 135–64.

———. "*Simon Boccanegra* I.10–12: A Generic-Genetic Analysis of the Council-Chamber Scene." *19th-Century Music* 13, no. 2 (1989): 101–28.

———. "'La solita forma' and 'The Uses of Convention.'" *Acta Musicologica* 59, no. 1 (1987): 65–90. Originally in *Nuove prospettive nella ricerca verdiana: Atti del convegno internazionale in occasione della prima del "Rigoletto" in edizione critica, Vienna, 12–13 marzo 1983.* Edited by Marcello Pavarani and Marisa Di Gregorio Casati, 74–105. Parma: Instituto di studi verdiani-Ricordi, 1987.

Pratella, Francesco Balilla. *Le Arti e le tradizioni popolare d'Italia: primo documentario per la storia dell'etnofonia in Italia.* Udine: Editrice IDEA, 1941.

Puccini: Le Prime: Libretti della prima rappresentazione. Milan: Ricordi, 2002.

Puccini, Giacomo. *Il trittico in Full Score: Il tabarro, Suor Angelica, Gianni Schicchi.* Mineola, New York: Dover, 1996. Reprint of *Il tabarro: opera in un atto* (Milan: Ricordi, 1918; reprint Milan: Ricordi, 1980); *Suor Angelica: opera in un atto* (Milan: Ricordi, 1918; reprint Milan: Ricordi, 1980); and *Gianni Schicchi: opera in un atto* (Milan: Ricordi, 1918; reprint Milan: Ricordi, 1980).

———. *Turandot: Dramma lirico in tre atti e cinque quadri.* Partitura: nuova edizione riveduta e corretta. Milan, Ricordi, 1958; reprint Milan: Ricordi, 2000.

Puccini, Simonetta, ed. *Giacomo Puccini: Lettere a Riccardo Schnabl.* Milan: Emme Editori, 1981.

———, ed. "Lettere a Luigi de' Servi." *Quaderni pucciniani* 1 (1982): 17–46.

———, ed. "Lettere di Giacomo Puccini ad Alfredo Caselli: 1891–1899." *Quaderni Pucciniani* 6 (1998).

———. "Puccini and the Painters." *Opera Quarterly* 2, no. 3 (1984): 5–26.

Puccini, Simonetta, and Michael Elphinstone, eds. *Quaderni Pucciniani 4: Lettere di Ferdinando Fontana a Giacomo Puccini, 1884–1919.* Milan: Instituto di studi pucciniani, 1992.

Quaderni Pucciniani 3: Convegno su Puccini giovane a Milano: L'opera Edgar e le composizioni giovanili. Milan: Instituto di studi pucciniani, 1992.

Ratner, Leonard G. *Classic Music: Expression, Form, and Style.* New York: Schirmer, 1980.

Ravenni, Gabriella Biagi, and Daniela Buonomini. "'Caro Feruccio . . .': Trenta lettere di Giacomo Puccini a Ferrucio Giogi (1906–1924)." In *Giacomo Puccini: L'uomo, il musicista, il panorama europeo: Atti del convegno internazionale di studi su Giacomo Puccini nel 700 anniversario della morte, Lucca, 25–29 novembre 1994,* ed. Gabriella Biagi Ravenni and Carolyn Gianturco, 169–209. Lucca: Libreria Musicale Italiana, 1997.

Review of Puccini, *La fanciulla del West. New York Times,* December 11, 1910, 2.

Ricci, Luigi. *Puccini interprete di se stesso.* Milan: Ricordi, 1954. Translated and annotated in Harry Nicholas Dunstan, "Performance Practices in the Music of

Giacomo Puccini as Observed by Luigi Ricci." Ph.D. diss.: Catholic University of America, 1989.

Robinson, Paul. *Opera, Sex, and Other Vital Matters.* Chicago: University of Chicago Press, 2002.

Roccatagliati, Alessandro. "Librettos: Autonomous or Functional Texts?" Translated by William Ashbrook. *Opera Quarterly* 11, no. 2 (1995): 81–95.

Rosch, Eleanor, and Barbara B. Lloyd, eds. *Cognition and Categorization.* Hillsdale, N.J.: Lawrence Erlbaum Associates, 1978.

Rosch, Eleanor, and Carolyn B. Mervis. "Family Resemblances: Studies in the Internal Structure of Categories." *Cognitive Psychology* 7, no. 4 (1975): 573–605.

Rosch, Eleanor, Carolyn B. Mervis, Wayne D. Gray, David M. Johnson, and Penny Boyes Braem. "Basic Objects in Natural Categories." *Cognitive Psychology* 8, no. 3 (1976): 382–439.

Rosen, David. "How Verdi's Operas Begin: An Introduction to the 'Introduzione.'" *Verdi Newsletter* 16 (1988): 3–18.

———. "Le quattro stesure del duetto Filippo-Posa." In *Atti del II Congresso internazionale di studi verdiani, 30 luglio–5 agosto 1969,* ed. Marcello Pavarani, 368–88. Parma: Instituto di studi verdiani, 1971.

———. "'La solita forma' in Puccini's Operas?" *Studi Pucciniani* 3: *"L'insolita forma": Strutture e processi analitici per l'opera italiana mell'epoca di Puccini: Atti del Convegno internazionale di studi Lucca, 20–21 settembre 2001.* Edited by Virgilio Bernardoni, Michele Girardi, and Arthur Groos, 179–99. Lucca: Centro studi Giacomo Puccini, 2004.

Rosen, David, and Carol Rosen. "A Musicological Word Study: It. *cabaletta." Romance Philology* 20, no. 2 (1966): 168–76.

Rosenberg, M. Lignana. Review of Girardi, *Puccini. Opera News* 66, no. 9 (2002): 94.

Rosenthal-English, Mirjam. *Giacomo Puccinis "La fanciulla del West": Eine neue Opernkonzeption Oeuvre des Komponisten.* Musicologica Berolinensia: Texte und Abhandlungen zur historischen, systematischen und vergleichenden Musikwissenschaft no. 3. Berlin: Kuhn, 1996.

Rosenwald, Lawrence. Review of Abbate, *Unsung Voices. Opera Quarterly* 10, no. 3 (1994): 149–52.

Rosolato, Guy. "La voix: entre corps et langage." *Revue française de psychanalyse* 38 (1974): 75–95.

Ross, Alex. "Puccini Remixed: A Fresh Approach to Opera's Crowd-Pleaser." *The New Yorker,* February 27, 2006: 84–85.

Ross, Peter. "Der Librettoovers im Übergang vom späten Ottocento zum frühen Novecento." In *Tendenze della musica teatrale italiana all'inizio del Novecento: Atti del 40 convegno internazionale "Ruggero Leoncavallo nel suo tempo," Locarno, Biblioteca Cantonale, 23–24 maggio 1998,* edited by Lorenza Guiot and Jürgen Maehder, 19–54. Milan: Sonzogno: 2005.

———. "Studien zum Verhältnis von Libretto und Komposition in den Opern Verdis." Inauguraldissertation: Bern, 1980.

Ross, Peter, and Donata Schwendimann Berra. "Sette lettere di Puccini a Giulio Ricordi." *Nuova Rivista Musicale Italiana* 13 (1979): 851–65.

Rothstein, William. *Phrase Rhythm in Tonal Music.* New York: Schirmer, 1989.

Rummelhart, David E. "Schemata: The Building Blocks of Cognition." In *Theoretical Issues in Reading Comprehension: Perspectives from Cognitive Psychology, Linguistics, Artificial Intelligence, and Education,* edited by Rand J. Spiro, Bertram C. Bruce, and William F. Brewer, 33–58. Hillsdale, N.J.: Lawrence Erlbaum Associates, 1980.

Sachs, Harvey. "The Practical Puccini." Review of Girardi, *L'arte internazionale di un musicista italiano. TLS: The Times Literary Supplement* (March 8, 1996): 23.

Saffle, Michael. "Exotic Harmony in La fanciulla del West and Turandot." In *Esotismo e colore locale nell'opera di Puccini: Atti del I convegno internazionale sull'opera di Puccini a Torre del Lago,* edited by Jürgen Maehder, 119–30. Pisa: Giardini, 1985.

Said, Edward. *On Late Style: Music and Literature Against the Grain.* Foreword by Mariam C. Said. Introduction by Michael Wood. New York: Pantheon, 2006.

Salvetti, Guido. "Come Puccini si apri un sentiero nell'aspra selva del wagnerismo italiano." In *Giacomo Puccini: L'uomo, il musicista, il panorama europeo: Atti del convegno internazionale di studi su Giacomo Puccini nel 700 anniversario della morte, Lucca, 25–29 novembre 1994,* edited by Gabriella Biagi Ravenni and Carolyn Gianturco, 49–79. Lucca: Libreria Musicale Italiana, 1997.

Samarotto, Frank. "A Theory of Temporal Plasticity in Tonal Music: An Extension of the Schenkerian Approach to Rhythm with Special Reference to Beethoven's Late Music." Ph.D. diss., City University of New York, 1999.

Sanguinetti, Giorgio. "Puccini's Music in the Italian Theoretical Literature of its Day." In *Tosca's Prism: Three Moments of Western Cultural History,* edited by Deborah Burton, Susan Vandiver Nicassio, and Agostino Ziino, 221–45. Boston: Northeastern University Press, 2004.

Sansone, Matteo. "Verismo: From Literature to Opera." Ph.D. diss., University of Edinburgh, 1987.

———. "The *Verismo* of Ruggero Leoncavallo: A Source Study of *Pagliacci.*" *Music and Letters* 70 (1989): 342–62.

de Saussure, Ferdinand. *Course in General Linguistics.* Edited by Charles Bally and Albert Sechehaye. Translated by Wade Baskin. New York: McGraw-Hill, 1966. Originally in French as *Cours de linguistique générale.* Edited by Charles Bally and Albert Sechehaye, with the collaboration of Albert Riedlinger. Paris: Payot, 1916.

Schachter, Carl. "Rhythm and Linear Analysis: Aspects of Meter." *The Music Forum* 6, no. 1 (1987): 1–59.

———. "Rhythm and Linear Analysis: Durational Reduction." *The Music Forum* 5 (1980): 197–232.

———. "Rhythm and Linear Analysis: A Preliminary Study." *The Music Forum* 4 (1976): 281–334.

———. *Unfoldings: Essays in Schenkerian Theory and Analysis.* Edited by Joseph N. Straus. New York: Oxford University Press, 1999.

Schickling, Dieter. "Carteggi Pucciniani inediti sul *tabarro,* e altri." *Studi Pucciniani* 2 (2000): 210–19.

———. "Ferdinando Martini librettista e collaboratore di Puccini." *Studi Pucciniani* 2 (2000): 205–20.

———. *Giacomo Puccini: Biographie.* Stuttgart: Deutsche Verlags-Anstalt, 1989.

———. *Giacomo Puccini: Catalogue of the Works.* Co-author of the English translation: Michael Kaye. Kassel: Bärenreiter, 2003.

———. "Die Urfassung von Giacomo Puccinis *Le villi*: Eine Rekonstruktion." In *"Una piacente estate di San Martino": Studi e ricerche per i settant'anni di Marcello Conati,* edited by Marco Capra, 307–14. Lucca: Libreria Editrice Musicale, 2000.

Seligman, Vincent. *Puccini Among Friends.* London: Macmillan, 1938.

Shapiro, Michael. *Asymmetry: An Inquiry into the Linguistic Structure of Poetry.* Amsterdam: North-Holland, 1976.

———. *The Sense of Grammar.* Bloomington: Indiana University Press, 1983.

Sheppard, W. Anthony. "Cinematic Realism, Reflexivity, and the American 'Madame Butterfly' Narratives." *Cambridge Opera Journal* 17, no. 1 (2005): 59–93.

———. *Revealing Masks: Exotic Influences and Ritualized Performance in Modernist Music Theater.* Berkeley: University of California Press, 2001.

Shreffler, Anne C. "The Coloratura's Voice: Another Look at Zerbinetta's Aria from *Ariadne auf Naxos.*" In *Richard Strauss und die Moderne: Bericht über das International Symposium München, 21. bis 23. Juli 1999,* ed. Bernd Edelmann, Birgit Lodes, and Reinhold Schlötterer, 361–90. Berlin: Henschel, 2001.

Silverman, Kaja. *The Acoustic Mirror: The Female Voice in Psychoanalysis and Cinema.* Bloomington: Indiana University Press, 1988.

Simms, Bryan R. "Berg's *Lulu* and the Theatre of the 1920s." *Cambridge Opera Journal* 6, no. 2 (1994): 147–58.

Sisman, Elaine. *Mozart: The "Jupiter" Symphony, no. 41 in C major, K. 551.* Cambridge: Cambridge University Press, 1993.

Smart, Mary Ann. "'Dernières Pensées': Questions of Late Style in Early Nineteenth-Century Italian Opera." Conference paper delivered to "Rethinking Late Style: Art, Literature, Music, Film." London, November 16–17, 2007.

———, ed. *Siren Songs: Representations of Gender and Sexuality in Opera.* Princeton, N.J.: Princeton University Press, 2000.

Smith, Patricia Juliana. "'Gli enigmi sono tre': The (D)Evolution of Turandot, Lesbian Monster." In *En Travesti: Women, Gender, Subversion, Opera,* ed. Corinne E. Blackmer and Patricia Juliana Smith, 242–84. New York: Columbia University Press, 1995.

Snook, Lynn. "In Search of the Riddle Princess Turandot." In *Esotismo e colore locale nell'opera di Puccini: Atti del I convegno internazionale sull'opera di Puccini a Torre del Lago,* ed. Jürgen Maehder, 131–42. Pisa: Giardini, 1985.

Specht, Richard. *Giacomo Puccini: The Man, His Life, His Work.* Translated by Catherine Alison Phillips. New York: Alfred A. Knopf, 1933.

Starr, Lawrence. *A Union of Diversities: Style in the Music of Charles Ives.* New York: Schirmer, 1992.

Steane, John. "Controlling Forces." Review of Girardi: *Puccini. Musical Times* 142, no. 1874 (2001): 64–65.

Stoïanova, Ivanka. "Remarques sur l'actualité de Turandot." In *Esotismo e colore locale nell'opera di Puccini: Atti del I convegno internazionale sull'opera di Puccini a Torre del Lago,* ed. Jürgen Maehder, 199–210. Pisa: Giardini, 1985.

Strasser-Vill, Susanne. "Exoticism in Stage Art at the Beginning of the Twentieth Century." In *Esotismo e colore locale nell'opera di Puccini: Atti del I convegno internazionale sull'opera di Puccini a Torre del Lago,* ed. Jürgen Maehder, 53–64. Pisa: Giardini, 1985.

Straus, Joseph N. "Disability and Late Style in Music." *Journal of Musicology* 25, no. 1 (2008): 3–45.

———. "Normalizing the Abnormal: Disability in Music and Music Theory." *Journal of the American Musicological Society* 59, no. 1 (2006): 113–84.

———. *Remaking the Past: Musical Modernism and the Influence of the Tonal Tradition.* Cambridge, Mass.: Harvard University Press, 1990.

———. *Stravinsky's Late Music.* New York: Cambridge University Press, 2001.

Strauss, Franz, and Alice Strauss, eds. *Richard Strauss und Hugo von Hofmannsthal: Briefwechsel.* Arranged by Willi Schuh. Zurich: Atlantis, 1952. In English as *The Correspondence Between Richard Strauss and Hugo von Hofmannsthal.* Translated by Hanns Hammelmann and Ewald Osers. Introduction by Edward Sackville-West. Cambridge: Cambridge University Press, 1980.

Stravinsky, Igor, and Robert Craft. *Conversations with Igor Stravinsky.* Berkeley: University of California Press, 1980.

Swigart, Jane. *The Myth of the Bad Mother: The Emotional Realities of Mothering.* New York: Doubleday, 1991.

Tarasti, Eero. *A Theory of Musical Semiotics.* Bloomington: Indiana University Press, 1994.

Taruskin, Richard. *Oxford History of Western Music.* 6 vols. Oxford: Oxford University Press, 2005.

———. "She Do the Ring in Different Voices." Review of Abbate, *Unsung Voices, Cambridge Opera Journal* 4, no. 2 (1992): 187–97.

———. *Stravinsky and the Russian Traditions: A Biography of the Works Through Mavra.* Berkeley: University of California Press, 1996.

Tomlinson, Gary. *Metaphysical Song: An Essay on Opera.* Princeton, N.J.: Princeton University Press, 1999.

———. "Opera and *Drame:* Hugo, Donizetti, and Verdi." In *Studies in the History of Music,* vol. 2, *Music and Drama,* 171–92. New York: Broude, 1988.

———. "Puccini Turns Respectable." Review of Phillips-Matz, *Puccini* and Budden, *Puccini. New York Times,* December 15, 2002, sec. 7, p. 14.

———. "Verdi After Budden." *19th-Century Music* 5 (1981): 170–81.

Tommasini, Anthony. "Puccini at 150, Still Capable of Revelations." *New York Times,* August 17, 2008, AR16.

Toolan, Michael. *Narrative: A Critical Linguistic Introduction.* 2nd ed. New York: Routledge, 2001.

Torrefranca, Fausto. *Giacomo Puccini e l'opera internazionale.* Turin: Bocca, 1912.

Trubetzkoi, Nicolai. *Principles of Phonology.* Translated by Christine A. M. Baltaxe. Berkeley: University of California Press, 1969. Originally *Grundzüge der Phonologie.* Prague: Travaux du Cercle Linguistique de Prague, 1939.

Tunbridge, Laura. *Schumann's Late Style.* Cambridge: Cambridge University Press, 2007.

Turandot: Dramma lirico in tre atti e cinque quadri (full score). Milan, Ricordi, 1926; reprint Milan: Ricordi, 2000.

Uvietta, Marco. "'È l'ora della prova': un finale Puccini-Berio per *Turandot*." *Studi Musicali* 31 (2002): 395–479. In English as "'È l'ora della prova': Berio's Finale for Puccini's *Turandot*." *Cambridge Opera Journal* 16 (2004): 187–238.

Valente, Richard. "From Scapigliatura to Expressionism: The Verismo of Giacomo Puccini. A Study of the Impact of Realism on Opera, with Consideration of the Influence of Scapigliatura on *Le villi* and Edgar and the Expressionism on *La Turandot*." Ph.D. diss., University of Freiburg, 1970. Reprinted as *The Verismo of Giacomo Puccini: From Scapigliatura to Expressionism*. Ann Arbor, Mich.: Braun-Blumfield, 1971.

de Van, Gilles. "Fin de Siècle Exoticism and the Meaning of the Far Away." *Opera Quarterly* 11, no. 3 (1995): 77–94.

———. "La notion de *tinta*: mémoire confuse et affinities thématiques dans les opéras de Verdi." *Revue de musicologie* 76 (1990): 187–98.

Visentini, Olga. "Movenze dell'esotismo: 'il caso Gozzi.'" In *Esotismo e colore locale nell'opera di Puccini: Atti del I convegno internazionale sull'opera di Puccini a Torre del Lago,* ed. Jürgen Maehder, 37–51. Pisa: Giardini, 1985.

Walsh, Steven. *Stravinsky: A Creative Spring: Russia and France, 1882–1934.* New York: Knopf, 1999.

———. *Stravinsky: The Second Exile: France and America, 1934–1971.* New York: Knopf, 2006.

Waterhouse, John C. G. "Italy from the First World War to the Second." In *Modern Times: from World War I to the Present,* ed. Robert P. Morgan, 111–27. London: Macmillan, 1993.

Watkins, Glen. *Pyramids at the Louvre: Music, Culture, and Collage from Stravinsky to the Postmodernists.* Cambridge, Mass.: Harvard University Press, Belknap Press, 1994.

Weaver, William. *The Golden Century of Italian Opera: From Rossini to Puccini.* London: Thames and Hudson: 1980.

Webern, Anton. *The Path to the New Music.* Translated by Leo Black. Edited by Willi Reich. London: Universal Edition, 1975.

Webster, James. "The Analysis of Mozart's Arias." In *Mozart Studies,* edited by Cliff Eisen, 101–99. New York: Oxford University Press, 1991.

———. "Mozart's Operas and the Myth of Musical Unity." *Cambridge Opera Journal* 2, no. 3 (1990): 197–218.

———. "To Understand Verdi and Wagner We Must Understand Mozart." *19th-Century Music* 11, no. 2 (1987): 175–93.

Weiss, Piero. "Verdi and the Fusion of Genres." *Journal of the American Musicological Society* 35, no. 1 (1982): 138–56.

Wheeldon, Marianne. *Debussy's Late Style.* Bloomington: Indiana University Press, 2009.

Wilson, Alexandra. "Modernism and the Machine Woman in Puccini's *Turandot*." *Music and Letters* 86, no. 3 (2005): 432–51.

———. *The Puccini Problem: Opera, Nationalism, and Modernity.* Cambridge: Cambridge University Press, 2007.

———. "Torrefranca vs. Puccini: Embodying a Decadent Italy." *Cambridge Opera Journal* 13, no. 1 (2001): 29–53.

Wimsatt, William K., and Monroe C. Beardsley. "The Intentional Fallacy." *Sewanee Review* 54 (1946): 468–88.

Wintle, Christopher. "Wotan's Rhetoric of Anguish." Review of Abbate, *Unsung Voices. Journal of the Royal Musical Association* 118, no. 1 (1993): 121–43.

INDEX

Page numbers in italics refer to musical examples and tables.

ANDREW DAVIS is Associate Professor of Music Theory and Director of Graduate Studies at the University of Houston Moores School of Music. His research focuses on late nineteenth- and early twentieth-century opera, including the music of Puccini, Verdi, Strauss, and Gershwin, among others.